CAPITALIST PUNISHMENT

CAPITALIST PUNISHMENT
Prison Privatization & Human Rights

edited by

Andrew Coyle
Allison Campbell
Rodney Neufeld

Clarity Press, Inc.
Atlanta

Zed Books
London

© 2003 HRI / Human Rights Internet

ISBN: 0-932863-35-3

In-house editor: Diana G. Collier

Cover photo: Alan Pogue, Texas Center for Documentary Photography
http://www.documentaryphotographs.com

Capitalist punishment : prison privatization & human rights / edited by Andrew Coyle, Allison Campbell, Rodney Neufeld. -- 1st ed.
   p. cm.
   Includes bibliographical references and index.
   ISBN 0-932863-35-3

   1. Prisons--United States. 2. Privatization--United States. 3. Corrections--Contractingout--United States. 4. Prisoners--Civilrights--United States. 5. Human rights--United States.

HV9469.C37 2003   365'.973
                         QB102-701901

Published outside of North America by Zed Books Ltd, 7 Cynthia Street, London, N1 9JF, UK, in 2003.

A catalogue record for this book is available from the British Library.

ISBN 1 84277 290 2 hb
ISBN 1 84277 291 0 pb

CLARITY PRESS, INC.   ZED BOOKS
Ste. 469, 3277 Roswell Rd. NE   7 Cynthia Street
Atlanta, GA. 30305   London N19JF

http://www.claritypress.com   http://www.zedbooks.demon.co.uk

Table of Contents

Foreword

Sir Nigel Rodley

During my tenure as United Nations Special Rapporteur on Torture I visited prisons around the world and all too often I was disappointed and discouraged by what I saw. From Russia to Brazil and from Cameroon to Pakistan, I was witness to prison conditions which in no way live up to internationally recognized minimum standards. In many nations, torture and abuse of prisoners are endemic.

The situation is one which should concern all advocates of human rights. Clearly something needs to be done to reform a significant proportion of the world's prisons. However, as this publication clearly illustrates, privatization is not the answer. As the authors of *Capitalist Punishment* so strongly argue, the profit motive of privately operated prisons in the United States and elsewhere has fostered a situation in which the rights and needs of prisoners and the direct responsibility of states for the treatment of those they deprive of freedom are diminished in the name of greater efficiency. I believe that the publication is a valuable contribution to the debate on this important subject.

Introduction

Andrew Coyle, Allison Campbell and Rodney Neufeld

The purpose of this book is to fill the relative void on the subject of prison privatization within a literature on incarceration that is otherwise vast and varied. Over 100,000 people in the United States are currently detained in prisons owned and operated by private corporations, but the phenomenon is not limited to the US. Private prisons have been opened in the United Kingdom, Australia and New Zealand. They have most recently been introduced in Canada and South Africa, and they are in the process of being exported to developing countries. Although the most recent form of prison privatization dates back to the 1980s, it is important to recognize that only a few countries are involved and they are still in the experimental stages of privatization. As they test the waters, undoubtedly looking to the US as a model, it is crucial that they be able to weigh all of the evidence.

Supporters of prison privatization have argued that private prisons make good sense. Private prison corporations promise reduced costs to governments, better and more cost-effective services to prisoners, and increased security for people living in communities where prisons are located. Much of the evidence throughout this book, however, does not support their position. Instead, it points to decreased security, poor employment standards and inadequate protection of prisoners' human rights. The first chapters locate the US experience with prison privatization in its recent historical context.

For Philip Wood, in chapter 1, prison privatization is part of the development of the "prison industrial complex", a term used to describe the multifaceted growth in the American criminal justice system as an industry. In his opinion, increased private sector involvement is one of three interrelated trends that have contributed to the complex. It needs to be understood alongside and together with increased incarceration rates and "penal regression", which entails a shift away from social and moral considerations towards a tolerance of violence as a means of social control, racism, and the tendency towards punishment rather than rehabilitation. He examines various explanations for the emergence of these trends and concludes that the prison industrial complex rose to prominence alongside a transformation of both economic development models and popular forms of social control that allowed Southern traditions of penal racialization and criminalization to come to the forefront of national policies in the 1960s. In the national penal system the tendency towards punitive policies in response to the social rebellion of the era, intertwined with economic restructuring after an economic crisis, reinforced racial considerations and criminalization.

In chapter 2, Christian Parenti argues that incarceration rates in the USA increased as part of a movement that employs incarceration as a means of state-managed social control, which divides and maintains social stratifications such as race and class. During the 1980s and 1990s, the number of for-profit private prisons increased across America, but contrary to initial optimistic expectations, private prisons have encountered an increasing number of dilemmas as well as much resistance to their operation. The charges of abuse, coupled with resistance from powerful unionized prison guards have played a large part in halting the further expansion of private prison companies. Parenti describes many examples of abuse in the private prison system in the US. The drive to lower costs and thus increase profits has resulted in irresponsible cuts to expenditures that have led to degrading prison conditions, a disregard for human rights, and a myriad of problems with prison security, including inadequate staff training and equipment as well as low accountability. According to Parenti, abuse is widespread, prompting riots, prison escapes, suicides and lawsuits. This translates into higher costs. Where it does not, cost savings do not go to the state, but towards enhancing corporate profit. However, Parenti does not blame the direct profit motive of the specific prison corporations for the massive growth in incarceration. Instead, he sees the push for privatization as part of the same process of social control which has been managed by the state with violence and incarceration.

According to Jeff Sinden, in chapter 3, privately run prisons are not a new phenomenon in the Western world. They existed in medieval England and in 17th and 18th century US, and it was in the early 20th century that their ownership and operation was fully transferred to US government agencies. Their re-emergence in the 1980s, he explains, was a response to a rise in the use of incarceration, which resulted in overcrowded prisons. Increased incarceration was brought about by a change in sentencing policies, not by rising crime, and has especially been related to the war on drugs and the 'get tough' approach to crime best exemplified by the Three Strikes legislation. As public facilities such as immigration detention centers struggled to cope with the increased numbers, private companies emerged to fill a newly found niche. Although delegating the operation of prisons to corporations has been proclaimed to be an improper abdication of an inherent government function, Sinden admits that there is probably nothing illegal about it. Typically, state governments enter into contracts with private institutions, then carry out monitoring through inspections. According to Sinden, this is where the major problems lie, since the incentives provided by the market to cut costs are stronger than the performance monitoring mechanisms that seek to keep this tendency in check.

The same thesis is picked up by Alex Friedman who argues in chapter 4 that some of the worst examples of neglect and abuse are found in privately-operated juvenile facilities. This is due in part to the fact that they have an "inherent motivation to cut corners in order to reduce costs—particularly in regard to employee training, wages and staffing levels". As examples, he points to the excessive force used by staff in a South Carolina training center, the failure to provide education, medical and mental health care in Louisiana, death by neglect at the Arizona Boys Ranch, and unsafe conditions and inadequate care in a center in Colorado. In addition to poor staffing, he cites an unwillingness to rehabilitate prisoners and the inability of privately-managed facilities to deal with the large numbers of mentally ill detainees as contributing factors to the overall mistreatment of juvenile prisoners. Despite the poor record of privatized juvenile facilities, they continue to expand and their misconduct and inadequate performance continue to make the headlines.

The effectiveness of incarceration, questionable in the best circumstances, comes seriously under scrutiny when the private sector becomes involved. Judith Greene's research, described in chapter 5, involved site visits, prisoner interviews and review of facility records by a team at the University of Minnesota. It shows that privatization of adult correctional facilities significantly reduces not only the possible effectiveness of incarceration, but also the security of facilities and public safety. The study compares the performance of one private facility in Minnesota to three public prisons in the state, tracing the lack of effective correctional services directly to the private operator's efforts to control costs. Services to prisoners are among the first budget items to be cut when a prison comes under private-sector management. Moreover, when private prisons are built on the outskirts of small towns, it becomes difficult for non-profit organizations to offer volunteer-run programs at the prisons. Service provision was also hindered by low staff salaries, contributing to a high turnover and lack of sufficient experience among the guards. Prisoners were occasionally misclassified, and education and health services were not adequate. Despite these problems, she argues that support for privatization has not been deterred. Officials ignore the growing body of evidence which suggests that the deficiencies are due to structural differences in how the private sector approaches prison management.

With prisoners' personal safety already in jeopardy, and little or no programming available, life in private prisons becomes much more tenuous for people with health concerns, as described in chapter 6. The imperative of corporations to operate profitably, and the business approach of treating every expenditure as potentially unnecessary, has had dire consequences for prisoners, whose access to adequate health care is dramatically reduced. Elizabeth Alexander cites numerous examples of inadequate heath care in private prisons, including the denial of necessary medical care, improper monitoring of prisoners with chronic diseases, and overmedicating patients. She points to the case of John Malesko, a man who suffered permanent head injuries resulting from a preventable heart attack while imprisoned at a privately run community corrections center in New York. Although his injuries allegedly related to the failure of prison staff to guarantee his constitutional right to heath care, the lawsuit against the corporation was thrown out. The case demonstrates that not only are private prisons less accountable for the provision of adequate services, they enjoy a degree of immunity from legal challenges founded upon constitutional guarantees.

Chapters 7 through 11 pay special attention to particularly affected communities. Statistics demonstrate that the people most adversely affected by the privatization of the prison system are immigrants, indigenous peoples, blacks, latinos, women and children. The US now incarcerates 690 people per 100,000, the majority of whom are people of color, and most of whom are incarcerated for non-violent offences. Nationwide, black men are eight times more likely than white men to be in prison, with an incarceration rate of 3,408 per 100,000 black male residents in 1998, compared to a white male incarceration rate of 417 per 100,000.

Mark Hecht and Donna Habsha consider the treatment of youth in private facilities in chapter 7. Unlike Friedman in chapter 4, their case studies do not focus on the US, but on Canada and the UK where, despite a decline in violent crime involving youth, the number of youth in custody has increased. The authors examine the performance of a privately run young offender institution in each country in light of international legal obligations set out mainly in the Convention on the Rights of the Child. They claim that Canada and the UK are in patent violation of their legal obligations under the Convention. They point specifically to the institutions' failures to guarantee quality education standards and to maintain an independent monitoring body to assess programs and accept complaints from youth.

In 2000, the US incarcerated over one million Black women and men. According to Monique Morris, in chapter 8, the disproportionate number of blacks in prison reflects the way the prison industrial complex and the American criminal justice system reinforce and perpetuate racial disparities between African Americans and Euro-Americans. Since African Americans are over-represented in the prison system, they are more likely to fall victim to the negative effects of prison privatization. Morris looks first at historical trends, including slavery, the convict-lease system and economic exploitation, that have led to the marginalization of African American communities and the tendency of the justice system to favor incarceration over rehabilitation. She looks at the repercussions of incarceration on groups within the African American community, such as women and children, and she explains how mistreatment in private prisons often does not remain inside prison walls. When people return to their communities from prison, they often bring the effects of that abuse and neglect home with them. Children of prisoners lack adequate care and access to familial relationships; inmates suffer from physical, mental and emotional health problems lack medical services and post-incarceration support; and the civic voice is lost or weakened with the disenfranchisement of a large portion of the community. Thus the employment of the private prisons serves to maintain the racial disparities that have existed for centuries.

Katherine van Wormer looks at the particular effects of prison privatization on female inmates in chapter 9. She argues that women arrive in prison with more social and health problems than men and that private prisons have failed to deal adequately with those needs. Imprisoned women are often poor, uneducated, and have small children who are negatively affected by the incarceration of their mothers. Due to more stringent, gender-neutral sentencing policies, women are being incarcerated at increasing rates mostly for non-violent crimes, such as substance abuse. In violation of international and national laws, female inmates in prisons around America have been subjected to degrading conditions in prisons and are not supervised by female guards. Private prison corporations have been dogged by many accusations of sexual abuse of female inmates by prison guards. Van Wormer also discusses problems faced by immigrant women in detention, and the ambiguity that surrounds their rights as non-citizens. She concludes with suggestions for reducing costs in the justice system through rehabilitation and preventive measures.

Frank Smith's chapter 10 concentrates on the ramifications of the increase in private prisons on Native Americans. He acknowledges the need to understand the current situation within a historical context of discrimination against and persecution of indigenous people. Smith then highlights three issues pertinent to the incarceration of Native Americans. First, Native Americans are dispro-portionately incarcerated in the US, at a per capita rate second only to African Americans. Second, the government's institutionalization of "color-blindness" has been coupled with a disregard for traditions and cultures, and has incurred a failure to recognize the negative effects of prejudice. Third, the effects of a lack of access to religious instruments and to home communities, central to Native American notions of healing, has created a cultural chasm. Smith charges that private prisons ignore traditional practices and healing methods, such as sweat lodges, and that the act of institutionalization interferes with the traditional healing process. He notes that prison facilities are often located far from the home community, disengaging inmates from the traditional process of rehabilitation within the community. He describes the support in the justice community that native justice traditions have gained, which unlike prisons, focus on rehabilitation and integration. Nevertheless, funding and political support for the integration of these traditions within the incarceration system remain weak. According to Smith, the system must begin to respect a diversity of cultures and traditions to be truly effective.

Significantly, non-citizens were the first to be jailed in privately owned facilities. In the US, Immigration and Naturalization Service (INS) used privately run detention centers in the early 1980s to incarcerate undocumented migrants and refugees. Detention of immigrants remains common practice in the US, and it has spread to other countries such as the UK and Australia, as outlined by Rodney Neufeld and Bente Molenaar in chapter 11. In Australia, the mandatory detention of all asylum seekers is not only expensive and unnecessary, but it also violates international law, as set out in the 1951 Refugee Convention. The authors point to official reports in both Australia and the UK which chronicle long lists of abuse and neglect of the detainees, some of it racially motivated, by staff who are paid poorly, overworked and given little training. In a number of instances, this has led to hunger strikes, riots and lawsuits. Following the Campsfield riot in the UK, the staff of the private detention center pushed for the rioters to be prosecuted. Their attempted prosecution collapsed upon the court's determination that the evidence of staff was untrustworthy and their conduct 'wicked'. Then, when one of the detainees attempted to attain judicial recourse for malicious prosecution, not only did he discover that the government's use of private prisons distanced it from liability, but as a non-citizen he was forced to continue to battle against the government's attempts to deport him. The case demonstrated how privatization of detention has allowed governments to pass off their responsibilities of caring for asylum seekers, while maintaining its role in deciding who qualifies as a refugee. The result is one of decreased transparency and accountability in a public function that arises out of an international legal obligation. According to Neufeld and Molenaar, it is wrong that the governments can be aware of the fact that guards are overworked and under-trained, but that it cannot be held accountable for the abuse inflicted by those guards upon the detainees. Ultimate responsibility and control of detention centers must lie with the government.

While the negative effects resulting from the reduction of labor costs by prison corporations have been touched on by many authors, they are the focus of Joshua Miller's chapter. He argues that companies typically pay significantly lower wages and benefits than public sector facilities, resulting in less qualified personnel and lower employee retention rates. Meanwhile, corporate executives, insiders and consultants receive exorbitant salaries. Companies also deliberately cut back on front line staffing, diminishing security and jeopardizing the safety of guards, prisoners and the community. Chronic staff shortages cause many employees to work extra long shifts without breaks and make adequate training difficult, as pre-service training gives way to on-the-job learning. The result is an insecure, unsafe working environment for employees and improper treatment of the people whose lives they control.

In chapter 13, Dawn Moore, Kellie Leclerc Burton and Kelly Hannah-Moffat describe the situation in Canada, where Ontario singles itself out as the only province that has opted for privatization. It has been promoted alongside the provincial government's push for a "no frills" system of punishment, which the authors evaluate in light of the 1957 UN Standard Minimum Rules for the Treatment of Prisoners. The new system of punishment has meant drastic cuts in educational programs, the erection of generic super-jails, and a proposed study of privatization, using Penetanguishene as the test site. Although Penetanguishene has only been opened recently, the authors catalog a series of troubling incidents, which they argue have led to hunger strikes and rioting. The authors conclude that this early record coupled with broader changes to the system of punishment in Ontario, which are making it increasingly harsh, austere and vengeance oriented, places the province on a perilous trajectory.

In the United Kingdom, privatization was first contemplated in 1986 as part of much needed prison reform, as described in chapter 14. According to Stephen Nathan, the Parliamentary Select Committee looked solely to the US as a model, and relying heavily on evidence provided by the Corrections Corporation of America, it found three principal advantages to privatization: the taxpayer could be relieved of the initial capital cost of building new prisons, the prisons could be built more quickly, and it produced enhanced architectural efficiency and excellence. After providing a brief history of prison privatization in the UK, Nathan attempts to disprove these and other supposed advantages of corporate involvement. As in Ontario, the British government decided to experiment with privatization without setting down any timelines or evaluation processes. By 1992, the first private prison was open, and plans for two more were in place. Once elected, Prime Minister Tony Blair immediately rescinded his pre-1997 election promise to return privately owned prisons to public ownership. Nathan argues that the UK has its own private prison industrial complex. Contracts are shared among the same small number of companies that are marketing their services worldwide. These companies argue cost savings and the easing of overcrowding as the primary advantages of corporate involvement, but Nathan claims that these conclusions are either flawed or not representative of the entire picture. He cites numerous fines, failures and controversies, focusing especially on HMP Blakenhurst. Despite the poor record of privatization and the general desire among the British public to see prisons brought back into the public sector, it looks set to remain.

The incorporation of the private sector into incarceration in South Africa is even more recent compared to the UK. The first private prison opened in South Africa in July 2001, if one discounts the small detention facility for 'illegal immigrants' which Julie Berg describes as "a human rights disaster". Noting that South Africa is a developing country with a prison system that is in a critical condition, Berg asks in chapter 15 whether prison privatization is a viable solution. She describes the unique situation of South Africa by pointing to its transition to democracy, the adoption of a new constitution and the demilitarization of the penal system. She explains that despite this transformation, some prisons are trapped in a style of prison management that is not in line with internationally accepted penal standards. The government, she argues, has had to be creative, which has included resorting to prison privatization. Like the UK, South Africa looked to the US model. However, Berg questions whether a 'First World solution' is appropriate. She points to the shaky introduction of prison privatization in South Africa, but she also recognizes the possibility for success. She believes that private prisons will inevitably be of higher quality than the extremely over-populated and squalid conditions of public prisons, but that this will produce an unacceptable inequality between prisoners held in public as opposed to private prisons. Moreover, she recognizes that experimentation and debate are necessary. It was wrong for South Africa to begin with the privatization of a maximum-security prison. In the end, for the system to work, it must uphold prisoners' rights, avoid corruption, and allow the government to retain ultimate control over the situation.

In chapter 16, Stephen Nathan takes a more skeptical approach to the privatization of prison services in developing countries. He is much less optimistic about the increasing private sector involvement in prisons in emerging economies, drawing his critique from an open letter from the Director General of Prisons in Lesotho. The letter expresses grave concern that a proposal for privatization will be approved and requests people to do anything in their power to frustrate the efforts of the proponents of Group 4, the European company wishing to export its services. According to Nathan, Lesotho is another example of how the private prison industry that emerged in the US is looking to the international market for growth. He lists the countries to which prison privatization has been exported, as well as the countries that have opted for the French semi-private model. Despite commercial secrecy and claims by some companies of their disinterest in expanding to certain types of countries, Nathan claims that there are important clues that suggest that the industry is headed in the direction of emerging economies. These countries have dire human rights records and are in serious need of assistance with criminal justice reform. They face demands from the World Bank and the IMF in relation to their serious debts, which require them to cut public spending and to privatize assets and services. Nathan cautions, however, that privatization schemes have dire social, economic and political implications, including the loss of public accountability, poorer wages and conditions for employees, fewer jobs than before, and inadequate service provision. If Lesotho gives in to the "terrible pressure" to have its entire prison service privatized, it would invite these and other problems. Instead, Nathan promotes an alternative strategy, supported by the UK's Department for International Development. The strategy promotes local solutions over those promoted by foreign companies.

In chapter 17, Amanda George recounts one Australian experience with prison privatization. The Deer Park Women's Prison has become known throughout the world as an example of how prison privatization can fail. In October 2000, the government of Victoria used its emergency powers to take over the management of the facility, putting a stop to the former government's most controversial prison privatization. George argues that from the moment it opened, the prison proved to be a disaster. Despite alleged intentions to reduce costs, the price paid by incarcerated women has been great. She documents a list of concerns: increased rates of self-harm, reduced visitations, unsafe surroundings for children, poor health treatment, lack of education programs and poor location, leaving many women far from home and unable to see maintain contact with their families. The promise of improved accountability also proved hollow as demonstrated by the three-year legal battle by a community legal center to seek the disclosure of operational standards, manuals, contracts and monitoring reports.

While prison corporations and the governments that support them argue that private prisons make sense, the privatization of punishment services is problematic. This book details some of the many problems created by the process. Contrary to the opinion of those promoting the privatization of prisons, the US model does not make sense for people or for communities. Prison corporations have not lived up to their promises. They have not saved governments substantial amounts of money, nor have they proven to be more secure. Instead, they have contributed to an unacceptable level of neglect and violence against inmates and detainees, diminished rights for the guards and other employees, a risk to the community, and are set to be a heavy burden for the public purse over many years in those countries which have experimented with them.

The responsibility that comes with incarceration and detention belongs to the state, and the manner in which it has been delegated to commercial enterprises in the US, Australia, the UK, Canada, New Zealand and South Africa amounts to an improper abdication of that responsibility.

CHAPTER ONE

The Rise of the
Prison Industrial Complex
in the United States

Phillip J. Wood

Introduction

If, as some historians suggest, the spirit of an age is revealed in its public works, the causal chain that connects the two is nevertheless long and complex. This is particularly true with respect to the recent emergence of the prison industrial complex in the United States. In the first place, the process itself is multifaceted, combining a number of interrelated quantitative and qualitative tendencies. Second, the range of forces that connect the prison industrial complex with the spirit of the age is both wide and subject to debate.

The term "prison industrial complex" refers to an American criminal justice system that has been substantially transformed by almost three decades of rapid growth and by the increasing importance of private interests in criminal justice policy.[1] The term originates from critical perspectives on the American state, which see corporate colonization of decision-making structures as the key to an adequate understanding of American public policy. By using their resources to serve the needs of state and local politicians and bureaucrats, business interests and/or wealthy individuals are able to exercise a disproportionate influence over policy decisions and contribute to the development of a corporate welfare state. The "revolving door" between government service and the private sector, substantial bureaucratic autonomy and the domination of electoral politics by corporate money all contribute to relative immunity from democratic accountability and recent attempts at "downsizing". Public funds thus continue to be diverted into activities that swell corporate coffers either in the absence of any compelling public purpose, or long after the purpose of the original policy decision has been overtaken by events. The classic case is that of the military industrial complex, but scholars have pointed to other similar systems in agriculture, transportation, health and elsewhere.[2]

This chapter will describe the rise of the prison industrial complex in the United States, and compare explanations for its emergence. The first section disaggregates the rise of the prison industrial complex into three main historical tendencies and demonstrates their mutual interdependence. The second section builds on this historical reconstruction and discusses different ways of explaining the rise of the prison industrial complex. The rise of the prison industrial complex can be seen as a response to rising crime rates, as a product of America's violent culture or as a result of the range of material and other benefits to be gained by powerful social actors from prison expansion. The analysis developed here argues, in contrast, that the rise of the prison industrial complex is part of a more profound transformation that has re-structured both the American pattern of economic development and its characteristic forms of social control.

The Prison Industrial Complex: Historical Trends

The idea of a prison industrial complex combines three tendencies: expansion, privatization and regression. In historical terms, they are closely interrelated. The discussion that follows treats each separately however, partly for purposes of exposition and partly because they each make distinct contributions to an adequate description of the rise of the prison industrial complex.

Increased Incarceration

The first historical tendency is the rapid expansion of prison populations. Figure 1 uses data from the US Bureau of Justice Statistics[3] to chart the growth of the incarceration rate in the US during the last three quarters of the twentieth century. It shows a period of substantial growth (73.4 percent) from 1925 to 1939. This is followed by a rapid decline during the Second World War and a long period of relatively slow growth from the end of the war through to about 1961. The 1960s saw the rise of the civil rights and other social movements, a period of progressive Supreme Court decisions on a variety of fronts and a growing commitment to political reform by the Democratic Party. As a result, a period of liberal criminal justice policy emerged from 1961 to 1972, causing a 22 percent drop in the incarceration rate.[4] After 1972, the graph is dominated by a sharp upward trend.

FIGURE 1:
The Growth of the US Prison Population, 1925-2000

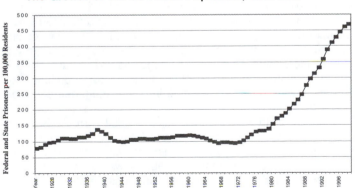

For most of the period between 1925 and 1972, the prison population had fluctuated between 100,000 and 200,000 inmates. From 1972 to 2000, with only a brief hesitation in the late 1970s, the total number of state and federal prisoners increased about six and a half times, from less than 200,000 to over 1.3 million, and the incarceration rate increased from 93 to 478. On a decade-by-decade basis, the prison population grew by 53 percent in the 1970s, more than doubled (+115 percent) in the 1980s and increased by a further 77 percent in the 1990s. This growth has been regionally uneven. At the end of 2000, thirteen states exceed the national rate. Nine of them were in the South where, from 1990 to 2000, the incarceration rate grew faster than in any other region: from 391 to 539.[5]

By 2001, the United States had about 5 percent of the world's population but was estimated to account for nearly a quarter of its prisoners and, though comparative data is not altogether reliable, some estimates indicate that its incarceration rate may have overtaken that of Russia to become the highest in the world.[6] If we add the jail population to those in prison, the total number of people incarcerated in the US passed the two million mark in February 2000, and by the end of the year reached almost 2.1 million.[7]

The annual rate of growth of the prison population has been falling since it peaked at 8.7 percent in 1994, but the numbers are now so large that even a 1.3 percent growth rate in 2000 (the lowest since 1972) added about 27,000 inmates to the prison population.[8] The broader population of those under correctional supervision (all those in prison or jail; on parole or probation) grew by about 117,000 in 2000 and now stands at about 6.5 million people, or 3.1 percent of the adult population.[9] Reflecting these trends, spending on corrections by all levels of government increased from less than $7 billion in 1980 to $43.5 billion in 1997. Total spending on criminal justice in 1997 reached $130 billion, or about half of that year's spending on "defense".[10]

Increased Private Sector Involvement

The second tendency is the increasing weight of private interests in the penal economy. In part this is simply a quantitative matter. More prisoners and prisons mean more and bigger contracts for a variety of private interests traditionally involved in incarceration, especially construction companies and architectural firms that have built more than a thousand prisons in the last two decades. In addition, a myriad of other companies provide food, health, education, drug treatment, laundry, garbage collection, transportation, communications and other services. These services were together worth about $1.1 billion in 1995.[11]

Beyond this there have been significant qualitative transformations, however. The incarceration boom not only created a vast increase in demand for prison space, but also coincided with a long period of economic crisis, middle class tax resistance, increasing pressure on public resources, and the growth of an international privatization movement. All these factors combined to provide an opening for private sector involvement in prison management and speculative prison building.

The modern history of the privatization of adult corrections in the US can be dated to 1979, when the Immigration and Naturalization Service began to hire private companies to detain illegal immigrants waiting for deportation hearings. The real expansion began in the mid-1980s however, a period in which public authorities were unable to keep up with the incarceration boom. By 1986, 38 states were operating at or above prison capacity, seven of those by more than 50 percent. Two years later, prisons in 39 states were operating under court order to remedy overcrowding and other constitutional violations. In difficult economic circumstances, many states had reached their debt limits and could no longer issue the bonds needed to finance construction. Contracting out to private companies became a relatively quick way to respond to overcrowding. Moreover, it could be charged to operating rather than capital budgets, thus avoiding the problem of debt ceilings.

The largest of the private corrections companies, Corrections Corporation of America (now part of the Sodexho/Marriott multinational empire) incorporated in Tennessee in 1983 and opened its first immigrant detention center in 1984. Its rise to national public prominence came with an offer in the same year to take control of the Tennessee prison system, which had recently been found to be in violation of the Constitution because of conditions for prisoners. Wackenhut, a well-established private security firm based in Florida, also entered the corrections business in 1984, to be followed by a dozen or so others. Rapid growth in demand and expanding "markets" caused the value of private corrections companies to soar during the 1990s. Revenues passed $1 billion in 1996.[12]

By the end of 2000, according to the Bureau of Justice Statistics, 87,369 prisoners were detained in private facilities in 31 states and the federal prison system. Almost 6 percent of all state prisoners and nearly 11 percent of federal prisoners are privately housed. Southern states use private contractors more than other regions, with 8.3 percent of their prisoners so housed.[13] According to other data reported by the Bureau, in 2000 fourteen companies ran 153 private facilities with a total capacity of 119,442 prisoners. Corrections Corporation of America (CCA) has a capacity of over 60,000, while the state with the largest private sector is Texas, with a capacity of over 30,000 inmates.[14]

In addition to the private prison contractors themselves, several other private interests have expanded their role in the penal economy. Some of the largest Wall Street investment firms began to compete for private prison business in the 1990s, buying bonds and securities from prison companies and re-selling them to individual investors, mutual funds and others. According to one estimate, this business was worth $2 to $3 billion per year in the mid-1990s.[15] In addition, the growing numbers of inmates have become a target for a variety of public-private partnerships designed to exploit their labor. Microsoft, Boeing, TWA, Starbucks and other companies pay minimum wage (to the state, not the inmates) to "hire" inmates to produce a growing range of low value-added goods and services.[16] Finally, in their efforts to cut costs through the use of sophisticated surveillance and control technologies, the private corrections companies have stimulated the interest of defense contractors looking for new post-Cold War outlets for their wares.[17] Many of these issues will be taken up in later chapters of this book.

Penal Regression

The third tendency at work in the transformation of the American corrections system can usefully be referred to as what Sir Leon Radzinowicz calls "penal regression". By this, Radzinowicz means the tendency of the system to become "more crude and cynical, displaying an increasing disregard for those fundamental considerations of a political social and moral nature from which ...the machinery of justice in a democratic society should never be cut off."[18] In the American case, massively disproportionate incarceration rates among communities of marginalized peoples, a growing tolerance for violence as a means of social control, and the replacement of rehabilitation with punishment and warehousing as the system's primary ethics, seem to be the main regressive tendencies.

The racist application of law and order has a long pedigree in the United States. The racial construction of criminality may no longer have goals as harsh as those under slavery or the post-Reconstruction struggles that gave rise to the

Black Codes, the convict-lease system, the Magnolia formula or Jim Crow. It remains nevertheless a systemic construction essential to an understanding of the American penal system. Racial profiling, a "war on drugs" that targets African American neighborhoods and the drug dependencies of the poor, zero-tolerance urban policing and "three strikes" legislation have created a prison system whose demographics are wildly at odds with the social profile of modern America.

In the 1990s, African Americans made up about 12 percent of the US population. On December 31, 2000, 46.2 percent of prisoners under state or federal jurisdiction were Black, up from 44.5 percent in 1990. Another 18 percent were Hispanic. For Black males in age categories 20-24, 25-29, 30-34 and 35-39 incarceration rates at the end of 2000 were 7,276, 9,749, 8,690, and 7,511 respectively, compared with 886, 1,108, 1,219, and 995 for white males.[19] According to a 1997 Bureau of Justice Statistics study based on 1991 rates of incarceration, the probability of a Black male doing time during the course of his life was 28.5 percent, compared with 16 percent for Hispanics and 4.4 percent for whites.[20] In some parts of the country, the disparities are even larger. In 1997 in the South, 63 percent of state prison inmates whose race was known were Black.[21] African Americans make up 63 percent of North Carolina's prison population, 76 percent of its drug offenders and 92 percent of those imprisoned for selling and possessing schedule II narcotics.[22]

Race and drugs may be the most visible markers of the incarcerated, but they are not the only ones. According to the Sentencing Project, a Washington-based prison reform organization, a third of inmates in 1999 had been unemployed before their imprisonment. Of those who had been free for at least a year before their sentence, almost a third had incomes less than $5,000. Sixty-five per cent of inmates had failed to complete high school.[23] Writing in 1998, Eric Schlosser estimated that 70 percent of inmates were illiterate, while as many as 200,000 suffered from mental illnesses.[24]

If the raw materials of the prison economy—its inmates—betray one side of penal regression, prison conditions betray the other. Faced with a nexus of huge numbers, increasingly problematic levels of public spending, and the need to satisfy shareholders, costs in both private and public systems must be cut to the bone. Since services and manpower are the main expenses, both have become targets. According to Schlosser, drug treatment has been cut back to the point where it is available to only about a tenth of those who need it. For fear of graduating jailhouse lawyers, prison libraries and educational programs have been reduced dramatically. Exercise facilities are either eliminated or rationed. In a context of enforced idleness, shrink-wrapping software for Microsoft, sewing "Prison Blues" and perhaps even the recently reintroduced chain gang must appear attractive alternatives. Private companies, in particular, have adopted the goal of supervising the largest number of inmates with the smallest number of officers and staff. Increasing reliance on electronic surveillance cuts costs but raises stress and contributes to escalating levels of violence by both officers and prisoners. Order is maintained as much by the indirect rule of prison gangs as by prison administrators. Predictably, recidivism rates are high and the prison comes to resemble a factory for crime rather than a way to limit it.[25]

Explaining the Rise of the Prison Industrial Complex

How do we account for the combination of expansion, privatization and regression that make up the transformation of the American corrections system?

Conventional approaches explain large prison populations as necessary reflections of high rates of crime in American society. In turn, the explanation for these high crime rates is to be found, according to some observers, in America's cultural exceptionalism, which has its roots in the frontier, rugged individualism and easy court-protected access to weapons. Others explain America's historically high crime rates as a consequence of fluctuations in the business cycle and their effect on choices about work and its alternatives. Each of these arguments however fails, either in whole or in part, to fit the available evidence.

FIGURE 2: Historical Trends in rates of Crime and Imprisonment, United States, 1960-1999

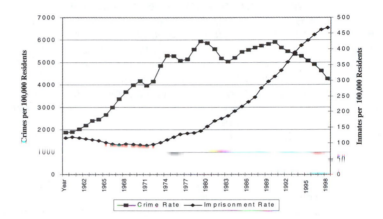

Figure 2 charts the relationship between the overall crime index and the incarceration rate in the US since 1960.[26] While it indicates that both the crime rate and the incarceration rate have risen in the last four decades, it also suggests that the relationship between the two is far from direct. The overall crime index fell in fourteen of the 27 years since the incarceration rate began its increase in the early 1970s. It peaked in 1980, and by 1999, stood at 71.7 percent of its peak– ower than in any year since 1973.[27] There is no clear relationship between the two sets of data. Nor do variations in the crime and incarceration rates fit well with the usual indicators of the business cycle, such as the unemployment rate. As several critics stress, the incarceration boom is not a direct product of variations in crime rates. Rather it is a product of almost three decades of criminal justice legislation that have transformed the relationship between crime and punishment in the United States.[28] And if the data fail to support the argument that high incarceration rates are caused by high crime rates, they equally fail to support the reverse, "prison works", argument favored by many neo-conservative scholars.[29]

The evidence is also unkind to those who argue that the real effect of America's cultural exceptionalism is on violent crime rather than crime in general. If the violent and non-violent components of the overall crime rate are disaggregated, the pattern described above is not dramatically altered. Property crime peaked just prior to the Reagan era in 1980. By 1999 it had fallen to less than 62 percent of its peak, lower than at any time since 1967. The index of violent crime peaked later (in 1991), but has also fallen since then, to 75 percent of its apex in 1999, at a level similar to those in the early 1980s.[30] Moreover, the percentage of offenders imprisoned each year for violent crimes has fallen consistently throughout the incarceration boom. By the 1990s, more than two thirds of those sentenced to prison in any given year were convicted of non-violent property, drug or public order offences, many of which would not result in prison time elsewhere in the world. Drug offenses alone made up nearly 31 percent of all new state admissions in 1998, 21 percent of the state prison population, and almost 58 percent of those incarcerated at the federal level.[31]

The second problem with the American exceptionalism argument is that with respect to the broad tendencies described above, it no longer appears to stand the test of international comparison. The American pattern of decreasing crime rates, increasing policy-driven rates of incarceration, prison privatization, disproportionate victimization of racial and ethnic minorities and deteriorating prison conditions is also the pattern in several other countries, including Canada,[32] Australia[33] and the United Kingdom.[34] The organization of criminal justice in a country may well be an expression of its culture and history. But if this is the case, the United States has more in common with the UK and other white settler former colonies than the exceptionalism argument allows.

As the above suggests, a compelling account of the rise of the prison industrial complex in the United States must be able to do more than explain the disproportionate size of the prison population. It must also explain a specific historical pattern: a three decades-long, uninterrupted expansion that is apparently independent of short-term economic fluctuations and is a political artifact rather than a reflection of crime rates. In addition, it must also deal with the qualitative dimension—the privatization and regression components of the problem. Finally, an adequate account of the rise in the prison industrial complex must be able to address both the international character of the new criminal justice regime and the fact that the American case is quantitatively different from other liberal democracies.[35]

Such an explanation is to be found in the way questions of crime and punishment have been constructed as political issues in the context of two fundamental crises that have afflicted the United States since the late 1960s: the crisis of democracy that began with the civil rights movement and the rise of the new left in the 1960s, and the economic crisis that began in the early 1970s and gave rise to a long period of economic restructuring. These crises have together given rise to a new political formula, of which the expansion-privatization-regression syndrome in corrections is a part. This new formula has transformed the American state in part by undermining faith in the effectiveness of many postwar liberal and/or Keynesian policy preferences. In the process, it has re-legitimized the use of prisons, punishment and private interests as mechanisms for dealing with a wide range of public policy problems beyond those specific to the criminal justice system.

The Crisis of Democracy and the Politics of the "Southern Strategy"

The crisis of democracy of the 1960s and early 1970s first led to the articulation of a punitive politics of law and order with what came to be known in the Nixon era as the "southern strategy".[36] This strategy was an attempt to criminalize where possible, and demonize where not, a range of activities that challenged the limits of American democracy and especially the large-scale political demobilization that was its foundation. Chief among these were civil rights and antiwar demonstrations, civil disobedience of all kinds and Supreme

Court decisions that expanded rights for defendants, African Americans and women.

The symbolic goal of this strategy was to present a political challenge to the status quo as evidence of a complete social breakdown by means of a rhetorical politics that associated the new left and the civil rights movement with crime and moral decay. In this way, popular support could be mobilized behind a punitive response. Its narrower political purpose was to detach Southern white conservatives from the Democratic Party, thus enabling the rolling back of the liberal reforms of the 1960s. Barry Goldwater, whose 1964 presidential candidacy married a law and order campaign with support for states' rights and opposition to the 1964 Civil Rights Act, made the first, unsuccessful, foray. In the presidential elections of 1968 and 1972 George Wallace took up the theme, demonizing civil rights activists and antiwar demonstrators in the same breath as muggers, pornographers, the hypocritical liberal elite, the Supreme Court and the federal bureaucracy.[37]

This nostalgic authoritarian populism, calling for a return to the political and moral order of an earlier America, had two political effects, one short-term and one longer-term. First, it forced Richard Nixon to play the same game in 1968 to avoid losing support to the right. Second, it set the political agenda of the Republican Party for the next generation. Though the primary audience was Southern, both Wallace and Nixon discovered that closet racism played well in other parts of the country. Racial backlash, politicized by Wallace's tirades, institutionalized in Nixon's Southern strategy and "spruced up and vetted by a team of pollsters and political marketing experts, [has] become the common currency of American political rhetoric."[38]

In the process, a host of questions of social policy—taxes, welfare and welfare "dependency", crime and policing, prison construction, individual rights versus social responsibility, affirmative action, drug enforcement, public housing —came to be seen in racialized terms.[39] And conversely, debates about social policy became tools for racial backlash. Angry taxpayers came to be persuaded, even though most of the "facts" are incorrect, that their efforts were supporting socially undesirable lifestyles, as young, single, addicted, inner city Black women, encouraged by the welfare state, gave birth to children who would grow up into an unsocialized and violent criminal "underclass". Taking this view to its extreme, Richard J. Herrnstein and Charles Murray argued that the welfare state is not only immoral in that it subsidizes unacceptable behavior, but also futile, since it cannot alter facts about the race-structured inheritability of intelligence which "keep most members of the underclass from fending for themselves".[40]

The traditional defect of reactionary populism is that while it identifies scapegoats, it has little to offer in terms of solutions. Modern versions like that of Herrnstein and Murray are no different. They make white, racist backlash politically acceptable by re-coding it or gathering spurious "scientific evidence" to "prove" it. But the clock cannot be turned back—the moral order of the past is no longer available. Beyond some vague proposals to "make life easier" for those of perceived low intelligence by returning social policy to states and communities, simplifying rules and clarifying penalties, they have nothing to offer. All that remains is punishment. For Herrnstein and Murray this takes the form of an emerging "custodial state", which would segregate and warehouse the "underclass" while relieving it of child-rearing responsibilities, improve and extend the technology of surveillance, take over welfare provision, and enhance penalties and build more prisons. What they have in mind is "a high-tech and more lavish version of the Indian [*sic*] reservation for some substantial minority of the nation's population, while the rest of America tries to go about its business."[41] As the authors admit, this is only part forecast since, with the rise of the prison industrial complex, much of it is already in place.

Economic Crisis, Restructuring and Social Control

The transformation of the penal economy can be explained only in part by the reactionary response to the political rebellions of the 1960s. A second crucial factor is the economic crisis that began in the late 1960s and the economic restructuring that followed. The material reinforcements of racial backlash and criminalization, in other words, are to be found in labor market policy and the social marginalization associated with the new accumulation strategy that emerged in the 1980s.

Accounts of this crisis and restructuring often contrast a "Golden Age" of American capitalism that lasted from the end of World War II to the late 1960s with a succeeding age usually described as one of crisis, decline or insecurity.[42] In the first period, social and political order was maintained primarily by means of a "Fordist" virtuous circle of rising productivity, profits, wages, standards of living, high levels of employment and mass consumption and an increasingly interventionist and redistributive state. Since work and the incentives associated with it are forms of social control, incarceration rates were low and falling. In contrast, rising unemployment, longer hours, falling real wages, insecure work, increasing poverty rates, dangerous levels of consumer debt, more competitive labor markets, and relative economic stagnation have characterized the second. Control by incentives has given way to control by the "stick."

This conventional account both exaggerates the dominance of the Fordist regime prior to the late 1960s and fails to address the social origins of the restructuring program that emerged from the crisis. The cultural and racial backlash that began in the Southern states in the late 1960s and has become the driving force of national social policy, has its economic counterpart in a Southern strategy of accumulation that has similarly come to dominate economic policy. This Southern accumulation strategy has its roots in the period after Reconstruction, and was based on low-wage, labor-intensive, high exploitation production, and hostility to unions. Since social and political control were achieved through the cultivation and preservation of historic racial antagonisms, industries and labor markets were in most cases racially segregated.[43] The South's "de facto industrial policy" was to provide a safe haven for "footloose" capital by providing an extensive package of relocation incentives and a business climate that protected low-wage, labor-intensive, non-union employers from the regulatory and industrial relations regime and tax structures of the Northeast and Midwest.[44]

In addition to low wages, the South was a region committed to low taxes, especially on capital, and limited social service provision, especially for African Americans and poor whites.[45] It also had a long tradition of using the law as a tool to build and protect a racialized political and economic order. In the nineteenth century for instance, the convict-lease in Alabama was used to create a coerced Black working class for use in the coal and iron industries.[46] The Magnolia formula was a complex menu of legal, constitutional and political provisions pioneered in Mississippi in 1890 and copied in whole or in part throughout the South in the next decade and a half. It was designed to disfranchise those who had least to gain from low-wage accumulation in the South and who had demonstrated a dangerous willingness to consider interracial cooperation and radical reform.[47] Unable to establish control by economic means, Southern planters and industrialists used a combination of coercion and racism. Consequently, the South was a region with disproportionally high prison populations who often lived under brutal conditions. In 1971, towards the end of the period of criminal justice policy liberalism, the rate of incarceration in the South was 220 percent higher than that in the Northeast. Some states, such as Georgia, Texas and North Carolina, had rates that were considerably higher than the regional average.[48]

From the New Deal on, the Southern accumulation strategy was threatened by, but managed to resist, a variety of attempts to nationalize the Fordist regime— the Wagner Act, the Fair Labor Standards Act, Operation Dixie and so on. Later, during a period when the South had lost much of its political strength, the 1964 Civil Rights Act and the Voting Rights Act of the following year promised to destroy the foundations of the Southern model. Southern sociologists began to speculate about the "Americanization of Dixie".[49] But the Southern accumulation strategy survived and, in the context of the economic crisis that emerged in the late 1960s and early 1970s, became the template for the national economic restructuring that took place after 1980.

Reaganism, like its counterparts in the UK and elsewhere, was a strategy to deal with the growing economic crisis by moving to a low-wage, export-oriented accumulation strategy, which required a significant shift in the balance of power between capital and labor.[50] In order to achieve this, the Reagan administration legislated tax reforms that were ostensibly dedicated to removing the state from the backs of all people but were, in reality, heavily skewed to benefit corporations and the wealthy. The distributions of income and wealth were consequently polarized. Federal Reserve decisions to raise interest rates contributed to a large industrial shakeout, increased unemployment and underemployment, a growing poverty rate, large increases in the ranks of the working poor and a general decrease in quality of life. In addition, the labor and civil rights movements came under attack, part-time and "flexible" work was expanded, and the threat and reality of unemployment in an already slack labor market was used to maximize insecurity and reduce wages and benefits of those still employed. Environmental, workplace and consumer protections were weakened and public services-- especially at the state and local levels--were cut back or privatized. Within the corporation, as David Gordon has documented, there was a significant expansion of managerial and supervisory cadres as management by threat (the "stick" strategy) gradually displaced management by incentive. As Gordon's analysis of the relation between managerial expansion and incarceration rates demonstrates, the use of the "stick" by managerial bureaucracies is generally closely related to its use in society.[51]

Since the 1970s, sociologists and other observers report the "Dixification of America" rather than the reverse,[52] suggesting that in the battle between regional accumulation and control strategies, the South has won, at least for now. According to Stephen Cummings, "the economic development policies that we have implemented in the United States over the past three decades have taken on the characteristics of an up-to-date, modified version of those that have been in effect in the American South for decades."[53]

The anti-democratic racial/cultural backlash that began in the 1960s and the economic restructuring program of the 1980s are clearly related, as Parenti and others indicate. To the extent that it involved a general remoralization of society, the former also served to justify a broader set of traditional cultural beliefs that reinforced the restructuring of economic life, emphasizing hard work, discipline and personal responsibility. Moreover, the climate dominated by the social ontology of Thatcherism—that only individuals and families can be said to exist, not communities or societies—justified individual punishment rather than social change as the way to deal with "unacceptable behavior."

It was within this context that the rapid acceleration of the incarceration rate began to take place in the 1980s. A decade later, the Clinton administration's "triangulation" and "third way" politics signaled its acceptance of the main components of Reaganomics, simultaneously destroying one of the few remaining potential obstacles to neo-liberal hegemony, and leaving African American communities more isolated and exposed than they had been for decades. Penal expansion continued to accelerate, reaching unsustainable growth rates by the middle of the decade, ironically almost coinciding with Clinton's signing the law that abolished federal welfare provision. Only in the late 1990s, with the economy approaching full employment, did the rate of expansion begin to slow.

Conclusion

Some observers of the prison industrial complex in the United States have begun to suggest that there is hope for a halt to the inexorable march of the penal economy. In the late 1990s, growth in the incarceration rate faltered, and in 2000 there was an apparent reduction in the private share of the prison system.[54] Some communities now question the balance of costs and benefits to small towns and rural areas that accrue from prison-building, while conditions in some super-maximum security institutions have given rise to federal civil rights suits by the American Civil Liberties Union. California's Proposition 36 replaces imprisonment with mandatory drug treatment for possession offences, and is thought likely to reduce the state's annual prison intake by up to 37,000 a year.[55] In November 2001, a federal appeals court in California ruled that a fifty-year sentence under the state's 3-strike law for stealing a videocassette was cruel and unusual punishment.[56]

Isolated statistics and events need to be treated with some caution however, given the haphazard and incoherent pattern of legal and political decisions that underpins the rise of the penal economy. A few months before the passage of Proposition 36, for instance, Californians voted in favor of Proposition 21, which drastically expanded penalties for gang-related offences while simultaneously lowering the thresholds used to define those gang-related offenses.[57] But suggestions like this do raise the question of how we can assess the life expectancy of the prison industrial complex in its current form.

One way to do this is to examine the self-regulating and self-expanding qualities that derive from the fact that the prison industrial complex is a system whose participants interact symbiotically. The list of beneficiaries is as long as the range of financial and other benefits is wide. Increased incarceration provides corporate participants expanded opportunities for profit making. Politicians and bureaucrats benefit from financial campaign contributions, the "endless dramaturgical possibilities"[58] that result from being "tough on crime" and the revolving door at the end of the public part of their careers. Southern politicians, in particular, benefit from the huge reductions in the size of African American electorates that result from felony disfranchisement laws.[59] Correctional Officers' Unions oppose privatization, but welcome the increased political power that expansion brings and lobby aggressively for more prisoners and more prisons.[60] Small town and rural communities see in the "strategic dispersal"[61] of prisons the possibility of reversing decades of deindustrialization and decline by virtue of job creation and the transfer of population and tax dollars from urban areas where most of their inmates formerly lived.[62] For the nation as a whole, the prison industrial complex, apparently unresponsive to the business cycle, may act like its military counterpart as an automatic Keynesian stabilizer in the event of recession.[63]

If the above analysis is correct however, the most compelling reasons for thinking that the prison industrial complex is here to stay have less to do with its effects than with its roots in historical structures and dynamics that continue to shape American development. A disproportionately large and racialized penal system has been a permanent part of the Southern landscape since the end of the nineteenth century. It reflects a political ideology designed to preserve peculiar Southern race and class structures and reinforce a low-wage, high-exploitation accumulation strategy. In the twentieth century, incarceration rates began to rise during what Cummings calls "the first conservative era" from 1921 to 1933, a period like the present characterized by the neo-liberal model that dominated the South: tax cuts, anti-unionism, income polarization, and so on.[64] Depression, war and Keynesianism created the conditions for a different accumulation strategy during the middle third of the century, confining the neo-liberal model to the South and largely discrediting the notion that imprisonment was the answer to all social problems. A combination of democratic rebellion, economic crisis and globalization in the last three decades of the twentieth century created the conditions that permitted the nationalization of the Southern accumulation strategy and its associated racial political ideology and re-asserted the neo-liberal nexus of "free economy, strong state". Prison expansion to Southern levels across the nation soon followed.

Ideas, institutions, policies and the like are rendered powerful not so much by the number of people and organizations they reward, but by their degree of fit with the dominant social and political structures and tendencies at work in the world. The structures and tendencies that have given rise to the prison industrial complex–the uneven development of American capitalism, global overproduction, privatization, rentierization, flexibilization, neo-liberal restructuring and zero-sum politics at the national level–remain the dominant ones at work in the world today. That being the case, the prison industrial complex will have plenty to do in the foreseeable future, "while the rest of America tries to go about its business".

Endnotes

1. Mike Davis, "Hell Factories in the Field: A Prison industrial complex" (1995); Steven Donziger, "The Prison industrial complex," *Washington Post*, 17 March 1996; Eric Lotke, "The Prison industrial complex," *Multinational Monitor* (1996) <http://www.igc.org/ncia/pic.html>; Angela Davis, "Masked Racism: Reflections on the Prison Industrial Complex" (1998), <http://www.arc.org/C_Lines/CLArchive/story1_2_01.html>; Eric Schlosser, "The Prison industrial complex," *The Atlantic Monthly* (1998) <http://www.theatlantic.com/issues/98dec/ prisons.htm>; Christian Parenti, *Lockdown America: Police and Prisons in the Age of Crisis* (1999): ch. 11.
2. Bertrand Bellon and Jorge Niosi, *The Decline of the American Economy* (1988); Michael Perelman, *The Pathology of the U.S. Economy* (1996): chs. 4 and 5; Grant McConnell, *Private Power and American Democracy* (1966); Theodore J. Lowi, *The End of Liberalism: The Second Republic of the United States* (1979); Philip Beardsley, *Whose Country America?* (1973).
3. US Department of Justice, Bureau of Justice Statistics, *Sourcebook of Criminal Justice Statistics Online* <http://www.albany.edu/sourcebook/index.html>: Table 6.26; Allen Beck and Lauren Glaze, *Correctional Populations in the United States, 1980-2000* (2001) <http://www.ojp.usdoj.gov/bjs/glance/tables/corr2tab.htm>.
4. The incarceration rate is defined as the number of prisoners per 100,000 residents.
5. Allen J. Beck and Paige M. Harrison, "Prisoners in 2000" (2001), August.

6. Human Rights Watch, *World Report 2001* (2001) <http://www.hrw.org/wr2k1>; Secretary of State for the Home Department, *Prison Statistics, England and Wales 2000* (2001), Cmnd 5250, Table 1.21.

7. "US Jails Two Millionth Inmate," *Manchester Guardian Weekly*, 17 February 2000: 1.

8. Allen Beck and Paige Harrison, "Prisoners in 2000," *supra* note 5.

9. US Department of Justice, "National Correctional Population Reaches New High," Press Release, 26 August 2001.

10. Sidra Lee Gifford, *Criminal Justice Expenditures and Employment* (US Department of Justice, Bureau of Justice Statistics, 2000) <http://www.ojp.usdoj.gov/bjs/data/eetrnd06.wk1>.

11. Eric Schlosser, "The Prison industrial complex," *supra* note 1; LIS Inc., "Privatization and Contracting in Corrections: Results of an NIC Survey," *Special Issues in Corrections* (1996), February.

12. Douglas McDonald et. al., *Private Prisons in the United States: An Assessment of Current Practice* (Cambridge, MA: Abt Associates, 1998): 5-7.

13. Allen Beck and Paige Harrison, *supra* note 5.

14. US Department of Justice, *Sourcebook of Criminal Justice Statistics Online, supra* note 3 at Tables 1.82 and 1.83.

15. Eric Lotke, "The Prison industrial complex," *supra* note 1; Steven Donziger, "The Prison industrial complex," *supra* note 1; Carol Strick, "The Ties That Bind," *North Coast Express* (1998), Winter <http://www.sonic.net/~doretk/Issues/98-12 percent20WIN/tiesthatbind.html>.

16. Julie Light, "The Prison Industry: Capitalist Punishment," *North Coast Express* (2000), Spring <http://_www.sonic.net/~doretk/Issues/00-03-SPR/thepris.html>; Christian Parenti, *Lockdown America: Police and Prisons in the Age of Crisis, supra* note 1 at ch. 11.

17. Eric Bates, "Private Prisons," *The Nation*, January 5, 1998 <http://www.thenation.com/>; Steven Donziger, "The Prison industrial complex," *supra* note 1.

18. Sir Leon Radzinowicz, "Penal Regressions" (1991): 431.

19. Allen Beck and Paige Harrison, "Prisoners in 2000," *supra* note 5.

20. Thomas P. Bonczar and Allen J. Beck, *Lifetime Likelihood of Going to State or Federal Prison* (1997).

21. US Department of Justice, Bureau of Justice Statistics, *Correctional Populations of the United States 1997* (2000): Table 5.6.

22. Ned Glasscock, "Blacks behind bars in record numbers," *Raleigh News and Observer*, 22 July 2001 <http://www.newsobserver.com/standing/collections/census/1100000026231.html>. Schedule II narcotics include both powdered and freebase (crack) cocaine. Although drug use rates among African Americans and whites are similar, federal guidelines use five grams of crack cocaine to trigger the same five-year mandatory sentence as 500 grams of powdered cocaine, the recreational drug of choice for affluent whites.

23. The Sentencing Project, *Facts about Prisons and Prisoners*.

24. Eric. Schlosser, "The Prison industrial complex," *supra* note 1.

25. Christian Parenti, *Lockdown America: Police and Prisons in the Age of Crisis, supra* note 1 at chs. 9 & 10; Eric Bates, "Private Prisons," *supra* note 17; Mike Davis, "Hell factories in the field," *supra* note 1; Eric Schlosser, "The Prison Industrial Complex," *supra* note 1; David Downes, "The Macho Penal Economy: Mass Incarceration in the United States: A European Perspective" (2001): 219; David Ladipo, "The Rise of America's Prison industrial complex" (2001): 109-123; Jenni Gainsborough and Marc Mauer, *Diminishing Returns* (2000).

26. See Endnote 3 above.

27. Bureau of Justice Statistics, *Sourcebook of Criminal Justice Statistics Online:* Table 3.120.

28. Christian Parenti, *Lockdown America: Police and Prisons in the Age of Crisis, supra* note 1 at chs. 1-5; Ladipo (2001); David Downes, "The Macho Penal Economy," *supra* note 25.

29. Jenni Gainsborough and Marc Mauer, *Diminishing Returns, supra* note 25; David Ladipo, "The Rise of America's Prison industrial complex, *supra* note 25.

30. Bureau of Justice Statistics, *Sourcebook of Criminal Justice Statistics Online:* Table 3.120.

31. Eric Schlosser, "The Prison Industrial Complex," *supra* note 1; Human Rights Watch, *World Report, supra* note 6; The Sentencing Project, *Facts about Prisons and Prisoners, supra* note 23.

32. In 2000, the Canadian crime rate was at its lowest since 1979, and its murder rate had been falling since the mid-1970s. Canada's prison population increased by 53.2 percent from 1978 to 1996, before falling by 6.2 percent from 1996 to 1999. On average, Aboriginal people are over 8 times as likely to be imprisoned as non-Aboriginals in Canada (Statistics Canada, *Canadian Socio-economic Information and Management Database*, Matrix 312, Series Nos. 91343, 91348, 91353, 91358, 91363, 91368, 91373, 91378, 91383, 91388, 91393, 91398).

33. From 1982 to 1999, the Australian prison population increased by 119.2 percent and the incarceration rate from 90 to 145. Although crime rates rose overall, the pattern during those two decades is one of increases and declines rather than a steady upward trend. From 1993 to 1998 there were no significant increases in the main crime categories. The incarceration rate for Indigenous Australians was almost 15 times higher than for non-Indigenous Australians in 2000 (Carlos Carcach and Anna Grant, "Imprisonment in Australia: Trends in Prison Populations and Imprisonment Rates, 1982-1998" (1999); Australian Bureau of Statistics, *Prisoners in Australia* (2000) <http://www.abs.gov.au/ausstats>; Cheryl

McDermid, "A precipitous increase in Australia's prison population" *World Socialist Website* 1 (2000), November <http://www.wsws.org/articles/2000/nov2000/pris-n01_prn.shtml>.

34. The British Crime Survey recently found that in 2000 the chance of becoming a victim of crime was at its lowest in 20 years. Between 1990 and 1998, the British prison population increased by 46 percent before leveling off until 2000 and then rising by 5.3 percent in 2000-2001. For whites in the UK, the incarceration rate was 188; for all Black Britons: 1,615; for Afro-Caribbean Britons: 1,704 ("Crime rate survey claims record fall," *The Guardian*, 25 October 2001 <http://www.guardian.co.uk/crime/article/ 0,2763,580678,00.html>; Secretary of State for the Home Department, *Prison Statistics, supra* note 6; Home Office, UK, *Monthly Prison Population Brief* (2001), August <http://www.homeoffice.gov.uk/rds/ pdfs/prisaug01.pdf>.

35. Sir Leon Radzinowicz, "Penal Regressions," *supra* note 18 at 39.

36. Christian Parenti, *Lockdown America: Police and Prisons in the Age of Crisis, supra* note 1 at xii.

37. Dan T. Carter, "Legacy of Rage: George Wallace and the Transformation of American Politics" (1996): 3-26.

38. *Id.*, 19.

39. Thomas B. Edsall and Mary D. Edsall, *Chain Reaction* (1991).

40. Richard J. Herrnstein and Charles Murray, *The Bell Curve* (1994).

41. *Id.*, 526.

42. Stephen A. Marglin and Juliet B. Schor, *The Golden Age of Capitalism: Reinterpreting the Postwar Experience* (1990); Samuel Bowles, David M. Gordon and Thomas E. Weisskopf, *Beyond the Waste Land: A Democratic Alternative to Economic Decline* (1984); David M. Gordon, *Fat and Mean: The Corporate Squeeze of Working Americans and the Myth of Corporate Downsizing* (1996).

43. Phillip J. Wood, *Southern Capitalism: The Political Economy of North Carolina, 1880-1980* (1986); Mike Davis, *Prisoners of the American Dream* (1986): ch. 5.

44. Thomas A. Lyson, *Two Sides to the Sunbelt* (1989).

45. V. O. Key, *Southern Politics in State and Nation* (1949).

46. Alex Lichtenstein, "Through the Rugged Gates of the Penitentiary: Convict Labor and Southern Coal 1870-1900" (1994).

47. James E. All, *The Impact of the Voting Rights* Act on Black and White Voter Registration in the South" (1994): 354-6.

48. These statistics are from incarceration rate data kindly provided to me by Paige Harrison of the Bureau of Justice Statistics.

49. John Egerton, *The Americanization of Dixie* (1974).

50. Robert Brenner, "Uneven Development and the Long Downturn" (1998): 1-264.

51. David Gordon, *Fat and Mean, supra* note 42 at ch. 5.

52. Peter Applebome, *Dixie Rising: How the South is Shaping American Values, Politics and Culture* (1996); Ron Nixon, "The Dixification of America" (1996): 19-22.

53. Stephen D. Cummings, *The Dixification of America* (1998): x.

54. *Sourcebook of Criminal Justice Statistics Online:* Table 1.82

55. Fox Butterfield, "Number of People in State Prisons Declines Slightly," *New York Times*, 13 August 2001; Barry Yeoman, "Steel Town Lockdown: Corrections Corporation of America is trying to turn Youngstown, Ohio into the private-prison capital of the world" *Mother Jones*, May/June 2000 <http:// www.motherjones.com/mother_jones/MJ00/steeltown.html>; "Lawsuits Against Prisons," *North Coast Express* (2001), Spring: <http://www.sonic.net/~doretk/Issues/01-03-SPR/lawsuits.html>; William Booth and Rene Sanchez, "Drug Reform Initiatives Receive Support of Voters," Washington Post, 9 November 2000: A48.

56. Greg Winter, "California Appellate Court Ruling Aids Foes of 3-Strike Law", *New York Times*, December 10, 2001 <http://www.nytimes.com/2001/12/10/national/10stri.html>

57. "California Youth Incarceration Initiative," *North Coast Express* (2000), Summer <http:// www.sonic.net/~doretk/Issues/00-06 percent20SUM/california.html>.

58. David Downes, "The Macho Penal Economy," *supra* note 25 at 213.

59. Andrew Shapiro, "The Disenfranchised" (1997): 60-62; Somini Sengupta, "Felony Costs Voting Rights for a Lifetime in 9 states," *New York Times*, 3 November 2000; Jamie Fellner and Marc Mauer, *Losing the Vote: The Impact of Felony Disfranchisement Laws in the United States* (1998).

60. Mike Davis, "Hell Factories in the Field," *supra* note 1.

61. This is the term used to denote the common practice in the military industrial complex of cultivating Congressional support for weapons systems by dispersing contracts and sub-contracts in as many congressional districts, states and regions as possible. See, for example, Hedrick Smith, *The Power Game: How Washington Works* (1988): ch. 8.

62. Tracy Huling, "Prisoners of the Census," *Mother Jones*, May 10 2000, <http:// www.motherjones.com/reality_check/census.html>.

63. David Downes, "The Macho Penal Economy," *supra* note 25 at 220.

64. Stephen Cummings, *The Dixification of America, supra* note 53 at ch. 4.

CHAPTER TWO

Privatized Problems:
For-Profit Incarceration in Trouble

Christian Parenti

Anti-prison activists in the US commonly blame over-incarceration on private prisons and the 'new slavery' of prison labor. The argument runs as follows: the 'prison industrial complex' is a replacement for the allegedly decimated military industrial complex——that constellation of civilian government, military power and private capital given its name by Eisenhower—which for two generations has been America's de facto industrial policy. This same line is argued by writers in the *Wall Street Journal* and *Atlantic Monthly* and in most books on prisons. But this analysis is factually wrong and politically stunted. Fundamentally this line of argument is economistic, focusing on the role of specific corporate interests at the expense of examining the capitalist system as a whole and the political (not always directly economically rational) policies that drive prison expansion.

First, the military industrial complex—driven by the Pentagon budget—is not withering. The last several years of Pentagon budgets have ranged from US $297 to $325 billion, some of the greatest even in real terms. Nor is prison labor a large or profitable piece of the economy, or even of the prison economy. Most prison labor is conducted for the public sector and operates at a loss. Only about 3000 prisoners work for private firms and that number has been stable for most of the last decade.[1] More important however, is the question of private prisons.

During much of the 1980s and nineties, the number of private prisons grew at almost 20 percent annually. Through assiduous cultivation of state officials, the private prison industry helped shape criminal justice policy in a few states. These factors made the emerging private prisons look like the new military industrial complex. But now the for-profit jailers' partnership with government faces very serious problems: private prison growth has stopped and even gone into reverse, as major firms sell off facilities around the country. Why has this industry, once the darling of Wall Street, gone into a tailspin? The short answer is that recent events have unveiled private jailers as cheats, liars and liabilities and all of this, plus huge debts, has been bad for business.

Anatomy of the Private Gulag

At their peak, for-profit lock-ups controlled about five percent of all US prison beds. The current private incarceration industry began with a humble Reagan-sponsored experiment to house INS detainees in two for-profit detention centers in Houston and Laredo, Texas. The architect of the plan was Attorney General

Meese (who now works at a pro-privatization think tank). In response to the federal government's broad invitation to capital, a pair of Tennessee entrepreneurs using money from Kentucky Fried Chicken and the know-how of several public sector corrections veterans, established the first private prison company: Corrections Corporation of America (CCA). At the apex of this fast-growing empire sat a troika of well-connected 'good old boys': Doc Crants, CCA's president and visionary; his old Westpoint roommate, CCA co-founder Tom Beasley who quite conveniently served a stint as chairman of the Tennessee Republican Party; and finally, providing the technical expertise, T. Don Hutto, former Commissioner of the Virginia and Arkansas Departments of Corrections.[2] Other board members include corrections veterans such as Michael Quinlan, former director of the Federal Bureau of Prisons. CCA's American empire consists of 64 prison and other facilities in 21 states, down from 78 a few years ago. However the company's political and geographic stronghold remains Tennessee where it dumps inmates from Wisconsin, Hawaii, Montana, the District of Columbia and Puerto Rico into a sprawling, barely regulated, private prison system.

The next largest private jailer is Wakenhut Corrections, with about 17,000 beds at 24 facilities. Named after its founder, former FBI agent George Wakenhut, the firm is a subsidiary of Wakenhut's private security service, which made it big more than forty years ago by scooping up contracts to guard America's nuclear waste dumps and testing installations. Since going public in 1994, Wakenhut's stock price has soared 800 percent and split once.[3] Behind CCA and Wakenhut is a hungry pack of some sixteen other firms that run local jails, private prisons, and INS detention centers. Underwriting the growth of both public and private prisons is a battery of mainstream financial houses. It is estimated that giant Wall Street firms such as Goldman Sachs and Merrill Lynch write between 2 and 3 billion dollars in prison construction bonds every year.[4]

Financially CCA, Wakenhut and the other private prison firms performed handsomely for almost two decades. One financial analyst dubbed CCA "a theme stock for the nineties."[5] In 1995 the company went public at $8 per share; by year's end the price had soared 385 percent to $37 per share. As late as 1998, CCA was still capitalized at $3.5 billion, and considered a 'secure' investment with growth potential.[6]

But all that has changed. CCA stock plunged in 2001 to below $1 per share. It has since bounced back somewhat, thanks to post-September 11security concerns and a federal bailout in the form of two long-term contracts to jail immigrant federal prisoners.[7] The fundamental problems remain: private prisons are too abusive, chaotic and poorly run to be the super profitable growth machines once imaged. For private prisons these problems are inextricable. To maintain market dominance, CCA and other firms do things the old fashion way: giving generously to politicians and buttering up the press while overcrowding and viciously abusing prisoners.

Private Hell

The root cause of the financial crisis facing for-profit dungeon keepers is the appalling disregard for basic human rights. Looked at from another angle, you might say private prisons produce a unique set of economic 'externalities.' CCA, like its peer firms, had started out by cherry picking—taking on easy to handle minimum-security contracts. Once they set off after bigger economic prizes, trouble began.

The first political rumblings from within the bowels of the CCA Empire came born on clouds of pepper spray and smoke in the summer of 1995. Prisoners from North Carolina—homesick, ill-treated and packed into a Tennessee house of corrections—trashed and burned two of their dorms. The riot lasted several hours and was only put down when CCA's overwhelmed guards finally handed off operations to local SWAT commandos.[8]

Another dent in the image of for-profit prisons was the riot at an INS detention facility run by Esmor Correctional Services, which housed non-criminals–would-be migrants awaiting immigration hearings. The "facility" in question was actually nothing more than a Motel Six retrofitted with bars, bunks, and fences. Packed into tiny rooms with no access to exercise or other activities, the detainees endured endless months of stultifying boredom, bad food, smelly toilets and humiliation at the hands of Esmore rent-a-cops. On June 18, 1995, desperation peaked: the 300 detainees finally exploded, trashing their rooms, smashing up toilets, and burning mattresses. After the riot was suppressed, 25 immigrants were transferred to the Union County jail where guards administered methodical punishment beatings.[9]

Since these first conflagrations, private prisons have become known for their deprivation, brutality, frequent escapes, and inmate violence. But the industry's reputation reached a new nadir on July 25, 1998, when six Washington, DC prisoners busted out of the CCA-owned Northeast Ohio Correctional Center in Youngstown, Ohio. Built to house 1,700 medium security prisoners from DC and other states, the Youngstown joint, Ohio's only private dungeon, was plagued with problems from the moment it opened in May1997. Poorly constructed, under-staffed, and immediately filled to capacity with both medium *and* maximum security convicts, the CCA prison became a chaotic gladiator's pit where nonviolent burglars and crack addicts were haphazardly thrust into cells with seasoned rapists, habitual killers and other high security predators. The fifteen months of operations preceding the escapes had seen forty-four assaults, sixteen stabbings (including one guard), and two murders. When state inspectors finally did arrive, they were turned away at the gate.[10]

But it was the news that six very angry young men from Washington, DC, had cut open CCA's chain link fence, crossed an electrified barrier, plowed through yards of razor wire and were now at large among the good people of Youngstown that *really* sent shock waves of fear throughout Ohio and, for different reasons, throughout the ranks of CCA investors.[11] For almost a week, regular police, tactical squads, canine teams, and helicopters combed an ever-widening circle around the prison in search of the runaways. One by one cops busted the desperate, exhausted escapees, some of whom had been badly wounded by the razor wire. The last departed inmate, Vincent Smith, was finally taken down in the backyard of Susie Ford's house. A 54-year-old grandmother of three living on the outskirts of Youngstown, Ms. Ford got the news live, when her frantic sister telephoned telling her to turn on the television: "That's our building! That's our building!" Indeed it was. And the Ford sisters watched their screens in amazement as police swarmed through the shrubs out back.[12]

The next months brought a cascade of revelations and inquiries. It seemed CCA's rent-a-cop security force was not only ill equipped and poorly trained, but battered by employer racism and reckless penny-pinching. The new prison was so unsafe, staff were soon deserting in droves. "I stopped counting at 70," said Victoria Wheeler, a former CCA guard. Another former correctional officer (CO), Linda Carnahan, recalled how she was sent—completely untrained in the use of firearms—to patrol the perimeter with a shotgun. "I told my captain that if we had an escape, I didn't know how to pick up a gun and shoot it. He said go out there anyway." CCA had deliberately skipped firearms training because state certification costs up to $3,000 per person.[13] A later report by the U.S. General Accounting Office found, among other things, that 80 percent of CCA guards had no corrections experience; many of the guards were only eighteen and nineteen years old; medical records went unaccounted for while more than 200 chronically ill prisoners were left untreated in the general population; and almost no effort was made to separate violent psychopaths from peaceful convicts. Later inmate civil rights suits alleged: that guards violated regulations by using tear gas inside; that prison tactical teams dragged inmates naked and shackled across floors; and that during cell searches convicts were forced to strip, kneel, and were shocked with stun guns if they moved. One female clerical worker—made to inventory inmate processions during such a cell raid—summed it up: "I told my roommate that the guards here are like people who got beat up in high school and this was their way of getting back at the world."[14]

The on-going pandemonium in the Youngstown joint was rooted in CCA's greed. So eager were the boys in Tennessee to start counting ducats that they rushed to fill the new prison by importing 150 convicts per day until the prison was full. Normal procedure in opening a new penitentiary is to process only 80 to 100 inmates *per week*, so as to check for security flaws.[15] But CCA was reimbursed per day, per inmate. Adding insult to injury, CCA had won handsome concessions from Youngstown just for building the penitentiary. Battered by deindustrialization, with an official unemployment rate of over 10 percent, the city had supplicated in the usual fashion: fawning city officials gave CCA 100 acres of prime real estate (much of which it had aggressively annexed from a smaller town) and an $11 million tax break.[16] Coincidentally, the tax abatement was directly proportional to that year's Youngstown City School District budget deficit. In fact the city's public schools—which had just eliminated 149 jobs and *closed* six schools—were in such horrible condition that Ohio State Auditor Jim Petro declared a "fiscal emergency."[17]

Even before CCA inmates had "hit the fence", local police and Democratic lawmakers were having second thoughts about the efficacy of hosting scam artists from Tennessee and their captives from DC. For one thing, neither the city nor the state had any regulatory control over CCA, in part because none of the convicts were from Ohio. When a state legislative bill designed to impose limited control on CCA was set to become law, the company's president, David L. Myers, killed it with a lobbying blitzkrieg that included personally calling lawmakers at home with threats to abandon the Youngstown prison and take its 400 jobs elsewhere.[18] Nonetheless the breakout caused a change of heart among legislators, and all further moves to expand private prisons in Ohio were blocked. In response to this and other political heat, CCA began experimenting with public relations retailing in the form of 'fuzzy' TV commercials intoning: "CCA. Quietly going about the business of public safety."[19]

The Youngstown debacle was not particularly unique, just well publicized. Despite the fact that for-profit jailers try to keep their captives away from the press, (in Youngstown, CCA put a gag order on prisoners), there is mounting evidence that private prisons are rife with abuse. For example, at Brazoria County Detention Center in Angleton, Texas, a Capital Correctional Resources Incorporated (CCRI) facility, guards made a "training video" of themselves beating, stun-gunning, and unleashing dogs on naked prisoners from Missouri. Injured inmates were dragged face down back to their cells. After the guards' rampage, cellblock telephones were cut off, preventing the Missouri captives from calling home.[20] The video was later obtained by lawyers and broadcast nationally. On it a guard taunts, "Gentlemen, you might not like it here, but this is the way it is. Do what you're told."[21]

The sadism of Brazoria was the hybrid result of power-tripping guards and institutional greed: CCRI paid its guards only $8 an hour, gave them little training, and hired convicted felons. One of the video's star performers, the CO Wilton David Wallace had served six months in federal prison in 1984 for abusing inmates while employed as a Texas state prison guard. The CCRI-leased jail was also abusing its charges in less dramatic ways: a typical menu revealed endless lunches of black-eyed peas, corn bread and water. The punishment diet was peanut butter sandwiches and water.[22] Similarly, in 1996, 14 convicts and two guards were injured at a CCA prison in Texas when prisoners rioted to protest poor food, inadequate recreation and other bad conditions.[23]

At a Wakenhut facility in New Mexico, a supervisor ordered his subordinates to beat a verbally belligerent prisoner. According to a state investigation, inmate Tommy McManaway was restrained and repeatedly kicked in the groin while lying face down on the floor. When the assault was exposed, the supervisor told two lieutenants and a sergeant to "stick to their stories and he would back them up."[24] Most of the time, abuse in private pens is kept hidden by just this method.

Not long ago, more bad news emerged from a CCA joint in Tennessee, housing exiles from Wisconsin. The trouble began when a CCA guard was attacked, beaten, and left in a coma. The subsequent 'investigation' took a brutal and arbitrary form. A seven-member paramilitary style tactical team based outside the prison was called in to do the heavy lifting: they ended up torturing between 15 and 20 prisoners with beatings and electric shock.[25] At first, both CCA and Wisconsin officials dismissed inmate complaints and suits, but as evidence mounted and family members protested, the cover-up collapsed. Wisconsin State officials and the FBI began investigating and several CCA staff were fired.[26] Over all, Tennessee officials say the rate of serious incidents in CCA prisons is sometimes as much as 28 percent higher than in state prisons.[27]

Private juvenile facilities have also been exposed as abusive. One such outfit in Colorado, operated by Rebound Corporation and housing 184 teenage felons, was shut down because it over-utilized restraints, allowed sex between staff and inmates, and in other ways physically abused its wards (all of which culminated in the preventable suicide of a 13-year-old boy). In 1998, South Carolina canceled a juvenile contract with CCA after numerous escapes, allegations of excessive force, and documentation of torture by claustrophobia in which as many as 18 boys were packed into a one-person cell with only cups for toilets. [28]

The problem, as far as prison corporations are concerned, is that such abuse creates bad press and hampers the expansion of private prisons. Even Tennessee Governor Don Sundquist, an ardent supporter of for-profit incarceration, was moved to propose a ban on private prisons releasing out-of-state inmates in Tennessee and denying such prisons the ability to house out-of-state sex offenders or habitual escapees. He also called for private prisons to reimburse the state for the costs of post-escape manhunts and riot suppression.[29]

Guards vs. Investors: Resistance to Privatization

The most important direct check on the expansion of private gulags is the growing political muscle of unionized prison guards. As incarceration in general increases, so too do the ranks, assets, and raw power of organized corrections officers, and in recent years guards have taken tentative steps to halt the expansion of for-profit jailers. The union that set the model and still leads the fight against privatization is the super powerful California Corrections Peace Officers Association (CCPOA), the largest political action committee in California. "We call them dungeons for dollars because their allegiance is to stockholders, not to the public," says CCPOA spokesman, Lance Corcoran.[30] Guards in other states around the country are beginning to follow the CCPOA template.

In most states, the COs' road to political power leads through the American Federation of State, County and Municipal Employees (AFSCME), whose Corrections United subdivision represents 100,000 publicly-employed prison guards. Calling private prisons "a threat to public safety" and "a taxpayer rip-off", AFSCME president Gerald McEntee has stepped into the fray, producing a 16-page report and a video on problems associated with private pens.[31] Even more interesting, AFSCME actions against the for-profit jailers are happening on the ground, at the local level. In Pennsylvania, for example, 300 guards marched outside the Pennsylvania Department of Corrections shouting "Death to Privatization." This, combined with intensive lobbying, forced free market-loving Governor Tom Ridge to kill plans for leasing the state's newest lock-up to a private company.[32]

In Wisconsin, the State Employees Union, led by Green Bay prison guard Gary Lonzo, has effectively blocked privatization. "These privateers come in, and they're only in it for one reason," says Lonzo. "They're not going to build a prison in Wisconsin unless they make money. And to make money, they have to pay generally substandard wages, [and provide] less training and less programming."[33] Privatization in Virginia, with one for-profit dungeon, has also run into opposition from angry AFSCME guards. And when Nebraska guards flexed, state legislators shut the door on Wakenhut, which had been trying to grab a piece of that state's prison system. Privatizers in Iowa are also facing well-organized COs who decry privatization as a "prescription for disaster" and use their weight with the board of corrections to shut out for-profit jailers. "This isn't for rent-a-cops," explained prison guard Wade Erickson.[34] Even before the Youngstown escape, 400 Ohio guards protesting any further privatization converged on the Statehouse. "The next thing you know, they're going to want to privatize another, then another one, then another," said a guard in a skunk-skin hat, which, as he explained, signified the odor of CCA.[35]

Perhaps the most dramatic campaign against prison privatization occurred in Tennessee, CCA's own gently rolling Siberia. In 1997, the company launched plans to take over the state's *entire* prison system. For a moment, CCA-drafted legislation was teetering on the brink of passage—it even seemed that the company had won the consent of union leadership. But a counter-offensive involving churches, student groups, and the 2,000 rank and file prison guards of the Tennessee State Employees Association, tipped the scales. Using the Internet to link forces and disseminate information (much of it leaked by CCA prisoners and disgruntled employees), the coalition forced the pro-privatization politicians and waffling union leaders to back down. In October 1998 there was another attempt at total privatization, which triggered a protest by some 2,000 guards at the governor's office and the nearby CCA world headquarters. As political backdrop, the COs had the spectacle of yet another big escape: four inmates had just busted out of CCA's South Central Correctional Facility in Clifton, Tennessee and were believed to be at large.[36]

The politics of guard unionism is wrought with contradiction: they have been instrumental in creating and shaping the prison industrial complex by bolstering hawkish anti-crime politicians and lobbying for get-tough legislation like three strikes. Moreover the CO unions in California and elsewhere have protected their rank and file members against any and all disciplinary procedures. However in their fight against privatization, the guards not only defend their own interests, but inadvertently the larger agenda of public accountability and democratic control over state functions. As bad as public prisons are, private ones are worse: both in fact and in principle.

Conclusion: A More Efficient Gulag?

Abuse, the lawsuits resulting from it and opposition from guards all translate into higher costs for private prison corporations. The most definitive test of such assertions was a broad 1996 study by the Government Accounting Office (GAO), which reviewed and compared all the major studies of the costs and quality of private prisons, conducted since 1991. The GAO found that in the end, public and private prisons cost taxpayers roughly the same. [37]

To the extent that private prisons do save on expenses, most of the surplus goes not to the state but rather takes the form of corporate *profit*. Moreover, the drive toward lowering costs—that is, the drive toward greater profit—engenders various other problems. As will be explored in other chapters of this book, private prisons make money by cutting corners, which means skimping on food, staffing, medicine, education, and other services for convicts. It also means fielding poorly trained, ill-equipped, non-unionized and often brutal guards (see Chapter 9). Exploitation of staff leads to high turnover rates, while the drive to keep overhead low means that many open positions remain vacant for months on end. One private prison in Florida, according to state audits, had an annual staff turnover rate of 200 percent.[38]

So, if we don't blame the *direct* profit motive of *specific* firms such as prison corporations, how do we explain the massive growth of incarceration? A better analysis of the American prison state uses as its analytic crowbar the concept of society-wide *class struggle*. This model understands incarceration, directly profitable or not, as part of a larger circuitry of social control in which the poor are blamed for their own plight, class privilege is protected by force, and a portion of the population who cannot find work because of the market economy's metabolic need for unemployment, are managed by the state with violence and incarceration.

Since the late 1960s when the new crackdown took place, the American political and economic system has faced two domestic challenges, both of which have been managed with criminal justice repression. The first challenge was the political rebellion of the Vietnam era: the Black power movement, mass community organizing, the antiwar movement and regular rioting. The state's response to this kaleidoscopic wave of rebellion was a massive police buildup beginning with the Omnibus Crime and Safe Streets Act of 1968. An economic crisis existed parallel to this political upheaval manifest as plunging profits and stagnant growth. By the early 1980s, the political challenges of the late sixties and early seventies had been vanquished but the economic crisis was just being tackled. To restore profits and growth Reagan unleashed a massive and brutal economic restructuring: unions were smashed, health and safety standards rolled back and social spending gutted. As a result, wages declined and profits recovered, but poverty surged. To manage this class of new paupers, politicians and corporate media fixated on drugs and the alleged moral deficiencies of the poor. The 'rabble' needed controlling and criminal justice repression was the tool for the job; the war on drugs its justification. What ensued was a massive increase in the rate of incarceration, most of it handled by states not private firms.

This analysis is less about "bad corporations" and more about *the role of state violence in reproducing capitalism*. Incarceration is seen as just one piece of a larger system of physical and discursive social control. Prison is the motherboard. Other components include: county jails, INS detention centers, psychiatric wards, halfway houses, hospital emergency rooms, homeless shelters, skid row and media demonization of the poor. All of these locations share populations and mark, segregate, contain and *process* not just people but also the social symptoms of poverty, racism and exploitation—all of which are essential to a healthy capitalist society. Thus, state repression (which is always articulated through racism) is intimately linked to the power of the working classes, the economic regulation of labor and the accumulation of surplus value throughout the whole society.

Endnotes

1. For a version of this argument see: Christian Parenti, *Lockdown America* (2000).
2. Chris Bryson, "Crime Pays For Those in the Prison Business," *National Times*, September 1996; Ken Silverstein, "America's Private Gulag," *Prison Legal News*, June 1997; Stephen Handelman, "Prisons for Profit," *Toronto Star*, 25 September 1994.
3. Andrew Billen, "A Man Called Wackenhut," *The Observer*, 3 November 1996; Randy Gragg, "A high-security, low-risk investment: private prisons make crime pay," *Harper's Magazine*, August 1, 1996.
4. Paulette Thomas "Making Crime Pay: Triangle of Interests Creates Infrastructure To Fight Lawlessness" *Wall Street Journal*, 12 May 1994.
5. *Id.*
6. Eric Lotke, "The prison-industrial complex" Multinational Monitor, November 1, 1996.
7. Judith Greene "Bailing out private jails," *American Prospect*, 10 September 2001.
8. Shirley Downing, "Officials still seek causes of riots at two prisons; FCI reports 'semi-lockdown'; Mason facility back to normal," *Commercial Appeal Memphis*, 31 October 1995; Shirley Downing: Bartholomew Sullivan, "Prison riot unleashes questions," *Commercial Appeal Memphis*, 13 November 1995.
9. MaryAnn Spoto, "Victim saw jail officer during day of beatings," *Star-Ledger Newark*, NJ, 4 February 1998; David Stout, "Detention jail called worse than prison," *New York Times*, 19 June 1995.
10. Martin Weil, "Six D.C. Inmates Escape Ohio Prison," *Washington Post*, 26 July 1998; Ann Fisher, "Questions Raised Over Thwarted Prison Inspection," *Columbus Dispatch*, 8 May 1998; "CCA Prison off to a Rocky Start," *Prison Legal News*, October 1997.
11. Eleena de Lisser, "Prison's Woes Spur Sell-Off In CCA Shares," *Wall Street Journal Europe*, 29 July 1998.
12. Cheryl W. Thompson, "Ohio Sours On Prison Managed by Private Firm; D.C. Inmates Live In Troubled Facility," *Washington Post*, 19 October 1998.
13. Quotes from: "CCA-Run Prison Under Attack by Former Employees," *The Tennessean*, August 31, 1998; Mark Tatge, "Private Prisons: A Growth Industry Youngstown: Lock-up Would be Ohio's First," *Plain Dealer*, 26 December 1995.
14. *Id.*, Mark Tatge, "Private Prisons: A Growth Industry Youngstown: Lock-up Would be Ohio's First".
15. Cheryl W. Thompson, "Report Galvanizes D.C. Prison Critics," *Washington Post*, 10 December 1998.
16. Michael Scott and Janet Tebben, "Prison project: Annexation clears the way," *Tribune Chronicle* (Warren Ohio), 29 March 1996; Mark Tatge, "Private Prisons: A Growth Industry Youngstown: Lock-up Would be Ohio's First," *supra* note 13; Cheryl W. Thompson, "Ohio Issues Restraining Order for Prison Firm; Control of Facility Cannot Be Changed," *Washington Post*, 19 November 1998.
17. "Schools in Crisis," *Cincinnati Post*, 20 September 1996. Around the same time, drug treatment and poison controls services were also being slashed. Sue MacDonald, "Poison Hotline: Not just for emergencies, it's a source for prescription drugs and substance abuse information," *Cincinnati Enquirer*, 19 March 1996.
18. Dan Egbert, "Ohio CCA facility hit by inmates' lawsuit," *Nashville Banner*, 24 November 1997; Mark Tatge, "Prison Control Bill Dies in Senate: Private Operator Blocks Attempt at Regulation," *Plain Dealer*, 25 November 1997.
19. Tom Humphrey, "Private prison backers adopting new tack," *Knoxville News-Sentinel*, November 22, 1998.
20. Kim Bell, "Missouri Says Texas Attack Was Planned: Distance Makes Keeping Track of Out-of-State Inmates Dfficult," *St. Louis Post-Dispatch*, 24 August 1997.
21. "Shakedown; Closer look at a private prison in Texas that videotaped guards' abuse of inmates," Dateline NBC, Tuesday, 23 September 1997.
22. Barbara Hoberock, "Removal of Inmates Not Linked to Tape," *Tulsa World*, 21 August 1997;

"Guard in jail video guilty of past beating," *Austin American-Statesman*, 21 August 1997.

23. Greg Jaffe and Rick Brooks, "Hard Time: Violence at Prison Run By Corrections Corp. Irks Youngstown, Ohio," *Wall Street Journal*, 5 August 1998.

24. "Prison supervisor ordered inmate beating, N.M. finds," *Denver Post*, 28 November 1998.

25. "Corrections officials to seek money to send more inmates out of state: $3.2 million request includes funds to move 519 additional prisoners," *Milwaukee Journal Sentinel*, 27 November 1998; "FBI Probe at Prison Praised: Lawyer Claims Client Beaten at CCA Facility," *The Tennessean*, 12 November 1998.

26. "Inmate Abuse Denied by Prison in Tennessee Complaints Probably Groundless, Wisconsin Officials says," *Wisconsin State Journal*, 8 October 1998; Richard P. Jones, "State now admits private prison abuse: Seven employees of corrections firm fired as result of Tennessee incident," *Milwaukee Journal Sentinel*, 11 November 1998.

27. G. Jaffe and R. Brooks, "Hard Time: Violence at Prison Run By Corrections Corp. Irks Youngstown, Ohio," *supra* note 23.

28. "Former High Plains Officials Regroup Company Applies to Open Private Youth Prison Under New Name," *Denver Rocky Mountain News*, 8 November 8, 1998; G. Jaffe and R. Brooks, "Hard Time: Violence at Prison Run By Corrections Corp. Irks Youngstown, Ohio," *supra* note 23.

29. Bonna M. De la Cruz, "Sundquist Offers Private-Prison Rules," *The Tennessean*, 19 December 1998.

30. Daniel B. Wood, "Private Prisons, Public Doubts: As California's first big private prison goes up, questions surface on profits vs. safety," *Christian Science Monitor*, 21 July 1998.

31. David Judson, "Guards' union attacks prison privatization," Gannett News Service, 6 May 1998.

32. Peter Durantine, "Ridge Now Against Private Firm to Run a New Prison," *Pittsburgh Post-Gazette*, 27 February 1997.

33. "Governor Waffles on Private Prison Plan: the Proposal: Build Them in Wisconsin," *Wisconsin State Journal*, 9 December 1998.

34. Laura LaFay, "Private VA. Prison Targeted by Group of Public Workers: The Emphasis is Placed on Profit Rather than Safety, the Group says," *Virginian-Pilot and The Ledger-Star*, (Norfolk, VA) 14 May 1998; Robynn Tysver, "State Workers Decry For-Profit Prisons," *Omaha World-Herald*, 14 May 1998; "Prison Guards in Union Call Privatization Bad Idea for Iowa," *Omaha World-Herald*, 13 May 1998.

35. Ann Fisher, "Correction Officers Protest Push for Private Prisons," *Columbus Dispatch*, 18 March 1998.

36. Alex Friedman, "Tennessee Prison Privatization Bill Fails to Pass," *Prison Legal News*, September 1998; Bonna M. De La Cruz, "Corrections Officers Plan Prison Privatization Protest," *The Tennessean*, 15 October 1998.

37. "Private and Public Prisons: Studies Comparing Operational Costs and/or Quality of service" (1996): 7, 20.

38. Ken Silverstein, "America's Private Gulag," *supra* note 2 ; Stephen Handelman, "Prisons for Profit," *supra* note 2.

CHAPTER THREE

The Problem of Prison Privatization: The US Experience

Jeff Sinden

The past two decades have witnessed a disturbing trend in the American criminal justice system. From immigration detention centers and work farms to county jails and state prisons, private corporations have entered the incarceration 'business' en masse. In fact, there are currently more than 100,000 people incarcerated in private prisons in the United States.[1] Privatization of the criminal justice system has been driven largely by the currently dominant ethos of a neoliberal agenda in which a wide variety of traditionally public goods have been transferred to the supposedly more efficient and less corrupt private sector. However, correctional services are fundamentally different from other goods, such as garbage collection, which have been transferred into private hands. Providing correctional services is a vastly complex and difficult task. Institutions are charged with the task not only of protecting society but also caring for the physical, psychological and emotional needs of inmates so that they may one day successfully return to the community. Unfortunately, private corrections firms have failed miserably in the task they were so eager to take on, as systematic human rights abuses have become the rule and not the exception.

Various forms of private sector involvement in the corrections industry exist in the United States, some more problematic than others. The most common and least controversial involves the private delivery of goods and services in publicly run prisons. According to a report by the US Bureau of Justice Assistance, during the past twenty years, "the practice of state and local correctional agencies contracting with private entities for medical, mental health, educational, food services, maintenance, and administrative office security functions has risen sharply."[2] For example, Sodexho Marriott Services provides food services for public correctional institutions (and college and university campuses) across North America.[3] Generally, this practice is not incompatible with a healthy respect for prisoners' rights.

As will be explored in later chapters, however, many aspects of privatization have been much more problematic. For example, the private delivery of medical services in correctional institutions, both public and private, has caused significant problems as every dollar of a fixed annual stipend not spent on health services for prisoners benefits the company's bottom line, encouraging an unacceptable incentive to skimp on critical care.[4] In fact, a 1998 independent prison health care audit found that "more than twenty inmates died as a result of negligence, indifference, under-staffing, inadequate training or overzealous cost-cutting."[5]

The use of prisoner labor by the private sector to produce goods and services has also been controversial. There has been a long tradition of exploiting prison labor in the United States and throughout the world by governments and corporations alike.[6] For example, during the 19th century, inmates at the Kingston, Ontario penitentiary in Canada "were either leased out to farmers, or their work was contracted to provide industry with cheap labor."[7] While this practice was largely abolished during the early twentieth century, it has returned as of late. In 1986, former US Supreme Court Justice Warren Burger called for prisons in the United States to be transformed into "factories with fences" in order to reduce the costs of incarceration.[8] Prison administrators have taken his advice to heart as many states have allowed corporations to purchase convict labor at cut-rate prices. For example, in California, prisoners who make clothing for export make between 35 cents and $1 an hour.[9] Similarly, in Ohio, prisoners are paid approximately 50 cents an hour for data entry work.[10]

The most controversial form of private sector involvement in correctional services is the management and operation of entire correctional facilities by for-profit corporations. In some cases, private firms have taken over the operation of public facilities; in others, corporations have constructed and then managed entire sites. This type of involvement has fostered situations in which a myriad of human rights abuses have occurred.

In many cases, the corporation's desire for cost-effectiveness has led to simple corner-cutting, which in turn fosters abuses. For example, low pay and a subsequently high turnover rate has led to a grossly underqualified and inexperienced staff at many institutions.[11] Far too often, this has resulted in the flagrant abuse of prisoners. In 1997, a videotape surfaced in the media that showed guards at a private facility in Texas shooting unresisting prisoners with stun guns and kicking them to the ground. One of the guards involved had recently been fired from a government-run prison for similar conduct.[12]

Rehabilitation costs have also been systematically slashed by the prison firms. In many of the institutions, opportunities for meaningful education, exercise and rehabilitation are virtually non-existent. For example, in 1995 a private jail in Texas was investigated for diverting $700,000 intended for drug treatment when it was found that inmates with dependency problems were receiving absolutely no treatment.[13] This type of flagrant neglect amounts to abuse and almost certain recidivism as job training and education programs, drug and alcohol rehabilitation services, as well as social and psychological counseling, are absolutely critical if the transition back into society is to be successful.

Neoliberalism, Increased Criminalization and the Drive to Privatize

Privately operated prisons are not a new phenomenon in the United States or in the Western world. In fact, privately run jails were in operation centuries ago in medieval England.[14] In the US, the seventeenth and eighteenth centuries witnessed the private ownership and operation of prisons in several states.[15] During this period, the Texas state penitentiary was leased out to a private business, which in turn subleased inmate labor to farms and industry. Similarly, the California state penitentiary at San Quentin was constructed and operated by private business.[16] "Conditions were so horrid" in these facilities, states John Dilulio "that some inmates were driven to suicide while others maimed themselves to get out of work or as a pathetic form of protest."[17]

Partly as a result of poor conditions and systematic abuse, the ownership and operation of private correctional facilities were transferred to the state in the early 20th century and thereafter "the operations and administrative functions in correctional facilitates were delegated to governmental agencies, authorized by statute, staffed by government employees, and funded solely by the government."[18] During the ensuing period, there was virtually no private sector involvement in correctional services. This changed rapidly in the 1980s.

The 1980s saw the return of neo-liberal, market-driven policies championed by President Reagan in the United States and Prime Minister Thatcher in the United Kingdom. In 1980, Ronald Reagan roared into the White House, riding a wave of popular anti-government sentiment and Cold War fear. His promise to get the government "off the backs" of the American people was welcomed by many in the US who were tired of the deep economic recession and growing public debt. Reagan's neoliberal mantra included deregulation, free trade, a hostility towards taxes and the labour unions and an almost maniacal desire for defense spending.[19] However, the central value of Reagan's doctrine and of neo-liberalism itself is the notion of free-market competition.

In championing an agenda whereby the public delivery of goods was viewed as inherently inefficient and necessarily corrupt, the Reagan administration sought to curtail all forms of government activity. Even the most basic government functions came under attack, as the administration argued that they could be more efficiently performed by the private sector. To this end, Reagan created a "privatization czar" post in the Office of Management & Budget and appointed a President's Commission on Privatization.[20] A wide array of government services, from health care to garbage collection, were subsequently sourced out to the more 'efficient' private sector; it was not long before many policy makers were advocating for privatization in the criminal justice system. A 1985 National Institute of Justice (NIJ) report explains that despite continual increases in taxpayer dollars spent on the criminal justice system, "neither local, State, nor Federal resources had seriously affected the problem of crime" and yet still "conspicuously absent from …crime prevention …is the input of private industry."[21]

The American criminal justice system was seen as ripe for privatization by Reagan's supporters largely as a result of the rapid and steady increase in the cost of correctional services over the previous several years. According to the US General Accounting Office (GAO), total prison operating costs (for both federal and state) grew from about US $3.1 billion in 1980 to more than $17 billion in 1994, an increase of nearly 550 percent based on inflation-adjusted dollars.[22]

These increasing costs were a direct result of a similar rise in the prison population as the past twenty years has seen an explosion in the number of individuals incarcerated in America. The number of prisoners–with 2 million currently behind bars–has increased three fold since 1980.[23] This scale of imprisonment is unmatched throughout the world (with the possible exception of Russia); in 1998, the US incarcerated 690 residents per 100,000, compared with 123 per 100,000 in Canada and 60 per 100,000 in Sweden.[24]

How can this huge increase in the prison population be explained? Rising crime and arrests are clearly not the cause. Douglas McDonald documents that "the annual number of arrests nationwide rose only slightly during this period."[25] The increase is due mainly to sentencing policies. According to a 1996 report by the US GAO, "inmate population growth in recent years can be traced in large part to major legislation intended to get tough on criminals, particularly drug offenders. Examples of this new "get tough" policy include mandatory minimum sentences and repeat offender provisions."[26]

The War on Drugs, Mandatory Minimums, and Three Strikes Legislation

In the early 1980s, President Reagan began a concerted 'war on drugs', which he and First Lady Nancy Reagan pursued with enthusiasm throughout their tenure in the White House. Anyone involved with the drug trade—producers, traffickers, dealers and users—was to be identified, criminalized and harshly punished. To this end, Reagan significantly increased the budget of law enforcement agencies, doubling the FBI's funding and increasing the resources of the Drug Enforcement Administration.[27] Additionally, he oversaw the creation of new institutions such as the Organized Crime Drug Enforcement Task Force (OCDETF), whose mandate is to coordinate the efforts of the multitude of agencies that fight the war on drugs.[28] Federal legislators also embraced the drug war, enacting comprehensive laws to deal with convicted offenders.

In 1984 the US Congress enacted both the Comprehensive Crime Control Act and the Sentencing Reform Act. These laws eliminated federal parole and established mandatory minimums for many drug-related offences.[29] Mandatory minimum sentences impose a strict lower limit on the number of years an individual convicted of a particular crime must serve in prison. Regardless of their assessment of the appropriateness of the punishment, judges must sentence convicted defendants to the minimum prison term.

Two separate Anti-Drug Abuse Acts—one passed in 1986 and a second in 1988—established a strict regime of drug-related mandatory minimums. While these were supposedly designed to punish those who produce and distribute drugs, the amounts that trigger mandatory sentences were in many cases small enough to affect users. For example, the simple possession of five grams of 'crack' cocaine was to elicit a mandatory sentence of five years in prison.[30] According to the Sentencing Project, in 1999 sixty-two percent of federal offenders convicted of a drug offense received a mandatory minimum prison term. More than 50 percent of these received at least five years.[31]

The harsh and often arbitrary nature of mandatory minimum sentences has come under sustained criticism by advocacy groups, legislators and judges alike. Many feel that justice is not achieved when judges have no discretion when deciding upon the terms of punishment. During one such sentencing, Judge Thelton Henderson, a US district court judge in San Francisco, was quoted as saying, "[t]his is the first time since the sentencing guidelines have been imposed that I find myself having to impose a 20 year mandatory minimum. While my opposition has been academic thus far, I now find that I join a long list of judges who are appalled at what they have had to do, and I am appalled at what I feel I am required to do right now."[32]

The war on drugs continues unabated to this day. According to the Office of National Drug Control Policy, the US federal government will spend over $19.2 billion on the war on drugs in 2001.[33] This massive amount of funds is not without result. It is estimated that more than 1.5 million people were arrested for drug-related charges in 2001 alone.[34]

The war on drugs and its cohort, mandatory minimum sentencing, are together part of a broader trend which, during the past two decades, has seen politicians across the US clamoring to 'get tough on crime'. One of the most dramatic illustrations of this has been the so-called 'Three Strikes' legislation, first passed by the state of California in 1994. Under this law, individuals convicted of a third felony offense are automatically sentenced to twenty-five years to life in prison. Since 1994, half of the states in the US have enacted similar laws.[35]

While the three strikes law was ostensibly designed to isolate and punish the most serious, habitual offenders, far too often this has not been the case as "an ever increasing number of 'three strikes' prosecutions are for crimes as menial as petty theft of a can of beer or a few packs of batteries."[36] For example, one California man is currently serving a sentence of 25 years to life after being convicted of stealing a pair of sneakers (he was previously convicted twice for theft).[37] In 2000, another man's appeal of a three strikes sentence for the theft of $20 worth of instant coffee was denied.[38]

Clearly, the three strikes regime has significantly impacted the scale of imprisonment in the US. As of June 2001, more than 50,000 offenders had been admitted to prison under the law in California alone.[39] Most of those sentenced to 25-year terms are convicted of nonviolent crimes. In fact, according to the *Contra Costa Times*, in California "the crime that most frequently led to a three strikes conviction that garnered 25-to-life or more was robbery at 18.2 percent, followed by first-degree burglary (11.2 percent) and drug possession (9.8 percent)."[40]

The 'war on drugs', featuring mandatory minimums and other 'tough on crime' legislation such as the three strikes law, has been largely responsible for the explosive scale of incarceration in the US since the 1980s. The public corrections system was overwhelmed by the huge influx of inmates during this period. The system, it was argued, simply could not accommodate the sheer number of prisoners as prisons were consistently overflowing. This overcrowded system, coupled with ballooning costs and the rise of neo-liberalism, set the stage for private sector involvement in American corrections in the early 1980s. The market was quick to react, and a number of firms emerged to fill the newly found niche. These corporations promised to provide the same level of correctional services for substantially less money—predicting savings to be between 5 and 15 percent.[41]

It was argued that privately operated facilities could perform more efficiently than their public counterparts for several reasons. Firstly, public agencies are believed to have few incentives to reduce costs. In fact, many public administration experts argue that public bureaucracies have a natural tendency to seek to increase their own budgets.[42] Conversely, in the private sector, competition in the marketplace and the possibility of loss and bankruptcy require managers to minimize costs. According to privatization advocates, pressure from shareholders to provide dividends will lead to more cost-effective operations.[43]

Another major advantage of the private sector often cited by prison privatization advocates is the speed and efficiency with which the market can finance and construct new prison facilities. The rapidly increasing prison population has necessitated the construction of countless new facilities throughout the US. In fact, the annual cost of building new penitentiaries in the past decade has been approximately $7 billion per year.[44] While state governments have generally taken five to six years to construct each new facility, private companies claimed to be able to do the same job in half the time.[45]

The Re-emergence of Private Prisons in the US

Privately owned and operated prisons first re-emerged in the US in the early 1980s in response to an acute overcrowding problem in Immigration and Naturalization Service (INS) facilities in Texas and California. State governments transferred some of their detainees to institutions run by Behavioral Systems Southwest (BSS), a for-profit firm, for a daily fee of $2 per prisoner plus costs.[46]

While the lifespan of BSS was relatively short, the practice of detaining undocumented people in private institutions quickly became commonplace. By 1986, 25 percent of all INS detention facilities were operated by private firms.[47]

State governments soon followed suit. By 1989 private correctional firms were operating approximately two dozen major facilitates, including three medium or maximum adult correctional institutions.[48] Today there are approximately 102 private facilities, holding more than 100,000 prisoners across the US.[49] Texas currently has the most facilities (43), followed by California (24), Florida (10), and Colorado (9).[50] In 1999, a corporate plan to take control of the entire Tennessee prison system was narrowly averted, as anti-privatization advocates succeeded in having the enacting legislation quashed in the state legislature.[51]

A few major players have emerged in the private prison industry, the oldest and largest of which is the Tennessee-based Corrections Corporation of America (CCA) established by the same entrepreneurs as was the Kentucky Fried Chicken fast-food chain. CCA currently controls approximately half of the private prison beds in the United States and has operations in the United Kingdom and until recently Australia.[52] The next largest prison corporation, controlling about a quarter of the private prison beds in the US, is Wackenhut Corrections, a subsidiary of the well-established Wackenhut private security service.[53] In addition to CCA and Wackenhut, there are about a dozen other for-profit prison firms currently operating in the US.[54]

Most private institutions are located in small towns in the southern and western United States. Politicians offer tax breaks and low, non-union wages in order to attract investment and jobs to their often poverty-stricken jurisdictions. A prison can literally 'make' a small town, providing hundreds of jobs and millions of tax dollars.[55] In order to fill the facilities, prisoners are often shipped in from out of state. Private prisons in Arizona, for example, have been stocked with Native Americans from as far away as Alaska.[56]

The private corrections industry quickly became a favorite on Wall Street. From an initial public offering price of $8 per share in 1995, the price of CCA stocks quadrupled in less than a year and hit highs of more than $100 in 1998 as investors rushed to secure their place in the booming industry.[57] Similarly, Wackenhut investors were treated to skyrocketing share prices in the mid 1990's.[58] While both have come down from their dizzying heights (CCA shares are currently at approximately $13 while Wackenhut's are at about $16), they are still seen by experts as secure investments[59] with excellent fundamentals: a recent report by the US Department of Justice estimates that annual total revenues for the industry are approximately $1 billion.[60]

Legal and Human Rights Issues

The emergence of the private prison industry in the US has fostered a tense legal debate. Many have questioned whether it is legal for federal and state governments to source out correctional services. One of the major features of the modern nation state is its monopoly on the legitimate use of violence and coercion in society. Only the state can detain, arrest and punish criminals. Many argue that "to continue to be legitimate and morally significant, the authority to govern those behind bars, to deprive citizens of their liberty, to coerce (and even kill) them, must remain in the hands of government authorities."[61] The American Bar Association has pointed out that "incarceration is an inherent function of the government and that the government should not abdicate this responsibility by turning over prison operations to private industry.[62] However, most legal scholars have suggested that private prisons are in fact legal in the US, unless specifically prohibited within a jurisdiction: "the question of whether a state can delegate the task of imprisonment has been raised occasionally, but thus far no authoritative court ruling or constitutional provision has been cited to prevent such delegation."[63]

Each new for-profit institution generally requires the consent of the state legislature.[64] Once the decision has been taken, a call for bids is made, encouraging corporations to submit proposals. Based on the promised level of service and associated costs, the government awards the contract to the firm with the strongest bid. Each state has adopted statutes that regulate their public correctional facilities, which governments attempt to apply to the private institutions through the contracting process. Contract provisions often——though not always ——stipulate minimum service levels such as the provision of educational and rehabilitation services.

However, performance monitoring and accountability are major problems in the industry as privatization encourages cost efficiency and not necessarily quality services or safety. The most common means of state monitoring of private facilities is through inspection. Typically, government inspectors visit a private operator's facility once a year to conduct an in-depth inspection and analysis including "structured interviews with administrators, staff, and clients; physical inspections of facilities; direct observation of services and programs; and attendance at hearings and meetings."[65] This is the case in Florida where the statute authorizing privatization calls for annual inspections. A report follows inspection "which serves to uncover or anticipate problems, initiate technical assistance, or promote the modification or termination of the contract."[66]

However, as J. Keating Jr. puts it "annual or semiannual inspections of privately operated secure correctional facilities are simply not enough."[67] For this reason, several states, including California, require full-time government monitoring staff in all private facilities. However, "there is no magic in the use of a full-time monitor, who may be seduced by the contractor's overt corruption or subtle cooptation."[68] Further, full-time monitors significantly increase costs and have been resisted by the corrections corporations.

The monitoring mechanism favored by the corporations has been facility accreditation. CCA officials boast that the independent American Correctional Association (ACA) has accredited all of their facilities.[69] While this may be the case, John Dilulio argues that this means little as "accredited facilities have been and are among the worst in the nation."[70] It is clear that as of yet there are no adequate solutions to the problem of corporate accountability. The incentives provided by the market to cut costs are stronger than the monitoring mechanisms that seek to keep this tendency in check. Meanwhile, it is the human rights of prisoners that suffer due to physical abuse and a serious lack of essential services.

Conclusion

An exploding prison population in the US and the rising costs accompanying it, coupled with a neoliberal reliance on the market for the provision of traditionally public goods and services, provided an impetus for prison privatization in the early 1980s. State and federal legislatures were lured by the promise of substantial savings made by for-profit jailers. Interestingly, the cost savings that were promised by the industry have not materialized. In 1996, the US GAO "could not conclude whether privatization saved money."[71] Similarly, a 2001 study commissioned by the US Department of Justice concluded that "rather than the projected 20 percent savings, the average saving from privatization was only about 1 percent, and most of that was achieved though lower labour costs."[72]

The private prison industry has clearly not achieved the substantial cost savings that were billed as a major feature in the drive to privatize. Nevertheless, free-market advocates may be inclined to argue that the services provided by private facilities are more efficient and of a higher quality than that provided by government-run operations. However, as subsequent chapters will clearly show, human rights abuses in for-profit correctional institutions have been systemic.

Endnotes

1. J. Austin and G. Coventry, *Emerging Issues on Privatized Prisons* (2001): x.
2. *Id.*, 2.
3. <www.sodexhousa.com/>.
4. W. Allen and K. Bell, "Death, Neglect and the Bottom Line: Push to Cut Costs Poses Risks," *St. Louis Post-Dispatch*, 27 September 1998.
5. *Id.*
6. D. Shicor, *Punishment for Profit: Private Prisons/ Public Concerns* (1995): 31.
7. J. Gandy and L. Hurl, "Private sector involvement in prison industries" (1987): 186.
8. P. Wright, "Slaves of the State," Prison Legal News, May 1994.
9. *Id.*
10. D. Cahill, "The Global Economy Behind Ohio Prison Walls," *Prison Legal News*, March 1995 / April 1996.
11. J. Greene, "Prison Privatization: Recent Developments in the United States," Presented at the International Conference on Penal Abolition, 12 May 2000.
12. S. Smalley, "For-profit prisons offer privatization lessons," *National Journal*, 3 May 1999.
13. K. Silverstein, "America's Private Gulag," *Prison Legal News*, June 1997.
14. R. Pugh, *Imprisonment in Medieval England* (1968).
15. J. DiIulio, "The duty to govern" (1990): 158.
16. J. Austin and G. Coventry, *Emerging Issues on Privatized Prisons, supra* note 1 at 10.
17. J. DiIulio, "The duty to govern," *supra* note 15 at 159.
18. J. Austin and G. Coventry, *Emerging Issues on Privatized Prisons, supra* note 1 at 11.
19. J. Karaagac, *Between promise and policy* (2000).
20. *Id.*
21. William C. Cunningham and Todd H. Taylor, *Crime and Protection in America* (1985): 2.
22. *Id.*, 1.
23. "US Jails Two Millionth Inmate," *Manchester Guardian Weekly*, 17 February 2000: 1.
24. R. Walmsley, *World Prison Population List* (2000).
25. D. McDonald, ed., *Private Prisons and the Public Interest* (1990): 5.
26. United States General Accounting Office, "Private and public prisons – studies comparing operational costs and / or quality of service," (1996).
27. C. Parenti (1999): 17.
28. *Id.*
29. *Id.*, 50.
30. Families Against Mandatory Minimums <www.famm.org>.
31. Sentencing Project <www.sentencingproject.org>.
32. Families Against Mandatory Minimums, *supra* note 30.
33. Office of National Drug Control Policy <www.whitehousedrugpolicy.gov>.
34. Federal Bureau of Investigation,Uniform Crime Reports <www.fbi.gov/ucr/99cius.htm>.
35. Sentencing Project, *supra* note 31.
36. *Id.*
37. *Id.*
38. *Id.*
39. *Id.*
40. Contra Costa Times, Three Strikes Facts, 27 February 2000 <www.contracostatimes.com/>.
41. J. Austin and G. Coventry, *Emerging Issues on Privatized Prisons, supra* note1 at 22.
42. Public choice theorists argue that the self-interest of public bureaucrats leads them to maximize their bureau's budget because larger budgets are a source of power, prestige and higher salaries. Please see Iain McLean, *Public Choice: An Introduction* (Oxford: Basil Blackwell, 1987).
43. C. Thomas, *Corrections in America* (1987).
44. C. Parenti, *supra* note 27 at 213.

45. J. Austin and G. Coventry *Emerging Issues on Privatized Prisons, supra* note at 15.

46. A. Press, "The Good, the Bad and the Ugly" (1990): 25.

47. *Id.*, 25.

48. D. McDonald, *Private Prisons and the Public Interest, supra* note 25 at 1.

49. J. Austin and G. Coventry, *Emerging Issues on Privatized Prisons, supra* note 1.

50. *Id.,* ix.

51. A. Press, "The Good, the Bad and the Ugly," *supra* note 46 at 28.

52. C. Parenti, *supra* note 27 at 218.

53. *Id.*

54. *Id.*

55. *Id.,* 212.

56. *Id.*

57. S. Smalley, "For-profit prisons offer privatization lessons," *supra* note 12.

58. *Id.*

59. C. Parenti, *supra* note 27 at 219.

60. J. Austin and G. Coventry, *Emerging Issues on Privatized Prisons, supra* note 1 at ix.

61. J. Dilulio, "The duty to govern," *supra* note 15 at 159.

62. D. Shicor, *Punishment for Profit, supra* note 6 at 52.

63. A. Press, "The Good, the Bad and the Ugly," *supra* note 46 at 25.

64. J. Keating, "Public over Private: Monitoring the Performance of Privately Operated Prisons and Jails" (1990): 145.

65. *Id.*

66. *Id.*

67. *Id.*, 147.

68. *Id.*, 146.

69. *Id.*, 153.

70. *Id.*, 163.

71. J. Austin and G. Coventry, *Emerging Issues on Privatized Prisons, supra* note 1 at iii.

72. *Id.*

CHAPTER FOUR

Juvenile Crime Pays–
But at What Cost?[1]

Alex Friedmann

The National Juvenile Detention Association estimates that 5 percent of the nation's juvenile facilities are privately operated. The construction of for-profit prisons, detention centers and boot camps for youthful offenders has become a rapidly expanding industry as youths are channeled from the schoolhouse to the jailhouse in ever-increasing numbers. By slashing operating costs and providing subsistence level services, companies can reap handsome profits from the millions of dollars they receive through government contracts.

'A Growth Industry'

According to a study by the Office of Juvenile Justice and Delinquency Prevention (OJJDP), from 1991 to 1995 the population of youthful offenders held in privately-operated facilities grew 9.6% to an estimated 35,600.[2] In 1997, Equitable Securities Research released a report entitled "At-Risk Youth: A Growth Industry," which indicated there were 10,000 to 15,000 private juvenile justice service providers nationwide; publicly traded juvenile corrections companies made $75 million in net profit in 1996 alone. An estimated $3 billion is spent each year on services for juvenile offenders at the federal, state and local levels, and up to $50 billion is spent annually on programs for at-risk youth.

Private-sector companies that provide primarily adult corrections services have jumped on the "jails for juveniles" bandwagon. Corrections Corporation of America (CCA), Wackenhut and Corrections Services Corp. have all expanded their incarceration services to include for-profit juvenile facilities. In May 1997, Cornell Corrections, another private prison contractor, announced its acquisition of the Abraxas Group, a leader in juvenile supervision services that provides residential, educational and treatment programs to over 1,300 youths.[3]

Most privatized services for youthful offenders, however, are provided by companies that specialize in that field. One of the industry leaders is Youth Services International (YSI). YSI manages over 20 juvenile facilities with more than 4,000 beds; the company has annual revenues of approximately $100 million.[4] YSI was bought out by Correctional Services Corp. in 1999.[5] Other established companies in the for-profit juvenile corrections industry include Rebound, Inc., Youthtrack, and Nashville, Tennessee-based Children's Comprehensive Services.

Mixed Reviews

The privatization of corrections-related services for youthful offenders, including incarceration, has received mixed reviews. Cash-strapped state and local governments faced with burgeoning juvenile offender populations have embraced the concept. "The private sector is financially better able to fill the immediacy of the need to offer the kinds of programs that are necessary," says John Joyce of the Florida Department of Juvenile Justice. Judy Brisco with the Texas Youth Commission agrees: "They fill a vital role because we can't meet the needs of every kid."

The public's reaction to private juvenile justice services has been less enthusiastic. In 1997, for example, YSI's plans to build and operate detention centers in Pennsylvania and New York were withdrawn after the company met stiff resistance from local community members.[6] Such opposition is partly a "not in my backyard" attitude, while other criticisms mirror those leveled against private companies that operate adult prisons: an industry that profits from imprisonment has an inherent conflict of interest in rehabilitating offenders. It is immoral for companies to reap profits from incarcerating inmates, and it is improper for the government to contract its responsibility for the custody and control of prisoners to the private sector.

Communities have also voiced concerns about safety and security issues, and these concerns are entirely justified in light of past incidents that have occurred at private juvenile centers. In 1994, Rebound lost a three year, $150 million contract with Baltimore County, Maryland to manage the Charles R. Hickey School, a facility for serious youthful offenders, after the company allowed too many escapes.[7]

Other juvenile justice service providers have had similar problems. In July 1994, the same week that YSI assumed Rebound's canceled contract to operate the Charles R. Hickey School, a juvenile escaped from the facility. Four months later, a female employee was raped by a youth at the school's sex offender unit. She had been left alone with the juvenile, which was a violation of the terms of YSI's contract. The senior staff member at the school was fired. Finally, on 5 June 1995, seven juveniles overpowered a bus driver and three counselors, and escaped as they were being driven across campus; several other youths were injured when the bus crashed.[8]

Sometimes the problem is not with the juvenile offenders but instead with the company contracted to incarcerate them. The worst-case scenario in this regard resulted in South Carolina's June, 1997 decision not to renew a $14 million contract with CCA to operate the 400-bed Columbia Training Center. Seven youths escaped in August 1996 and the facility's administrator was replaced. A review of operations at the training center three months later found that staff members had used excessive force. This was confirmed in an independent evaluation commissioned by the governor's office in January, 1997. CCA employees were accused of hog-tying juveniles, and several of the youths claimed they had been subjected to physical abuse and were denied food, medical care and toilet facilities.[9]

After eight more juveniles escaped from the center in February, 1997, CCA agreed to withdraw from the contract, stating it was "inordinately distracting to both parties". CCA later lost a civil rights lawsuit brought by juveniles formerly incarcerated at the center. A federal jury awarded over $3 million in damages against the company and found that CCA had a policy and practice of mistreating youths at the facility.[10]

Despite these setbacks, the private juvenile corrections industry continues to grow as state and local governments attempt to cope with decreasing budgets and increasing numbers of juvenile offenders–the latter being driven by politically-motivated 'tough-on-crime' legislation. As in any industry, the operational emphasis is on generating profit, often to the exclusion of other, more humane factors such as rehabilitation or ensuring a safe environment for incarcerated youth. As a direct result of this profit-margin mentality, an increasing number of privately operated juvenile detention facilities have been cited for abusive conditions, illustrated by the following case studies involving for-profit juvenile facilities in Louisiana, Arkansas and Colorado.

Fear and Loathing in Louisiana

The U.S. Justice Department filed suit on 5 November 1998, against the state of Louisiana for failing to protect juvenile prisoners from brutality and for failing to provide adequate education, medical and mental health care.[11]

"It's incredibly unusual," said David Utter, director of the Juvenile Justice Project of Louisiana, which also filed suit against the state over conditions at one of its four juvenile prisons, the privately-owned Tallulah Correctional Center for Youth. "I don't even know when the Justice Department ever filed suit in a case like this."[12]

"Over the past two years," the Justice Deptartment told the *New York Times*, "the Justice Department has repeatedly advised state officials of the specific deficiencies and the corrective action needed. The state has failed or refused to address the Justice Department's finding in many critical ways."[13]

A 1997 investigation by the Deptartment of Justice (DOJ) found that guards at the Tallulah prison routinely beat juveniles at the facility, and a 1998 DOJ report cited Tallulah's lack of treatment for mentally ill adolescents who, investigators say, were dumped into the general prison population where they were frequently victimized.[14]

In a one-week period in May 1998, seventy of the 620 boys at Tallulah were sent to the infirmary after being involved in fights. Many had cuts and bruises; one had been raped. Another youth begged not to be returned to a dormitory where he said a fellow prisoner had been sexually abusing him for weeks. And a former juvenile offender, a 16-year-old who served 18 months at Tallulah for stealing a bike, said youths often fought each other over food and clothes.[15]

State corrections officials disputed many of the DOJ findings but conceded that mentally ill juveniles had been improperly placed in the general prison population. Investigators said many of the deficiencies were due to high employee turnover, which was as high as 100 percent in one year. Tallulah guards were only paid $5.77 an hour.[16]

Tallulah was operated by TransAmerican Development Associates Inc., which received $16 million a year, or $71 a day per juvenile. The company's principle owners/directors included George Fischer, a campaign manager for former Gov. Edwin Edwards, Verdi Adams, a former state highway engineer who had other business dealings with Fischer, and James R. Brown, the son of late state senator Charles Brown.[17]

Louisiana has repeatedly claimed that it has tried to make changes at Tallulah and its three state-run juvenile prisons, and that federal investigators have exaggerated the problems. The owners of Tallulah have complained that improvements demanded by the Justice Department would be so expensive that it would put them out of business.

On 22 July 1998, Louisiana officials took temporary control of the Tallulah facility following a disturbance by 15 youths and the resignation of the prison's warden. The facility was later turned over to Correctional Services Corporation.[18] On April 2, 1999, a former Tallulah guard was convicted of civil rights charges stemming from an assault on a youth at the facility.[19]

Death by Neglect in Arizona

On 2 March 1998, Nicholaus Contreraz, 16, collapsed and died after being forced to do strenuous exercise at the Arizona Boys Ranch (ABR) in Oracle, Arizona. The Pima County Medical Examiner determined that Nick's death was a result of empyema, a build-up of fluid in the lining between the lungs and the chest cavity. He also suffered from strep and staph infections, chronic bronchitis and pneumonia.[20]

In the days prior to his death, Nick had complained to ABR employees about being sick. He had been defecating and urinating on himself and was vomiting. Staff members responded by making him perform calisthenics and subjecting him to humiliation. He was accused of faking ill health. Even after he collapsed, ABR staff ordered him to do more exercises. The last word he spoke was "no".[21]

Nick Contreraz was one of more than 1,000 California juveniles sent to privately-operated out-of-state facilities. Following Nick's death, Arizona and California agencies began investigating ABR, which had had approximately 100 child abuse claims lodged against it within the previous five years.

Company officials, who temporarily closed the Oracle ranch to improve staff training and medical care, placed the blame on employees who "totally disregarded established disciplinary practices." Several staff members were fired and four were placed on administrative leave, including the camp director.[22]

ABR, based in Queen Creek, Arizona, operates seven wilderness/boot camp-type facilities for juvenile offenders. The company recruits nationally and charges $3,700 per month for each youth. On 26 August 1998, the Arizona Dept. of Economic Security canceled the Oracle facility's operating license after determining that abuse and neglect by 17 employees had contributed to Nick's death.[23]

Manslaughter charges were brought against five former ABR employees in connection with Nick's death. When the charges were later dismissed due to a technicality, the district attorney's office announced its intention to pursue first degree murder indictments. As a direct result of Nick's death, the California legislature passed a bill to increase control and supervision over out-of-state privately-operated juvenile facilities that house California youths.[24]

Nick Contreraz had been sent to the Arizona Boys Ranch for stealing a car and failing rehabilitation programs. According to Joe Contreraz, Nick's uncle, company officials initially told the family that Nick had committed suicide by going on a hunger strike.

Misconduct in Colorado

The High Plains Youth Center in Brush, Colorado, a 180-bed facility operated by Denver-based Rebound, Inc., was closed by state officials in April 1998 following an investigation that revealed abuse and mismanagement. Three years earlier the facility had been criticized in an independent evaluation that found "a consistent and disturbing pattern of violence, sexual abuse, clinical malpractice and administrative incompetence at every level of the program."[25] Colorado's juvenile corrections division admitted that it had to lower its contract performance standards for the facility because the state was dependent on Rebound to provide bed space.[26]

Juveniles at High Plains told investigators they had been choked and kneed in the back by company guards. Records indicate that some youths were physically restrained up to five times a day. Several female staff members were suspected of having sex with children at the facility and two employees were fired for sexual misconduct. From January to April 1998, state officials documented seven cases of physical abuse, four of sexual abuse and ten of neglect.[27]

Colorado authorities finally took action and began an intensive investigation after 13-year old Matthew Maloney, a mentally ill youth from Utah, committed suicide. He hung himself, and had been dead for almost four hours before his body was found.[28]

According to state investigators, many of the problems at High Plains were related to low pay and excessive staff turnover. Twenty-five out of 164 employees had left the facility within a three-month period. The workforce was stretched so thin that juveniles said they had to help staff members restrain other prisoners. Only half the required number of employees were on duty the night that Matthew died.[29]

Other problems were attributed to mentally ill juveniles housed at the facility. Rebound had advertised High Plains as providing services for youths with mental illnesses, although the center did not have adequate mental health care and was not licensed to provide such services. State investigators found 22 youths on psychotropic medication when they audited the facility.[30]

The Colorado Dept. of Human Services revoked Rebound's operating license for High Plains on 20 April 1998, citing unsafe conditions and inadequate care. Company officials called the closing of the center "inappropriate." The opinion of Rebound spokesperson Tom Schilling at the time was that "High Plains remains a safe facility for youths and always has been safe."[31]

Other Rebound facilities have been closed by state authorities in Florida and Maryland. Florida officials described one of the company's programs as being "largely out of control."

Business as Usual

It seems that the private juvenile prison industry has not learned from its mistakes. Reports of systemic abuse, misconduct and inadequate performance continue to make the headlines in states where juvenile offenders are housed in privately-operated facilities.

In 1998, Wackenhut agreed to pay $1.5 million to settle a lawsuit filed by Sara Lowe and joined by 11 other girls who had been held at the Coke County Juvenile Justice Center in Coke Bronte, Texas. They claimed they had been sexually, physically and mentally abused; at least one Wackenhut employee pled guilty to criminal charges of sexual assault. The day of the settlement, which included a confidentiality agreement and no admission of guilt by Wackenhut, Sara committed suicide. When asked whether Wackenhut owed an apology to Sara or the other girls involved in the suit, Wackenhut chairman George Zoley said, "not that I'm aware of. I don't know what you mean by that."[32]

Another Wackenhut facility, the Jena Juvenile Justice Center in LaSalle Parish, Louisiana, experienced a near-riot on December 19, 1998 involving 108 of 144 juveniles at the facility. The center was criticized by a court-appointed monitor who found poorly trained staff, lax security and inadequate education programs. The monitor noted that the vocational job training classes consisted entirely of showing tool-handling safety videos. When the youths finished viewing the videos, they watched them again.[33]

On 9 January 2000, Bryan Dale Alexander, an 18-year-old prisoner at a Mansfield, Texas boot camp operated by Correctional Services Corporation, died of antibiotic-resistant pneumonia caused by a staph infection, despite having requested medical treatment. A grand jury indicted CSC nurse Knyvett Jane Reyes on negligent homicide and manslaughter charges in connection with Bryan's death, and a judge described the medical neglect as "modern-day torture."[34]

In February 2000, a judge awarded $2.8 million in damages to three girls who had been incarcerated at the same CSC facility in Mansfield. They had been intimidated by a maintenance worker at the camp into disrobing, showering and touching themselves while he watched. Two other girls and three boys later filed suit claiming they had been mistreated. In June 2001, the Board of Criminal Judges voted to cancel CSC's contract to operate the facility.[35]

When state officials audited the Victor Cullen Center in Maryland in 2001, they found an insufficient number of staff, a failing education system, inadequate mental health services, and excessive violence. The facility is operated by CSC. In August 2001, the company agreed to repay the state more than $600,000 for services that were promised but never delivered at the center.[36]

On 1 June 2001, twenty juveniles at the CSC-operated Summit View Youth Correctional Center in Las Vegas, Nevada escaped to the facility's roof. There they aired a lengthy list of grievances, including being held past their release dates so the company would make more money (CSC had previously been cited for just such a practice at a Florida juvenile facility).[37] Additionally, two CSC employees were convicted and sentenced to probation for having sex with youths at the center. The company quit its contract with the state to operate the Summit View facility soon after the rooftop protest, claiming it was unprofitable.[38]

Inherent Problems with For-Profits

Such incidents do not mean that privately-operated juvenile facilities have a monopoly on abuse and malfeasance as opposed to their public counterparts. Gross deficiencies exist in many state juvenile justice departments, largely the result of a politically-driven 'tough-on-crime' trend to incarcerate more and more youthful offenders. When lawmakers authorize spending for the construction and expansion of juvenile prisons, they often neglect to appropriate funds for educational, vocational and treatment services. According to Georgia Dept. of Juvenile Justice Chairman Sherman Day, it is "much easier to get new facilities from the legislature than to get more programs."

Some of the worst forms of abuse and neglect, however, are found among privately-operated juvenile facilities because they are accountable to corporate stockholders rather than the tax-paying public. As such, they have an inherent motivation to cut corners in order to reduce costs—particularly in regard to employee training, wages and staffing levels—which, as amply demonstrated in the above examples, results in a plethora of extremely serious problems.

Another contributing factor to the mistreatment of juvenile offenders in private facilities is the presence of a large number of youths with mental disabilities. Mental health authorities estimate that up to 20% of incarcerated juveniles have serious psychiatric problems. Privately-managed facilities accept mentally ill youths because they charge higher fees to house them, even though they are frequently unable to provide adequate mental health care or treatment services.

Lastly, there is no indication that rehabilitation, or offering programs and a safe environment conducive to rehabilitation, is a priority for for-profit companies that provide juvenile justice services. Private prison operators may see rehabilitation as being counter-productive since they require a constant flow of youthful offenders to ensure a steady stream of revenue.

"Is It Worth It?"

So why, given the built-in profit-motivated deficiencies of private-sector juvenile corrections services, do local and state governments continue to contract with such companies? Allegedly to save money. After all, if a company skimps on everything from wages (no combative unionized state employees to deal with) and staffing levels (fewer staff members to pay) to educational/vocational programs and staff training (less overhead), it indeed can charge less to operate juvenile jails, boot camps and detention centers. However, the long term costs to society are much higher when juveniles leave privately-operated juvenile prisons more traumatized, neglected and brutalized than when they went in. Without addressing the emotional, social, educational and vocational needs of juvenile offenders, they face an increased chance of continuing the cycle of abuse and delinquency, eventually becoming adult criminals.

To quote Louisiana Corrections Secretary Richard Stadler, "There's no question the state is saving money" by using private juvenile corrections services. "The question is: is it worth it?"[39]

Endnotes

1. An earlier version of this chapter appeared as two articles in *Prison Legal News*.
2. Prison Privatization Report International (PPRI), London, May 1997 <www.psiru.org/justice>.
3. *Id.*, July 1997: 4.
4. *Id.*, August 1996.
5. *Id.*, March 1999; April/May 1999: 8.
6. *Id.*, March 1997.
7. *Id.*, August 1996.
8. *Id.*
9. *Id.*, March 1997; *Chattanooga Times* (TN), May 5, 1997.
10. See *William P., by and through his GAL Lesly A. Bowers* v. *CCA*, Case No. 3:98-290-17, U.S. District Court, Columbia, South Carolina.
11. *The New York Times*, 6 November 1998; *USA Today*, 11 December 1998, *Dallas Morning News*, 6 & 15 November, 1998.
12. *Id.*
13. *Id.*
14. *Id.*
15. *The Jackson Sun* (TN), 5 July 1998; *Corrections Digest*, 10 July 1998; *New York Times*, 15 & 24 July, 1998; *USA Today*, 29 July 1998.
16. *Id.*
17. *Id.*
18. *The Times-Picayune* (LA), Dec. 12, 1998.
19. *Id.*, April 3, 1999.
20. *Id.*
21. *Boston Sunday Globe*, 5 July 1998; *The New York Times*, 9 July 1998; *Corrections Digest*, 10 July 1998.
22. *Id.*
23. *Id.*
24. *USA Today*, 27 August 1998.
25. *Los Angeles Times*, 30 March 1999; *Dallas Morning News*, 27 August 1998; *USA Today*, 2 October 1998
26. PPRI, *supra* note 2, April 1997.
27. *Rocky Mountain News* (CO), 13 June 1998, 15 & 23 April, 1998; *Denver Post*, 21-22 April 1998.
28. *Rocky Mountain News* (CO), 25 & 26 February 1998; *Denver Post*, 25 February 1998.
29. *Rocky Mountain News* (CO), 13 June 1998, 15 & 23 April, 1998; *Denver Post*, 21-22 April 1998.

30. *Id.*
31. *Id.*
32. *Sixty Minutes II*, 15 January 2001 <http://cbsnews.cbs.com/now/story/0,1597,193636-412,00.shtml>; *San Angelo Standard Times*, 27 January 1998.
33. *Id.*; *The Times-Picayune* (LA), 26 June 1999; *The Advocate* (LA), 13 June, 5 & 8 July 1999.
34. *Fort Worth Star-Telegram*, 8 March, 26 April, 5 May 2001.
35. *Id.*, 26 February, 6 March 2001.
36. *The Sun* (Baltimore, MD), 30 November, 1 & 5 December 2001.
37. PPRI, *supra* note 2, Jan. 1999: 1; *Palm Beach Post* (FL), 23 November 1998.
38. *Reno Gazette-Journal,* 28 January 2002; *Las Vegas Sun*, 13 June, 23 July 2001.
39. *The Times-Picayune* (LA), June 26, 1999; *The Advocate* (LA), 13 June, 5 & 8 July 1999.

CHAPTER FIVE

Lack of Correctional Services

Judith Greene

Introduction

The private prison industry emerged in the US amid a rising tide of neo-liberal free-market economic ideas and neo-conservative zeal for moralistic discipline that propelled the country's criminal justice system through a series of campaigns to "get tough on crime." Reagan Administration officials' ardor for mandatory prison sentences and zero-tolerance approaches to crime control and drug enforcement launched a national crusade to "take back" criminal justice policies and practices from the hands of a supposedly liberal elite of criminologists and a defense-oriented legal establishment. The rapid embrace of their ideas by the public sent prison population levels shooting through the roof.

The Reagan Administration introduced a broad program of privatization to make good on their president's promise to "get government off our backs and out of our pockets."[1] But the US government had few state-owned enterprises such as were being sold off to private corporations by the Thatcher government in Great Britain. Privatization in the US was to be accomplished largely by contracting out public services. Federal policymakers urged both the US Marshals Service and the Immigration and Naturalization Service to contract for detention beds for pretrial prisoners and undocumented immigrants. Both the Corrections Corporation of America and the Wackenhut Corrections Corporation—the two firms which together hold three-quarters of the current US market for private prison beds—were launched into business with contracts from the INS.

Prison privatization was touted by policy analysts at conservative think tanks as a prison reform panacea. They championed the notion that privatization could and would solve seemingly intractable problems of deteriorating prison facilities, crowded conditions, and rising correctional costs, blindly believing that private-sector competition and profit incentives inevitably yield efficiencies that lie beyond the reach of government bureaucrats. While the industry was still in its infancy, with just a handful of facilities in operation, the national business press published glowing accounts of how private firms were using innovative building techniques, and media pundits predicted that private prisons would soon meet higher performance measures than could be met in the public sector.[2]

Corporate prison pioneers pledged that their industry would revolutionize the "business" of corrections. Tom Beasley, one of the founders of CCA, promised that private management of prisons would improve correctional practices across the board. Private prison guards would receive higher wages. Prisoners would get better living conditions, improved programs, and full-time assignments to work or educational activities—all this, while saving taxpayers millions of dollars.[3]

Academic experts rode to prominence on these issues, providing testimonials for policymakers and the media that privatization would indeed lead to better prisons and substantial savings.

As the industry matured, however, the promise of higher quality services at a lower cost was not demonstrated by solid evidence. Research findings about cost savings were mixed, inconclusive, and sometimes contradictory.[4] Comparative evaluations of prison performance were few and far between, and those that existed were plagued with a variety of methodological shortcomings.[5]

During rapid expansion of the industry over the 1990s, it became abundantly clear that private prison management is far more challenging than private collection of solid waste, private repair of potholes, or even private provision of security in public buildings. As private prison executives began to press government officials for contracts to take on more challenging types of prisoners, the operational flaws and deficiencies that critics had cautioned against from the very beginning became all too evident.

When, in July 1998, six prisoners fled to freedom through the security fences surrounding a CCA prison in Youngstown, the largest private prison company in the world found itself at the center of a media maelstrom. A series of operational disasters over the next three years kept the industry in the bright light of public scrutiny. By the end of 2000, the private prison industry experienced a "market slump." With prison populations beginning to level off in many states, and public officials terminating contracts where scandals erupted or poor performance was chronic, opportunities for new business contracts at the state level evaporated.

Because advocates for privatization of prisons placed so much emphasis on the putative cost-benefits, the relatively scant body of research and evaluation of private prisons has focused primarily on the issue of correctional costs. A fast-growing stack of newspaper accounts of operational difficulties, routine monitoring reports, security audits, and special inquiry documents offer increasing evidence that the industry's performance record does not engender much confidence. Nevertheless, questions about whether cost savings and profit-taking entail a significant sacrifice of performance quality–in terms of programs, facility security, and public safety–have not received much rigorous examination by researchers.

In 1998, this author designed and directed a performance evaluation of a CCA prison located in Minnesota with the goal of determining whether, as the company claimed, privatization was providing higher quality correctional services. The research project was sponsored through the University of Minnesota Law School Institute on Criminal Justice. Correctional services and programs offered at CCA's medium-security Prairie Correctional Facility (PCF) in Appleton were compared with those offered at three medium-security prisons run by the Minnesota Department of Corrections (DOC). All four prisons had been operating for many years, and their administration and programs were well established.

The research plan entailed both review of facility records and site visits, but the primary component of the study was survey research. A detailed questionnaire was used to conduct structured interviews with Minnesota prisoners housed at PCF, and with a carefully matched set of prisoners at the public prison who fully met the screening criteria used by DOC case managers to select prisoners for transfer to PCF whenever a bed became available at the private prison. The survey was designed to explore prisoners' perceptions about all aspects of prison operations: health care, counseling services, educational and treatment programs, work assignments, recreation, routine daily activities, and prison safety and security. Information was collected about the extent of their participation in these activities and services. Through the use of questions requiring a graded response (e.g., from one to five) or an answer of true or false, the questionnaire made it possible to compare the responses of prisoners at PCF with those in the public prison facilities, and to use standard statistical methods to test the significance of their responses.[6]

The Prison in Appleton

The Prairie Correctional Facility, now owned and operated by the Correctional Corporation of America, was originally established as a city-owned non-profit private prison facility. This municipal venture was initiated in 1990 with the formation of the Appleton Prison Corporation as a not-for-profit corporation by the City of Appleton, Minnesota. The corporation was used to finance prison construction through lease-revenue bonds. The prison was built purely "on speculation," which is to say that the facility was planned, financed, and fully constructed without a contractual agreement having been secured from any government agency to house prisoners there.

Appleton is a small farming community located in southwestern Minnesota, about 20 miles east of the South Dakota border. The town was established in 1872 when the settlers built a flour mill and a schoolhouse on the banks of the Pomme de Terre River. By the 1880s, the town had become the area's major distribution point for farm machinery. Sustained by a booming farm economy founded on the production of wheat and the sale of farm machinery, Appleton thrived for a century until low grain prices and the economics of corporate agriculture brought that era to a close. With foreclosures of family farms and a population exodus to other communities to find jobs, farm equipment stores were shuttered and the town appeared to be relegated to an inexorable decline.

The Appleton City Coordinator, Bob Thompson, chased after a variety of economic development schemes to restore the town's employment base. Thompson pursued plans for a gambling casino and a furniture manufacturing plant, before hitting on the prison development idea in 1989. By the spring of 1990, Thompson had recruited a corporate board of directors to finance construction of the $28 million private prison through sale of $5,000 revenue bonds. The prison development board would operate under the aegis of the city council, with profits, if any, accruing to the city treasury. The board was headed up by Mark Stromswold, the local "Culligan Man." Major investors included IDS Financial Services in Minneapolis, as well as the banks with local branch offices in Appleton.

The project developer was Dominion Leasing, an Edmund, Oklahoma-based group that had gained the necessary experience through development of the nation's first city-owned private prison in its home state. The firms that provided planning and architectural design were also Oklahoma-based, as was the construction contractor. The original proposal envisioned operation of 472 beds, a staff of 160, and a $3 million annual payroll. Construction of the Prairie Correctional Facility was begun in November 1990, with the opening slated for June 1992.

Section 241.021, Minnesota Statutes, requires that the Minnesota Department of Correction inspect and license all facilities, public or private, for detention or confinement of persons in the state. The city applied for and received a license to operate the new facility as a medium-security prison. The license required that the prison maintain at least a partial staff of 80 on the payroll before it could open for business. No contracts to house prisoners had been secured, however, and the facility was operated without a revenue source at a loss of nearly $10,000 a day for more than 10 months.[7]

In January 1993, the Appleton Prison Corporation officials approached Minnesota's governor with a blanket offer to either provide prison beds on a contract basis, or to lease or sell the facility to the state. But Minnesota DOC managers had prison expansion plans of their own, already well underway, involving conversion of regional treatment centers at Moose Lake and Faribault. The offer was quickly declined.

The following month the prison development board defaulted on a total of $1.5 million in interest and principal payments which had come due. By this time the spectacle of a prison running on empty attracted international attention. Appleton was flooded with media, including reporters from both the *New York Times* and the *Los Angeles Times*. Michael Moore filmed a segment of his TV Nation show at the prison site, interviewing correctional officers and townspeople about the empty facility.

Finally, in March of 1993, the board secured a three-year contract to house prisoners from Puerto Rico. The start-up problems common to other "spec" prisons were equally evident in early operations at the Appleton prison: prison officials were willing to take whatever inmates they could get; insufficient information from the Puerto Rico corrections department impeded proper classification of prisoners; and inexperienced staff grappled with very seasoned, difficult prisoners. Added to this volatile mix were cultural and language issues stemming from the complete lack of familiarity between prison staff and prisoners. DOC licensing inspectors complained that the facility was understaffed and lacked Spanish-speaking officers.[8]

The experience over the next 19 months with these prisoners was extremely difficult. There were riots. The FBI investigated allegations by ex-employees that prisoners had been beaten and abused by a "Special Operations Response Team" wearing black face masks. Within the same time frame, four wardens were hired and terminated by the city.[9]

By August 1994, a fifth warden, Hoyt Brill, had been recruited from Colorado, and a second contract had been secured to house prisoners from that state. By October, 287 prisoners had been received from Colorado, and 100 more were on the way when Appleton city officials decided to evict the Puerto Ricans, demanding that the government of Puerto Rico remove them as soon as possible. Puerto Rican officials managed to obtain a temporary restraining order to block removal of their prisoners, but ultimately they were removed.

Minnesota DOC officials expressed concern that housing units were not properly staffed to accommodate the influx of new prisoners, sufficient vocational programs were not available to them, and again, in-coming prisoners were not being screened with proper classification methods. They placed a temporary ban on acceptance of more inmates until these problems were addressed.[10]

After the removal of convicts from Puerto Rico, the operational crises subsided somewhat. However, in July 1996, the Appleton Development Corporation remained in default on the prison bonds, owing $26.7 million principal debt and $9.7 million in unpaid interest. Eventually Warden Brill was able to secure a multi-million dollar "bail-out" deal with the Corrections Corporation of America that allowed the non-profit corporation to make good its obligation to the bond-holders on their original investment, with a one percent return. As part of the deal, CCA was granted rights for a $25 million expansion of the facility as they assumed operations. The same year, PCF was finally able to secure a small contract to house Minnesota state prisoners under funding expressly appropriated for that purpose by the Minnesota legislature. A contract was drawn up for 95 beds at $55 per day.

By the winter of 1998, when the University of Minnesota research team conducted interviews with prisoners, CCA was housing inmates from a number of different state and federal sources and the daily prison population at PCF had reached 1,250. Seventy were held under the contract with the Minnesota DOC. Almost 1,000 were prisoners shipped in from Colorado, and the remainder were housed under contracts with Hawaii, North Dakota, and the US Marshals Service. About 2,700 Minnesota prisoners were being held at the three medium-security public prisons, where the prisoners that comprised the matched comparison group were confined.

The Research Findings

Many significant differences in correctional service delivery and program operations were revealed by comparing data from operational records and in-depth interviews with prisoners confined in PCF and the DOC prison system. The differences favored the public system for the most part, and prisoners also rated the public prison system higher on most performance measures.

Levels of medical care delivery appeared more or less the same in the two systems. Ninety-one percent of those interviewed in the DOC prisons had been seen by medical staff at least once, compared to 88 percent of those interviewed at PCF, and the average number of medical visits was similar between the two groups. But prisoners in the public prison system received significantly more dental care. The proportion of prisoners who received dental care was about the same (52 percent at PCF and 55 percent at the DOC prisons), but over the same period of time the DOC prisoners had averaged 3.3 sessions with the dental staff, while prisoners at PCF averaged just 1.6 sessions.

The DOC prisons also provided significantly more instruction for prisoners about general health issues. The public prison system provided HIV/AIDS education to most prisoners, with seventy percent of the DOC prisoners reporting being given information about the disease and how to avoid it. No prisoners at PCF reported receiving this type of education at the private facility.

DOC prisoners gave significantly higher ratings to the education programs in their prisons than the ratings given by prisoners at PCF—and they were more than twice as likely to assert that prisoners were being given a good opportunity to prepare themselves for new employment opportunities upon release.

General academic education classes were offered in both the private and public facilities, and most prisoners who were enrolled in either system said they attended classes five days a week. The teachers who provide academic education in the DOC system were state-certified. The Minnesota Department of Children, Families and Learning conducted periodic compliance audits to assure that the education programs met state standards, and that students requiring special education services were receiving them. Data obtained from CCA's company-wide computerized education information system, called "Roll Call," revealed that of six academic education teachers, just half possessed an academic certificate from the state.

The duration of daily classes was much longer in the DOC system. At PCF, all educational programs were just part-time. Participating prisoners attended only one three-hour class per day—a single morning, afternoon, *or* evening session. More than half of those enrolled in DOC classes reported participation in full-day classes – morning *and* afternoon sessions. With these differences it came as no surprise that state education records showed that the academic programs at the DOC facilities produced a much higher annual rate of General

Education Diplomas earned by students—74 GEDs per 1,000 prisoners, compared to the 55 GEDS per 1,000 prisoners at PCF.

A similar contrast pertained to vocational classes. These were offered in both systems, and most prisoners who were enrolled attended classes five days a week. But again, at PCF, participating prisoners took just one three-hour class per day, while two thirds of those enrolled in vocational training in the DOC system were enrolled in a full-time program of study. Moreover, the vocational programs at DOC facilities are fully accredited by the State of Minnesota. The students earned transferable classroom credits and authentic, recognized certificates from the state's technical college system upon completion, giving graduates an important advantage over those who graduated from the training programs offered at PCF, where none of the vocational instructors was licensed by the state, and where graduates could only obtain a CCA institutional certificate of completion. Fifty-three percent of the prisoners interviewed in the DOC prisons reported that it was easy to get enrolled in a good vocational program, while just 23 percent of those at PCF reported this to be the case.

Few prisoners in either system felt that adequate attention was being given to preparing them for release. Nevertheless, more prisoners at the DOC prisons reported that planning for release was a required activity (35 percent, compared to only six percent at PCF), but few prisoners were enrolled in programs geared specifically to prepare them. Prisoners in *both* systems voiced a strong desire for more help with housing arrangements and job contacts.

As to treatment for substance abuse—a problem plaguing a high proportion of Minnesota's prisoners—the contrast between CCA's prison and the public prisons was stark. The DOC chemical dependency treatment programs met state licensing requirements, and were designed to provide prisoners with the high level of treatment that is mandated by law for all who need it. The treatment programs at the DOC facilities provided a full day of therapeutic sessions, five days a week. Thirty-six percent of the prisoners interviewed at the DOC prisons had been enrolled in full-time treatment. Eighty-six percent of the DOC prisoners said that prisoners had easy access to substance abuse treatment services, and almost two-thirds of those who participated reported the experience had been "very helpful." A full-time chemical dependency treatment program had never been established at PCF, even though the contract required it. Treatment for substance abuse at PCF consisted of weekly Alcoholics or Narcotics Anonymous meetings, and a sporadic offering of "drug education" classes.

The proportion of prisoners who reported performing a daily work assignment was significantly higher at PCF than at the DOC prisons, but this comparison was affected by the higher proportion of DOC prisoners who were enrolled in daily, full-time education and treatment programs, and who therefore did not have a prison work assignment. Moreover, the prisoners with daily work assignments at PCF were significantly more likely to report assignment to part-time work activities, and many of them complained that most work assignments in the CCA prison were "just keep-busy jobs."

One aspect of the work assignments available to prisoners at PCF stood out as exceptional, however. CCA had established a private-sector prison industry shop at PCF, through an arrangement with Jacobs Trading, an employer based in Minneapolis. Jacobs Trading hired about 100 prisoners at PCF to refurbish and repackage damaged consumer goods for sale in job-lot, discount, or close-out stores. The few Minnesota prisoners who worked in the Jacobs Trading shop expressed strong appreciation for the opportunity to do "real work for real wages." Even though a large portion of their wages were deducted to offset the costs of their incarceration, they were happy to be making more money than other prisoners, and some were pleased that they were able to meet child support obligations.

Important differences between how prisoners perceive the requirements placed upon them by private and public systems indicated that the public system maintained a significantly higher degree of authority and control over the daily activities of prisoners than was the case at PCF. Two-thirds of the DOC prisoners agreed with the statement that "[p]risoners are kept busy all day," while 78 percent of prisoners at PCF judged this to be *untrue*. And while 85 percent of DOC prisoners agreed that prisoners in the public prisons "must work, study, or be in treatment," only a tiny fraction, nine percent, asserted that this was so for prisoners at PCF. Some prisoners confined in the DOC prisons expressed resentment about the degree of control exerted by prison staff, stating the following: "You don't have a choice whether to work or not;" and "Staff treat you like a little kid." In contrast, some prisoners at PCF appreciated the relative freedom afforded by CCA: "My day is not structured – I can set my own schedule;" and "It's easy time – you have more time for recreation."

Although it not possible to determine the exact effects of weaker control on prison safety and security, it is interesting that prisoners' assessments about security issues in the two systems responses indicated significant, disturbing differences. Asked to rate their facilities on measures of safety and security, prisoners in DOC facilities gave them a significantly higher average rating over those given by prisoners at PCF. In their responses to questions about institutional control and facility safety, many prisoners at PCF observed that the CCA prison staff were less experienced than those at the DOC, and that many were not up to the job of handling difficult situations:

> "I like the independence I have here – they give you enough rope to hang yourself – but they shouldn't bring younger prisoners to a place like this – the staff aren't adequately trained to prevent the most obvious problems."

> "Minnesota DOC staff are more professional, more qualified, better trained – if private prisons are going to be used, they should be just as good as the public side."

Most Minnesota prisoners at PCF expressed dissatisfaction about being confined with prisoners from other jurisdictions. CCA was operating PCF along the lines of other "spec prisons," mixing prisoners from Colorado, Hawaii, Minnesota, North Dakota, along with detainees sent to PCF by the US Marshals Service. Some prisoners complained that with prisoners constantly coming and going from different jurisdictions with different laws, rules, and regulations, the prison routine was continually disrupted:

> "This place is unstable and unorganized [*sic*] – the rules change too often—based on the majority of the prisoners' state laws."

Many prisoners expressed concern and resentment about the lack of a uniform custody classification policy at PCF. Many prisoners complained that their safety was being jeopardized by CCA's willingness to admit prisoners with high custody classifications from other states:

"Some of these guys are never getting out, and they have nothing to lose."

This issue had long been a sore point between the PCF managers and the licensing staff at the Minnesota DOC. In numerous letters and memos, DOC staff warned the managers at PCF that classification matters were not being handled in a careful and timely fashion. Spot checks of files for prisoners imported from other states had repeatedly revealed that some did *not* meet Minnesota's criteria for medium custody classification. The typical response from CCA prison managers was that perhaps there might have been a lapse, or an oversight, but that the matter would be rectified. The response was consistently coupled with assurances that, with rare exceptions, the prisoners at PCF *were* medium-custody.

During the course of the study, however, researchers obtained data that demonstrated that CCA was not taking the classification issue seriously. In February 1998, PCF staff had provided data about prisoner classification for a national survey of private prisons under sponsorship of the US Department of Justice's Bureau of Justice Assistance. They reported that on 31 December 1997 just 48 percent of the prisoners in their facility were classified as medium custody. They said that 586 prisoners, 45 percent of those confined at PCF, were in fact classified as "maximum/close/high" custody, while another eight percent were classified "minimum/low."

Beyond Appleton

Proponents of prison privatization have insisted that introduction of market competition into the field of corrections would help to solve many chronic problems in correctional practice. The introduction of competition would spur improvements in the public sector. Technical innovation and effective business practices would inevitably produce both increased efficiencies and higher performance. The freedom to manage personnel without the fetters of union contracts and civil-service rules would promote both higher productivity and a more humane prison environment. Some continue to make these claims.

Taken together, the findings from the Minnesota study provide strong empirical evidence supporting the opposite view: that privatization significantly *lowers* the level of correctional effectiveness, facility security, and public safety compared to what is now provided by the public system. The comparative deficiencies at the CCA prison in Minnesota can be traced to the company's efforts to control costs, thereby increasing profits. Skimping on program services expenditures to increase profits is no way to improve correctional practice. The bulk of correctional costs are labor costs, and the effect of privatization on expenditures for staff compensation and training is of paramount importance.

The entry-level salary paid to guards by private prison firms in the US is just $17,628, compared to the public prison average of $23,002. The average *maximum* salary differential is far steeper: $22,082 to $36,328.[11] Low pay leads to high turnover. Prisoners' complaints that PCF guards lacked a sufficient level of experience were supported by data that showed that the annual rate of turnover at the prison was 42 percent, compared to just 13 percent at the comparable public prisons. The latest national figures show that the problem of high turnover at private prisons is reaching crisis proportions. The turnover rate for private prison guards reached 52 percent in 2000, compared with 16 percent for public prisons.[12]

The types of deficiencies found at PCF have been documented elsewhere. The most severely troubled private prisons have been found to have very high rates of turnover—sometimes in excess of 100 percent. Many private prison managers have been willing to solicit and accept prisoners whose custody classification exceeds the control capacity of their facilities in terms of both design and staffing. Pressure to maximize profits by filling prison beds as fast as possible and keeping them as full as possible can lead to very serious problems. Problems with hasty start-up of prison operations and misclassification of prisoners' custody levels has been cited by national prison experts to have led to a series of prison disasters, including escapes, stabbings, and homicides, at both CCA and Wackenhut prisons.[13]

In the summer of 2001, the last prisoners from Washington DC were removed from the Northeast Ohio Correctional Center (NOCC), the Corrections Corporation of America's prison in Youngstown. The history of escapes, violent assaults, 20 stabbings, and two homicides that brought a national media spotlight to that prison need not be retold here. Suffice it to say that in July 1998 when six prisoners escaped from the prison in broad daylight, Ohioans were shocked to discover that the prison had been in turmoil from the day it was opened for business, 15 months earlier.

Corrections Trustee John Clark's thorough investigation of NOCC for the Justice Department turned up more shocking evidence:[14]

- the prison staff was woefully inexperienced;

- many prisoners had been wrongly classified;

- predatory prisoners with serious records of institutional violence were being housed together with vulnerable low-risk prisoners;

- prisoners were not provided adequate medical care; and

- prison programs were not in place to provide education and treatment.

The lessons from this experience were abundantly clear. Yet the learning has evidently been lost. More recent audits of another CCA prison in Florence, Arizona read like a "Youngstown" just waiting to happen. The Florence Correctional Center (FCC) held almost 600 male prisoners from Hawaii, along with women detained by the INS. In April 2001, the FCC erupted in violence – a string of serious assaults, and a riot on the prison yard that left a prison guard and three prisoners with serious injuries. That same month, a prisoner died at FCC of a heart attack that prison officials say was caused when he swallowed a packet of drugs to conceal it.

When prison auditors flew in from Hawaii to inspect the prison they found "a prison in turmoil," with an atmosphere so hostile that most areas of the prison were deemed too dangerous to be toured. They determined that a prison gang had taken control and was running the prison. Gang members were said to be attacking other prisoners and staff, dealing drugs, and having sex with the women housed there by the INS. Some staff were said to be "working" for the prison gang. One guard admitted providing drugs for prisoners in exchange for protection.

The auditors raised a variety of familiar complaints: security staff were inexperienced and under-trained, and they were neglecting the most basic security measures, like failing to search prisoners for contraband, or neglecting to exert adequate control over their movement within the facility. There were discrepancies with regard to the security classification system, and prisoners in different custody levels were not being separated as required to protect low-risk prisoners from predatory gang members. The medical unit at the prison was "grossly understaffed." Education and treatment programs were operating far below the contractors' expectations. The cultural gap between the Hawaiian prisoners and the CCA staff was wide. Many prisoners complained of racial slurs, alleging among other things that they had been called "beach niggas" by staff.[15]

There is a growing body of empirical evidence that the types of deficiencies documented at PCF are due to structural differences in how the private sector approaches prison management. Both Wackenhut and CCA, the industry "giants," have been cited repeatedly for chronic understaffing, deficient work assignments and education programs that result in widespread prisoner idleness, lack of compliance with proper procedures for inmate classification and discipline, sub-standard medical treatment and inadequate mental health care.

New research reports have documented the deleterious effects of these problems on prison operations. Rates of prison violence are much higher in the private prisons. The BJA national survey findings indicated that there were 65 percent more inmate-on-inmate assaults and 49 percent more inmate-on-staff assaults in private prisons than in comparable public prisons.[16] A study by researchers at the Federal Bureau of Prisons Office of Research and Evaluation concluded that the security problems in private prisons are systemic. They cited the much higher rates of security staff turnover, and attributed the much higher rate of escapes, and of drug use by prisoners (as evidenced by higher rates of positive "hits" from random urine screening) to the "greenness" of the work force, including both line staff and mid-level supervisors and managers.[17]

Conclusion

The US prison system, private and public prisons alike, has far to go before it will meet the basic correctional standards that human rights activists and penal reformers have long advocated. After 25 years of booming capacity expansion, too many American prisons remain plagued with overcrowding. Understaffing, sub-standard healthcare, insufficient programs, and human rights abuses are still widespread. However, prison privatization has not only failed to alleviate these problems, the industry has actually produced a much *worse* record of deprivation, violence and abuse than is found in the *public* prison system.

Slackened rates of prison population growth have allowed state-level correctional officials to shy away from further reliance on this very high-risk proposition. Thankfully, poor performance has not gone totally unnoticed. State-level contracting for new private prisons has ground to a halt. Private prison contracts in Arkansas, Louisiana, North Carolina, Ohio, South Carolina and Texas have been ended where chronic under-performance has resulted in serious problems.

Yet this poor performance history has yet not yet extinguished support for privatization at the federal level in the US. In May 2002 the Federal Bureau of Prisons awarded a three-year $109 million contract to CCA to house 1,500 federal prisoners in an empty facility the company had built "on spec" in Georgia. Citing a declining rate of federal prison population growth, BOP officials cancelled plans to contract for more private prison beds in the foreseeable future. But the same ideological winds in Congress and the White House that propelled the birth of the private prison industry are likely to continue to push its growth. Regardless of their sorry track record, private prison industry executives predict that the "post 9/11" crackdown on undocumented immigrants will produce a steady flow of new contracts for housing detainees for the INS.

Endnotes

1. E.S. Savas, *Privatization and Public-Private Partnerships* (2000).
2. P.E. Fixler, "Behind Bars We Find an Enterprise Zone," *The Wall Street Journal,* 29 November 1984.
3. A. Weston, "Would You Stay In One of This Man's Prisons?" *Advantage Magazine,* February 1986.
4. U. S. General Accounting Office, *Private and Public Prisons: Studies Comparing Operational Costs and/or Quality of Service* (1996); J. Nelson, "Appendix 1: Comparing Public and Private Prison Costs" in D. McDonald, *et al., Private Prisons in the US: Assessment of Current Practice* (1998); T.C. Pratt, "Are private prisons more cost effective than public prisons? A meta-analysis of evaluation research studies." (1999).
5. G.G. Gaes, *et al.,* "Appendix 2: The Performance of Privately Operated Prisons: A Review of Research" in D. McDonald *et al., Private Prisons in the US: Assessment of Current Practice* (1998).
6. J.A. Greene, "Comparing Private and Public Prison Services and Programs in Minnesota: Findings from Prisoner Interviews" (1999).
7. B. Robson, "Little Big House on the Prairie," *City Pages,* 8 February 1995.
8. P. Doyle, "Inmates at Appleton allegedly terrorized," *Star Tribune,* 14 October 1994.
9. B. Robson, "Little Big House on the Prairie," *supra* note 7.
10. J. Ojeda-Zapata, "Puerto Rican prisoners kicked out of Appleton," *Pioneer Press,* 19 October 1994.
11. C.G. Camp & G.M. Camp, *The Corrections Yearbook: 2000* (2001).
12. *Id.*
13. J. Clark, "Report to the Attorney General: Inspection and Review of the Northeast Ohio Correctional Center" (1998); J. Austin, *et al., The Consultants' Report on Prison Operations in New Mexico Correctional Institutions* (2000).
14. J. Clark, "Report to the Attorney General," *supra* note 13.
15. P. Kawai, Memo to HCF Warden Nolan Espinosa "Summary of identified Security Threat Group (STG) at Florence Correctional Facility (FCC)," Hawaii Department of Public Safety, 16-20 April 2001; J. Martinez, "After Action Report — Florence Correctional Center, June 4, 2001 – June 6, 2001," Hawaii Department of Public Safety; C. Zembik, "Briefing Report – Florence Correctional Facility, 4/16 – 4/20 Monitoring Trip," Department of Public Safety inter-office memo to Ted Sakai, 30 April 2001.
16. J. Austin and G. Coventry, *Emerging Issues on Privatized Prisons* (2001).
17. S.D. Camp, & G.G. Gaes, "Growth and Quality of US Private Prisons: Evidence from a National Survey" (2001).

CHAPTER SIX

Private Prisons and Health Care: The HMO From Hell

Elizabeth Alexander

In 1994, John Malesko was serving an eighteen-month sentence for securities fraud in the federal prison system. The Bureau of Prisons rewarded him for his satisfactory behavior by transferring him to a half-way house, the Le Marquis Community Corrections Center in New York City. As it turned out, he might have been better off if his behavior had been worse.

If Malesko had been a trouble maker, he would have stayed in a more secure facility, where he might have had a chance to receive the medical care he needed for his previously-diagnosed congestive heart failure. But it was his misfortune that the Le Marquis facility was operated by the Correctional Services Corporation. CSC, as it is usually called, is a publicly traded for-profit prison corporation, and Malesko's health care was now the corporation's responsibility.

About six weeks after Malesko arrived at Le Marquis, he notified CSC that his heart medication had run out, but he was not provided with a refill. Moreover, CSC had a policy that all prisoners who lived below the sixth floor of the building were required to use the stairs rather than an elevator available to staff. For a while Malesko was able to persuade sympathetic staff members to allow him to use the elevator despite the policy, but then another staff member ordered him to use the stairs. While attempting to comply with that order, he had a heart attack and fell on the stairs, suffering permanent head injuries.[1]

When Malesko filed suit against the corporation, the corporation's lawyers claimed that, like the United States government itself, the corporation was not subject to suit for any violations of Malesko's constitutional right to health care. The federal trial-level court threw out his lawsuit on that basis, but an appellate court ordered that the case go forward for trial. Now the Supreme Court has ruled that for-profit corporations like CSC who run prisons under contract with the federal government are protected from suit for their constitutional violations.[2]

The *Malesko* case raises fundamental questions about the dangers of turning over core government functions to private prisons. When the government decides to vest its power over prisoners in a for-profit corporation, that decision represents a formidable transfer of public authority. If a private company contracted with the government to deliver the mail, the potential for violation of constitutional rights would be inherently limited. However, there are few spheres, if any, in which power to control private citizens is ceded to private entities in a manner comparable to the power that for-profit prisons exercise. The victory by CSC in the *Malesko* case will give the private prison industry a political and economic shot in the arm, but prisoners, jail detainees and incarcerated juveniles will be even more likely to be denied necessary health care.

It is important to remember that denying necessary medical and mental health care to prisoners is particularly dangerous since prisoners suffer in disproportionate numbers from many diseases. Because they are more likely to have a history of intravenous drug use and unsafe sexual practices, prisoners are five times more likely to be diagnosed with AIDS than the general population.[3] Prisoners are also substantially more likely to be infected with hepatitis C.[4] They also have elevated risk for chronic illnesses such as diabetes, cardiovascular disease, pulmonary disease, and cancer because of life style factors such as smoking, heavy alcohol consumption and poor nutrition.[5]

Unfortunately these lifestyle risk factors are even more important now because newer, more severe sentencing policies have resulted in longer sentences and have thus drastically and disproportionately increased the number of prisoners over fifty,[6] the prisoners who are at greatest risk for chronic diseases. Finally, prisoners suffer from serious mental illness far more frequently than the general population.[7]

Aside from the obvious humanitarian reasons to be concerned about the health of the two million people in prison in the United States, public health officials have long argued that prison health care must also be seen as a public health priority because the health problems of prisoners do not stay permanently walled off from the broader community. Tuberculosis provides an appropriate illustration. As is the case with so many infectious diseases, prisoners are more likely than other members of the community to be infected.[8] The higher rate of tuberculosis infection is probably consistent with the fact that prisoners typically come from lower socio-economic backgrounds. Since tuberculosis is an air-borne infection, overcrowded housing conditions associated with poverty promote its spread. Unfortunately, if tuberculosis infection is not correctly assessed and treated among in-coming prisoners, and an infected prisoner develops active tuberculosis, the extraordinarily high-density prison environment is the perfect setting for the disease to spread.[9]

For example, in one case a court ordered the Pennsylvania prison system to implement an appropriate tuberculosis control program throughout the state.[10] That order led to the discovery of over 400 prisoners in just one prison who, unknown to any prison authority, were infected with tuberculosis. The medical records of the prison were not complete enough to determine how many of these infections had resulted from the spread of tuberculosis within the prison, but there was little doubt that at least some of the active cases of tuberculosis within the system had resulted from exposure within the prison system.

Moreover, it has been repeatedly demonstrated that tuberculosis, including highly dangerous multi-drug resistant tuberculosis, can and does spread from prisons and jails to the community. A study in San Francisco during the period 1997-1999, for example, demonstrated that just under 44 percent of all persons with active tuberculosis had been incarcerated at some point before their diagnosis. Moreover, medical researchers analyzed the DNA strains involved and concluded that tuberculosis from the jail had infected the community; indeed sixty-three percent of persons who had never been incarcerated but had developed active tuberculosis had been infected with the strain of tuberculosis associated with the jail outbreak.[11] An earlier Centers for Disease Control study concluded that an outbreak of multi-drug resistant tuberculosis in the New York State prison system involved two hospitals where prisoners were treated. The outbreak also resulted in the deaths of thirty-six prisoners and a correctional officer, and the infection of a number of health care workers with multi-drug resistant tuberculosis.[12]

Prisoners confined at for-profit prisons, just like those held in public facilities, are at heightened risk for many diseases, including communicable diseases. But there is substantial reason to be even more concerned about the health care offered in private prisons. Whatever the failings of publicly-operated facilities, they do not operate under the same set of incentives as for-profit prisons. Officials who run public prisons are not ordinarily judged primarily on the basis of the bottom line. Indeed, controversies about publicly-run prisons rarely focus directly on costs; instead controversies tend to concern whether a prison is fulfilling its functions, which range from preventing escapes to maintaining constitutionally required services, including medical care.

In contrast, private prisons, like other business corporations, are organized and carried on primarily for the profit of the stockholder. Indeed, corporate officials have a legal duty to act in the interest of the corporation and its shareholders.[13] Accordingly, private prisons have an economic motive to cut costs in every area of operations, whether they involve security, programs or health care, as long as the savings in cost do not result in penalties under their contract with the governmental agencies or increases in the cost of litigation that outweigh the savings.

Nevertheless, the first constraint on reducing costs, the prospect of governmental monitoring, is unlikely to prove a substantial deterrent. While private prisons typically agree in their contracts that the contracting governmental agency can monitor the company's performance of the contract, the private prison is usually not subject to the same general oversight that a prison operated directly by the agency would face.[14] For example, the federal Bureau of Prisons is covered by the Freedom of Information Act,[15] the Administrative Procedures Act,[16] and the Government in the Sunshine Act.[17] These statutes require agencies to answer requests for information, to publish their rules and regulations, and to allow public scrutiny of internal decisions and records. In the words of the Supreme Court, the basic purpose of such laws is to "ensure an informed citizenry, vital to the functioning of a democratic society, needed to check against corruption and to hold the governors accountable to the governed."[18] Private prisons are exempt from all these laws.[19]

Similarly, private prisons that hold federal prisoners are exempt from regulation under state prison regulatory standards. For example, in New York City, where CSC's Le Marquis Community Center operates, there is both a Board of Correction that promulgates minimum standards and inspects local jails[20] and a New York State Commission of Corrections that has authority over prisons and local jails,[21] but neither of these regulatory bodies could have acted to ensure health care for a federal prisoner like Mr. Malesko.

Moreover, there are structural barriers to effective governmental monitoring of private prison contractors. When a governmental agency contracts with a private firm in other areas, such as constructing a public road, taxpayers can readily observe the results. Prisons, in contrast, are closed institutions and the general public has almost no ability to evaluate the quality of the services purchased with its money. In economic theory, this problem is known as the "hidden delivery" problem, in which the quality of the goods sold cannot be effectively observed by the buyer, so that the seller has the opportunity to substitute goods of less value than those specified in the contract without the normal risk of detection.

It is true that neither public nor for-profit prisons are open to substantial citizen scrutiny, so there is always the risk that prison managers will betray the public trust by utilizing the difficulty of detection to misuse their budget, or that they will abuse the extraordinary power they are granted over their charges. However, the risk of misuse of public funds is particularly great in the case of private prison operators. If the official in charge of a private corporation saves money on a contract with the government by failing to provide medical staff, and that failure is not detected, the company will be more profitable and those profits are likely, in some form, to benefit the manager. In contrast, it is generally extremely difficult for an official of a publicly-operated prison to transform funds that were appropriated for prisoner services to the official's private benefit. If, for example, the warden of a publicly-operated prison decided to cut the budget by refusing to hire necessary medical staff, the warden would still find it difficult to transform the saved funds into personal gain.[22]

There are other reasons to expect that governmental agencies will not perform adequate monitoring of contracts with private prison companies. First, once the agency has selected the company to perform the contract, the agency may have reason to expect that the company's failure to perform the contract satisfactorily will reflect badly on the agency, so the agency may be motivated to ignore failures to comply with the contract. In addition, there may be high transaction costs to attempting to change companies, particularly because the private prison market is dominated by a small number of big companies. Once a particular private company is entrenched in a contract, the governmental authority is likely to be resistant to changing contractors. The company can then generate excess profits, not by raising its contracting price, but by reducing the services to which it is obligated under the contract.[23]

Aside from monitoring by the governmental agency, with the possibility that the company will lose the contract or suffer other penalties, the only other deterrent to failing to provide adequate health services is litigation. But litigation, while it has had a substantial effect of ameliorating conditions of confinement,[24] by itself will not effectively deter denials of necessary medical care in either public or private prisons. Among the reasons for the only partial effectiveness of litigation is the Prison Litigation Reform Act (PLRA). Passed by Congress in 1996, the PLRA restricts the ability of federal courts to issue injunctive relief to prisoners (including incarcerated youth and jail and immigration detainees); it restricts the ability of state and federal prisoners to seek damages; and it makes it substantially more difficult for prisoners to obtain lawyers.[25]

In addition to the PLRA, prisoners face other barriers to successful suits for damages when their health needs have been ignored. The constitutional standard to establish liability on the part of the officials is quite high. Staff must be "deliberately indifferent" to a "serious medical need". To prove deliberate indifference, the prisoner must establish that the staff member knew of a substantial risk of significant harm; the fact that the staff member should have realized there was a risk is not enough. Thus, for example, if a prisoner dies of untreated appendicitis, and most physicians would have realized that the symptoms of appendicitis required checking, the prison physician will not be liable if he or she in fact did not recognize the need to check. Ordinary negligence is not enough.[26] Moreover, juries may be unwilling to award a prisoner substantial amounts of damages, regardless of circumstances, in light of the fact that the prisoner's criminal conviction may make him appear undeserving.

Accordingly, neither the threat of governmental monitoring of private prisons nor the litigation costs of failing to provide necessary medical care provide sufficient incentives to prevent such denials. Indeed, there is overwhelming evidence that cost-cutting measures by private prisons have led directly to failures to provide care. As one writer put it, "[p]rivate prisons essentially mirror the cost-cutting practices of health maintenance organizations: Companies receive a guaranteed fee for each prisoner, regardless of the actual costs. Every dime that they don't spend on food or medical care or training for guards is a dime they can pocket."[27] Typically, private prisons strive for cost reductions by minimizing labor costs, since about 75 percent of total operating costs involve labor costs.[28] These reductions in labor costs are achieved in two ways: hiring fewer staff and hiring less qualified staff. Both methods can and have led to disasters.

CSC, the private corporation that confined Mr. Malesko when he was injured, has a history of using both methods to reduce costs at the price of services. At a Texas boot camp run by CSC an eighteen-year-old boy died after he developed pneumonia and was denied treatment despite requests for medical attention and obvious symptoms.[29] Prior to this death, a girl had died of a brain aneurysm; her repeated complaints of headaches had been ignored by staff. Another girl was not taken to a hospital, despite weeks of complaints of breathing problems, until she lost consciousness. Both former staff and youth who had spent time at the camp said that youth were discouraged from seeking medical care.[30]

At the Pahokee Youth Development Center in Florida, a youth tied a sheet around his neck and jumped from the second floor of the dormitory. While he hung there, a CSC staff member cut the sheet, causing him to fall and strike his head. He was given an ice pack and returned to his cell. Only after he experienced a seizure in his cell and began foaming at the mouth was he taken to a hospital. The same institution allowed staff to give youth psychotropic medications without an examination by a psychiatrist.[31]

At another youth facility run by CSC, a Maryland state audit described a pattern of understaffing, employment of medical personnel with expired licenses, a lack of mental health services, and three-month waits for youth in need of drug treatment.[32] Indeed, CSC was formerly known as Esmor; it changed its name after publicity about bad conditions within one of its facilities that had contracted with the federal government to hold illegal immigrants. The government eventually canceled the contract after the detainees rioted in response to the bad conditions.[33]

Other private prison corporations have been charged with similar failures to provide medical and mental health care to the prisoners in their custody. The Corrections Corporation of America, which is the largest private prison company in the United States, has repeatedly been charged with denying necessary medical and mental health care to those placed in its charge. For example, a twenty-three year-old woman confined at CCA's Silverdale Work Farm near Chattanooga, Tennessee died of an undiagnosed complication of pregnancy. According to a staff shift supervisor, the woman suffered in agony for twelve hours before CCA officials allowed her to be taken to a hospital.[34] In March 2000, a prisoner from Alaska was acquitted of a charge of escape from a CCA facility in Florence, Arizona after presenting evidence that staff had denied him medicine for his heart condition.[35] A state audit of care given to prisoners transferred from Hawaii to the same facility noted the lack of substance abuse programs required under the contract with the state.[36]

Perhaps CCA's most infamous prison is the Northeast Ohio Correctional Center in Youngstown, Ohio. The District of Columbia contracted in 1997 to send medium security prisoners to the facility, but instead CCA accepted every prisoner sent to them, and failed to develop a working classification system to separate dangerous prisoners from others, with the result that two prisoners were stabbed to death in less than a month. The prisoners filed a lawsuit comprehensively challenging conditions in the prison, including medical care. The Corrections Trustee for the District of Columbia subsequently issued a report documenting that, at the time the facility was opened, medical staffing was deficient in numbers, training and experience. Medical services were so overwhelmed when the first 900 prisoners arrived that basic intake procedures were not followed. Many of the prisoners, including 250 prisoners with chronic diseases, needed special medical attention that the staff was not prepared to provide. Like the failures of CCA to screen arriving prisoners for suitability for confinement in a medium security facility, the failures to deliver medical care to prisoners with special needs appear to have resulted from CCA's drive to boost the prison's occupancy rate and the resulting payments to the corporation.[37]

The District of Columbia prisoners transferred to Youngstown filed a lawsuit comprehensively challenging conditions in the prison, including medical care. The prisoners charged that access to health care was delayed by staff; prisoners with chronic diseases were not monitored properly; there was no infection control system; there were too few staff physicians; and sick call was performed in a barber shop lacking an examination table or other basic equipment.[38] CCA eventually settled the litigation against the facility for the largest class action money damages ever recovered in a prison case and comprehensive changes in practices.[39]

Similar problems have beset facilities operated by Wackenhut Corrections Corporation, which has the second largest share of the private prisons market in the United States. One of the facilities operated by Wackenhut under a contract with the state in 1996 was the McPherson Unit in Arkansas, housing 685 women. By 1998, officials from the state correctional system discovered that 70 percent of the women were being given psychotropic medications, a rate of medication many times higher than the rate for women prisoners in the state's custody. Two years later, when state officials attempted to verify the company's schedule for programming, they found that the programming, including substance abuse programs, did not exist. Wackenhut blamed the state, saying that its contract did not produce enough money to allow it to offer programs.[40]

Wackenhut also operated a particularly notorious juvenile facility in Jeno, Louisiana. Although the worst conditions at Jeno involved deliberate abuse of youth and failure to provide them with necessities such as shoes, underwear, and blankets, a report by the Department of Justice also found that, not surprisingly, the company cut costs by failing to provide necessary medical care. When the facility opened, its ostensible purpose was the provision of substance abuse treatment. The Department of Justice found, however, that virtually no substance abuse programs actually operated at Jena.[41] After extensive media coverage of the abuses at the facility, Louisiana took over its operation in April 2000.[42]

After Wackenhut began running Texas pre-release centers, the Texas Board of Criminal Justice found that the corporation had collected excessive profits from its operations at the same time as medical and dental care, among other services, were deficient.[43]

Unfortunately, the events of September 11 in the United States are likely to combine with the Supreme Court's decision in the *Malesko* case to exacerbate the problem of the denials of medical care in private prisons. Prior to September 11, private prisons in the United States were in deep trouble. The nation's two largest private prison corporations, CCA and Wackenhut, together account for about 75 percent of all private prison beds. CCA was on the verge of bankruptcy.[44] Although Wackenhut was in better financial shape, by May 2001 its stock had fallen from around thirty-five dollars a share in 1998 to about eleven dollars a share.[45]

After September 11, however, the Bureau of Prisons issued its two largest requests of the year for bids on the operation of facilities in Georgia to lock up non-citizens charged with crime. The Bureau of Prisons also intends to solicit bids in early 2002 for fifteen hundred detainees to be held in the deserts of the southwest United States.[46] Prospective investors sense a potential bonanza in running prisons for profit. CCA stock has risen over 300 percent from its low during the year, as CCA among other private prison companies positions itself to cash in on the new federal contracts. Wackenhut, the second-largest prison corporation, hopes to capitalize on its experience in Australia of converting military bases to immigrant detention camps. Moreover, even before September 11, prisoner population within the Bureau of Prisons was continuing to grow, although population trends in the state corrections system were almost flat.[47] Accordingly, the future of private prisons appears to lie increasingly in housing federal rather than state prisoners.

For this reason, the victory by private prisons in the *Malesko* case is critical to their future. Although, for the reasons given earlier, the potential threat of prison litigation is not sufficient by itself to deter for-profit prisons from cutting health care services, litigation does have some deterrent effect. Litigation offers the possibility of drawing public attention to the facilities' deficiencies and presents opportunities to examine documents for evidence of corporate decisions to cut costs by denying care. Certainly the successful case against Youngstown's CCA facility, which resulted in damages of over a million and a half dollars[48] as well as substantial adverse publicity, contributed significantly to the collapse of CCA's fortunes in the late 1990's.

With the victory in the Supreme Court, however, CSC and the other prison corporations will benefit from corporate immunity from legal challenges to their failures to provide constitutionally mandated care as long as they operate under contracts with the federal government. In light of the dismal history of for-profit prisons even in the absence of this legal shield, it is safe to predict that corporate profits will be paid for in prisoner lives and prisoner suffering.

Endnotes

1. *Malesko v. Correctional Services Corporation*, 229 F.3d 374, 376 (2d Cir. 2000).
2. *Correctional Services Corporation v. Malesko*, 122 S. Ct. 515 (2001).
3. L. Maruschak, "HIV in Prisons and Jails, 1999" (2001): 1-2.
4. J. Mandak, "Hepatitis C Spreads in U.S. Prisons," Associated Press, 4 Sept. 2001.
5. C. Massie Mara and C. McKenna, "Aging in Place in Prison: Health and Long-Term Care Needs ofOlderInmates" (2000): 1, 3.
6. R.B. Hudson, "Aging and Criminal Justice: Images and Institutions" (2000): 2.
7. P.M. Ditton, "Mental Health and Treatment of Inmates and Probationers" (1999): 2.
8. T.M. Hammett, P. Harmon and L.M. Maruschak, *1996-1997 Update: HIV/AIDS, STDs, and TB in Correctional Facilities* (1999).
9. K. Wilcock, T.M. Hammett, R. Widom and J. Epstein, "Tuberculosis in Correctional Facilities 1994-95" (1996): 1.
10. Austin v. Pennsylvania Department of Corrections, 1999 WL 277511 (E.D. Pa. September 29, 1992).
11. "Tuberculosis Can Spread from Jail to Community," *Reuters Health*, 29 Oct. 2001.
12. S.W. Dooley, W.R. Jarvis, W.J. Martone and D.E. Snider, Jr., "Multidrug-Resistant Tuberculosis"(1992): 257.
13. *United States v. Bynum*, 408 U.S. 125, 137-38 (1972).
14. P. Belluck, "As More Prisons go Private, States Seek Tighter Controls," *New York Times*, 15 April 1999.
15. 5 U.S.C. §552.
16. 5 U.S.C. §500 et seq.

17. 5 U.S.C. §551 et seq.

18. N.L.R.B. v. Robbins Tire & Rubber Co., 437 U.S. 214, 242 (1978).

19. N.B. Casarez, "Furthering the Accountability Principle in Privatized Federal Corrections: The Need for Access to Private Prison Records" (1995): 264-272.

20. New York City Charter Section 626.

21. N.Y. Correction Law Sections 40, 45.

22. J. Gentry, "The Panopticon Revisited: The Problem of Monitoring Private Prisons" (1986): 356-357.

23. *Id.*, 357-358.

24. S.P. Sturm, "The Legacy and Future of Corrections Litigation" (1993): 662-681.

25. P.L. 104-134, effective 26 April 1996. The restrictions on injunctive relief are codified in 18 U.S.C. § 3636. The Act also prohibits prisoners from filing suit for damages until after they have presented their claims to internal grievance systems, even if the system does not award damages. See *Booth v. Churner*, 121 S. Ct. 1819 (2001). This restriction makes filing a damages action particularly difficult, since many grievance systems have deadlines for filing as short as one or two weeks. Another section of the PLRA, codified in 42 U.S.C. Section 1997e(e), prohibits a prisoner from seeking damages for mental and emotional injuries unless the prisoner has already suffered physical injuries; it is unclear whether physical pain is considered a "physical injury" under the statute. Another section of the statute places several restrictions on the fees that a prisoner's lawyer could otherwise recover directly from the defendants in a successful lawsuit for violations of the prisoner's constitutional rights. 42 U.S.C. Section 1997e(d). Since prisoners are almost always indigent, these limitations make it much more difficult for a prisoner to persuade a lawyer to take the case.

26. *Farmer v. Brennan*, 511 U.S. 825 (1994).

27. E. Bates, "Prisons for Profit," *The Nation*, 5 Jan. 1998: 14.

28. J. Austin and G. Coventry, Emerging Issues on Privatized Prisons (2001).

29. N.Y. Correction Law Sections 40, 45.

30. *Id.*

31. D. Jackson, "Broken Teens Left in Wake of Private Gain," *Chicago Tribune*, 27 Sept. 1999.

32. New York City Charter Section 626.

33. *Id.*, 15.

34. E. Bates, "Prisons for Profit," *The Nation*, 5 Jan. 1998: 13-14.

35. S. Toomey, "Unusual Defenses Work for Alaskans Charged with Prison Escape," Daily News, 1 Mar. 2000. A state audit of care given to prisones transferred from Hawaii to the same facility noted the lack of substance abuse programs required under the contract with the state.

36. K. Dayton, "Arizona Prison in Turmoil," *Honolulu Advertiser*, July 2001.

37. "Report of the Corrections Trustee for the District of Columbia to the Attorney General" (1998): 24-25,53.

38. "It's Murder at CCA's Ohio Jail" (1998) 18 Prison Privatisation Report International: 1-2.

39. A. Gerhardstein, "Private Prison Litigation: The Youngstown Case and Theories of Liability" (2000): 62.

40. C. Frye, "Board Finds Private Units of Prisons Poorly Run," *Arkansas Democrat-Gazette*, 21 Oct. 2000.

41. F. Butterfield, "Privately Run Juvenile Prison in Louisiana Is Attacked for Abuse of 6 Inmates," *New York Times*, 16 Mar. 2000.

42. F. Butterfield, "Private Company to Pull Out of Operating Troubled Prison," *New York Times*, 27 April 2000.

43. M. Ward, "Private Prisons Faulted on Services, Discipline," *Austin American Statesman*, 16 May 1990; "Wackenhut Corrections Corporation — the Stories They Won't Tell You," (1999) Corrections USA.

44. P. Tharp, "Prison Companies Get Hot," *New York Post*, 4 Oct. 2001.

45. E. Perez, "For-profit Prison Firm Wackenhut Tries to Break Shackles to Growth," *The Wall Street Journal*, 9 May 2001.

46. P. Tharp, "Prison Companies Get Hot," *supra* note 44.

47. *Id.*

48. A. Gerhardstein, "Private Prison Litigation: The Youngstown Case and Theories of Liability" (2000): 62.

CHAPTER SEVEN

International Law and the Privatization of Juvenile Justice

Mark Erik Hecht and Donna Habsha

Introduction

The incorporation of specific rights of children into the administration of justice is a recent development in international law. Although significant advancements in due process were achieved with the adoption of the Universal Declaration on Human Rights[1] at the United Nations (UN) in 1948, in reality the vast majority of these entitlements were accorded only to adults. Whether this was due to the fact that offences for young offenders often carry lighter sentences or whether it was because of a belief that children are insensitive to the concept of fairness is unclear.[2]

In 1980, the UN organized the sixth Congress on the Prevention of Crime and Treatment of Offenders. As a result of the conference, a set of guidelines for children in conflict with the law was drafted and adopted in 1985. The Standard Minimum Rules for the Administration of Juvenile Justice, or the Beijing Rules, provides a framework within which a national juvenile justice system should operate and establishes a model for fair and humane responses to juveniles involved with the justice system.[3] Four years later, the UN opened for signature the Convention on the Rights of the Child.[4] This one document redefined the way children's rights were understood by states and placed new obligations on countries with regard to their younger citizens accused of criminal activity.

In the early 1990s, as a consequence of the advancements in international law and domestic pressure from child advocates and civil libertarians, many states began redrafting their national statutes on juvenile delinquency. The objective of the legislators was to ensure compliance with the new universal set of standards. Many young offender acts, particularly in the wealthier Northern nations, made specific reference to the CRC in their preambles.

Despite the advancements noted above, a new trend has emerged within the last five years involving private corporations operating state-owned children's institutions. Because the privatization of young offender facilities is a relatively recent phenomenon, there is a lack of empirical evidence that examines in detail the effects of private prisons on incarcerated juveniles. The information that has been reviewed thus far, however, suggests that even if a state's domestic legislation is in keeping with the spirit of its international obligations, the reality of privately-run penal facilities creates a greater likelihood for violations of these requisite protections. Accordingly, young people eventually released from these institutions do not receive adequate care and service. As a result, society and the youth themselves are less protected from the harms associated with juvenile crime.

A Primer on Juvenile Justice

In the 2002 edition of *The State of the World's Children*, Carol Bellamy, the Executive Director of UNICEF, asserts that, "[g]overnments, as well as international institutions, must be held accountable for their leadership in putting the rights and well-being of children above all other concerns. And those that fail to do so must also be held accountable."[5] Since UNICEF began publishing its annual report in 1980, world leaders have made considerable advancements in the protection and promotion of children's rights, perhaps the most significant of which was the creation of the Convention on the Rights of the Child (CRC) in 1989. Despite a movement over the past ten years for domestic implementation of the CRC's provisions, coupled with the work of non-governmental organizations (NGOs) in raising awareness of children living in difficult circumstances, the area of international juvenile justice has remained relatively static. As Kirsten DiMartino, editor of *Juvenile Justice Worldwide*, describes: "Juvenile justice...ten years on...what has changed for children who come into conflict with the law? Not as much as expected. The challenge has proved more demanding than anyone could have imagined...when the [CRC] was adopted."[6]

In a recent study published by the International Network on Juvenile Justice of Defence for Children International, the author describes juvenile justice as being the "unwanted child" of states when it comes to their obligations under the CRC. Several reasons are cited for the negative attitude. For example, juvenile justice is not a popular topic. Minors in conflict with the law do not receive the same sympathetic understanding that is often afforded to other youngsters. The juvenile justice system is also very complex and as a result quite difficult to reform since it involves a very diverse set of actors, including the police, judiciary and social service agencies. Finally, juvenile justice often reflects an over-representation of marginalized groups and is therefore much more difficult to "fix" compared to other areas of children's rights such as access to health.

When drafting the CRC and similar international agreements and guidelines that focus on young offenders (i.e., the Beijing Rules), a fundamental concern was the treatment of children and youth deprived of their liberty. Deprivation of liberty is still a frequently applied measure for young people found guilty of committing a crime. The reality is the rights described in international law have not been adequate to eliminate the worst forms of detention and imprisonment. In many countries, for example, children can still be found in adult jails and "rehabilitation centers" are nothing more than teen jails by another name. In recent years, most often due to an extreme but exceptional incident of juvenile delinquency, a call for a tougher approach on youth crime has resulted in more closed and secure institutional settings.[7] In a study on juvenile justice ten years after the CRC, the investigator states that

> [c]omplying fully with the provisions of the [CRC]...means first and foremost to take more time and spend more energy on the promotion and development of non-residential alternatives, including prevention policies based on the objective of realizing a respectful society for children and families as a whole.[8]

Despite international obligations and the national legislation which often reflects the norms contained therein, many states have failed to submit to calls for better compliance and have retreated from discussions of alternative measures. In their place, a greater emphasis has been put on incarceration. To meet the demand for more jails, governments have been choosing to establish private systems and allow corporations—which by their very nature are in the profit making business—to take responsibility for young offenders. As Carol Bellamy explains, "[g]overnments who fail to put the rights and well-being of children above all other concerns must be held accountable." As the trend of incarceration continues, more child advocates will no doubt draw attention to the violations caused by this policy.[9]

International Law and Juvenile Justice

A decade before the establishment of the CRC, the 6th Congress on the Prevention of Crime and the Treatment of Offenders called for the preparation of minimum rules regulating the administration of juvenile justice.[10] Following these preparatory meetings, the UN General Assembly adopted the Standard Minimum Rules for the Administration of Juvenile Justice, known as the Beijing Rules.[11] Generally speaking, the rules do not legally bind a country; however, they are a reflection of commonly recognized "best practices" or customary international law.[12] The provisions of the Beijing Rules call for a strict limitation on the use of juvenile detention, maximum use of community-based modalities, separate juvenile courts and detention facilities, professionalization of personnel, the provision of specialized facilities, and programs and services aimed at reintegrating youth back into society.[13] In 1987, the UN Secretary-General initiated a dialogue with governments, government-appointed national correspondents, NGOs and experts concerned with children's rights and juvenile justice in order to encourage the worldwide application of the Beijing Rules.[14] As of 30 April 1988, communications were received from 34 governments on the most effective ways and means of implementing the principles contained in the Beijing Rules.[15]

The Beijing Rules were reinforced for countries that signed and ratified the CRC one year later in 1989. The signing and ratification of an international convention establishes a state's legally binding obligation to uphold the provisions of the document. The need to grant children special legal protection is contained in the preamble to the CRC that states, "The child, by reason of his physical and mental immaturity, needs special safeguards and care, including appropriate legal protection".[16] This is further emphasized by Article 40, which requires states to seek to establish laws and institutions specifically applicable to children in trouble with the law. Despite the existence of such institutions, Article 37 requires that detention and imprisonment be imposed "only as a measure of last resort and for the shortest appropriate period of time".[17] Further to this end, a state must make available a variety of dispositions and alternatives to institutional care that are suitable to the child.[18] The CRC instructs that the ultimate objective of a state that involves children in the penal process is to rehabilitate them so that they may pursue a constructive role in society.[19]

Regarding the potential dispositions applicable to juveniles, a number of studies which have examined the issue of juvenile delinquency conclude that the best deterrent is the establishment of programs to ensure healthier children, stronger families, better schools, and more cohesive communities.[20] This is based on research that demonstrates that the children most likely to be charged with juvenile offences are those that have experienced parental rejection, neglect, abuse or harsh corporal punishment.[21] Given this reality, international law took on an unaccustomed role by providing guidance to states on developing policies aimed at preventing children from coming into conflict with the law. Although there was a risk that the aims of prevention would appear to be indoctrination, the UN believed that the advantages of developing such standards would outweigh the risks.[22] The General Assembly resolution, the Development of Standards for the Prevention of Juvenile Delinquency, highlights the need for states to adopt measures aimed at protecting youth who are at "social risk" as a result of abandonment, neglect, abuse or exploitation and therefore more likely to become involved in criminal activity.[23] In 1990, the UN formally adopted the Guidelines for the Prevention of Juvenile Delinquency, otherwise know as the Riyadh Guidelines.[24]

The weakness of the Riyadh Guidelines results from the lack of agreement between states over appropriate approaches to prevent juvenile delinquency. Generally, the division exists between those states which support a "clinical approach" to prevention[25] and those that believe in the power of deterrence that is only available through the use of penal sanctions. The Riyadh Guidelines focus on early prevention and protection by paying particular attention to children in situations of "social risk" and encouraging the development of programs related to social welfare, education, labor and health.[26]

Given the lack of widespread international support for "clinical prevention," it may be more fruitful to examine international conventions and treaties regarding the treatment of juveniles for whom the last resort of institutionalized custody has been applied. There is very little binding treaty law setting out the objectives and standards of institutions that deprive children of their liberty. As a result, in 1981 Amnesty International produced a draft Standard Minimum Rules for the Protection of Juveniles Deprived of their Liberty.[27] The work done by Amnesty International was used in drafting parts of the CRC, namely Articles 3 and 40. However, neither the CRC nor the Beijing Rules provide a thorough and systematic approach related to the conditions necessary for children who are deprived of their liberty. Thus, at the 8th Congress on the Prevention of Crime and the Treatment of Offenders held in Havana in 1990, a number of states adopted a set of Rules for the Protection of Juveniles Deprived of their Liberty (JDL Rules).[28]

In recognizing the negative effects of depriving children of their liberty, the JDL Rules recommend that states counteract such effects and recognize that the care of children and youth involved in crime is a social service of great significance. JDL Rules provides a legislative framework within which the Secretary-General of the UN was able to appoint a Special Rapporteur on the Application of International Standards Concerning the Human Rights of Detained Juveniles.[29] This framework relates to such things as the management of juvenile facilities, classification and placement of young offenders, physical environment and accommodation, education, vocational training and recreation. For example, Rule 27 explains that staff within youth detention facilities should be competent and suitably trained to deal with the individual needs of each child with the aim of rehabilitating and reintegrating the child back into society.[30] Consistent with the objective of assuming a constructive role in society, the right of children to education as enshrined in a number of other treaties and declarations is not limited by virtue of the child's deprivation of liberty. Integration with the State's education system is emphasized so that the children's learning may continue without interference upon their release from a detention facility.[31] In short, the JDL Rules recommendations are in keeping with the rehabilitative aim of the institutionalization of young offenders.

International Law and Private Sector Responsibilities

There have been a number of recent developments in international law that undertake to strengthen the linkages between corporate responsibility and the protection of children's rights. Much of the basis for this framework is found in the Universal Declaration itself. Notably, its preamble states, "every individual and every organ of society, keeping this Declaration constantly in mind, shall strive by teaching and education to promote respect for these rights".

The wide-reaching ambit of responsibility outlined in the Universal Declaration suggests that even corporate bodies are seized with the obligation of such protection. Further, Article 30 of the Universal Declaration indicates, "[n]othing in this Declaration may be interpreted as implying for any state, group or person any right to engage in any activity or to perform any act aimed at the destruction of any of the rights and freedoms set forth herein". Enumerated rights specifically include freedom from cruel, inhuman or degrading punishment and access to education. Although this document is non-binding, it is widely recognized as customary international law, and its provisions are implemented in the International Covenant on Economic, Social, and Cultural Rights[32] and the International Covenant on Civil and Political Rights,[33] both of which are binding upon ratification by states.

Multilateral declarations have been developed to place checks upon the work of private sector industries, in particular those that are multinational in origin. These declarations recognize not only the need for private industries to respect rights, but that their position in society places a strong obligation to promote and enhance respect for human rights. An example of this is seen in the Organization for Economic Cooperation and Development (OECD) Guidelines for Multinational Enterprises[34] and the OECD Principles of Corporate Governance,[35] which require businesses to recognize the greater context in which they operate and thus contribute to the greater benefit of society.

In furtherance of such stated principles, the UN has undertaken an initiative called the "Global Compact" which requests that businesses show good "global citizenship" in the nations in which they operate. This source document explains that businesses should support and respect the protection of internationally proclaimed human rights within their sphere of influence and ensure they are not involved in human rights abuses.[36]

Although the primary responsibility to administer juvenile justice lies with the state, the trend in international law to place assurances on the business community is relevant in the context of prison privatization. If governments choose to delegate their public duties to the private sector, they must ensure the service delivery is in keeping with their laws, both at the state and international level. The fact that a company contracting with government has parallel legal commitments should suggest a greater level of protection be placed on those individuals affected by the contract. In reality, many of these private sector guarantees are voluntary in nature and are therefore difficult to enforce. However, the fact remains that international legal protections cannot be said to end with the state. Private companies are not absolved from their fundamental human rights obligations.

Case Studies: Canada and the United Kingdom

As previously mentioned, Article 40 of the CRC requires states to draft criminal legislation and operate penal institutions within the parameters established in the

Convention and, wherever appropriate and desirable, provide alternative measures to judicial proceedings. Both Canada and the United Kingdom (UK) asserted their commitment to implementing a youth justice system by ratifying the CRC in 1991.[37] The Beijing Rules, the Riyadh Guidelines and the JDL Rules were established as non-binding minimum standards upon which member states of the UN could build their juvenile justice systems.[38] Aspects of the Beijing Rules, the Riyadh Guidelines and the JDL Rules were incorporated into the CRC. Thus, when Canada and the UK ratified the CRC in 1991, many of the standards and norms established in the abovementioned General Assembly resolutions became legally binding upon their government. Canada and the UK submitted their initial reports to the UN Committee on the Rights of the Child in 1994 and 1995 respectively. The Committee's primary criticism of both governments was their lack of coordinating mechanisms or independent monitoring bodies to promote the general implementation and incorporation of the CRC.[39] In recent years, both countries have attempted to address the Committee's concerns.

In 1997, the new Labour Government took office in the UK and adopted a more open approach to reporting to the CRC Committee.[40] Currently, advisory groups representing key government departments, NGOs and children and youth all play a part in scrutinizing government policy and legislation to ensure compliance with its international obligations.[41] In 1998, the UK government introduced the Crime and Disorder Act,[42] which mandated greater monitoring of the youth justice system to ensure compliance of international standards when depriving juveniles of their liberty. The Youth Justice Board (YJB) is a national public body that was established under the Crime and Disorder Act in order to ensure that basic principles are met in the youth justice system.[43] The YJB encourages the youth justice system to deliver its aim of prevention by providing support for the implementation of early intervention in the lives of young people, effective community programs and services, a coordinated approach across government departments to tackle the issue of youth offending and strong intervention by the YJB where local agencies are failing. In addition to the establishment of the YJB, the Crime and Disorder Act also provides a new range of non-custodial sentences. If a custody order is made, the act mandates that community supervision must be provided for at least the same period of time.[44]

The Government of Canada has created a Children's Bureau to ensure consistency and provide coordination for federal, provincial and territorial programs and policies concerning children.[45] Further, in 1998, Canada showed particular progress in relation to its juvenile justice policy, by introducing the Youth Criminal Justice Act (YCJA).[46] The YCJA represents a positive development for children's rights in a number of ways. Firstly, the statute acknowledges the Government's international commitment to children's rights by stating in its preamble that the CRC ought to be used as a guide for judicial interpretation. Further, the YCJA places greater emphasis on rehabilitation, treatment and social reintegration of youths involved in criminal activity with concomitant reduced use of custody.[47] For example, for non-violent, low-risk offenders, the use of alternative measures and programs of restorative justice such as community service and restitution is encouraged.[48] For violent offenders, special sentencing is available which requires intensive treatment and long-term supervision.[49] Thus, the YCJA's focus on rehabilitation and reintegration of young offenders accounts for the developmental needs of each child and ensures that custody is a measure of last resort exercised for the shortest appropriate period of time as established in Article 37(b) of the CRC. Unfortunately, the recent steps taken by Canada and the UK to strengthen their commitment to the CRC and the needs of youth involved in criminal activity has been somewhat defeated as a result of their support for privately operated young offender facilities.

In the past decade the UK has witnessed a reduction in the rate of violent crimes committed by 10- to 17-year olds.[50] Nevertheless, numerous highly publicized acts of violence have distorted the reality of youth involved in crime and have led to intense public debate on the matter. Politicians have been driven to introduce harsher sentencing policies and legislation as a result of public pressure to "get tough on crime".[51] To this end, the UK has abandoned its commitment to base youth justice upon principles of diversion and minimum intervention. A punitive approach based on greater use of custody has resulted in a rapidly increasing prison population. In order for the UK government to cope with the cost of expanding the number of youth prison facilities, there has been a move toward handing over the financing, design, construction and operation of such facilities to the private sector. Generally, the argument made in favor of privatization is that it is cost efficient, innovative and more likely to reduce rates of recidivism.[52]

Hassockfield Secure Training Centre is a privately run young offender institution in the UK that began operating in September 1999. Hassockfield houses 40 youth between the ages of 12 and 17. The average length of a sentence in Hassockfield is 8.6 months for offences such as criminal damage, theft, robbery and driving offences.[53] The first half of an order made in a secure training center is served in detention by way of the Criminal Justice and Public Order Act[54]. The second half of the order involves compulsory supervision in the community by Youth Offending Teams. Community sentences, also known as Detention Training Orders, include supervision orders, probation orders, community service orders, combination orders and curfew orders. Detention Training Orders were made available to UK courts in April 2000 under the Crime and Disorder Act.

Similar to the UK, serious violent crime involving youths has been declining in Canada since 1995 and property crime has fallen since 1990.[55] Notwithstanding this fact, increasingly punitive public attitudes have increased the number of youths in custody. To alleviate the financial strain this places on the government, Canada has supported the move toward privatizing young offender institutions. Canada's first privately owned and operated young offender facility named Project Turnaround opened in Ontario in 1997. Project Turnaround is an all boy facility, which aims to provide an intensive and regimented program that will instill self-discipline and responsibility in high-risk young offenders.[56] The program has two phases. The first phase is a secure custody phase that has a distinctive military style. It places the youth on a highly structured schedule of activities beginning at 6:00 am and continuing until 10:00 pm. The custodial component is from 4 to 6 months long and includes rehabilitation programming based on the participant's particular needs. The second phase is a community after-care program, whereby youth released on probation are offered supervision and services in their respective communities. The after-care program augments the custodial component of the program in order to facilitate and enhance the skills necessary for successful reintegration into society.[57] Encourage Youth Corporation, the company which owns and operates the facility, contends that the Project Turnaround program is very effective in refocusing the lives of "misdirected young men" and is keeping with national and international objectives of rehabilitating and reintegrating young offenders back into society.[58]

The following analysis shall focus on the failure of Project Turnaround and Hassockfield Secure Training Centre to maintain quality education standards, and an appropriate independent monitoring body to assess programs and accept complaints from youth. Such failures patently violate international minimum standards related to juvenile justice and reflect the trend that privately operated prisons conflict with international standards, norms and obligations related to children's rights.

The JDL Rules provides that every juvenile of compulsory school age has the right to education suited to his or her needs and abilities and designed to prepare him or her for return to society.[59] Moreover, the CRC has been declared a holistic document that regards all enumerated rights to be of equal value and importance. In other words, the CRC must be read as a whole and as such Article 28, which recognizes the right of a child to an education suited to his/her needs, must be equally granted to youth in custody or deprived of their liberty. The social services inspectorate of UK young offender institutions has recently issued a report stating that the quality and quantity of education and training provision in custody are inadequate. The report found that teaching was unsatisfactory and some staff had difficulty keeping the students under control. The approach by staff was reported to be inconsistent, as some staff responded to misbehavior very firmly while other staff completely avoided any challenging behavior.[60] The incompetence of the instructors was mainly accounted for by the fact that they were not trained to work with youth in custody. The report also stated that the curriculum in Young Offender Institutions such as Hassockfield is limited and often inappropriate to the needs of young people in custody.

Untrained staff and an inappropriate curriculum explain why youth attendance at education and training in custody was erratic and not properly monitored. Further, only 60% of the youth discharged to the community component of their Detention Training Order had education or vocational training and 58% had no education or training one month following their release into the community.[61] Private young offender institutions that have not made the educational needs of the youth a spending priority will not achieve their stated objective of rehabilitating and reintegrating youth back into society. Youth who are not receiving adequate educational training lack the qualifications necessary to find employment and are therefore more likely to reoffend.[62]

Despite the fact that educational achievement has been established as a crucial factor in the successful rehabilitation of young offenders, an examination of the educational opportunities available to youth in private facilities reveals that the economic success of private corporations will override the rights and needs of youth. The strict discipline milieu of programming appears to appease the voting public and is therefore given more attention than the academic pursuits of the youth in boot camps or secure training centers. Hassockfield maintains that they are interested in helping youth advance their future employability. However, if the cost of offering co-op programs or certificates in commercially viable enterprises is not recouped by the corporation which owns the facility, then there will be pressure by shareholders to abandon such practices. The profit motive of private prisons is in direct conflict with the interests of youth and the objective of rehabilitation.

Project Turnaround is also indicative of the inherent conflict of interest between young offenders and the private sector. In order for the facility to renew its contract with the government, it is in its best interest to ensure that occupancy is maintained. Thus, the incentive of reintegrating offending youth back into society is weakened, as a radical reduction in the number of repeat offenders would in effect reduce the supply of profit-producing "patrons" to Encourage Youth Corporation. In light of such issues, a request was made by the opposition government in the provincial legislature to view Encourage Youth Corporation's contract with the provincial government in power that had signed the agreement.

While a copy of the contract was received, it concealed the facilities' daily operating costs. Thus, it is unclear whether the contracting parties have established a cap on the percent of government funds provided to Project Turnaround that may be deemed as profit. The deliberate omission of such information begs the question of whether financial losses by Project Turnaround may be compensated by cutting back on food, health care, and programming, potentially resulting in further violations.

The JDL Rules and the CRC require that youth have access to the contact information of authorities competent to receive complaints by juveniles deprived of their liberty in order to ensure the protection of youth caught up in such a situation.[63] Qualified inspectors, not belonging to the administration of the facility, must conduct periodic and unannounced inspections with unrestricted access to everyone working in the facility.[64] Unfortunately, Project Turnaround does not have a complaints procedure in place through which youth are able to ensure that their rights are being upheld. Project Turnaround officials maintain that the rights of youth are protected and monitored because the facility receives regular review and evaluation of the effectiveness of its programs by independent persons or agencies.

Last year an evaluation of Project Turnaround was released which examined whether or not a military model custody facility, delivered in the context of appropriate correctional interventions, would decrease recidivism rates and enhance the children's psychological well-being and positive life skills.[65] The report concluded that only 33% of Project Turnaround participants re-offended compared to a 50% recidivism rate for young offenders in regular facilities.[66] Experts disagree with the report's conclusions. University of Toronto criminologist, Anthony Doob, explains that, "using traditional conservative, common–sense statistics, there is no difference [in recidivism] between boot-camp participants and a group the evaluators claim to be comparable".[67] Doob points out that the control group used in the evaluation was compared only to those Project Turnaround participants who completed their stay at the facility. The youth who dropped out of the program were ignored and they are the ones who would tend to have higher recidivism rates. Thus, when the dropouts are included in the boot-camp group, the actual rate of recidivism rises.[68]

An alternative report prepared by an independent research firm compared the recidivism rates of young offenders released from Brookside, a publicly run jail, with that of youths released from Project Turnaround. The alternative report, which is based on statistics from the provincial Offenders Management System, indicated that only 6 out of 21 youths reoffended upon release from Brookside while 7 out of 12 Project Turnaround youths reoffended within six months of their release.[69] The primary difference between Brookside and Project Turnaround is that Project Turnaround is based on a strict-discipline military style program whereas Brookside places greater emphasis on rehabilitative programming. This report supports the argument that public facilities' focus on case management while in custody and extensive after-care programming, are in fact more effective means for reducing recidivism rates than the boot camp model. There is a strong body of evidence that indicates that strict discipline facilities do not lower recidivism rates or enhance rehabilitation and the success of boot camps has been entirely attributable to rehabilitation programming and after-care programs. [70] Although Project Turnaround provides rehabilitation and aftercare programs, they have not invested in the quality of such programming. For example, post-release community supervision provided for Project Turnaround participants is subject to the location and remoteness of the participant's community.[71] Limiting the availability of after-care programs on the basis of community location will radically reduce rates of rehabilitation.

The JDL Rules state that the assessment of programs and institutions for young offenders ought to be conducted by independent persons or agencies in order to keep practices abreast of the changing needs of youth involved in crime.[72] Accordingly, the evaluation report of Project Turnaround should have been conducted by an agency that would not share in the economic interest of Encourage Youth Corporation. A private and independent consulting company called T3 Associates Training and Consulting Inc. conducted Project Turnaround's evaluation. Ironically, shortly after the favorable report was released, T3 was given a contract for the training of caseworkers at a recently opened private "mega jail" in Penetanguishene Ontario.[73] Such evidence suggests that the profit interest of private companies invariably subordinates the monitoring and maintenance of children's rights in privately run detention facilities. Jim Goetz, of the provincial opposition party stated,

> The fundamental conflict between public and private correctional facilities is whom the operators are ultimately responsible to. A public facility is responsible to the community in which it is located, the Ministry to which it reports, the Minister in charge and therefore ultimately the electorate. A private correctional facility adds the extra component of responsibility to stakeholders, which can affect decisions made for the sake of profit—decisions that may not be in the best interest of the public.[74]

In addition to the suspected bias of the report, the sample size used by T3 in their evaluation is far too small to be statistically significant or conclusive. There were only 158 Project Turnaround youth and 136 members of the comparison group that were examined. In fact, the report states "It must be underscored that the current results are based on small sample sizes that make it difficult to fully explore the properties of the composite scale that attempts to measure change."[75] The report further indicates that "higher risk" offenders such as those with charges of homicide, arson or sexual offences were excluded from the sample, as they tend to show lower rates of recidivism, and because the perception of their offences by the other youth in the group may have impeded them from fully engaging in the programming.[76] Youth with serious mental or health problems were also excluded from the evaluation, as doing so would drive up the cost of treatment programs and likely lower reported rates of rehabilitation.[77] The reporting agency's discretion suggests that the youth involved in the study were "cherry picked" in order to produce favorable results. Strategic research tactics strike at the credibility of the evaluation report and the general conclusion that privately operated strict discipline facilities successfully rehabilitate youth.

Conclusion

Over the past fifty years the international human rights movement has witnessed significant advancements in the field of children's rights. The Universal Declaration of 1948 laid a foundation for the levels of protection that followed thereafter. Although juvenile justice was for many years left behind, the Beijing Rules of 1985 and the Riyadh Guidelines and JDL Rules of 1990 did provide some protection for youth involved in criminal activity. With the adoption of the CRC, states were required to demonstrate a greater accountability as the international community began monitoring their compliance. As a result of these achievements, many governments, Canada and the UK among them, drafted domestic laws that mirrored their new international responsibilities. Child advocates were optimistic that the most vulnerable youth, particularly those being deprived of their liberty, would benefit.

The reality is that children implicated and involved in crime are not much better protected today than they were fifty years ago. Due to a variety of factors – public pressure, media campaigns, budgetary constraints – more governments are choosing to privatize their juvenile institutions. The result is fewer safeguards coupled with an increased risk of violations of the human rights of children placed in the care of these corporations. Unless this trend is reversed, the government promises taking place in public fora will not protect the youth involved in criminal activity from the intentions of the private sector.

Endnotes

1. UNGA Res. 217A (III) of 10 December 1948 [hereinafter Universal Declaration].
2. G. Van Bueren, *The International Law on the Rights of the Child* (1998): 169.
3. *Id.*, 170.
4. GA Resolution 45/112, 14 December 1990.
5. UNICEF, *The State of the World's Children 2002* (2002): 4.
6. K. DiMartino, "Juvenile Justice…ten years on…" (2000).
7. R. Abramson, "Juvenile Justice: The 'Unwanted Child' of State Responsibilities" (2001).
8. G. Cappelaere, Juvenile Justice 10 years after the CRC" (2000).
9. UNICEF, *State of the World's Children 2002, supra* note 5.
10. UN Doc. Resolution 4, 6th UN Congress on the Prevention of Crime and the Treatment of Offenders, United Nations Publications; no. E.81.IV.4, ch.1, sec.B.
11. GA Resolution 40/33, 29 November 1985; Canada voted for the rules and they were adopted by consensus [hereinafter Beijing Rules].
12. To be considered customary international law, the document must be adopted by a significant number of UN member states. All of the states adopted the Beijing Rules and no states abstained. Austria, Byelorussia, France, Germany, Greece, Hungary, Ukraine, UK and the USSR had undertaken a study and reported that some or all of the Beijing Rules found expression in their national systems and therefore opted not to adopt the Rules.
13. W.D. Angel, *The International Law of Youth Rights: Source Documents and Commentary* (1995): 867.
14. *Id.*, 867.
15. *Id.*, 868.
16. K.Covell & R.B.Howe, *The Challenge of Children's Rights for Canada* (2001): 91.
17. CRC Article 37; GA Resolution 45/112.
18. *Id.*, Article 40(4).
19. *Id.*, Article 40.
20. National Crime Prevention Council Canada, "Economic Analysis Committee Report", March 1996.
21. Department of Justice, Canada, "Toward Safer Communities," (1995): 77-87.
22. UN Doc. A/CONF/87/5, 6th UN Congress on the Prevention of Crime and Treatment of Offenders.
23. GA Resolution 40/35, 11 December 1985.
24. Adopted by the General Assembly 28 March 1991. General Assembly Resolution 45/112 [hereinafter "The Riyadh Guidelines"].
25. A clinical approach prevents social pathologies by identifying the characteristics of the population at risk and recommending specific counter measures such as special programs.
26. G. Van Bueren, *The International Law on the Rights of the Child, supra* note 2 at 196.
27. *Id.*, 208.
28. GA Resolution 45/113 [hereinafter JDL Rules].
29. See Resolution of the Subcommission 1985/19, 29 August 1985; Resolution of the Subcommission 1989/31, 1 September 1989, appointing Mary Conception Bautista as Special Rapporteur. See also UN Doc E/CN.4/Sub.2/1991 24.
30. JDL Rule 30, UN Doc. A/RES/45/113.
31. *Id.*
32. UNGA Res. 2200A (XXI), 16 December 1966.

33. *Id.*
34. 15 I.L.M. 9 (1976).
35. Available online at <http://www1.umn.edu/humanrts/links/oecdbusinessguidelines.html>.
36. Available online at <http://www.unglobalcompact.org>.
37. S. Muscroft, ed., *Children's Rights: Reality or Rhetoric?* (1999) <info@save-children-alliance.org>.
38. G. Van Bueren, *The International Law on the Rights of the Child, supra* note 2 at 170.
39. S. Muscroft, *Children's Rights, supra* note 37 at 105, 261.
40. *Id.,* 261.
41. *Id.*
42. 1998 (U.K.), 1998, c.37.
43. For an overview of the board visit <http://www.youth-justice-board.gov.uk/who/what.html>.
44. <http://www.youth-justice-board.gov.uk/who/what.html>
45. S. Muscroft, *Children's Rights, supra* note 37 at 105.
46. Bill C-7, *An Act in respect of criminal justice for young persons and to amend and repeal other Acts,* 1st Sess., 37th Parl., 1998, 3rd reading Senate, 18 December 2001 [hereinafter *YCJA*].
47. Sections 83 and 84.
48. Section 42(1).
49. Section 38(1).
50. S. Muscroft, *Children's Rights, supra* note 37 at 261.
51. *Id.*
52. "Making Crime Pay" at 93.
53. Available online at: <http://society.guardian.co.uk/crimeandpunishment/story/0,8150,537869,00.html>.
54. 1994 (U.K.), 1994, c.33.
55. S. Muscroft (1998): 105.S. Muscroft, *Children's Rights, supra* note 37 at 105.
56. R. Brennan, "Ontario Plans New Boot Camps in Facelift" *the Toronto Star* (2000).
57. Project Turnaround Outcome Evaluation-Final Report, T3 Associates Training and Consulting, 159 Gilmour Street, Ottawa, Ontario K2P 0N8 at 1.
58. Final Report T3 Associates.
59. JDL section 38, UN Doc. A/RES/45/113.
60. Available online at <http://society.guardian.co.uk/crimeandpunishment/story/0,8150,537869,00.html>.
61. Available online at <http://www.youth-justice-board.gov.uk/view_pr.cfm?PRID=97>.
62. Available online at <http://web.ukonline.co.uk/howard.league/press/1801.html>; The Howard League is a penal reform charity established in the UK in 1866. It works for humane and rational reform of the penal system by researching and commenting on criminal justice policy and practice, holding conferences and debates and publishing books and reports.
63. JDL Rule 77, 24 UN Doc. A/RES/45/113; CRC Article 37(d) GA Resolution 45/112.
64. JDL Rule 72, UN Doc. A/ RES/45/113, *supra* note 63.
65. Final Report T3 Associates at 71.
66. *Id., 73.*
67. A. Lindgren, "Boot-camp claims bunk: academic," *National Post,* 4 February 2002.
68. *Id.*
69. R. Brennan, "Study says boot camp has high repeat-offender rate," *The Montreal Gazette,* 7 October 1998.
70. Dr. Jalal Shamise, Professor of Child Psychology at the University of Toronto and Director of Toronto's Institute for the Study of Anti-social Behaviour in Youth.
71. Final Report T3 Associates at 2.
72. JDL Rule 74, UN Doc. A/RES/45/113.
73. Interview: Jim Goetz Executive, Assistant to Dave Levac, MPP Liberal Corrections Critic, 2 November 2001, (416)325-6261.
74. *Id.*
75. Final Report T3 Associates at 68.
76. *Id.* at 4.
77. *Id.*

CHAPTER EIGHT

Prison Privatization: The Arrested Development of African Americans

Monique W. Morris

Introduction: The Prison Industrial Complex, Private Prisons and African Americans

Each year, private prisons hold hundreds of thousands of African American men, women, and children. As with public facilities, African Americans are imprisoned in disproportionately greater numbers than any other ethnic group in private facilities, making them the group most likely to reap the ramifications of private facilities' poor administration, prisoner abuses, and problematic policies. While acknowledging the importance of holding the offender responsible for his/her actions, research continues to confirm that the best responses to non-violent delinquent and criminal behavior are those which are multi-modal (so as to address the multiple factors that contribute to aberrant behavior), and community-based. However, policy has erred to the side of incarceration as the leading response to crime and delinquency, particularly when the offender is African American. While the American justice system is premised on notions of honor, impartiality, and fairness, the legacy of African Americans' long and largely negative historic relationship to American law—commencing with their official enslavement, followed by legalized apartheid (segregation), and finally by a governmental policy of civil rights which has largely failed to redress the historic disadvantages produced by the preceding eras—has entrenched racial biases that continue to taint the administration of justice. African American offenders are often on the receiving end of less than impartial judgments, often resulting in lengthy prison sentences. These well-documented racial biases are important to examining the impact of private prisons on the development of the African American people.

Today, African Americans experience the highest representation in the criminal and juvenile justice systems, despite the fact that they do not commit the most crimes. African American males have a 1 in 4 chance of going to prison in their lifetime, compared to a 1 in 6 chance for Latino males, and a 1 in 23 chance for white males.[1] Institutionalization is often used as the solution for addressing the aberrant behavior of black people, supporting the burgeoning prison industrial complex, and thereby creating an economic system that is buoyed by the incarceration of African Americans.

In 2000, over one million African American men and women were incarcerated—the largest number ever in United States history. Annual expenditures on law enforcement have increased from US $5 billion to $27 billion over the past 20 years. It costs an estimated $30,000 to house a prisoner for one year, even with cuts in prison programs. In fact, the United States now spends over $100 billion annually fighting crime (e.g. through law enforcement, prison construction, etc.), prompting an entire industry to be developed around policies and practices that favor incarceration over rehabilitation.

The impacts on African American communities of the prison industrial complex in general and of prison privatization are inseparable in many ways. Indeed the two compound to significantly undermine African Americans' ability to exist and function in society. The rapidly-expanding private prison industry was responsible for 90,000 prisoners in 2000, up from approximately 5,000 prisoners in 1999.[2] As a significant component of the prison industrial complex, prison privatization is responsible not only for cementing the idea that prisons are the panacea for addressing crime. It is also responsible for supporting a documented history of inhumane conditions and brutality (i.e. starvation, filth, beatings, etc.) that have been inflicted upon black prisoners.[3] Instead of implementing more community-based prevention programs and culturally competent alternatives to incarceration, policies have favored the economically-driven prison industry at the expense of African Americans. Through the prison industrial complex and prison privatization, African Americans have continued to be a source of profit for major corporations while continuing to suffer from the deleterious attitudes and practices that entrench a low appreciation and quality of black life.

Through the criminalization and incarceration of African American people–men, women, and children–private corporations have profited enormously, while millions of people of African descent remain relegated to oppressive conditions reminiscent of slavery and the Antebellum South. Between 1994 and 1995, the nation's largest private prison developer, Corrections Corporation of America (CCA), enjoyed an increase in revenues from $152 million to $207 million—an increase of 36 percent. The interest on the loans financing the massive prison construction boom has also grown enormously. For example, lenders in California "earned" over $1.6 billion from prison construction in the state from 1982 to 1990.[4] In fact, private prisons–and those who invest in them–have directly benefited from punitive laws that feed on the perception of the innate criminality of people of African descent and the harsh sentences accompanying such a philosophy.

Race—a social construct based on biological and ethnic identity—and culture play a profound role in American society, especially where the prevalence of violence in communities of color is generated by the economic, political, and social stratification that makes them more vulnerable to involvement in the criminal or juvenile justice system (via incarceration, probation, parole, or trial). The "racialization" of urban space has ghettoized African American populations in the United States, seriously impeding their access to housing, adequate medical care, and education. The failed effort to adequately address this racialization has helped to engender in the minds of leading criminologists such as John DiIullio the notion that race is a minimal factor in the administration of justice and that a mythic "superpredator" exists who must be controlled or, in some cases, eliminated. Additionally, the failure of the effort to address this racialization has given rise to a climate that has supported the race to incarcerate, a race that explicitly depends upon the continued cheapening of African American life, community and place, and the varied responses to this socio-economic and cultural oppression by its victims.

Authors Michael Keith and Steve Pile once observed that, "for those who have no place that can be safely called home, there must be a struggle for a place to be." Feminist author bell hooks echoed that sentiment in her argument that historically, "African American people [have] believed that the construction of a homeplace, however fragile and tenuous (*i.e.*, the slave hut, the wooden shack) has a radical political dimension."[5] In the context of defining *space* and *place* in society, the prison industrial complex has been lethal in its ability to cripple African American communities as they struggle to participate fully in American society. The process of institutionalizing the space in which millions of African Americans dwell has had a significantly deleterious effect on the development of African Americans, impeding both black offenders' abilities to rehabilitate and the larger black community's capacity to fully participate in American culture.

Historical Context

Since landing in shackles on the shores of North America, African people have been at the center of the debate between punishment and rehabilitation, how justice should be administered in America, and who is most vulnerable to lifelong stigmatization and marginalization as a result of, and contributing to, their perceived criminality. To begin, it is important to acknowledge that it is those in power who determine who and what is "criminal" or "bad"—not those who are labeled by these monikers. In 1975, sociologist Robert Staples effectively discussed the relationship between race and crime in America using a colonial analogy. Staples asserted that as a function of African America's status as a culturally-colonized group, they suffer a constant victimization based on justice practices that are structured to support only what is determined to be favorable to white America.[6] As a result of this "colonization," African Americans are on the receiving end of policies and practices that reinforce their marginalization— through disproportionate unemployment, poor education, poor housing, and ongoing social stigmatization.

This marginalization is not new to the African American experience; rather, it is an amalgamation of years of educational, economic, and cultural oppression that have systematically demonized people of African descent as being incapable of rehabilitation, and that have further dehumanized the experience of being criminalized by repeatedly distorting the public understanding of who commits most crimes. Most people understand "criminality" according to who is arrested and punished, and do not consider the social factors that contribute to who is brought into the system (*e.g.*, over-policing, decisions based on race and appearance of the alleged offender, etc.) But historically, it has not only been the socio-economic and cultural situation of communities, but also, concomitantly, the decisions made along the justice continuum—by law enforcement, prosecutors, judges, etc.—that determine which populations will be over-represented in, and disproportionately punished by, the justice system. For example, African Americans are disproportionately arrested by law enforcement. As early as 1872, African American arrests were reported as being at a rate two and a half times greater than their proportion to the general population. In 1880, the rate of African American arrests was four and half times greater than their proportion to the general population, in 1890 it was seven times greater, and in 1892 it was nine

times greater. However, this disparity was not solely attributable to the disproportionate number of criminal acts being committed by African Americans.[7] While in
1892, Ida B. Wells-Barnett documented cases where white men committed crimes
with their faces painted black,[8] and it has been well documented that many police
officers harbor and openly express highly prejudiced feelings toward black people,[9]
it may be of greater causative significance that during this period, the convict-
lease system was in place. This practice of leasing the labor of mostly black
convicts to private bidders encouraged the increased conviction of African Americans for purposes of servitude under white "bosses" under conditions that were
arguably more deplorable than slavery. In 1901, W.E.B. Du Bois testified and
wrote about the criminalization of black people resulting from the crop-lien system—an "arrangement of fixed chattel mortgages that placed the housing, labor,
agriculture, and personal liberties of black laborers in the hands of white land-
owners and merchants" and the convict-lease system. In his pioneering work,
"The Spawn of Slavery," Du Bois pointed squarely to these two practices as being
responsible for cementing African Americans' conviction that both criminal justice and slavery were forms of "white men's oppression", and for destroying their
faith in the integrity of courts and in the fairness of juries.[10] The relative ease with
which alleged black offenders were convicted not only contributed to the climate
that favored incarceration and exploitation of African Americans, it caused much
of the distortion in public perception which today so easily equates perpetrators of
crime with being of African descent.

Further compounding the marginalization of African people in America is the
status of black females. African American girls have a history of unequal sentencing and treatment by the justice system, as well as increased victimization because of their double status as a black person and a woman in American society.
Black females have not been perceived as a group worthy of study, therefore
information about African American females is usually presented in the context of
their position relative to Black males and white females, creating images of black
womanhood that are distorted and falsified.[11] These images have influenced the
way in which African American female victims and offenders have been treated by
the criminal justice system.

This history has haunted the arrest trends of African American females, and
contributed to their criminalization—whether innocent or guilty—for possessing
the same qualities that have kept them alive under the oppressive legacy of
slavery in their lives. For example, African American females were seven times
more likely to be arrested for prostitution than women of other ethnic groups in the
1970s.[12] It has not been established whether they were disproportionately more
prevalent than prostitutes of other racial/ethnic groups, however. Moyer and White
in 1981 suggested that police officers applied more severe sanctions to a black
female if she was perceived as "loud, boisterous, aggressive, vulgar, and disrespectful."[13] So then, as a function of being loud and aggressive—signs of strength
and positive resistance in African American culture—thousands of black females
are criminalized into becoming the casualties of this ongoing war of contradictions.

More recently, the inaccurate representation of who commits crimes has
increased throughout the media, which over-reports crimes committed by African
Americans while under-reporting crimes where African Americans are victims,
and under-representing crimes committed by whites. This disparity generates
significant consequences because approximately 76 percent of the American
public formulate their opinions about crime based upon what they see or read in

the news.[14]   Through this greater preoccupation with African Americans as perpetrators of crimes, and lesser attention to their increased vulnerability as crime
victims, the notion is reinforced in the American public psyche that African life is of
lesser value than white life, and therefore not as important to protect.

The egregious use of incarceration and institutionalization in response to
crime and delinquency in black communities may be seen as a continuation of
the American cultural legacy of slavery and creation of an economy that thrives on
the continued subjugation of people of color–largely people of African descent.
Current racial disparities in the rates of incarceration are exacerbated by this
history of criminalizing and subjugating African Americans. In 1931, the Scottsboro
Trials in Alabama became a powerful illustration of how the *perception* of African
American male criminality has historically contributed to a criminal justice climate that rallies for their incarceration and death. In the trials, the nine African
American teenagers accused of raping two white girls suffered from many of the
same challenges that continue to result in partial and incorrect verdicts, including
incompetent legal representation and foregone conclusions regarding culpability based upon appearance. During the several years that it took to complete their
lengthy trial, the nine boys were imprisoned, left to contend with conditions of
confinement–alcoholism, disillusionment, disease, and suicide–that further cemented their marginalization and social stigmatization. The Scottsboro trials remain an example of how little African American life has been valued by the criminal justice system, and by those charged to uphold justice, perpetuating the
expendability of African Americans, which is the bitter legacy of labor exploitation
and brutality institutionalized during the Transatlantic Slave Trade.

The Black Codes enacted in the South in 1865 were designed to restrict the
activity and rights of newly emancipated slaves. While laws varied by state, most
were designed to compel African Americans to work as regulated domestics,
laborers or agricultural workers so as to support the continuing agricultural society of the slave-owning South. During that time, many African Americans who had
no homes, jobs, or other "legitimate" places of refuge were targeted under these
codes and incarcerated for such "criminal acts" as vagrancy and unemployment.
For example, in South Carolina a special license and a certificate from local
judges were necessary in order to confirm a freedman's skill and ability to pursue work in any occupation other than in agriculture or domestic work. In short,
these codes sent a strong message that African American activity and lifestyle
needed to be strongly regulated in order to support private businesses. This
message is again being reinforced by the current prison industrial complex.

Mississippi, which has also had a long and problematic legacy of using
African American prisoners to bolster the economy, historically imprisoned large
numbers of recently emancipated African American men for the purpose of exploiting their labor. After the practice of leasing prisoner-laborers to private businesses ended at the turn of the twentieth century, prisoners continued to provide
unpaid plantation-like labor for the state. Until the 1970s, Mississippi's Parchman
Prison Farm stood as a national symbol of brutal and corrupt prison rule–colored
by the harsh legacy of slavery–where its prisoners donned the infamous striped
uniforms and its armed guards were referred to as "trusty shooters."[15]

In 1994, the Mississippi legislature enacted a new package of laws designed to "get tough" on crime that included increasing the capacity for 4,000 new
prisoners, half to be held in new state prison beds and half to be held in two new
private prisons. While increasing bed space, the state also implemented laws
that eliminated parole for all offenders sent to prison, both violent and nonviolent,

and required that they serve at least 85 percent of their sentence before gaining release. By so doing, the state of Mississippi implemented a series of ineffective and punitive measures that sent the state's prison population–nearly 75 percent of it African Americans–soaring. Such ineffective planning has continued. In March 2001, while more than 2,600 beds in Mississippi's state prisons were empty, the state legislature committed $6 million in public funds to increase the capacity of private prisons and county correctional facilities.[16] The apparent commitment to private prisons–even in the absence of need–as demonstrated by the Mississippi example, illustrates the degree to which the exploitation of African American offenders for the direct economic benefit of large corporations has been preserved—and anticipated.

Juvenile Injustice and Adult Criminal Disparity

The racial disparities prevalent in private prisons affect African American men, women, and children alike. According to Poe-Yamagata and Jones [2000], African American youth make up 15 percent of the youth population (age 18 and under) in the United States, but represent 26 percent of youth arrested and 40 percent of youth in residential placement.[17] While private juvenile residential facilities are often less restrictive and less prison-like than public institutions, there remains a tremendous racial disparity between the proportion of African American youth in the US population and the rate at which they are placed in private correctional institutions. For example, on October 29, 1997, African American youth represented 39 percent of all youth in private residential placement, more than twice their proportion of the US youth population.[18]

There is no definitive explanation for why African American youth are incarcerated at levels that far surpass those of their counterparts of other racial and ethnic affiliations. However, much of the racial disparity in sentencing can be attributed to increased police surveillance in African American communities–making them more vulnerable to arrest–and the discretionary decision-making throughout the juvenile and criminal justice systems that criminalizes them. For example, a 1998 study in Washington State found that probation officers consistently portrayed black youth differently from white youth by attributing their crimes to internal factors (*i.e.*, attitude) as opposed to external factors that might influence their behavior (*i.e.*, the environment). In the study, probation officers were more likely to interpret a young black person's perceived disrespectful attitude toward the current offense or a court official as proof of his or her lack of internal restraints against committing future crimes.[19] This interpretation was more common among black youth than among white youth. Never did they consider that this "attitude" might be a result of ongoing strains between African American communities and law enforcement, or a symptom of these black youths' own environmental risk factors. For instance, over one-fourth of African American youth who have been exposed to violence exhibit symptoms severe enough to warrant a diagnosis of Post-Traumatic Stress Disorder.[20] However, instead of this a condition warranting evaluation and treatment, the justice system shuffles African American children as offenders, with little or no responses given to their mental health needs. As a result, these needs increase and become more severe, making these youth more likely to re-offend and become "career criminals." However, insofar as private prisons are designed to *save* money by cutting costs in prison administration and services, they are notoriously permitted to be unresponsive to the health needs of inmates. Further, because these facilities are designed to profit from the

"career criminality" of offenders, it is in their interest to be unresponsive to inmates' rehabilitative needs.

By allowing this injustice to continue, the criminal and juvenile justice systems, particularly through the use of private prisons, cripple the already tenuous
grasp that African Americans have on the construction of their "place" in society.
This is accomplished by defining their place through degrees of culpability rather
than by the true merits of their character in relation to their environmental circumstances. African American communities grapple with systemic racism and discrimination that leave them disproportionately represented among this nation's
poor, uneducated, unemployed and disenfranchised. In this context, character
becomes secondary to circumstance, rendering many innocent African Americans vulnerable to being labeled as criminal or suspect. Even worse, these
factors produce environmental circumstances that criminalize entire communities for the acts of a relatively few. This criminalization has led to the over-reliance
on incarceration as a means by which to correct aberrant behavior among African
American youth, who are deemed "superpredators" and often considered incapable of rehabilitation through community-based alternatives.

However, not all disparities are attributed to discriminatory attitudes among
justice professionals. In 1902, author H. C. Cooley coined the term "looking
glass self," referring to the idea that an individual's self-perception is largely
determined by the way others relate to him or her. This theory, when applied to
racial and ethnic minority groups, suggests that if a community is treated as
inferior or inhumane, that will subsequently affect how people within that community view themselves.[21] For many African American youth, being perceived as
"useless predators" contributes to a climate where to have participated in violent
or criminal behavior is perceived as a rite of passage rather than an indiscretion.
Even further, many of these youth accept abuses that occur in and out of private
prisons as normal occurrences rather than as serious human rights violations,
which leads to their further demoralization as human beings.

Recently, the Jena Juvenile Justice Facility in Jena, Louisiana, operated by
the Wackenhut Corporation, was closed as a result of gross human and civil
rights violations that left thousands of African American children subject to Post-
Traumatic Stress Disorder as a result of having been so terribly abused. Youth at
this facility were subjected to corporal punishment, excessive force, and gas
grenades rather than given access to rehabilitative services. One US Department of Justice report confirmed that youth at the Jena facility–overwhelmingly
African American males–were at "substantial risk of harm due to unreasonable
levels of violence from juvenile-on-juvenile assaults and the use of excessive
force and abuse from staff."[22] Further, in December 2000, a juvenile prison in
Columbia, South Carolina, operated by CCA, was found to have subjected abuses
so egregious and "repugnant to the conscience of mankind" upon its largely
African American youth population that punitive damages were awarded against
the offenders in the amount of $3 million.[23]

***

Such abuses are not only witnessed at juvenile facilities. Private adult prisons
also have a higher rate of inmate-on-inmate homicides than government-run
facilities. A 1997 survey conducted by George Washington University Professor
James Austin found that there were 65 percent more inmate-on-inmate assaults
in medium- and minimum-security private facilities than in government-run me-
dium- and minimum-security prisons. Between 1998 and 1999, the Wackenhut

Corporation's New Mexico facility had a homicide rate of one for every 400 prisoners, compared to state-run prisons, which had a homicide rate in 1998 of one for every 22,000 prisoners.[24]   Being subjected to this level of physical abuse and violence can also have devastating physical and psychological effects. For example, a 2001 study by the American Society of Hypertension found a direct correlation between constant exposure to violence and increased risk of hypertension and cardiovascular disease in urban African American males.[25] Private prisons, through their higher incidences of acts of random violence, are contributors to these health crises affecting African American communities. As more black males, and increasingly black females, return to their communities after having been subjected to this violence, more black communities must grapple with the short-term and long-term effects of these health risks, including future institutionalization, family fragmentation, and unemployment. The lingering physical and psychological effects that plague prisoners returning to their home communities are often inadequately addressed by programs not equipped to handle them. As a result of the lackadaisical health policies and practices in use by private prisons, more black communities are vulnerable to behavior resulting from inadequate rehabilitation which threatens community development as a whole, and in turn perpetuates cycles of violence.

The degree to which violence appears to be tolerated in private facilities not only sets a bad example for inmates (whose own behavior was ostensibly to be "corrected" during their time of incarceration), but it reinforces the age-old racist sentiment that the African American life is useless and expendable. When this sentiment has been allowed to fester in the past, crimes committed within the African American community or committed against African people have not been considered crimes at all—a notion currently sustained by the rampant violence allowed in private penal institutions. When such a disregard of life becomes commonplace, African American people suffer from an extremely dangerous and vulnerable state of perpetual dysfunction – one that affects not only those who are incarcerated, but the larger community as well.

The Greater Community Impact

The criminal and juvenile justice systems' tendency to rely on institutionalization and prison privatization in response to African American crime and delinquency has had a devastating impact on the rights of the black community. Specifically, as part of the prison industrial complex, prison privatization exacerbates the civic demise of millions of black people—whether or not they have been convicted of a crime.

As a result of the inadequacies and violations discussed above, the impact of the prison industrial complex has been devastating to African American communities' health and families, as well as their economic and civic development. It is important to note that many of the ramifications of the over-reliance on incarceration affect ethnic and racial groups other than African Americans. However, due to the *degree* to which African Americans are particularly over-represented in these institutions, the impact of their incarceration–and the development of an economic system reliant on that incarceration–is tantamount to genocide. Below are specific areas where prison privatization and the prison industrial complex threaten the livelihood and development of African American offenders and the communities from which they come.

Increased Vulnerability of African American Children

Millions of African American men and women sentenced to prison are parents. It is estimated that 7 in 10 women under correctional sanction have children under the age of 18. An estimated 72 percent of women on probation, 70 percent of women in local jails, 65 percent of women in state prisons, and 59 percent of women in federal prisons have young children. This translates into more than 1.5 million minor children,[26] disproportionately African American, who are the offspring of women and men under private and public correctional sanction.

Children of incarcerated parents suffer from trauma related to events surrounding parental crime and arrest. They become vulnerable as a result of separation from their parents, and experience an inadequate quality of care due to extreme poverty. A 1993 National Council on Crime and Delinquency (NCCD) study found that 43 percent of the children of incarcerated mothers were African American, and 52 percent of those black children were female. Upon parental arrest, 65 percent of the children were placed with a relative other than the child's father, and most of these placements were with the maternal grandmother.[27] Unfortunately, some states do not allocate foster care funds for these families because they are relatives, creating an even stronger likelihood that these children will be reared in poverty. Further, these children born to incarcerated mothers are at increased risk of being born drug-exposed to mothers who were not given proper prenatal care. Consequently, they are at increased risk of experiencing poor peer relations and school performance, enduring a severed relationship with their parent(s), and experiencing an increased risk of being institutionalized themselves. All of these factors exacerbate their already marginalized status in American society.

Perhaps one of the most distressing results of parental incarceration, particularly for out-of-state placement, is that children rarely, if ever, visit their parent(s) once that parent is incarcerated. In the 1993 NCCD study, 54 percent of the mothers interviewed reported that their children *never* visited them in the jail or prison.[28] Because many African American parents rarely or never see their children due to the distance between these private facilities and their home communities, the bonding necessary to foster healthy family relationships is severely damaged. This level of family dysfunction, supported by the prison industrial complex, is reminiscent of slavery – when families were separated to support the sharecropping needs of slave-owners – and is contributing to millions of African American children growing into a redefined family structure conducive only to future institutionalization, poverty, or death.

Health Risks

In addition to the mental health risks resulting from the violence discussed above, which impact incarcerated African American males and their home communities, inmates are at higher risk of contracting infectious diseases during incarceration than their counterparts of other ethnic and racial groups. This increased risk is born from the disproportionate degree to which black prisoners are represented among America's incarcerated populations and the lack of adequate culturally-competent services—in youth and adult prisons as well as in home communities—to address their needs. So visible are these inadequacies that elected representatives are beginning to challenge institutions to be more responsive to the health needs of inmates. For example, in June 2002, US

Congressman Bernie Thompson (D-MS) requested that the Department of Justice investigate the inadequacy of medical facilities for confined youth in the Oakley and Columbia Training Schools in Mississippi.[29]

There is a basic inadequacy of prisons' educational, counseling, and treatment programs in addressing the particular health risks of African Americans, and the cultural relevance of a problematic history of racist, immoral "medical" experiments conducted on black men and women (*i.e.*, the Tuskegee syphilis experiment). Further, given the poor access to and administration of quality services in many black neighborhoods, prison treatment programs often do not attract black inmates who could benefit from rehabilitative and medical services, or are unsuccessful in rehabilitating them.

Millions of African American male inmates have been identified as HIV-positive. Because there are fewer women incarcerated than men, the number of HIV-infected women is also smaller, though they report higher percentages of infection relative to men. Approximately 3.3 percent of incarcerated women who were tested and reported their results were HIV-positive in 1995, compared to 2.6 percent of men.[30] HIV and other diseases are often communicable through unprotected sexual contact (voluntary and forced), shared proximity with infected or ill inmates, and inadequate responses by the facility to existing health crises.

The transmission of HIV and other diseases is just one of the many abhorrent health risks resulting from negligent conditions in US prisons. It is estimated that between one-quarter and one-third of male prisoners have either endured or fended off sexual attacks in US prisons. As Tom Cahill, President of Stop Prisoner Rape argues, prisoners are likely to bring this behavior back to their home communities after release, thereby further subjecting themselves and their communities to the inhumane existence that is allowed to fester in these institutions.[31] Cahill once confirmed that men and boys who are raped in prison "usually return to the community far more violent and antisocial than before they were raped. Some of them perpetuate the vicious cycle by becoming rapists themselves in a misguided attempt to 'regain their manhood' in the same manner in which they believe it was 'lost.'"[32]

Understanding the health risks associated with sexual abuse is critical to understanding the growing rate at which HIV is being spread among African Americans in jail and in the community. The struggle to tame the spread of this disease is compromised when private prisons cut back on costs that could facilitate better supervision of inmate activity–through the employment of qualified, permanent staff, the implementation of appropriate monitoring equipment, and so on – to ensure that no one must endure the experience and legacy of unwanted sexual activity.

Sexual abuse, moreover, disproportionately plagues incarcerated African American women. A 1996 Human Rights Watch report noted that male correctional employees have vaginally, anally, and orally raped female prisoners. These women then return to the community with damaged self-esteem that contributes to the deterioration of their perceived self-worth. Many female prisoners return to their communities with the erroneous perception that their power rests solely in their sexuality, as opposed to their intellect and personality. This inhumane exploitation reinforces the myth of the over-sexual African American woman, which not only cripples their ability to value their own lives and contributions to society, but sets the foundation for the cycle of abuse that makes African American girls the most victimized population in America.

Compounding this issue, a significant number of these women have a history of physical, emotional, drug, and/or sexual abuse. A 1996 NCCD study found that 44 percent of women under correctional authority report* that they were physi-cally or sexually assaulted at some time during their lives.[33] Sixty-nine percent of women reporting an assault in the 1996 NCCD study said that it happened to them before the age of 18.[34] Many women–again disproportionately African Ameri-can women–are subjected to emotional, physical, and sexual abuse as girls, and go untreated; many of these mistreated women have that abuse re-enforced in prison, as described in the 1996 report by Human Rights Watch.

The lack of adequate responses to these needs and to the compounding effects of sexual abuse also exacerbates mental health conditions of African American women who are haunted by soaring rates of hypertension, diabetes, and high blood pressure. The 1996 study by NCCD found that incarcerated women seem to have more health problems and require more assistance than their male counterparts. In fact, the percentage of women rated as minimally (60 per-cent) or mildly (17 percent) impaired with mental health problems is nearly 2 to 3 times that of men.[35]

Economic Development

As a function of being the first stock sold on the New York Stock Exchange, African people in America have been stigmatized and exploited in order to support the capitalist interests of America's "ruling class." Profits—or savings—realized through the privatization of the criminal justice system represent a con-temporary mode of structuring that interest. As a result of unemployment and limited access to skilled jobs with high-earning potential, African Americans are disproportionately represented among America's poor. However, according to the US Department of Commerce, African Americans accounted for 60 percent of the declining number of poor persons in America between 1996 and 1997. In 1997, the poverty rate for African Americans was at 27 percent, compared with 11 percent for whites, 14 percent for Asians and Pacific Islanders, and 27 percent for Hispanics (note that there was no statistical difference between the rates for African Americans and Hispanics).[36] Significantly, those who are incarcerated are not routinely included in unemployment and poverty statistics, which leaves over one million African American men and women unaccounted for among those who are unemployed. George Cave, an economist associated with the Joint Center for Political and Economic Studies in Washington, DC, argues that if African American men (and women) were not in jail, the rate of African American unemployment would be much higher. In fact, according to Princeton University sociologist Bruce Western and his colleague Becky Pettit of the University of Washington, once the figures are adjusted to account for incarceration, there is "no enduring recovery in the employment rate of young black high-school drop-outs."[37] Further compounding the issue is the fact that once released from pris-ons, many African Americans are unable to acquire employment in the commu-nity due to illegal racial discrimination, societal biases against prisoners, and/or their lack of employable skills in a competitive job market.

Additionally, according to a study conducted in March 2000 by Price-waterhouseCoopers for the US Census Monitoring Board, the federal govern-ment is estimated to distribute $185 billion annually to local jurisdictions based upon their census counts. Since many of the private prisons holding African American inmates are in white, suburban and rural communities, the population counts are raised in these communities, which then benefit from additional fed-eral financial support. While communities that house prisons reap political and financial rewards, prisoners' own communities, many of which are dilapidated and lacking in the resources needed for healthy and positive habilitation, continue to deteriorate – further exacerbating the conditions that contribute to delinquent and criminal behavior in the first place. Poverty, unemployment, poor access to quality education, health care, and other risk factors that thrive in neglected communities (e.g. substance abuse and malnutrition) remain intact and make African Americans disproportionately more vulnerable than other racial/ethnic groups to future incarceration. Private prisons are not only supported by the continued dilapidation of African American neighborhoods, but help to sustain this by removing offenders from their home communities during their incarceration, while planting the financial rewards of their incarceration elsewhere. Eerily reminiscent of the 3/5 clause in the U.S. Constitution which allowed white slave owners to claim 3/5 constituency for each African slave that he possessed, this trend of reaping franchise from the disproportionate incarceration of black inmates invokes more than just memories of enslavement.

Civic Involvement

Across the country, hundreds of thousands of African American felons are unable to participate in the important process of voting, thereby significantly crippling the impact of the civic voice of the entire African American community. In Washington, Wyoming, New Mexico, Texas, Iowa, Virginia, Mississippi, Alabama, and Florida, over 20 percent of African American males are temporarily or permanently banned from voting because of felony convictions.[38] Since there are disproportionate numbers of African Americans who have been indicted and found guilty for felony offenses, there are subsequently disproportionate numbers of African Americans rendered incapable of fully participating in society as citizens once their time has been served. This is particularly problematic given the degree of discretionary decision-making that takes place in the justice system to determine arrest, presumption of guilt or innocence, and sentencing.

While criminals should be held accountable for their actions, when racial bias compromises the integrity of the process determining culpability, the impact of having an impaired civic voice is amplified. For example, in Alabama and Florida, 31 percent of all African American men are *permanently* disenfranchised. In Iowa, Mississippi, New Mexico, Virginia and Wyoming, 1 in 4 African American men (24 to 28 percent) are permanently disenfranchised.[39] As a result of state restrictions and a prison industrial complex that keep a disproportionate number of incarcerated African Americans from voting, the 1965 *Voting Rights Act* is effectively being repealed – compromising the entire community's civic voice.

Public Perception of Culpability and People of African Descent

In 1987, Darnell Hawkins wrote "Devalued Lives and Racial Stereotypes: Ideological Barriers to the Prevention of Family Violence among Blacks," an essay printed in R.L. Hampton's (Ed.) *Violence in the Black Family* (Jossey-Bass, Inc.) that challenged the "normalcy" with which black criminality is understood in America. He presented several examples illustrating how violence among black communities is viewed as normal, due to the frequency with which black crime is reported and to the relatively limited law enforcement and judicial responses to acts of violence in African American communities. To be sure, it has been established that there are a disproportionate number of African Americans who are arrested and punished for committing criminal acts, but it is equally important that *most African Americans do not commit crimes*, are law-abiding citizens, and do not deserve to be criminalized or penalized in any way.

The manner in which crime in African American communities has been handled by the American media however contributes to the sharp contrast between how white offenders and offenders of African descent are perceived. As incarceration rates that reflect the *over-representation* of African Americans become confused with the incorrect notion that African Americans perpetrate most crimes, the association between black communities and criminality becomes cemented in the minds of the public. The fact that private prisons can openly bid and rely upon the future incarceration of black men, women, and children–with little outcry from the American public–is a testament to the media's power in contributing to the myth that race and culpability are connected. Through the use of language and visual images that associate innate violent or lawless behavior with "blackness," media-promulgated images support the lucrative "business" of so-called African American criminality—while, as collateral damage, projecting punitive and mean-spirited tendencies not only into American criminal justice in general, but also into US social consciousness and public policy as a whole. During the past several years, when several teen-aged white males have been arrested for the murder of schoolmates and teachers, newspapers and national magazines described the boys as "quintessentially American", using such language as "skinny", "slight" freckle-faced", and "intelligent but isolated". None of the national coverage referred to these youth as "superpredators," "maggots", or "animals"–language that is often used when the perpetrator of a violent crime is of African descent.[40]

Again, mass media shapes the ideas and often actions of the American public, thus the power of perception cannot be ignored. The perception that African American offenders are "animals," incapable of being rehabilitated, and therefore deserving of lengthy prison sentences, punitive policies and prison abuses, negatively impacts all people of African descent – American or otherwise – particularly when skin color becomes the proxy by which culpability is determined and justice is administered. When a perceived normalcy of violence is married to African Americans, not only is the integrity of the justice system compromised, but the notion of fairness becomes void as well. By extension, African Americans become distrustful of the justice system and its enforcement, and racial profiling plagues millions of innocent black people simply as a byproduct of walking or driving with dark skin. In an atmosphere where there is an increased probability of interacting with law enforcement and the criminal justice system if one is of African descent, negative stereotypes and public policy reinforce, in practice, that "justice" is not for all, but for some.

Conclusion

Prison privatization perpetuates the victimization and exploitation of African American communities by supporting and perpetuating many of the key injustices that sustain racial disparities in American justice system. Through its various civic, health, and economic abuses, the private prison industry has defined a new "code" for African Americans to carry—one that profits from the image of black criminality and that subjects millions of innocent black people to a punitive, ineffective, and inhumane panacea for crime.

The racial overtones of the abuses suffered by African Americans as a result of the prison industrial complex constitute one of the most flagrant assaults on the rights of human beings in the juvenile and criminal justice systems. Fueled by a legacy of slavery, the reliance on the incarceration of African Americans has not only adversely impacted the African American community's collective ability to function competitively in American society. It has also adversely impacted the lives of decent and innocent people of African descent as a result of socially perpetuated negative stereotypes and public images that equate "blackness" with criminality. The awareness that the struggle to develop "place" is occurring in a society that criminalizes them continues to press upon the psyche of an African American community grappling to define its identity.

Sociologist Stephen Nathan Haymes has stated that historically, African American "spaces" have been centered on daily survival. For millions of African Americans, prisons have become the space where they "develop self-definitions or identities that are linked to a consciousness of solidarity." [41] However, a new pedagogy must inform the politics that define "effective" criminal justice policy. By implementing a continuum of services that emphasize the accountability of the justice system and graduated sanctions–including objective decision-making tools–racial disparities and the over-reliance on incarceration could be greatly diminished. No longer can millions of African Americans suffer while the prison industry arrests their communities' development. The legacy of slavery that has made African Americans the incarcerated race must end somewhere, along with the economic incentives that perpetuate its existence. As long as the prison industrial complex is allowed to continue its exploitation of African Americans' educational, economic, health, and civic vulnerabilities, the abominable legacy of slavery remains intact.

Endnotes

1. T.P. Bonczar and A. Beck, "Lifetime Likelihood of Going to State or Federal Prison," Bureau of Justice Statistics, US Department of Justice (Washington, DC, March 1997).

2. Beckett and Sasson, *The Politics of Injustice.*

3. C. Richey Mann, *Unequal Justice: A Question of Color* (Bloomington and Indianapolis, IN: Indiana University Press, 1993), p. 254.

4. C. Booker, "The Profits of African American Male Criminalization," *African American Male Research* 1, no. 2 (1996).

5. S. Nathan Haymes, *Race, Culture, and the City: A Pedagogy of black Urban Struggle* (Albany, NY: State University of New York Press, 1995).

6. R. Staples, "White Racism, Black Crime, and American Justice: An Application of the Colonial Model." *Phylon, 36,* 14-22.(1975).

7. S. Gabbidon, H. Taylor Greene, and V. Young (Eds.), *African American Classics in Criminology & Criminal Justice* (Sage Publications, 2002), p. 72.

8. *Id.,* p. 38.

9. R. Staples, "White Racism, Black Crime, and American Justice: An Application of the Colonial Model," *supra* note 6 at 14-22.

10. W. Du Bois, "The Spawn of Slavery: The Convict-Lease System in the South," *The Missionary Review of the World* (New York, 1901) October: p. 737-745.

11. V. Young, "Gender Expectations and Their Impact on Black Female Offenders and Victims," *Justice Quarterly*, 1986, 3,3:305-327.

12. M. Haft, "Hustling for Rights, " L. Crites (ed.) *The Female Offender* (Lexington, MA, 1976).

13. I. Moyer and G. White, "Police Processing of Female Offenders," L. Bowker (Ed.), *Crime in America* (New York: McMillan, 1981).

14. L. Dorfman and V. Schiraldi, *Off Balance: Youth, Race & Crime in the News* (Washington, DC: Youth Law Center, 2001), April.

15. J. Greene, "Bailing Out Private Prisons," *American Prospect* 12, no. 16 (2001), September 10.

16. *Id.*

17. E. Poe-Yamagata and M. Jones, *And Justice For Some: Differential Treatment of Minority Youth in the Justice System* (Washington, DC: Youth Law Center, 2000), April.

18. *Id.,* 19.

19. G. Bridges and S. Stevens, "Racial Disparities in Official Assessments of Juvenile Offenders: Attributional Stereotypes as Mediating Mechanism," *American Sociological Review* 63 (1998), August.

20. Department of Health and Human Services, *Mental Health: Culture, Race, and Ethnicity* (Rockville, MD, 2001).

21. M. Williams and I. Sapp-Grant, "From Punishment to Rehabilitation: Empowering African American Youths," *Souls: A Critical Journal of black Politics, Culture, and Society* 2 (2000), Winter.

22. T. Frieden, "Justice Department sues over conditions at Louisiana Juvenile Center," (Washington, DC, 2000), <http://www.cnn.com>.

23. J. Greene, "Bailing Out Private Prisons," *supra* note 16.

24. *Id.*

25. Reuters Health Ltd., *Violence Linked to Heart Disease Risk in African American Teenage Boys* (San Francisco, CA, 2001), May.

26. T. Snell, ed., *Survey of Inmates of State Correctional Facilities*; Bureau of Justice Statistics (Washington, DC: GPO, 1996).

27. Reuters Health Ltd., *Violence Linked to Heart Disease Risk, supra* note 25.

28. B. Bloom and D. Steinhart, *Why Punish the Children? A Reappraisal of the Children of Incarcerated Mothers in America* (San Francisco, CA: National Council on Crime and Delinquency, 1993).

29. C. Tisdale, "Juvenile Centers Under Scrutiny," *Jackson Advocate* (Jackson, MS, 2002), Vol. 64, No. 34.

30. T. Snell, ed., *Survey of Inmates of State Correctional Facilities, supra* note 26.

31. P. Smith, "The Human Rights of Jail," (2001) <http://www.DRCNet.org>.

32. *Id.*

* This is the reported figure. Because not all women report their history of sexual and/or physical abuses the true percentage of women who have experienced this type of exploitation and abuse is likely to be much higher.

33. L. Acoca and J Austin, *The Crisis: Women in Prison* (San Francisco, CA: National Council on Crime and Delinquency, 1996), February.

34. *Id.*

35. T. Snell, ed., *Survey of Inmates of State Correctional Facilities, supra* note 26.

36. US Department of Commerce. *US Census* (Washington, DC, 1997) <http://www.census.gov>.

37. E. Crose, "America's Prison Generation," *Newsweek*, 13 September 2000.

38. *Id.*

39. M. Marable, "The Political Cultures of Incarceration," *Souls: A Critical Journal of black Politics, Culture, and Society* 2 (2000), Winter.

40. M. Williams and I. Sapp-Grant, "From Punishment to Rehabilitation," *supra* note 21.

41. S. Nathan Haymes, *Race, Culture, and the City, supra* note 5.

CHAPTER NINE

Prison Privatization and Women

Katherine van Wormer

Introduction

Compared to male prisoners, women come to prison with more pressing problems in need of attention. Female inmates are more likely to have severe substance abuse histories, co-existing mental disorders, lower self-esteem probably related to extensive victimization, and periods of chronic unemployment.[1] Owing to women's sexual vulnerability, moreover, and to their likely responsibility for the care of small children, any major changes in how services such as health care are delivered in prisons are apt to be far-reaching in their impact on women.

The first task of this chapter is to present the social and political context within which the upsurge in female imprisonment is taking place. The anti-feminist backlash in conjunction with the war on drugs is part of that context. We will look at the profile of the typical female inmate in terms of her pathway into prison, a pathway characterized by chronic victimization. We will then examine the costs of female imprisonment to society (in terms of tax dollars consumed and families broken), which have been considerable.

The impact of prison privatization on the human rights of women in confinement is introduced in the second portion of the chapter. Three major areas of human rights concern highlighted here are healthcare, prison labor and personal safety. That the problem of sexual abuse of female inmates is exacerbated under the dictates of "modern correctional management" is a major argument of this chapter. The same economic incentives that encourage departments of correction to cut back on costs in staffing and treatment resources are also responsible for placing women at risk of violation by male predators who take advantage of their positions of power. The chapter concludes with a discussion of particular issues faced by immigrant women in detention. Throughout the chapter, emphasis is on the role of privatization in the treatment of female inmates. To my knowledge, this is the first study specifically focused on the impact of prison privatization on women offenders.

Rapid Prison Expansion and Its Effects on Women

Whereas women were only 4 percent of the US incarcerated population in 1980, today they account for 6.6 percent of the prison total.[2] Between 1980 and 1995, the number of women entering US prisons rose by almost 400 percent, roughly double the incarceration rate increase in males. Since the crime rate has not increased and for women the murder rate has declined strikingly, how do experts account for this imprisonment binge?

The refusal to conceptualize substance abuse as a health care issue rather than as a criminal justice problem is at the heart of the phenomenal growth rate of female incarceration in US prisons. The profiles of women in prison, in contradiction to the myth of the new, violent female offender, confirm the detrimental impact of mandatory sentencing guidelines. Singling out crack cocaine–the one drug used most frequently in the inner city–for harsh penalties leads to desperate consequences for Black and Latina women. When their spouses and partners are arrested for drug dealing, these women are often brought down with them. Equality under the law may thus not adequately take into account the inequalities in most of these male/female relationships. In any case, the new sentencing guidelines weigh heavily upon the young women of color–most of them mothers–who are serving time in the nation's prisons. The backlash against affirmative action and women's 'creeping equality' that has played out in US courtrooms–termed "equality with a vengeance" by Chesney-Lind and Pollok[3]–is clearly in evidence within the prisons as well, where the view of women offenders as offenders first and as women second has led to the treatment of women according to an entirely inappropriate male standard.

Elsewhere, I make the case that today there is a backlash against affirmative action–a backlash caused in part by men's resentment of the strides made by professional women during the latter quarter of the twentieth century.[4] This backlash against women at the higher echelons who have reaped the benefits of affirmative action is played out against vulnerable women at the lower echelons. Consider, for example: the attempts to stymie women's reproductive freedom; the new coercive and highly punitive social welfare policies; the use of anti-conspiracy laws to punish the wives and partners of drug dealers for their role in perpetrating or covering up crime; extensive press coverage of domestic violence statistics which purport to show that women initiate violence against their partners as often as men do; and most tellingly, a resurgence in the previously discounted myth of the "new female criminal".

Sadly but predictably, the myth of the "new female criminal" has resurfaced in recent years to coincide with and justify women's harsh treatment by the courts, both civil (*i.e.* child custody) and criminal. Books such as *Abused Men*, *When She Was Bad: How and Why Women Get Away with Murder*, and the more scholarly *Shifting the Blame: How Victimization Became a Criminal Defense* unabashedly present the case that the female offender has special privileges that can exculpate her from crime.[5] Even *Psychology Today*, in an article entitled "Bad Girls", attempts to link "women's liberation" with violent crime.[6] Interestingly, the Canadian media are promoting some of the same claims about the supposed new wave of female violence. However, writing in the *Toronto Star* in 1999, Michele Landsberg sets the record straight through interviews with criminologists whose data on girls and violence had been distorted in other news reports.[7] To understand the true state of affairs for incarcerated women, let us turn to a profile of the typical female criminal.

Profile of the Female Inmate

About 75 percent of women prisoners are serving time for nonviolent offenses, most of which is results from enforcement of offenses mandatory drug-sentencing laws or 'zero tolerance' for drug use. During the period from 1990 to 1997, the number of female inmates serving time for drug offenses nearly doubled, while the number of comparable males increased by only 48 per-cent.[8] The new gender-neutral, mandatory minimum sentences provide the same punishments for conspiracy to commit crimes—such as driving the get-away car—as for playing the central role in the commission of crime. Almost half of the women in prison today, who were sentenced under these mandatory laws, have accordingly been convicted of conspiracy.[9] Often they are turned in by their partners or husbands who do so as the only means of getting their sentences reduced.

Women in prison are drawn from the ranks of the poor and uneducated.[10] Only four in ten women in state prisons were employed full-time prior to their arrests; this compared to 60 percent of male inmates. Furthermore, 30 percent of female inmates were receiving welfare assistance prior to arrest.[11] Classism, accordingly, is at least as pronounced in the criminal justice system as in any other social institution.

The racist element of crime and punishment is revealed in the fact that an African American is eight times more likely than a non-Hispanic white, and twice as likely as a Latina woman to be imprisoned.[12] Singled out for crack cocaine, the drug associated with inner city crime. The war on drugs has become a war on minorities and on women.

Nationwide, over 65 percent of women in state prisons are mothers of small children.[13] As an unintended consequence of harsh sentencing practices, the children of incarcerated mothers are placed at high risk of entering the vicious cycle of crime and punishment themselves.[14] With women's facilities often located in rural areas, the mothers can get completely out of touch with their children.

Drug use at the time of arrest was reported more often among female in-mates (about 40 percent) while alcohol use was more commonly reported among males. On a finding that may be indirectly related to substance abuse, 57 percent of women in state prisons reported that they were physically or sexually as-saulted at some time during their lives; most of those reported the assault oc-curred before age 18.[15]

In her explanation of the disproportionately high rate of multiple victimiza-tion for female compared to male offenders, Meda Chesney-Lind maps out the pathway that leads girls, desperate to escape sexual and physical abuse at home, to run away, seek solace in drugs and the company of drug users, gang members, and the like, and to survive on the streets through prostitution.[16] This pattern is exacerbated among inner-city females where prostitution may provide a means of survival in the face of extreme economic hardship. Garry Rolison stresses the role of sexual and physical abuse in women who in their economic oppression, come to assist the men in the commission of crime.[17] As Rolison explains, "[t]o the degree that cross-gender relationships are still relatively class and racially homogenous, then women involved with these men, on the one hand, become objects of discipline by public patriarchy due to their involvement with bad men, and on the other hand, become objects of discipline by these men because they are seen as bad or devalued women."[18] Their involvement in this vicious cycle of abuse by the state and by their partners is seen as primary in paving the way for a lifetime on the margins.

Costs of Prison Expansion–to Women and Society

To pay for the rapid and incredibly expensive expansion of the criminal jus-tice system, government services elsewhere are sacrificed. The hardest hit pro-grams are in the social services, especially means-tested programs. As military, corporate, or middle-class subsidy programs are off-limits in this time of fiscal conservatism, poor women and children are the losers.[19] The *Welfare Reform Bill* of 1996 has taken its toll on women who were receiving financial aid by forcing them into the lowest paying sectors of employment without adequate provisions for child or healthcare benefits. Money saved by the state in this maneuver is being funneled into the criminal justice system.

The new prison industrial complex will only impoverish communities as it enriches politicians and corporations, as Mona Danner suggests.[20] "Although women have largely been left out of the debate," Danner argues, "it is women who are the quiet losers–the big-time losers–in the crime bills. Criminal justice reforms such as these are politically motivated, unnecessary, ineffective, and far, far too costly."[21]

And who will take care of the children? When a woman is arrested, her children are typically sent to relatives or to an overloaded foster care system. Since these mothers are often the sole providers for their children, the impact on their kids can be devastating. Consumed by anger and rage, these children are clear candidates for developing emotional and legal problems down the road. In a 1999 nationwide poll by the *US News and World Report*, all but one of the juvenile justice agencies surveyed reported that more girls than boys had mothers who had been previously arrested. The state of Iowa reported that 64 percent of girls in that state who were in conflict with the law said their mothers had criminal records.[22] Several other states were not far behind. Most of these mothers in prison are sentenced for drug-related offenses. Mandatory drug treatment with close aftercare monitoring, therefore, could provide tremendous cost savings for the community, thereby sparing the succeeding generation from following their mothers' footsteps into crime.[23] One thing for sure: building more prisons will *not* reduce the rate of intergenerational crime.

Human Rights, Private Prisons and Women Prisoners

Under international law and the US Constitution, the rights of prisoners and of women are enunciated. The US was largely instrumental in the development of the United Nations *Universal Declaration of Human Rights*, which was enacted in 1948. Article 5 of that treaty states, "No one shall be subjected to torture or to cruel, inhuman or degrading treatment or punishment."[24] In 1994 the US ratified the Convention Against Torture and Other Cruel, Inhuman or Degrading Treatment or Punishment. The US government only signed this treaty with the stipulation that individuals would be given no more rights than those provided by the US Constitution.[25] This restriction has important implications for prisoners who are mistreated in the custody of the state.

US resistance to international human rights commitments was even more pronounced in the failure of the Senate to ratify the Convention on the Elimination of all Forms of Discrimination Against Women are of particular relevance to incarcerated women. This treaty's provisions of the right to adequate health care services and protection against gender-based violence are of particular relevance to women.[26]

In addition to these agreements, the United Nations has adopted standards that do not have the same legal clout as treaties but which nevertheless have moral power. The UN Standard Minimum Rules for the Treatment of Prisoners is relevant to women who are imprisoned.[27] Rule 53(3) provides that women should be attended and supervised only by women officers. In the US, however, nondiscrimination guidelines have removed most restrictions on women working in men's prisons and conversely, of men working in women's prisons. Accordingly, more often than not, women incarcerated in the US are guarded by men; violations against these women have been reported virtually in every state. Before returning to this issue, let's take a look at how crimes are prosecuted in the US and the causes and consequences of the current prison population explosion for women.

Prison Privatization–Implications for Women

From 1995 to 2000, the three major private prison companies–Corrections Corporation of America (CCA), Wackenhut, and Cornell–made a combined total of more than $528,000 in federal election campaign contributions, much of it directly to political parties. In light of the spate of scandals and lawsuits involving these for-profit enterprises and numerous cancellations of state contracts, this attempt to influence politicians is understandable. And it paid off. The headline from a 2001 *Wall Street Journal* article, "Federal Government Saves Private Prisons as State Convict Population Levels Off," tells all. According to the article, the contract signed with the Federal Bureau of Prisons was a bonanza for CCA.[28] Interestingly, the deal was signed despite initial resistance by the prison bureaucracy itself and, in an unprecedented arrangement, payment for 95 percent of the beds was guaranteed.

Meanwhile, the war on terrorism is likely to bring further revenues to CCA and other private corporations in the increased detention of immigrants. Even as new anti-terrorism legislation was passed in Congress, the value of stocks in some private prison corporations soared by as much as 300 percent.[29] In light of these recent developments, the earlier rumors of the demise of the prison industrial complex may have been premature.

According to the 2000 Census of State and Federal Correctional Facilities, a total of 120 privately operated facilities are authorized to house women.[30] Thirty-seven of these facilities are exclusively female. Entries on the 2000 Census listing range from the Des Moines Women's Residential Center, which has an excellent reputation in Iowa for gender-specific programming to the notorious correctional center at Florence, Arizona. Operated by CCA, this facility has been the subject of several successful lawsuits on behalf of sexually violated women.

The prison privatization movement has enormous implications for female offenders, first, with regard to the increase in the number of women being incarcerated; and second, in light of the recent history in private prisons of sexual abuse by male guards. If commercial enterprises take over the hiring and supervision of correctional staff, standards will be lowered. At the same time as the state relinquishes responsibility for the running of the prisons, public accountability for the abuses inflicted on female inmates will be even further reduced.

Prisons are as good (if they can ever be good) as the staff who run them, given adequate financial support and a progressive mandate from above. When profit motives dictate policies, one can predict that the focus on rehabilitation will wane. The *modus operandi* is to make the corporation money–usually through reduced wages, lower staff/inmate ratios, and reduced health care spending for inmates and employees alike. The risk is that the services provided for health care, vocational education and treatment, will all go to the lowest bidder.

International precedents for these concerns have already been set. In this age of globalization, corporations easily expand into foreign markets. Wackenhut and CCA, for example, both had some initial success in selling their prisons overseas; private prisons for women sprang up in Australia, New Zealand, and England. Women's prison activists had several major concerns, including: the removal of women to a large centralized prison far away from family; exemption of private prisons from freedom of information because of commercial confidentiality; the economic and political influence of the multinational corporations on Australian sentencing; and use of cheapened prison labor. In October 2000, complaining of serious breeches of contract, the government of the Australian state of Victoria seized control of the maximum-security women's correctional center at Deer Park.[31]

The profit motive not only provides an incentive to hold down costs at the expense of quality and care, but when punishment is an instrument of private business, there is a clear conflict of interest caused by the direct relation between profits, the prison occupancy rate, and cost-cutting in the provision of services. Won't corporations lobby for even harsher sentencing? Won't they then be tempted to find ways to increase an inmate's sentence and to thereby keep the beds occupied? What is most troubling about these developments, as Reiman indicates, is the corporations' vested financial interest in having a large and increasing incarceration rate. Not only do the rich get richer while the poor get prison, but under the forces of privatization, as Reiman declares, "the rich get richer *because* the poor get prison!"[32] According to American Federation of State, County, and Municipal Employees (AFSCME), the union to which many correctional officers belong, services provided by for-profit firms typically are protected from public scrutiny.[33] The only way to make information public concerning certain shady practices, for example, is through lawsuits against the for-profit prison operators themselves.

The Impact on Health Care

The physical and mental health needs of female inmates far exceed those of their male counterparts. Compared to men, women in prison have strikingly higher rates of illness in the three areas of substance abuse, mental health problems, and HIV infection. Furthermore, 6 to10 percent of women are pregnant when they enter prison.[34] Partly because of the explosion in the female prison population, there are too few staff to meet these physical and mental health needs.

The failure of the state to provide adequate medical care to meet the particular needs of female prisoners is highlighted in a 1999 report by the US General Accounting Office.[35] Whether the prison is privately operated or state owned and operated, medical services tend to be privatized through contractual arrangements. Firms receive a fixed rate to provide medical care to prisoners, so every dollar *not* spent benefits the company's profit margin.[36] The ideal arrangement of this kind is in Iowa where women at the Mitchellville prison receive specialized health care through the highly-rated University of Iowa Hospital. Another kind of arrangement is where the state contracts with a private medical company or hospital for services. The quality of such treatment for female inmates has been mixed.

According to a national study sponsored by the National Institute of Justice, prison administrations viewed the contracted services for health and mental health treatment and drug programming as beneficial to the institution.[37] Improved programs, the promotion of new ideas, and cost containment were cited as benefits of such arrangements with outside organizations. In my study of women's prison programming, I have indeed been impressed by certain advantages in the policy of subcontracting out to mainstream treatment services.[38] My basic rationale, which is couched in political terms, is: professional staff who are employed by medical and treatment centers answer to these agencies rather than to correctional staff. This external affiliation may provide at least some professional and legal protection to practitioners who wish to report human rights violations of inmates or who are called to testify in internal hearings or who are subpoenaed to testify in court. It is my impression, moreover, that when hospitals and mental health centers do the hiring, the independent thinker–the radical feminist as well as the recovering substance abuser, and even the ex-convict–stands a better chance of getting hired than does the professional screened by correctional administrators who tend to favor personnel who have "come up through the ranks". One might expect that practitioners (and educators) from outside agencies could build alliances with offenders more readily than staff who answer to the prison establishment. By the same token, staff external to the prison may be more amenable to innovative programming; they may even be in a position to advocate for changing problematic institutional policies, such as those that re-traumatize previously traumatized inmates.

Whatever the administrative arrangements, treatment providers are badly needed for women who, if they needed help before they got in trouble with the law, need help even more once inside. A promising development today is the legal mandate (arising out of the lawsuits) for institutions to provide counseling to inmates who were sexually exploited or abused within prison walls. Such counseling necessarily should be provided by externally employed professionals.

With regard to actual medical services however, privatization often results in a reduction in quality of services in the interest of saving the state money. In California, for example, an investigation of medical care offerings showed pre-natal care for pregnant women was lacking. Systemic problems at the contracting hospital included lack of coordination of services and medical information, as well as an abnormally high rate of miscarriage and babies who died at birth.[39] Dangerous methods of restraint such as use of leg shackles while women were in labor increased the health risks to mother and child. Similarly in Nevada, the medical services provided by CCA at the women's prison in Las Vegas have been completely inadequate to meet the women's needs. Such contractors save money by hiring LPNs rather than RNs and by reducing qualifications in other areas as well.[40] Critics point out that when services are contracted out, the state is still liable for inadequate or negligent patient care.

We are currently faced with a situation in which the entire prison system is in private hands. The national trend toward the privatization of women's correctional institutions, as Mary Faith Marshall indicates, results in reduced external oversight and scrutiny of health care and other services by outside professionals and by the media.[41] Yale law professor Ahmed White concurs,[42] arguing that private prisons tend to distance public officials from responsibility for the way private prisons are run. Under privatization, the internal mechanisms of punishment are cloaked in a veil of secrecy. When a scandal occurs, journalists and other observers will focus on the performance, efficiency, and services of the private prison, rather than on public officials for allowing the conditions to persist. Accordingly, the government is conveniently let off the hook.

Human Rights and Prison Labor

In 1979, to ensure a cheap labor pool, Congress began a process of de-regulation that allowed private corporations to exploit the captive labor market for profit. Modern day prison labor, as Levin argues, bears a frightening resemblance to slavery,[43] with wages as low as eleven cents an hour in some places with no benefits or vacations. The prisoners must choose between taking low paying jobs or serving longer sentences, since "good time" policies subtract days from one's total sentence for good behavior and days worked. In fact, while involuntary servitude as punishment for crime is legal under the US Constitution (13th Amendment) it is prohibited by the UN's Universal Declaration of Human Rights (1948) which outlaws slavery in all forms.

Consider the fact that prison-made goods were initially only manufactured for state agencies; now they flow into all sectors of the economy, competing with outside companies and jobs. The extent of this exploitation of involuntary labor is revealed in an article in the 1997 summer issue of *Iowa Commerce Magazine*: "Employers pay an hourly wage only. No workers' compensation. No unemployment. No health insurance. No benefits."[44] Corporations ranging from J. C. Penney and Victoria's Secret to IBM and TWA utilize prison labor to cut costs and increase profit margins, though some inmates are relatively well paid by the companies that employ them—well paid, that is, by prison standards. [45] In contrast, in countries with better welfare systems such as Sweden and Norway, prison workers are well paid, unionized, and receive paid vacation time. In Canada, prison workers are paid a living wage, even for schooling. For the smooth running of a women's institution, these kinds of incentives for work and education are immensely helpful to correctional authorities.

Private prison companies have been predictably enthusiastic about the booming market for cheap convict labor. Whether they sew clothes, engage in data entry or telemarketing, etc., inmates in the private system are paid far less than workers in the state or federal systems.[46] Women typically are paid 15 to 30 cents an hour and even female juveniles may be forced to work a 40-hour week if they have been tried and sentenced as adults.[47]

Sexual Abuse in Private Prisons

In a practice unique to North America, male guards are placed in contact positions over female inmates. The inevitable in scandals and lawsuits has happened. The facts are daunting; the individual stories more so. The stories come to light in lawsuits histories described in Human Rights Watch and Amnesty International reports and aired on national TV, and in personal correspondence from prisoners.[48]

If it had not been for the idealism and determination of legal aid lawyers and feminist organizations such as the National Women's Law Center, the stories might never have emerged. The stories of rape, revenge deprivations, forced nudity in lockup, pregnancies in a closed system where the only males are the guards, forced abortions, and solitary confinement of complainants and witnesses barely received notice until seven or eight years ago. Across the country, there were incidents of prison or jail staff sexually molesting inmates with impunity.[49] The situation in privately owned prisons, with their poorly paid and trained staff, and low accountability is the most unconscionable. Consider what happened at the predominately male-staffed, CCA-operated facility in Florence, Arizona.

Barrilee Bannister has written to me personally and been interviewed publicly concerning events that took place at the Central Arizona Detention Center.[50] When several female Oregon inmates were transferred to the for-profit, private facility in Arizona due to severe overcrowding in Oregon, they were subjected to some very unprofessional conduct. Bannister, one of the prisoners transferred to Arizona and then back again to Oregon when she spoke out, explained that a guard captain gave a marijuana joint to six women, then had men search their cells. They could avoid charges of drug possession, they were told, if they would perform a strip tease for the men. When they complied, the officers became sexually aggressive with them. After Bannister filed an official complaint, she was beaten by three officers.

A settlement reached in a suit filed by the Justice Department was flawed and weak, according to a Human Rights Watch 2000 report.[51] The Department of Corrections is allowed to continue to place women in solitary confinement after they have filed complaints of sexual abuse. No mechanism has been set up through which women can safely file complaints without fear of retaliation. In Texas, allegations of poorly-staffed prisons and rampant sex behind bars caused Wackenhut to lose one of its jails when the staff conducted an audit and transferred the women to another facility. Many of the women had been raped. Similar stories emerged from a Texas women's prison and the Juvenile Justice Center, both run by Wackenhut.[52]

Few such cases are officially reported, however. The passage of the Prison Litigation Reform Act in 1995 limits judicial supervision of prisons and thereby reduces the civil rights of inmates. The difficulty of litigation notwithstanding, a substantial settlement recently was awarded to five female prisoners who had been coerced into sex with a correctional officer at a privately owned halfway house in Anchorage.[53]

Immigrant Women in Detention

Amnesty International, in its 1999 report *"Not Part of My Sentence": Violations of the Human Rights of Women in Custody* expressed the following concern with reference to immigrants in detention:

> Women asylum seekers are often subjected to harsh treatment. While awaiting action on INS claims, they often languish in penal institutions facing the same human rights violations all women prisoners face. Many times they are placed in cells with hardened criminals.[54]

Because they are not US citizens, detained political refugees are curiously considered to exist outside the jurisdiction of the Constitution. Fauziya Kassindja's harrowing memoir, *Do They Hear You When You Cry?* graphically recounts the horrors of her oppression during confinement by the Immigration and Naturalization Service (INS).[55] Kassindja, who arrived in the US as a refugee from forced genital mutilation in Togo, Africa, was successful in gaining eventual release only because her story received rare national press coverage.[56]

New harsh sentencing laws have created a special population of prisoners –immigrant prisoners–whom the federal government segregates from the rest of the prison population and turns over to the private companies.[57] Since September 11 when US national security became the top priority of the nation, the numbers of immigrants in detention has increased in conjunction with new anti-terrorism laws. In a personal interview with a social worker from Elizabeth, New Jersey where immigrants, including refugees who request political asylum, are kept in lock-up, I have learned that conditions that would qualify as 'cruel and unusual' clearly apply. In the privately run Elizabeth Detention Center, women are kept all in one cell; no recreation is offered and telephone calls are priced at $1.00 per minute. One woman has been so detained for five years. To what extent the usual protections offered to Americans under the Bill of Rights apply to these non-citizens is still not completely settled.[58]

Conclusion

As compassion takes a back seat in this punitive society, women connected to crime through family ties–mothers who protect their drug-dealing children, or wives and girlfriends of drug-using men, for example–are now subjected to harsh punishment, often turned in by their menfolk. Gender-neutral sentencing policies have resulted in a growth rate in incarceration for female offenders that far exceeds the rate of increase for men.[59] Constructed architecturally according to the same designs used for medium-security men's prisons and run by male correctional staff, many of the new women's facilities are privately owned and operated. For female inmates, the effects of privatization have been uniquely devastating.

In this chapter we have seen the many ways in which the privatization of a nation's prisons is associated with the loss of human rights, particularly for female inmates. In health care, mental health and addiction treatment, vocation training and work, standards decline drastically when corporate interests supercede humanitarian concerns.

Far from being cost-effective, turning over of the prison system to private enterprise has been a disaster. The very low pay and poor benefits of staff that keep costs down have created a climate for dire neglect of inmates' health care needs while leaving them vulnerable to sexual abuse and corrupt practices by male guards. After being faced with expensive lawsuits and international human rights investigation, several states have cancelled their contracts and regained control of the women's prisons. A key fact that this story of privatization of women's prisons reveals is that once the state turns over accountability for the provision of services (mental health care, health care, etc.) to big business, the quality of care will slide to the lowest common denominator. The clientele are a captive audience, after all; they cannot successfully shop for services. The state may contract out for some services with good results, but only if state officials oversee the care that is provided.

Expansion of community corrections, use of drug courts in lieu of incarceration, an end to the war on drugs in both its military and harsh sentencing dimensions and a focus on rehabilitation and treatment rather than punishment–these are among the ways favored by experts to truly lower costs. We need policies that reflect what we know about drug addiction rather than policies that seek to punish. We need policies that take into account the special needs of women in conflict with the law, women who so often have been victimized by the men in their lives, women who so often are the mothers of small children.

Clearly it costs far less money to treat a woman offender for addiction than to incarcerate her, where she is sure to experience further victimization. Effective treatment results in savings to society that outweigh the costs of treatment by a factor of 4 to 1.[60] The cost savings of innovative, gender-specific programming such as that offered in Canada are incalculable.[61] Benefits include: prevention of the spread of HIV/AIDS, a sharp reduction in cases of fetal alcohol syndrome, a decrease in welfare and foster care costs, and a significant reduction in crime. What is good for mothers, in short, is good for children, and what is good for both mothers and children is good for the society as a whole.

Endnotes

1. Bureau of Justice Statistics, *Women Offenders* (1999); N. P. Messina and L. Prendergast, "Therapuetic Community Treatment for Women in Prison" (2001): 1-2 , 54-56.

2. Bureau of Justice Statistics, *Prisoners in 2000* (2001).

3. M. Chesney-Lind and J. Pollock, "Women's Prisons: Equality with a Vengeance" (1994): 155-177.

4. K. van Wormer, *Counseling Female Offenders and Victims: A Strengths-Restorative Approach.* Springer Publishing. (2001).

5. See P. W. Cook, *Abused Men* (1997); P. Pearson, *When She Was Bad* (1998); S. D. Westernelt, *Shifting the Blame* (1998).

6. B. Yeoman, "Bad Girls" (1999): 54-57, 71.

7. M. Landsberg, "Feminism and the Link between Girls and Violence," *Toronto Star*, 13 November 1999, L1.

8. Bureau of Justice Statistics, *DWI Offenders Under Correctional Supervision* (1999).

9. N. Siegal, "Women in Prison: The Number of Women Serving Time Behind Bars Has Increased Dramatically," *MS* 9, no. 2 (1998): 64-73.

10. In Canada, although drug violations bring large numbers of women to prison, most women get sent there for property crimes. Canada, unlike the US, relies heavily on short sentences for public intoxication and theft, many of the sentences being 14 days or less. See M. Shaw, "Women in Prison" (1994): 1-7.

11. Bureau of Justice Statistics, *Women Offenders* (1999).

12. Amnesty International, *Not Part of My* Sentence (1999).

13. Bureau of Justice Statistics, *Women Offenders, supra* note 11.

14. K. van Wormer, *Counseling Female Offenders and Victims, supra* note 4.

15. Bureau of Justice Statistics, *Women Offenders, supra* note 11.

16. M. Chesney-Lind, "Girls, Delinquency, and Juvenile Justice" (1995): 71-88.

17. G. Rolison, "Toward an Integrated Theory of Female Criminality and Incarceration" (1993): 137-146.

18. *Id.*, 37-146.

19. M. Danner, "Three Strikes and It's Women Who Are Out" (2000): 215-224.

20. *Id.*, 215-224.

21. *Id.*, 222.

22. T. Locy, "Like Mother, Like Daughter?" *US News and World Report,* 4 October 1999, 18-21.

23. K. van Wormer and D. Davis, *Addiction Treatment (forthcoming).*

24. United Nations, *Universal Declaration of Human Rights* (1948) Resolution 217A(III).

25. Amnesty International, *supra* note 12.

26. *Id.*

27. Human Rights Watch, *All Too Familiar* (1996).

28. J. T. Hallinan, "Federal Government Saves Private Prisons as State Convict Population Levels Off," *Wall Street Journal*, 6 November 2001, A1, A16.

29. M. Moorehead, "Ominous Growth Industry Mass Detention Push Up Prison Stocks," *Workers World Newspaper*, 25 October 2001<http://www.resist@best.com>.

30. From data provided by Bureau of Justice Statistics Statistician Tracy Snell in correspondence, 25 October 2001.

31. People's Justice Alliance, "Overseas News," *Newsletter*, 16 (1999), January <http://home.vicnet.net.au/~pjan/news/pja16005.htm>; A-Infos, "Private Australian Women's Prison," (6 March 1996) <www.hartfordhwp.com/archives/24/137.html>; "Victorian Government Plans Resumption of Privatized Prison," (10 October 2000) <www.abc.net.av/7.30/s195156.htm>.

32. J. Reiman, *The Rich Get Richer and the Poor Get Prison* (2001): 163.

33. "The Evidence Is Clear: Crime Shouldn't Pay" (2000) <http://www.afscme.org/private/evid05.htm>.

34. Amnesty International, *supra* note 12.

35. US General Accounting Office, *Women in Prison* (1999).

36. J. Sinden, "Capitalist Punishment" (2000).

37. M. Marash, T. Bynum, and B. Koons, *Women Offenders* (1998).

38. K. van Wormer, *Counseling Female Offenders and Victims, supra* note 4.

39. M. Marshall, "Health Care for Incarcerated Pregnant Women," (March 1999) <www.asbh.org/exchange/1999/ w99mar.htm>.

40. G. Dornan, "Privatization of Prison Medical Services Challenged," (29 January 1999) <www.tahoe.com/bonanza/ stories>.

41. M. Marshall, "Health Care for Incarcerated Pregnant Women," *supra* note 39.

42. A. White, "Rule of Law and the Limits of Sovereignty" (2001).

43. J. Levin, "Uncle Tom's Cell: Prison Labor Gives a Market Face to an Old Idea: Slavery," *Perspective Magazine* (February 1999) <www.digitas.harvard.edu/~perspv/issues/1999/feb/uncletom.shtml>.

44. R. Basu, "What's at Work in Iowa Prisons?" *Des Moines Register*, 15 March 1998, A6.

45. J. Levin, "Uncle Tom's Cell," *supra* note 43.

46. K. Silverstein, "America's Private Gulag," *Prison Legal News* 8, no. 6 (1997), June: 1-4.

47. L. Jordan, "Drugs, Minority Women, and the US Prison Economy," *Saxakali Magazine*, 2, no. 2 (1996) <http://saxakali.com/saxakali-magazine/saxmag3s.htm>.

48. Human Rights Watch, *supra* note 26; Amnesty International, *supra* note 12.

49. N. Siegal, "Women in Prison," *supra* note 9.

50. B. Bannister, personal correspondence, 21 June and 5 July 1998; D. Burton-Rose, "Our Sister's Keepers" (2000): 1-3.

51. Human Rights Watch, *Nowhere to hide* (2000).

52. J. McNair, "Wackenhut Prisons Mired in Abuse Scandals," *Miami Herald*, 16 April 2000 <www.oregonafscme.com/corrections/private/pri.1196.htm>.

53. "$1.4 Million Awarded to Raped Alaska Women Prisoners," *Prison Legal News*, July 2001, 21.

54. Amnesty International, *supra* note 12 at 2.

55. F. Kassindja, *Do They Hear You When You Cry?* (1998).

56. K. van Wormer and C. Bartollas, *Women and the Criminal Justice System* (2000).

57. J. Greene, "Bailing Out Private Jails," (2001): 23-25.

58. From personal interview with social work educator Patricia Levy, a resident of Elizabeth, New Jersey.

59. See Bureau of Justice Statistics, *Prisoners in 2000, supra* note 2.

60. P.A. Kassebaum, *Substance Abuse Treatment for Women Offenders* (1999).

61. M. Shaw "Women in Prison," *supra* note 10.

CHAPTER TEN

Incarceration of Native Americans and Private Prisons

Frank Smith

Introduction

There are currently slightly over two million inmates in local, state and federal jails and prisons. Of these, some 1.6 percent are Native Americans and Hawaiian Natives; in Federal institutions, Native Americans constitute 2 percent of the population, since the U.S. government is involved in criminal justice enforcement on reservations. Because approximately 6 percent of all U.S. inmates are held in private prisons, the total number of Native Americans in these for-profit prisons is comparatively rather small. For that reason, this article presents a picture of the conditions in which Native Americans are held given that limited experience.

Historical Perspective

In order to achieve an informed understanding of the current situation with regard to Native Americans in prison, it is necessary to place it within a larger historical and sociological context. While most residents of the US have the notion their country was founded on the principles of justice and freedom, closer examination reveals that perception is not accurate, particularly in the case of Native Americans.[1]

The more progressive of our founding fathers whom we remember so fondly as protectors of these ideals include Thomas Paine and Thomas Jefferson. Paine consistently referred to Indians as "savages", and used them as a negative comparative stereotype. Jefferson considered his contemporary Indians to be hindrances to colonial progress. The US only granted Natives citizenship in 1924, five years after women and 59 years after Black males were allowed to vote.

African Americans have undoubtedly been pervasively discriminated against in US history—their dehumanization was even embodied in the Constitution. Schoolchildren learn of the more egregious Supreme Court-approved violations of the rights of Blacks such as the *Dred Scott* decision or *Plessy v. Feurgeson*,[2] and that the Civil War was fought in part over slavery. They may have read the Emancipation Proclamation and even the Thirteenth to Fifteenth Amendments to the Constitution. The sordid history in America of slave owning, in the north and south, of lynching, of Jim Crow, is discussed in most schools. The role of such historic figures as Frederick Douglas or Sojourner Truth is widely recognized. Martin Luther King Jr., is certainly better known than many mediocre presidents.

Selma, Alabama, and Little Rock, Arkansas are familiar mileposts, as is *Brown v. Board of Education*.

Students may even understand the meaning of racial profiling, of the immense disparity between sentencing for crack cocaine, more prevalent in inner-city neighborhoods, and powdered cocaine, more favored by wealthier surburbanites. They may possibly be aware that a Black adolescent has perhaps a 50 times greater chance of being placed in an adult penal institution than a white youth who has been charged with exactly the same crime,[3] and that perhaps one of three young Black men has been subjected to some criminal sanction, such as probation, parole, jail or prison.

Yet how many Americans, young or old, fully understand that this same disenfranchisement; this same disproportionate treatment by the criminal justice system, has affected Native Americans since the Articles of Confederation were signed? How many realize that broken treaties have been the order of the day for over two hundred years? Do they know that the early settlement of this nation involved pushing indigenous peoples into ever smaller, less habitable reservations? How many school children are taught the cruel facts behind the genocidal removal of the inhabitants of the post-Revolutionary Southeast?

There is hardly a Native American tribe that does not have a history of broken treaties and persecution. What this long, troubled relationship between European Americans and Natives constitutes is deliberate disregard for and discrimination against Native culture, Theft of lands, exiles, dispossessions, and a prevailing condemnatory and paternalistic attitude provide the background for the problems of Native Americans in prisons, both public and private, today. It particularly pervades the conditions of confinement of Indians in private prisons.

Criminal Justice and Injustice

There are four especially salient issues regarding Native Americans and the criminal justice system. First is disproportionate incarceration: a much higher percentage of Native Americans are imprisoned, per capita, than any other ethnicity except African Americans. Second is disrespect by the government for traditions, including an institutional "color-blindness" which often fails to recognize the effects of prejudice and often disregards cultural beliefs and practices. Third: lack of access to spirituality and to home communities. Lastly, there is a higher percentage of alcohol-related behavior resulting in imprisonment. Let's examine how each of these factors operates, particularly in the context of private prisons.

Disproportionate Incarceration

There are approximately 26,000 Native Americans in US jails and prisons who have been sent there at a rate 38 percent higher than the general population.[4] However, if Blacks, who constitute about half of all prisoners are excluded from the calculation, it is clear that this disproportion is far more egregious, when compared to non-Black ethnicities.[5] In Alaska, for instance, if Natives do not already form a plurality in prison, they soon will, as Native incarceration rates are rising rapidly while white and Hispanic rates have remained relatively flat, and the incarceration of Black people has actually dropped in recent years. Natives are only 16 percent of the general population in that state, though they make up 40 percent of adult inmates. Between 1996 and 2000 in Alaska, the total of incarcerated white males rose just 6 percent, while the total number of Native males rose

23 percent. White female totals went up by 26 percent, but Native female inmates skyrocketed by 41 percent in just those four years.[6]

An examination of state-by-state totals shows remarkable disproportion in ethnic representation. In Arizona, where many reservations are policed by tribal authorities and hearings held in tribal courts, the rate of Indian incarceration appears not significantly higher than non-Natives.[7]

In other states, however, such is clearly not the case.[8] In South Dakota, where 10 percent of the state population is Indian, male and female Natives make up 23 percent and 35 percent respectively, of all inmates. In Wyoming, Indians make up 2 percent of the state population but 7 percent of prisoners. In Montana, though only 6.8 percent of residents are Native, they are 18.8 percent of men and 29.6 percent of women prisoners. Still more worrisome is the fact that in the last decade, the general prison population there less than doubled, but total numbers of Indian women went up from 17 to 81, an increase of 376 percent. An extensive search of the literature revealed no information about why rates of incarceration for women are rising far faster than for men, nor why rates for Native women are vastly outpacing those for whites. Native Hawaiians constitute almost 40 percent of prisoners in and from that state.

Similar disparities prevail among juveniles.[9] In Minnesota, 12 percent of the juvenile population is non-white, but they represent 46 percent of commitments to public facilities and 59 percent of secure placements. Minorities were 23 percent of juvenile arrests, but 70 percent of transfers to adult courts. In South Dakota, Native juvenile residential placements are at 27 percent. In Montana, 18 percent of all youthful inmates are Native. Alaska is at 36 percent and in 1997 (all) minority youth represented 47 percent of commitments to public facilities, and 57 percent of secure detention placements.[10]

Nancy Schafer of the University of Alaska's Justice Center reports, "It seems that Alaska Natives tend to accumulate extensive referral histories in rural areas for behaviors which would be ignored or dealt with informally by urban police. The history of prior referrals is a significant factor in adjudications for residential placement."[11] Alaska has reluctantly used private out-of-state "treatment" facilities for those youths who were not thought suitable for juvenile correctional institutions, but for whom no in-state alternative was thought to exist. It has had consistently poor outcomes involving the care and recidivism of such children. Because the per diem rates in some private facilities for minors run over $250 per day, these children represent significant "profit centers" to the private providers. Nationwide, many of these operations have been extremely troubled to the point where children have died in their custody from abuse and neglect at the hands of poorly trained and paid staff. Prisons have been taken back from substandard private operators. Official oversight of the conditions of confinement is often minimal, as states' prisoners are heavily subsidized by parents' insurance and by Medicaid payments—sending states are less likely to assess their "bang for the buck," and the geographic distance from the sending authority may be substantial.

This disproportionality has a powerful effect when one looks at the states that "transport" their prisoners. Montana, for instance, shipped large numbers of inmates to private prisons in Texas, and afterwards to Arizona after conditions in the Bobby Ross Group prison became explosive. Hawaii shipped its convicts to the same prison, but after racial altercations and poor treatment, the prisoners "voted with their matches" and twice burned down those Lone Star state facilities. After two deaths in the spring of 2001, a Hawaiian state audit team found that the CCA Florence prison essentially was being run by its inmates. Although the guards received far better wages than most private prison staff, due to prevailing wage standards in the community, they still lacked the experience and training to deal with problem prisoners. Chastened by these experiences, Hawaii has now removed most to Oklahoma, yet it is contemplating allowing another private operator to build on the Big Island near Hilo.

Institutional "Color-blindness"

In a US Senate debate over the Juvenile Justice Bill, the gulf between those who are empathetic to the inherent racism of the system and those who are not became crystal clear. Utah's Senator Orrin Hatch, trying to eliminate a standing requirement for tabulation of the ethnic disparity in juvenile justice in a system he saw as "color blind," is quoted in the *Los Angeles Times* as declaring, "I haven't heard one shred of information that proves there is discrimination here." Minnesota Senator Paul Wellstone responded,

> I cannot believe that I have heard on the floor of the Senate an argument that race is not the critical consideration…When we get to the question of which kids are arrested and which kids are not, you don't think that has anything to do with race today in America? When we get to the question of sentencing, you don't think that has anything to do with race? You are sleepwalking through history.[12]

Black youth self-report committing violent crimes about 50 percent more than do whites. But they are four times more likely to be arrested, and seven times more likely to be locked up for violent crimes as their white counterparts. White youths seem to mature out of violent behavior in their early twenties. But if Black youth have similar employment levels, their rate of violence declines also. No similar study has been done with regard to Native American violent crime patterns; however this chapter's analysis may shed some light on conditions that contribute to the high rate of Indian incarceration.

According to the 2000 US Commission on Civil Rights report on South Dakota there is "85 percent unemployment on the reservations compared to 2.7 percent unemployment for the non-Native population." "On any given day," it states, "an estimated one in 25 American Indians 18 years old and older is under the jurisdiction of the nation's criminal justice system."[13] This is 2.5 times higher than the rate for whites.

It is no wonder Natives have marginal faith in the criminal justice system, which they feel clearly discriminates against them. The Commission asked "why South Dakota incarcerates more than twice the number of criminals as its neighboring state and why Native Americans comprise 4 times the prison population compared to their percentage in the State's total population."[14] Racial profiling begins early, and suspects are much more likely to be charged. Ruth Steinberger reports[15] that of 41 incidents where Montana juveniles were pepper sprayed, "40 targeted Indian youth." She details accounts of the decision to place Native inmates in administrative segregation (ad-seg). It appears that the due process rights of Natives are disregarded and commitments of Natives to ad-seg and maximum units are frequently whimsical. Steinberger writes:

> Statistics show that from initial contact with police to length of sentence, the differences disproportionately punish Native

Americans, ultimately affecting families and communities as well...While the origins of the problems are complex, and it is impossible to highlight one particular fault, statistics reveal that the sum of those problems place Indians into confinement far earlier, and for less serious crimes than other Americans. Additionally, indications are that being denied parole opportunities may increase the sentences served by Indians even further.[16]

She also quotes numerous anecdotal reports of whites being given slaps on the wrist for offenses against Indians, as well as nationwide figures for granting of parole that are similar to those found on the State of Alaska's Department of Corrections website. There, it appears that Natives get parole at half the rate of whites, but have their paroles violated twice as often.[17] A public institution usually has a parole or probation officer to facilitate an inmate's transition back to "outside" life. Privates rarely provide such support.

Robert Guilfoyle, a Seneca who is a tribal consultant states: "The median (age) of a prisoner in the US is 34, yet the median age of an American Indian prisoner is slightly under 20 years of age."[18] Moreover, Scott Crichton of the Montana American Civil Liberties Union has said, "People...who claim that racism is not an issue in Montana, have their heads in the clouds. Racism here is real and it is profound, it's demonstrated in the prison system at each stage of the processing, from profiling and arrests and public defense to probation."[19]

While visibility in small towns is a factor in more frequent law enforcement referrals, Indians who are not "institutionalized" frequently tend to take blame for offenses on initial questioning, more so those who are less "assimilated" than those who are not. University of Alaska researcher Phyllis Morrow, who did an exhaustive study of Yup'ik in the state court system, found that both defendants and witnesses feel coerced, and expectations are quite different between them and whites.[20] This commonly results in acceptance of guilt, facilitating prosecution and eliminating plea bargaining chips for defendants. Carey Vicente, former chief judge of the Jicarilla Apache Tribe, wrote, "Among the Apaches the telling of truth is extremely important. ... The implications of such values in current legal process have been that few criminal cases are contested."[21] A former South Dakota correctional counselor who is Indian reported that his institution criticized him for starting the healing process with getting an inmate's acceptance of guilt for crimes.

Of the dozens of individuals consulted for this article about the issues facing Native people with regard to the criminal justice system, perhaps a third independently mentioned substance abuse. Inadequate legal representation, was frequently mentioned, and most interestingly, the propensity for Natives not only to confess, but to supply considerable details of the crimes for which they were being questioned.[22]

But private prisons, with their poorly trained, high turnover staff, fail to recognize the need for an environment that values and enhances the use of tradition in rehabilitation. In fact, the process of institutionalization, which proceeds from confinement which is disengaged from culture, interferes with the traditional function of honesty in the healing process.

Religious and Cultural Issues and Rehabilitation

Native American inmates often face significant cultural discrimination. Healing in their communities of origin requires utilizing traditional resources. Besides accepting responsibility for their crimes, offenders need to engage themselves in providing restitution to their victims, and in cleansing themselves of the behavior and attitudes that caused them to hurt others. This may involve receiving counsel from elders and spiritual guides, and participating in healing circles.

There often exist clashes between this culturally-based rehabilitative process and prison administration and rules. Although traditional healing is seen as a powerful deterrent to recidivism, Native inmates have been forbidden the use of sweat lodges and prisons have enforced grooming codes prohibiting long hair. Inmates have been made to prove their Native ancestry in order to participate in cultural activities, though this is not required of those of other ethnicities. The possession or use of materials central to the religious process such as cedar, sage and sweetgrass may not be allowed. In Montana, a Christian choir was allowed into a correctional facility without being searched, yet guards are alleged to have strip-searched a medicine man who had come to provide counsel to inmates. Guards examined the contents of guides' medicine pouches. Steinberger quotes Montana Lakota prisoner Manuel Redwoman as saying that the former prison chaplain claimed to be able to conduct traditional ceremonies, and tried to deny access to traditional items involved in worship. Redwoman remarked that while inmates were allowed to have four books on Christian or Muslim spirituality, only one was allowed on Native traditions.[23] Again, with private prisons, there is even less oversight concerning the conditions of confinement and adherence to law regarding prisoners' rights than in the public sector, so expectations of such protections are minimized. In many states there are no statutes governing the conduct of such institutions.

Cultural restoration has shown real and necessary restorative qualities for Indian prisoners. The world outside their villages and reservations is often a very foreign place, as the Yup'ik study cited above shows. Most of white Americans can't really understand and empathize with a people who have been dispossessed of their lands. Generations in the US and Canada were exiled without legitimate cause and punished for speaking their languages when they were forced to attend distant residential schools. Children who used to learn from their respected elders are now suffering the forced assimilation into the broader Western society. Television sets fill their dwellings with sitcoms, cartoons, exploding cars and game shows. Reservation and village Indians encounter a separate reality, a culture as foreign to them as if they were Laotian Hmong refugees, transplanted to America. This cultural intrusion dissolves the glue that holds their communities together.

The patent discrimination against inmates who desire to engage in traditional practices resulted in the 1993 passage of the Native American Free Exercise of Religion Act, authored by Hawaii Senator Daniel Inouye, a perennial champion of Indian issues. Six co-sponsors included Wellstone and Ben Nighthorse Campbell of Colorado, the only Native American Senator. The act ostensibly provided parity for Indian inmate religious observances, including access to spiritual leaders, materials used in ceremonies, food for religious diets, outdoor secure sweat lodges and teepees. It allowed inmates to wear long hair if the practice was part of their traditional beliefs. When signing the bill, President Clinton stated:

> The agenda for restoration of religious freedom in America will not
> be complete until traditional Native American religious practices
> have received the protection they deserve. My Administration has

been and will continue to work actively with Native Americans and the Congress on legislation to address these concerns.[24]

Though these are noble sentiments, it can be presumed they will be honored more in the breach than the observance. The initiative for the passage of the Act, ironically, was the US Supreme Court (5-4) decision in *Oregon v. Smith* [25] which allowed a state to discriminate against non-criminal Indian employees who had infrequently taken a small amount of peyote in a religious ceremony. The Court thus ignored its own precedent of the "compelling interest" standard. Earlier Congressional action in the 1978 American Indian Religious Freedom Act was unfortunately deemed to be policy rather than law in the 1988 decision *Lyng v. Northwest Indian Cemetery Association.*[26] Justice Blackmun, in dissent in *Smith*, commented that the state had never offered any evidence that peyote was harmful. The same "compelling interest" did not prohibit the Catholic Church's use of sacramental wine in masses during Prohibition, of course. Anthropologists feel that the spiritual use of peyote may date back thousands of years and stylized representations of the cactus appear in traditional southwestern art. In 1997, the Supreme Court once again overturned an act of Congress in deciding the obscure zoning case of *City of Boerne, Texas v. Flores*, when it found the Religious Freedom Restoration Act to be unconstitutional on Fourteenth Amendment grounds.[27] Dozens of liberal to conservative, religious and secular organizations had joined in an *amicus* brief, to no avail.

Compounding the denial of access to meaningful spiritual opportunities is the related issue of proximity to home communities. Ironically, Cornell Corrections made this argument in advocating for the return of Native inmates to Alaska from their competitor's facility in Arizona. Natives are closely bound to their communities of origin. To achieve their rehabilitation potential they need to maintain those connections to their extended families and support systems. Far too often they are incarcerated hundreds, if not thousands of miles from their homes and families. With the rise of private prisons, this situation has become particularly exacerbated as multinational corporations locate in the areas with the lowest taxes and wages. Prisoners of all ethnicities have been transported up to thousands of miles, such as Native Hawaiian prisoners who are now being held in Oklahoma after disastrous experiences in Arizona and Texas. Washington, DC prisoners have been held in another private prison in Florence also, as were more than 800 Alaskan prisoners, including over 300 Alaska Natives.[28] Dozens of these Natives have communicated their intense displeasure with their treatment in for-profit prisons. Inmate Harold Kankanton, the first chief of the Wildwood Prison Native Culture Club in Kenai, Alaska, having served five years in the Arizona private prison, stated, "All they do is warehouse you. ...They don't have a clue." Other Native inmates nodded in agreement. He remarked about private prison corporations, "They're using us as a pawn."[29]

During a recent attempt by Cornell Corrections to build a private prison adjacent to Wildwood, far from their Alaskan families' homes, many inmates wrote with specific complaints. They counterbalanced representations by a local tribal association that tried to get financially involved in the "Rent-A-Pen" business. Inmate Council President Michael Tebo listed a long series of complaints about treatment of himself and his fellow inmates in the care of the private companies and questioned the sincerity of the financially shakey local Native Corporation since it would have profited handsomely if the proposed prison were built on its land.[30] An earlier proposed venture with another Alaska Native corporation ended in disaster, partly because the remote prison site was relatively inaccessible to most families of inmates.

A private prison inmate's family member from Ketchikan, in Southeast Alaska, received documents that had been smuggled out of one of the Florence, Arizona Correctional Corporation of America prisons. They detailed outrageous punishments of Natives seeking respect for and observance of cultural rites and traditions. After a Cornell private prison was proposed for his own town, he turned them over to the local newspaper. Postings to the Native American Prisoner Support website by and about Alaska prisoners being held in CCA echoed similar complaints.

Indeed, since Alaskan "bush" natives often rely on four wheelers, boats and snow machines for home transportation, they were usually unable to visit a prison only 11 miles from Anchorage. There was no useful public transportation to the prison. Even though family members sometimes got to Anchorage for medical treatments and conferences, they often did not possess driver's licenses, insurance and credit cards necessary to rent a vehicle to visit their loved ones. In the lower 48, things are much the same: in South Dakota, Belva Black Lance noted that the prison was 350 miles from prisoners' homes. She said, "What this problem is doing is destroying our families. Children are the ones who lose the most."[32] A study of California inmates three decades ago showed that inmates who received visits from three or more people in the last three months of their incarceration recidivated at one sixth the rate of those who received no visits.[31] But incarceration in distant state, private and federal penitentiaries ruptures the bonds particularly needed to prevent the return of Native inmates to prison. More significantly, the states most heavily reliant upon private prisons to fill the gap between prison population and available in-state bed space are those transporting convicts the farthest, such as Alaska and Hawaii. Montana has brought its prisoners home by allowing the construction of a private prison within its borders. Wisconsin has just recently initiated attempts to return its prisoners, who are also disproportionately Native, back within its borders, by buying an empty, speculative prison.

Native communities have tended to seek and discover solutions for alcohol-related problems in what, in contemporary times, tend to be fairly unique ways. These interventions find little respect within a for-profit prison environment more interested in cutting expenses than in outcomes.

Native Justice Traditions

Traditionally, justice in the Native community has been of a reconciliatory rather than a retributive nature. Admissions of guilt are sought in order to resolve the offense, for the sake of the community, offenders and victims alike. If a tribal member's behavior was intolerable to the community of origin, and elder counseling, community shaming or other methods were not able to control the difficulty, exile was used as a last resort, and "meant severe hardship".[33] In Alaska, "blue ticketing" was the process of forcing an offender to leave his village.[34] But this was a last resort, the worst of punishments in a subsistence and cooperative society, and incarceration was a wholly foreign concept.

In 1996, an Alaska Justice Center survey reported:

> Many of the villages surveyed were found to have established
> ... their own policies and methods for dealing with most crime

and social control problems in the communities. Despite the importance of these extralegal local practices to villages, in general they seem to go unrecognized or ignored by justice system employees who are assigned to serve communities. ...Most respondents indicated a preference for having crime and social control problems handled by people in the community with support from the troopers. ...Eight times as many people identified tribal courts as identified state courts as the most effective group to stop drug and alcohol abuse.[35]

Ada Pecos Melton, former Director of the American Indian and Native Justice Programs at the US Department of Justice, expressed her concept of Eurocentric justice:

The American paradigm...is based on a retributive philosophy that is hierarchical, adversarial, punitive and guided by codified laws and written rules, procedures and guidelines... (D)ecision making (is) limited to a few. ...It holds that because the victim has suffered, the criminal should...as well. ...Punishment is used to appease the victim, to satisfy society's desire for revenge.[36]

By contrast, she writes,

The indigenous paradigm is based on a holistic philosophy and a world view of the aboriginal inhabitants of North America. These systems are guided by the unwritten customary laws, traditions, and practices...learned primarily by example and through the oral teachings of tribal elders. The holistic philosophy is a circle of justice that connects everyone involved with a problem or conflict on a continuum, with everyone focused on the same center. The continuum represents the entire process, from disclosure of problems, to discussion and resolution, to making amends and restoring relationships.[37]

The website RestorativeJustice.org chronicles the history of "Circles," and their adaptation to the criminal justice system in the last two decades. Their initial use in 1991 was by "Judge Barry Stuart of the [Canadian] Yukon Territorial Court, (who) introduced the sentencing circle as a means of sharing the justice process with the community." A grass roots effort to find solutions to alcohol problems in the Alkali Lake community guided a similar process in the Hollow Water First Nations Community in 1984-86. "In the safety of those circles, many began to disclose experiences with sexual abuse. This led to the development of healing circles as a way of dealing with the harm created by the offender, of healing the victim and of restoring the community." Circles have been developed most extensively in the Yukon, Saskatchewan, and Manitoba. In the US, Navajo peacemaking courts have also used circles. The initial use of circles in mainstream criminal justice was in 1996 in Minnesota. Everyone present, the victim, the victim's family, the offender's family, and community representatives are given a voice in the proceedings. Participation in the circle is voluntary. The victim must agree to attend without any form of coercion. The offender accepts his/her guilt in the matter and agrees to be referred to the circle. Especially for the native communities, it is important for the offender to have deep roots in the community. "After the healing circles, a sentencing circle determines the kind of response expected of the offender, although it may also contain commitments by the justice, community, and family members involved."

Referring to the healing circles process of the Mille Lacs Circle Sentencing Project, Kay Pranis of the Minnesota Department of Corrections observes, "Circles call people to more conscious awareness of our connections, our shared fate, our humanity, our spirituality. Awareness of connections is the foundation of authentic community."[38] It is simply inconceivable that private prison staff could facilitate such an intensely respectful process.

Treatment involving both traditional indigenous interventions and those accepted in more conventional substance abuse programs are integrated into the community healing process. One program, named for Alaska's first tribal judge, the late Gunaanasti Bill Brady, a Tlingit from Sitka, Alaska, is described as,

> ...a five week intensive residential program for adults with alcohol and/or drug problems. A holistic model that combines biological, psychological, social and internal spiritual elements is used for treatment, allowing the Center to address other major problems clients might have such as depression, low self-esteem, victimization issues and family problems.[39]

Alaska's Department of Juvenile Justice funded a pilot project involving miscreant juveniles appearing before councils of respected elders who decided on non-institutional resolution of offenses. This approach appears to be appropriate throughout North America. For instance, Navajo Nation Chief Justice Robert Yazzie wrote, "Navajo wise persons are called *naat'aanii*. Others call them an elder...They help plan decisions through guidance, but they don't make the decisions." Elsewhere he states, "Indians don't store their laws in books; they keep it in their minds and hearts. Everyone knows the law" and "Navajos believe that is wrong to use coercion on each other, so the legal process requires consensus."[40]

American Indian traditional responses to crime have found advocates from as far away as Belgium and Great Britain. These interventions require a bond formed with a proximate support system outside the walls, which is not found in the case of private institutions. Andrew Coyle, a former governor (warden) of a British prison, advocates that such methods include:

> • Creating more awareness amongst convicted prisoners of the impact of crime on victims and programs of direct mediation between victims and offenders.
> • Remodeling the way disputes are settled within the prison and incorporating restorative principles into grievance and disciplinary procedures.
> • Building a new relationship with the community outside the prison to emphasize the need for prisoners to be reconciled with the wider society and received back into it.[41]

Governmental and *ad hoc* Resistance to Native Community Initiatives

Unfortunately, though Congress and the Department of Justice have encouraged the development of community empowerment, alternatives to incarceration, and tribal courts, the funding to ensure their viability has been largely limited to rhetoric. Though many grants facilitating measures that might decelerate the swelling of the Native American incarcerated population have been approved, obligations of the government to support tribal courts themselves have been wanting. Judge Vicente writes, "Congress passed the Indian Tribal Justice Act...in 1993," but "[a]lthough it authorized up to $58 million to reinforce the funding of tribal courts to this day [in 1995] it remains unimplemented and unfunded."[42] He points out that the 1953 Public Law 280 (Ch. 505, 67 Stat. 588-90) has caused tribal authority to suffer except in limited instances, and the Indian Reorganization Act of 1934 (the *Wheeler-Howard Act*) overlaid structures that involved corporate or western organizations and frequently damaged traditional institutions.

Because of a Native cultural ethic which emphasizes cooperation, and which has antipathy for interpersonal confrontation, it has been difficult for indigenous communities like Barrow, Alaska, to mount resistance to these sorts of injustices and expressions of the dominance of majority culture. In the South Dakota Civil Rights Commission hearings, Elaine Holy Eagle said, "Native Americans, particularly 'full bloods,' are taught to respect authority, and out of this respect, they do not stand up for their rights."[43] For this reason, Natives are particularly vulnerable to exploitation in a unfamiliar environment such as a private prison in a distant state.

Judge Vicenti explains the dichotomy: "America, in its attempts to correct what it perceives as a rampant injustice in Indian America, creates a greater injustice by forcing its culture upon Indian peoples."

Summary

Native Americans have had a long and dismal history of negative interaction with the Euro-American legal system. The oppression that they have collectively experienced, the imposition upon them of an alien ideology, the clash of cultures, and their product, an intrinsic distrust of that criminal justice process, have helped cause disproportionate numbers of Indians to be incarcerated. If this process is to be reversed, respect for different traditions must be fostered. Traditional means of healing community trauma and discord need to be utilized and sovereign tribal powers need to be expanded. Most importantly, prisoners should be kept as close as possible to their families and support systems, and given access to those aspects of their culture that help keep them from endlessly recycling through the criminal justice system. Shipping them wholesale to faraway private penitentiaries that have no vested interest in rehabilitation and eventual return to inmates' home communities is a prescription for disaster.

Endnotes

1. The terms "Indian," "Native American," "indigenous, and "First Nation" in this chapter will be used interchangeably. It will not differentiate between Alaskan Indians and Aleuts. Native Hawaiians will be included; their situation is much the same as with Indians and Native Alaskans, and other US and Canadian indigenous peoples.

2. *Dred Scott* 60 US 393, 15L ed 691(1856) held that even if a slave was transported to a state or territory where slavery was illegal, it did not affect the slaveholder's property rights in the slave., 163 US 536 (1896) gave an imprimatur to the "separate but equal" doctrine, legitimizing segregation *Plessy v. Ferguson*, 163 U.S. 537 (1896) with a veneer of supposed equality of services. *Brown v. Board of Education* 347 US 483 (1954) finally forced desegregation by striking down *Plessy* as it applied to schools. A good study guide may be found at: <http://www.yale.edu/ynhti/curriculum/units/1982/3/82.03.06.x.html>.

3. Jason Ziedenberg, et al, Building Blocks for Youth: "Drugs and Disparity: The Racial Impact of Illinois' Practice of Transferring Young Drug Offenders to Adult Court." April 2001 <http://

www.buildingblocksforyouth.org/illinois/>

4. The *Foundation for National Progress* website posts current helpful charts showing incarceration rates for Black, white and other ethnicities on a state-by-state basis, obtained from Department of Justice and individual state statistics. <http://www.motherjones.com/prisons/atlas.html>. Also see Department of Justice, Office of Justice Programs, Bureau of Justice Statistics, "American Indians and Crime." Greenfield & Smith, Feb. '99, NCJ 173386.

5. It is also difficult to calculate the precise amount of the differential incarceration. Since many Natives are held in federal prisons, they may not be properly counted as coming from their sentencing state. This could also reduce the amount of the disparity that is found in state prison populations. Additionally, Hispanics are often inconsistently counted as whites, and Indians as Hispanics – the practice varying from state to state. If Blacks are eliminated from the prison population, and they constitute half of all prisoners, then the 26,000 Native Americans of the remaining million prisoners are 2.6% of the non-Black prisoners, though only .9% of U.S. population. U.S. Census Bureau.

6. From the Alaska Dept. of Corrections website: <http://www.correct.state.ak.us>.

7. Foundation for National Progress, <http://www.motherjones.com/prisons/atlas.html>.

8. *Id.*

9. The following numbers do not reflect a higher rate of Native adolescent referrals to adult courts, beyond the juvenile system, so the situation is likely worse than it appears to be.

10. Office of Juvenile Justice and Delinquency Prevention: *Census of Juveniles in Residential Placement Databook*, Race/Ethnicity by State, (1997): <http://www.buildingblocksforyouth.org/statebystate/>.

11. N.E Shafer. *A Comparison by Race of Juvenile referrals in Alaska*: Phase II Report, Anchorage Justice Center, University of Alaska Anchorage, (1998) May: <http://www.uaa.alaska.edu/just/reports/press/press10.html>.

12. Common Dreams Newswire (2000) March 21: <http://www.commondreams.org/pressreleases/may99/052199a.htm>.

13. Native Americans in South Dakota: An Erosion of Confidence in the Justice System. <http://www.usccr.gov/sdsac/ch2.htm>.

14. Rural Ethnic Institute, *Western Dakota's Pilot Project of the Evolving Roles of Tribal People in Nation States*, (1991) Document 09

15. Ruth Steinberger, Native Times.com. "Incarcerated Indians, Part I," 4-5, <http://www.okit.com/Justice4parts/justice1.html>. This four-part series speaks to the problem far more clearly than thousands of pages of government and academic reports. The reporter accurately describes the process that tips the balance of the scales of justice against Indians at every stage. From the initial decision to question suspects, to custody level decisions behind the walls and wires, Indians fare far more poorly than non-Native peers.

16. *Id.*, 4-5.

17. <http://www.correct.state.ak.us>. An Eskimo, for instance, can go back to prison simply as a result of a urinalysis containing a tiny trace of marijuana, though most of the people in his or her village smoke it, and such smoking is not associated with criminal conduct. Indeed, it was legal for any Alaskan to smoke marijuana until 1991.

18. Ruth Steinberger, "Incarcerated Indians," *supra* note 14 at 4-5.

19. Ruth Steinberger, "Lakota Man's rights Denied in State Penitentiary," <http://www.okit.com/news/2001/dec/lakotarights.html>.

20. A Sociolinguistic Mismatch: Central Alaskan Yup'iks and the Legal System, Phyllis Morrow, <http://www.uaa.alaska.edu/just/forum/f102su93/asocio.html>. See also Yup'ik Eskimo Agents and American Legal Agencies: Perspectives on Compliance and Resistance, Phyllis Morrow, University of Alaska, Fairbanks. J Roy. Antrop. Inst. (N.S.) 2, 405-423.

21. *Native Americans in South Dakota: An Erosion of Confidence in the Justice System*: <http://www.usccr.gov/sdsac/ch2.htm>.

22. People who were consulted included researchers, judges, attorneys, former prisoners, police and village public safety officers, probation officers and former correctional officers. Most of these persons were either Native themselves, or were empathetic to and had worked closely with Native communities. Most people also identified that Miranda warnings - notifications of the right to refuse to incriminate oneself – have minimal useful effect in Native communities; extension of civil liberties there is a mixed bag.

23. Ruth Steinberger, "Administrative Segregation common for Indian Prisoners in Montana," *We have many voices*: <http://www.turtletrack.org/ManyVoices/Issue_20/Prison_1027.htm>.

24. White House press conference, April 29, 1994.

25. 494 US 872 (1990)

26. At issue in *Lyng* was the construction of a paved two lane road, meant to facilitate access for timber harvesting, in proximity to a traditional California North Coast Indian sacred site. An excellent explanation of these Supreme Court cases, including *Lyng*, is at: <http://sorrel.humboldt.edu/~jae1/emenLyng.html>.

27. <http://www.washingtonpost.com/wp-srv/national/longterm/supcourt/stories/062697a.htm>.

28. Some of these prisoners are from the arctic, a polar opposite climate. Many never adapt to the baking desert.

29. Tom Kizzia, "KNA says rehabilitation utmost in prison pitch: inmates scoff," *Anchorage Daily News* 26 September 2001.

30. From an undated letter to the Kenai Borough Assembly in the summer of 2001.

31. Norman Holt, Donald MIller, California Department of Corrections. January, 1972. Report #46: Explorations in Inmate-Family Relationships. <http://www.fcnetwork.org/reading/holt-miller/holt-millersum.html>.

32. Ruth Steinberger, "Incarcerated Indians," *supra* note 14 at 4-5.

33. Guilfoyle. <http://nativenet.uthscsa.edu/pipermail/nn-dialogue/2001-April/000047.html>.

34. <http://www.uaa.alaska.edu/just/forum/f124wi96/a_village.html> and also "Elders Court works to save troubled village teens," *Anchorage Daily News*, 26 December 2001.

35. <http://www.uaa.alaska.edu/just/reports/press/press02.html>.

36. Ada Pecos Melton, *"Indigenous Justice systems and Tribal Society,"* Tribal Court Clearinghouse: 1, <http://www.tribal-institute.org/articles/melton1.htm>.

37. *Id.*, 2.

38. The exemplary protocol developed by Hollow Water, an Anishnaabe community, is remarkably thoughtful and professional, and mandates long-term involvement in the treatment process. Organizational staff understands that the healing process is necessarily lodged within a wide circle in the community and there is no magical "quick fix," especially in cases of sexual abuse. At the core of the process are the traditional cycles of ceremonies. It also recognizes that women are leading the healing movement.

39. Its umbrella agency, Southeast Alaska Regional Health Consortium (SAHRC), also sponsors Raven's Way, a program for juveniles. SARHC notes, "[i]n 1998, of all court referrals of Native youth in the state, 55 percent were for the offense of possession and/or consumption of alcohol." <http://www.ojp.usdoj.gov/americannative/promise.pdf>.

40. *Healing as Justice: The American Experience*: <http://www.usask.ca/nativelaw/jah_yazzie.html>.

41. *Restorative Justice in the Prison Setting*: Andrew Coyle, as presented to a conference of the International Prison Chaplains Association, Driebergen, The Netherlands, 13 May 2001.

42. From Tribal Court Clearinghouse: The Reemergence of Tribal Society and Traditional Justice Systems: <http://www.tribal-institute.org/articles/vicenti1.htm>. See also list of tribal law articles at <http://www.lawlink.nsw.gov.au/ajac.nsf/pages/usa>

43. *Native Americans in South Dakota: An Erosion of Confidence in the Justice System*: <http://www.usccr.gov/sdsac/ch2.htm>.

CHAPTER ELEVEN

The Use of Privatized Detention Centers for Asylum Seekers in Australia and the UK

Bente Molenaar and Rodney Neufeld

Introduction

Shocking accounts of detainees sewing their lips together and children threatening to commit mass suicide have brought the issues of detention of asylum seekers to the public's attention. In Woomera, a detention center referred to as a "hell hole" by former Australian Prime Minister Malcolm Fraser,[1] there have been allegations of child abuse and degrading treatment of detainees by employees. In the UK, hunger strikes and riots have embroiled detainees, guards and the Home Office in court proceedings. Group 4, a private company that runs Oakington, Yarl's Wood and Campsfield House detention centers, has been heavily criticized since it was first contracted to run Campsfield House in 1993. In February 2001, the government announced a revamp of asylum policy; however, detention will remain an important part of UK policy.

The detention of asylum seekers, a group of people who for the most part have not committed any offence, is in itself a controversial subject. It is not rendered any less controversial by the trend among governments to contract out their responsibilities for refugee protection to private firms, especially since there are but a few multinational firms that have a stranglehold on the industry. While it is outside the scope of this paper to provide a detailed analysis of the morality and legality of detention of refugees, an assessment of what is permissible under international law is necessary, along with a brief survey of state practice. This paper will then move on to discuss the privatization of detention services by considering the systems in Australia and the UK. Rather than providing an exhaustive analysis, the cases will highlight problems associated with the privatization of detention centers.

The Detention of Asylum-seekers: An Exceptional Measure

International law prohibits detention "except on such grounds and in accordance with such procedure as are established by law."[2] When a person arrives on British or Australian soil and applies forthwith for refugee status, with only minor exceptions, his or her detention cannot be in accordance with international law. This reality is accounted for in Article 31(1) of the 1951 Convention relating to the Status of Refugees (Refugee Convention).[3]

Article 31 provides that states "shall not impose penalties" on refugees who "enter or are present in their territory without authorization" so long as they have come "directly from a territory where their life or freedom was threatened" and "provided they present themselves without delay to the authorities and show good cause for their illegal entry or presence." The Convention does not define "penalties", but the term is thought to include prosecution, fines, imprisonment, and other restrictions on freedom of movement.[4] Article 31 also prohibits states from restricting the movements of refugees except where necessary and only "until their status in the country is regularized or they obtain admission into another country." Therefore, until a determination is made as to whether or not a person meets the definition of a refugee, it is impermissible to detain them unless it is "necessary". For an authoritative interpretation of what is meant by necessary we turn to the Executive Committee (ExCom) of the United Nations High Commissioner for Refugees (UNHCR).[5]

ExCom has concluded that detention should normally be avoided, but if necessary, it

> may be resorted to only on grounds prescribed by law to verify identity; to determine the elements on which the claim to refugee status or asylum is based; to deal with cases where refugees or asylum seekers have destroyed their travel and/or identity documents or have used fraudulent documents in order to mislead the authorities of the State in which they intend to claim asylum; or to protect national security or public order.[6]

Detention is therefore an "exceptional measure"[7] that may only be used for one of the above purposes, such as where there is a risk that the refugee applicant will abscond to remain illegally in the country. Once the refugee determination has been made and it is held that the applicant does not meet the definition of a refugee, the state is within its rights to temporarily detain anyone who is not lawfully on its territory until they are removed. However, as with detention prior to the refugee determination, detention prior to removal should not be longer than is necessary and otherwise in accordance with law.

Despite the understanding that detention is an exceptional measure that should be used only when necessary, detention is not being avoided in North America, Europe and Australia; it is being encouraged. The application of detention varies considerably by state, but in these three regions, the growing trend is to set up special detention or holding centers, which may be open, semi-open or closed. Sometimes mandatory detention is automatic pending a decision on the admissibility of the asylum application, as in Australia. It is sometimes imposed as a penalty for illegal entry or as a deterrent to potential asylum seekers.[8] Periods of detention also vary, from 48 hours to eighteen months. Moreover, in some states, judicial review of the decision to detain is not always available, as in Australia or in the case of the detention of suspected terrorists in the UK.[9]

Governments present the need for detention as an answer to the abuse and misuse of the refugee determination system by fraudulent applications. Not only do they often disregard the alternatives to detention that exist, but they fail to see that detention is often unnecessary and expensive. For instance, it is estimated that the US spent over $500 million on the detention of 24,000 immigrants and asylum seekers in 2001.[10] It is unclear what the total cost is for Australia, which has a fraction of the asylum claimants, but the new detention centers it will build in Darwin and Brisbane cost $30 million.[11] It is spending another $250,000 on its offshore "Pacific solution", money paid to Nauru, Papua New Guinea and other countries to take asylum seekers that have arrived in Australia.[12]

The purpose of this paper, however, is not to debate the morality of immigration detention.[13] While it is probably true that Australia's policy of mandatory detention without recourse to judicial review is a violation of the prohibition against "arbitrary arrest or detention,"[14] it is also clear that all states have the competence in exceptional circumstances to detain non-nationals pending removal or admission. The only requirement is that their competence must be carried out lawfully, according to human rights standards, which prohibit cruel, inhuman or degrading treatment,[15] which ensure that all persons deprived of their liberty shall be treated with humanity and with respect,[16] and which offer special protection of children and the family.[17] This paper will now consider the conditions of detention in privately run centers in Australia and the UK as measured against international human rights standards.

Background: Australia

Australian law requires the mandatory and non-reviewable detention of all unlawful non-citizens, prescribing that the unlawful non-citizen be detained until he or she is granted a visa, deported, or removed from Australia.[18] All 'unauthorized arrivals, people arriving without the required documents, must be detained under current legislation.[19] While the number of detainees fluctuated, there has been a steady increase in numbers over the years, and in April 2000, 3,791 people were held in immigration detention centers, hospitals and prisons.[20] In February 2002, the number of child detainees was estimated to be about 300.[21]

As part of the government's budget discussion of August 1996, it was decided that the provision of detention services should be contracted out as a measure to ensure more flexible and cost effective services.[22] In February of 1998, the Australian Department of Immigration and Multicultural Affairs (DIMA) contracted out the delivery of detention services to a private firm.[23] Australasian Correctional Services Pty Ltd (ACS), a subsidiary of the American-based company Wackenhut, was awarded the contract for an initial period of three years, with extension provisions.[24] The operational arm of ACS is Australasian Correctional Management Pty Ltd (ACM). The general agreement between DIMA and ACM obliges ACM to provide services in accordance with the Immigration Detention Standards. Although DIMA has the ultimate responsibility for the detainees, the service provider is under a duty of care to uphold the dignity of detainees in ways appropriate to their age, gender, religion, language and culture.[25]

In the years following the privatization of the delivery of immigration detention services, a wide range of problems have become evident. Problems seen in all detention centers include overcrowding, tendency towards self harm, conflict arising from the communal living arrangements as well as frustration and depression stemming from the delays in processing of applications.[26] As a result of the complaints and allegations, a number of inquiries and reviews of the immigration detention centers have taken place to evaluate the situation and determine whether ACM has failed to operate according to the Immigration Detention Standards. Woomera, an immigration detention center in South Australia has been the focus of many of the complaints and has been held up by activists as the worst one. The following section will consider some of the problems at Woomera and evaluate whether the situation is aggravated by the privatization of the detention center.

Woomera Immigration Detention Centre

The Woomera detention center, built in 1999, has the capacity to house up to 2000 detainees. It has seen a number of riots, and in January 2002, more than 200 detainees went on a prolonged hunger strike. Twenty-five of them swallowed a potentially lethal mixture of detergent and shampoo, forty-two of the detainees sewed their lips together while on hunger strike and fifteen were reported to have attempted to hang themselves.[27] Their frustration at the conditions and their uncertain future has led detainees to desperate acts, and to international criticism of the government's policies and ACM's practices.[28]

Although the Immigration Detention Standards state that the operator of the detention center must ensure that "the dignity of the detainees is upheld in culturally, linguistically, gender and age appropriate ways",[29] allegations of racial abuse and heavy-handed treatment by ACM officers towards the detainees have been widespread.[30] At Woomera, offensive drawings and poems penned by ACM staff were reported to be widely available. In a recent visit of parliamentarians to Woomera, the most common complaint of the detainees was that if they tried to advocate on behalf of anyone or went on hunger strike, they were harassed by staff.[31] Moreover, people were humiliated by officers in unnecessary room searches.[32] At Woomera, the employees had a greater tendency to address detainees by number rather than by name.[33]

Part of the problem at Woomera, as at other detention centers operated by ACM, is that the institution faces staff shortages and high staff turnover, as partly shown by the larger proportion of 6-week work contracts than at other centers. Many of the staff members previously worked at ACM's private prisons, which house convicted criminals. Some staff lacked the cultural awareness, and failed to appreciate that the nature of the detention is administrative rather than punitive.[34] Moreover, the training of officers is very limited in light of the complex issues with which they are faced. Asylum seekers have often escaped persecution by fleeing across borders in dangerous circumstances. Once having arrived, they may suffer post-traumatic stress at the same time as they live under the uncertainty of being accepted or rejected. Although Woomera has medical staff and a mental health nurse on site,[35] ACM officers are often the first point of contact when detainees are faced with anxieties, when there are tensions between different groups of detainees, or when there are allegations of abuse. The ACM staff receive only a 5-week pre-service course and forty hours of refresher training annually.[36] The combination of limited staff training, high staff turnover, the presence of former prison guards, and the remoteness of Woomera makes the reality of the detention punitive.

Children are especially vulnerable in the detention center environment. In a report prepared for the Minister of Immigration and Multicultural Affairs, it was stated that "the environment at the Woomera Immigration Reception and Processing Centre is such that this constitutes abuse of children (and women) who are obliged to spend long periods there."[37] While Australia is a party to the Convention on the Rights of the Child and as such has the obligation to keep the best interest of the child in mind under all circumstances, this has not always been the case at Woomera.

Children face a number of particular issues in relation to detention. The environment at the Woomera detention center is heavily male dominated. Under pressure of lengthy asylum application procedures and mental deterioration due to depression and pre-existing post traumatic stress, there has been a tendency to self-harm and many conflicts among groups of detainees. In the recent hunger strike, some children had sewn their lips together.[38] Children who may already have been separated from their parents or witnessed horrific incidents in their home countries should not fall victim, or bear witness to the tensions in detention centers.[39] The latest report by the Australian Human Rights Commissioner concludes that it is beyond doubt that "children are suffering psychological trauma" from their experiences in the detention center.[40]

There are also concerns that children in detention miss out on formal education, and that there is a lack of activities for them at the center. For instance, Woomera lacks appropriate outdoor space for children to play. The Human Rights Commissioner's February report notes that education is confined to those aged twelve and under, and is provided for a total of only two hours a day, four days a week.[41]

Although claims of sexual and other child abuse have been made against residents of the center over the past three years, the manner in which allegations have been dealt with by ACM officials has been at best neglectful. For instance, in March 2000, although the duty nurse reported to the ACM center manager that she suspected that a 12-year old boy had been sexually assaulted, the manager and ACM officials failed to immediately report the incident, ignoring established incident reporting procedures.[42] Moreover, staff at Woomera have generally failed to keep proper files and a report commissioned by the government concluded that the 'existing arrangement for the security of files was quite inadequate.' Things came to a head in January of 2002 when eleven child detainees at Woomera threatened mass suicide, leading the Australian Human Rights Commissioner to investigate. Among the 236 children still detained at Woomera, the Commissioner found 24 reported incidents of self-harm, including lip sewing, slashing and one attempted hanging, and concluded there were "clear breaches of the Convention on the Rights of the Child."[43]

Unrest and reports of violations continue to come out of Australia. There is little doubt that problems will persist as long as the government maintains its harsh asylum policies and continues to give a freehand to ACM or any other corporation operating on a for-profit basis.

Background: UK

The United Kingdom differs from Australia in that only 1 to 1.5 percent of all asylum seekers are detained at any given time.[44] UK law makes it possible to detain a person upon arrival, pending the applicant's examination and a decision to grant or refuse him or her leave to enter.[45] The detainees, however, are not given written reasons justifying their detention, and many are left feeling confused as to why they are being detained.[46] The government's current policy is "to introduce a fast-track procedure which involves detention of some applicants for a period of about a week in order to ensure speedy and efficient processing of their applications."[47] The new policy is a response to critics who have accused the government of detaining asylum seekers for unnecessarily long periods in appalling conditions, either among convicted criminals in public prisons or with failed refugee applicants in private detention centers.

In March 2000, the Oakington Reception Centre, run by Group 4, was made the "central plank" of the fast-track policy, enabling about 250 applicants to be processed each week, or up to 13,000 a year.[48] Despite fast-track processing, detention places have expanded from about 900 in 1997 to 2,800 in 2001.[49] In September 2001, about 1,850 people were detained, but new detention centers were being opened in Yarl's Wood (Bedford), to accommodate 900 women, children and men, and in Harmondsworth near Heathrow, to house another 550 detainees. These facilities are currently being operated by Group 4 and Sodexho respectively. Additional places are expected to be in operation by spring 2003, bringing the total number of available places to 4,000.

Unlike the system in Australia, detention centers in the UK are operated by a number of different for-profit companies. The major UK contractors are Group 4, the company that operates Campsfield House, Yarl's Wood and Oakington detention centers, Wackenhut, which has a contract to operate Tinsley House, and finally Sodexho, the company responsible for the operations of Hammondsworth. Although there have been problems at all the detention centers, the most serious allegations of human rights abuse and mismanagement have been directed at a Group 4-run detention center, Campsfield House.

Campsfield House

On 7 February 2002, the Home Secretary, David Blunkett, announced that Campsfield House detention center would be closed.[50] Campsfield House is located approximately 5 miles from Oxford. Built as a hospital in 1932, it was acquired by the prison service in 1952, and used to house young offenders. In 1993, the building appeared in its current incarnation as an immigration detention center with Group 4 running it. Until recently, Campsfield House was the largest immigration detention center in the country, equipped to house 200 detainees.[51]

Unfortunately, the decision to close Campsfield did not relate to a change in government policy to use detention only as an exceptional measure. It is, however, part of the government's latest policy to limit the use of detention to two categories of people: refugee applicants undergoing expedited refugee determination and failed applicants awaiting removal. Moreover, its decision to close Campsfield is undoubtedly related to the center's history of riots, hunger strikes and suicides, as well as the negative press coverage the center has received, helped along by persistent public protests at the site, among the public and on the Internet.[52] The information, as provided by protesters and official sources alike, highlights the long history of human rights abuses and poor conditions at Campsfield House. Much of the information relates to a large disturbance in March of 1997 which caused significant damage to the center and resulted in charges being brought against detainees. This event resulted in a series of court actions, which will be described at some length below, as well as an unannounced visit by the Prison Inspector to Campsfield House in October of 1997.

The report of the Prison Inspector is interesting since it substantiates the complaints of detainees and a number of pressure groups, including the problems associated with high staff turnover. It notes how staff turnover was at an all time high of 57 percent in 1996. Staff worked 12-hour shifts, and their salary was a mere £4 ($5.71) an hour.[53] In 2002, custody officers employed by Group 4 were paid slightly more, at £6.75 ($9.64) an hour, still not much more than the current minimum wage.[54] Employees were frequently required to work long hours and there was an inadequate number of staff on shifts. Staff complained that working conditions were poor, they received no lunch break or provision of a meal and they received holiday pay for 10 hours per day when each shift was in fact 12 hours.[55] To make matters worse, the shift pattern required each employee to work 7 consecutive shifts,[56] and the overworked, underpaid staff felt vulnerable because they believed they had no authority over detainees. Based on Group 4's working conditions, it is doubtful that the company is able to hire and keep qualified staff.

In addition to complaints about the conditions under which the immigration detention staff worked, there was a lack of appropriate training. The HM Chief

Inspector found that staff had little or no information about security issues, or about the possibility that detainees could carry communicable diseases. Originally the staff were trained to deal with static guard duties.[57] While training was improved to include suicide awareness training, health and safety, and training on security-related matters,[58] there was still limited understanding of different cultures and religions, and detainees complained of racial slurs and inappropriate language.[59] In 2002, lack of training for detention officers continues to be an issue.[60]

The general atmosphere of Campsfield House was punitive and detainees felt like criminals. Detainees complained that staff censored private letters, the food was of poor quality and variety, every medical complaint was treated with paracetamol, and they felt bored. There were occasions where detainees were told to go back to their own country if they did not like it here.[61] Detainees felt reluctant to complain, thinking that if they did they would be sent to prison, and grievance procedures were lacking. Forms were available from Group 4 staff, but upon completion they had to be returned to staff, whose responsibility it was to hand them to the supervisor. If the allegations contained in the grievance were serious, the grievance was referred to the manager.[62] The detainees had no confidence in the integrity of the system.[63]

The lack of confidence in the system leads to an atmosphere of mutual suspicion and high levels of tension. Detainees have little trust in Group 4 staff, and staff have little respect for the human rights of asylum seekers. Since the Home Office has failed to maintain a supervisory role over the privately run detention centers, it has failed in its obligation to ensure that the detainees' dignity is being respected and that their applications for asylum are not being jeopardized. This can be illustrated by the court proceedings involving John Quaquah.

John Quaquah and the Campsfield Riot

John Quaquah arrived in the UK seeking asylum in 1997 and was detained at Campsfield House. His asylum appeal was ultimately dismissed on 27 August 1997, exactly one week after he and eight others were charged with offences of riot and violent disorder in relation to serious disturbances at the detention center. The charges were brought by police on the basis of evidence obtained from Group 4 staff.

Quaquah and the others stood trial almost one year later, in June 1998, but the prosecution collapsed within one week on the basis that certain witnesses, who were Group 4 Security officers, were "shown to have fabricated their evidence."[64] The evidence was not only declared to be unreliable and false, but questions were also raised with respect to "the integrity of their conduct during the disturbances."[65] For instance, it was shown that staff, not detainees, were responsible for the destruction of telephones. Even the Secretary of State accepted that the conduct of the officers "both during the incident of unrest itself as well as their conduct in giving unreliable/false evidence satisfied the description of having been 'wicked'."[66] The outcome of the case prompted Quaquah to bring civil proceedings for malicious prosecution against Group 4 and the Home Office.

To date, the suit has not been resolved. However, in a hearing on 23 May 2001, Wright J. struck the Home Office from the claim. He held that it was within the power of the Secretary of State to delegate the running of an immigration detention center to an independent contractor, and given that the Secretary of State had exercised all reasonable care in the selection of such a contractor, he could not be liable for the torts of that contractor's servants or agents.[67]

The decision demonstrates how the process of privatization is allowing the government to pass off its responsibilities of caring for asylum seekers, while maintaining its role to decide who qualifies as a refugee. The result is that even if the government is aware of the fact that guards were overworked, underpaid and under-trained, it is not liable for the abuse inflicted by them upon asylum seekers, regardless of whether its legislation is the reason behind their detention in a privately run center. It is important to point out that after Quaquah brought the claim for malicious prosecution, the Secretary of State persisted in its efforts to deport him, despite the ongoing trial. The attitude of the Secretary of State throughout has been that Quaquah can pursue the litigation "from afar–from Ghana–with the possibility of a visit or visits" when necessary.[68] The Immigration Service expressed its view that "should his presence be required at any future proceedings it would be open to him to apply for the required entry clearance ... to enable him to return."[69] While it is not suggested that the Secretary of State was acting to protect Group 4, its actions appear to demonstrate that it is less concerned with the proper operation of the Campsfield detention center than with the deportation of John Quaquah. Turner J., the judge who overturned the Secretary of State's decision to deport Quaquah while the court action was ongoing, said the following:

> This was not just a simply straightforward case of infringement of a private right by a private individual. The case may be one in which the agencies of the state (the Group 4 custodians) have breached, in the public sphere, duties which they owed to those who were held in the Detention Centre and for which the respondent (the decision maker [on Quaquah's deportation]) had the overall legal responsibility.[70]

In the end, however, a different judge decided that the Secretary of State had delegated away its legal responsibility. The opening of new detention centers, like Yarl's Wood, demonstrates that the government is content to continue the process of delegating its legal responsibilities to companies with poor track records.

Yarl's Wood

In February 2002, a Group 4-run detention center was again at the heart of controversy, when a disturbance resulted in a destructive fire. The riot was reported to have been ignited by frustration over an elderly woman's lack of access to medical care.[71] When she became agitated, Group 4 staff handcuffed her. In the scuffle that resulted, guards were attacked, their keys stolen, windows were smashed, fires erupted and doors broken down. The damage was estimated at £38 million.[72] Tensions had been rising at Yarl's Wood, where detainees complained that they were being treated without respect, like prisoners, and that they often had to wait for health care and other services. Staff were concerned about lack of appropriate training, low salaries and inadequate staffing levels.[73] The company tacitly acknowledged it had been economizing on staffing numbers when, just three days after the incident, it announced that it would double staff numbers.[74] The disturbance provides further evidence that Group 4 has yet again failed to provide a secure environment for detainees and staff, and that the problems of Campsfield House will persist at other Group 4-run detention centers. The government in turn, failed to intervene in a timely manner to guarantee that safety was preserved.

Australia and the UK Are Breaching International Legal Standards

By encouraging detention and delegating those responsibilities to private companies, the UK and Australia have created a greater likelihood of human rights abuses. Although the services for operating the detention services have been contracted out, the governments must accept some of the responsibility for rioting and the destruction of detention centers. Instead, they dismiss their responsibilities, and continue to allow private companies to run detention centers in a neglectful and dangerous manner. The Australian Prime Minister has admitted that the conditions in the detention centers are deliberately harsh to act as a deterrent to other people considering trying to sneak into Australia.[75] In a bid to quell future riots, the Immigration Minister, Philip Ruddock, has even expressed support for the use of drugs to sedate "problem" detainees.[76] Although the UK cannot be said to be acting in the same intentionally abusive manner, it is interesting that the Australian minister has pointed to the UK's 2002 immigration reforms, suggesting that they reflected policies and practices already used in Australia.[77]

Ruddock has also responded to the detention center riots with threats of non-admission of refugees. Despite the Australian authority's decision to stop refugee processing for fear of terrorists being among the boatpeople,[78] and despite the dire conditions within some of the detention centers, Ruddock reacted to the riot by saying that the Refugee Convention makes it very clear that if people commit, or have committed, serious criminal offences, they have no lawful basis of obtaining status."[79] It is noteworthy that to support his position he invoked the same convention that makes mandatory detention illegal in the first place. His comments demonstrate that the Australian government accepts no responsibility for conditions in which asylum seekers find themselves. The critics have been boisterous, including Mr. Neville Roach, a senior advisor of Ruddock's until 23 January 2002, when he decided he could no longer support the government's harsh asylum policy.[80]

If the UK and Australia insist on contracting out detention services, they must maintain a supervisory role that extends beyond occasional site visits. Thankfully, changes brought to UK law by the Immigration and Asylum Act of 1999 go part way in recognizing this fact. In section 151(1) of the Act, the Secretary of State has been given the power to intervene, if

> (a) the manager of a contracted out detention centre has lost, or is likely to lose, effective control of the centre or of any part of it; or
> (b) it is necessary to do so in the interests of preserving the safety of any person, or of preventing serious damage to any property.

He may do so by appointing a "Controller" who is given the status of a Crown servant. The problem, however, is that the legislation merely provides that the Secretary of State "may" intervene. The Secretary of State should be given more than discretion to intervene; he or she should be obliged to step in, especially if it is "in the interests of preserving the safety" of the guards, visitors and detainees. Unfortunately, the wording of the Act leaves doubt as to whether another Quaquah situation will be averted in the future.

After all, it is the UK and Australia, not Group 4 or ACM, that are parties to the Refugee Convention. Accordingly, they bear the responsibility to ensure that applicants are treated fairly, and that their human rights are respected. By contracting detention services out to firms that pay their employees poorly, offer them little training, and force them to work long shifts, are the governments living up to the obligations they have undertaken? The fact that the British government has taken few steps to hold Group 4 officers accountable for the false testimony they provided or the questionable practices in which they engaged suggests that it is not.[81] No officer "has been charged, sacked or even disciplined."[82]

One of the most serious problems resulting from the privatization of immigration detention centers is that transparency of the system is compromised in favor of commercial confidentiality. A public system allows for greater scrutiny and hence increased accountability. Media, for example, have been limited in their access to report on public detention centers. While there are legitimate reasons for limiting detainees' exposure to journalists, detainees have felt that their plight is not being heard by the public, the taxpayers who fund the system. While media crews were allowed to visit Woomera in January of 2002, they were not allowed to speak to any of the detainees and the television crews had their footage screened. During the height of the hunger strike at Woomera in January 2002, the "Australian government officers imposed tough new restrictions aimed at preventing journalists easily filming from outside the perimeter of the center the protests occurring inside the razorwire-topped fence."[83]

In both countries, there is a lack of information available on the contracts that govern the relationship between the governments and the private for-profit companies that run the detention centers. There is, for example, no official information available on the salary levels of the detention staff. This may seem like an operational detail, but, as we have seen above, it may have serious implications on the ability to attract qualified staff. Also, there is a large degree of confusion regarding the powers of detention staff in both the UK and Australia. It is of crucial importance to have clearly defined operational guidelines that have been publicly scrutinized. Since it is the tax payer who funds the detention centers, they have a right to access information on their operation. It is unacceptable that corporate confidentiality gets in the way of public scrutiny and accountability of government legislation, enacted pursuant to international obligations.

The traditional argument raised by advocates of private prisons is that they are more efficient. In the case of immigration detention centers, this could not be further from the truth, since there are better alternatives to detention. According to Professor Goodwin-Gill, subjecting asylum seekers to penalties without regard to their claim to be a refugee is

> wasteful of national resources and an example of bad management. Where the penalty imposed is detention, it imposes significant costs on the receiving State, and inevitably increases delay in national systems, whether at the level of refugee determination or immigration control.[84]

The use of private detention centers to detain people who do not pose a security risk is not only inefficient, it also contributes to the greater likelihood of human rights abuses, as demonstrated by the track record of Group 4 in the UK and ACM in Australia.

Conclusion

Although international law stipulates that the detention of asylum seekers is an exceptional measure that should be avoided, it is increasingly popular in

Australia and the UK. Nevertheless, the immigration detention policies of these two countries differ enormously. Whereas Australia requires the mandatory detention without judicial review of all 'illegal' entrants, the UK detains only a very small percentage upon entry, as well as failed applicants awaiting removal. Therefore, although both countries detain between 2,000 to 4,000 asylum seekers per year, the Australian system, on its face, violates international guarantees accorded to refugees and other persons, while the British system does not necessarily do so. In the case of the UK, it is necessary to consider the specific treatment of detainees in order to determine whether it violates international legal standards.

The conditions of private detention centers and the treatment of detainees in Australia and the UK have been shown to be inadequate. While international standards guarantee the right of detainees to be treated with humanity and respect, official reports chronicle a long list of abuse and neglect by Group 4 and ACM staff. Admittedly, the situation is worse in Australia, where the government has openly encouraged substandard conditions, but the UK has also neglected to ensure the safety and respect of detainees.

The reasons behind the inadequate treatment of asylum detainees relate directly to the practices of the private companies running the centers. In both countries, detention staff are paid poorly, overworked and given little training, yet they have to deal with men, women and children who speak foreign languages and have special medical and psychological needs. The conduct of staff has proved to be untrustworthy and 'wicked', but the governments continue to entrust their responsibilities to the companies that hire them. This distances the governments from liability, as demonstrated by the Quaquah trial, as well as increases lack of accountability and transparency due to commercial confidentiality.

Endnotes

1. "Criticism grown over asylum seekers' detention," *Inter Press Service*, 6 February 2001.
2. *International Covenant on Civil and Political Rights (ICCPR)*, 1966, Art.9.
3. As of February 2002, 138 states have become a party to the 1967 Protocol to the Refugee Convention, ensuring that it applies without any geographic limitation.
4. G. Goodwin-Gill, "Article 31 of the 1951 Convention relating to the Status of Refugees: Non-penalization, Detention and Protection" (2001): 34, available at <http://www.unhcr.ch> [hereinafter Goodwin-Gill, "Article 31" (2001)].
5. The Executive Committee, or "ExCom", was established by ECOSOC at the request of the UN General Assembly. It is thus formally independent of the UNHCR, operating as a distinct body of the UN, but it advises the UNHCR on the exercise of its functions. It is currently made up of 57 states, and its Conclusions can therefore be said to constitute important *opinio juris* in the area of refugee law.
6. ExCom Conclusion No. 44 (XXVII) - 1986, para. (b).
7. Summary Conclusions on Article 31 of the 1951 Convention relating to the Status of Refugees, 8-9 November 2001, Geneva Expert Round Table as part of the UNHCR's Global Consultations on International Protection <http://www.unhcr.ch>; see also Guideline 3 of the UNHCR Guidelines on Detention of Asylum Seekers.
8. For instance, the Australian Prime Minister, John Howard, has admitted that conditions in the detention centers are deliberately harsh to act as a deterrent to other people considering trying to sneak into Australia, see "Australia's leader says he won't soften policy on asylum seekers," *AP World News*, 30 January 2002.
9. G. Goodwin-Gill, "Article 31," *supra* note 4 at 23.
10. Lawyers Committee for Human Rights, "Refugees behind Bars: The Imprisonment of Asylum Seekers in the Wake of the 1996 Immigration Act" (August 1999): 15 <http://www.lchr.org/refugee/behindbars.htm>.
11. "Criticism grows over asylum seekers' detention," *Inter Press Service*, 6 February 2002.
12. "Oxfam blasts Australia's Pacific detention centres," *Agence France Presse*, 4 February 2002; compare this amount to the $8.5 million Australia offered to help reconstruct Afghanistan, something that would assist in the avoidance of future refugee flows.
13. For a broader discussion of the detention of asylum seekers and refugees, see Amnesty International, "United States of America: Lost in the Labyrinth: Detention of Asylum-Seekers," Report

AMR/5151/99, September 1999; Helton, A., "Detention of Refugees and Asylum Seekers," in G. Loescher and L. Monahan, *Refugee Issues in International Relations*, Oxford, 1989; J. Hughes and F. Liebaut, *eds.*, *Detention of Asylum Seekers in Europe: Analysis and Perspectives*, 1998, which also appraises the Australian and Canadian approaches; Ramji J., "Legislating Away International Law: The Refugee Provisions of the Illegal Immigration Reform and Immigrant Responsibility Act" (2001) 37 *Stan.J.Int'l.L.* 117; Takkenberg, L., "Detention and other restrictions of the freedom of movement of refugees and asylum seekers: The European perspective," in J. Bhabha and G. Coll, *Asylum Law and Practice in Europe and North America*, (1992).

14. This principle can be found in Art. 9 of the *ICCPR*, to which Australia is a party.

15. Article 3 of the European Convention on Human Rights, 1950, and Article 7 of the *ICCPR*.

16. *ICCPR*, Article 10.

17. The Convention on the Rights of the Child (CRC) ensures the protection of the rights of child refugees or asylum seekers (Art. 22(1)), the right to play (Art. 31), the promotion of physical and psychological recovery from neglect and abuse (Art.39), and most importantly that detention "shall be used only as a measure of last resort and for the shortest appropriate period of time (Art. 37(b)).

18. Sections 189 and 196 of the Australian Migration Act, 1958.

19. There are some circumstances under which detainees, such as unauthorized boat arrivals who have not entered Australia lawfully, may be granted a Bridging Visa E (051). The exceptional circumstances are if the detainee: (a) is under 18 years old and it is considered to be in their best interests; (b) is over 75 years old; (c) has a medical condition that cannot be treated in detention; and (d) is a spouse of an Australian citizen. Please see Chapter 2 of the *Flood Report*.

20. P. Flood, "Report of Inquiry into Immigration Detention Procedures," (February 2001): para. 3.2 [hereinafter *Flood Report*].

21. "Criticism grows over asylum seekers' detention," *Inter Press Service*, *supra* note 11.

22. *Flood Report*, *supra* note 20 at paras. 4.1 and 4.4.

23. Commonwealth Ombudsman, "Report of an Own Motion Investigation into the Department of Immigration and Multicultural Affairs' Immigration Detention Centres" (March 2001): 9 [hereinafter *Ombudsman Report*].

24. *Flood Report*, *supra* note 20 at para. 4.2. The contract was extended for 12 months, and in January 2002, Prison Privatisation Report International reported that ACM was facing competition for the renewal of the contract. Serco, the Australian Protection Service and Wackenhut's British joint venture partner in Premier Custodial Group Ltd. and Chubb protective services are all thought to be considering a bid. *PPRI*, #45 <www.psiru.org/justice>.

25. *Id.*, para. 9.1.

26. Ombudsman Report, *supra* note 23 at 17; See also Rachel Nowak, "Detention destroys asylum seekers' mental health," in *New Scientist*, Melbourne, 19 December 2001.

27. "Canberra warned about asylum camp," *The Guardian*, 25 January 2002, at p.18.

28. See "Criticism grows over asylum seekers' detention," *Inter Press Service*, *supra* note 11; "Australia denies reputation hit by immigration controversy," *Agence France Press*, 7 February 2002; "Australia detention center criticized," *Associated Press*, 6 February 2002; "Australians rally for largest protest yet over refugee policy," *New York Times*, 12 February 2002.

29. *Flood Report*, *supra* note 20 at annex E.

30. Ombudsman Report, *supra* note 23 at 26.

31. "Criticism grown over asylum seekers' detention," *Inter Press Service*, 6 February 2001.

32. *Flood Report*, *supra* note 20 at para. 7.4.

33. *Id.*, para. 7.2.

34. See the immigration detention standards in *Flood Report*, *supra* note 20 at annex E.

35. Ombudsman Report, *supra* note 23 at 37.

36. *PPRI* no. 39 <www.psiru.org/justice>.

37. *Flood Report*, *supra* note 20 at para. 7.1.

38. Rachel Nowak, "Detention destroys asylum seekers' mental health," in *New Scientist*, Melbourne, 19 December 2001.

39. *Flood Report*, *supra* note 20 at chapter 8.

40. Pres. Prof. A. Tay and Dr. S. Ozdowski, Media Statement on "Woomera Immigration Detention Centre: Report of visit by HREOC officers," 6 February 2002 <http://www.hreoc.gov.au>.

41. *Id.*

42. *Flood Report*, *supra* note 20 at chapter 6.

43. Pres. Prof. A. Tay and Dr. S. Ozdowski, Media Statement on "Woomera Immigration Detention Centre: Report of visit by HREOC officers," 6 February 2002, available at <http://www.hreoc.gov.au>.

44. G. Goodwin-Gill, "Article 3," *supra* note 4 at 28.

45. *Immigration Act*, 1971, Schedule 2.

46. "Campsfield House Detention Centre," a report by Her Majesty's Chief Inspector of Prisons following an unannounced short inspection (1998): para. 1-22 [hereinafter *HM Chief Inspector of Prisons Campsfield Report*].

47. These are the words of Lord Phillips of Worth Matravers in his judgment in *R. (on the application of Saadi and others)* v. *Secretary of State for the Home Department*, CA (Civil Division), [2001] 4 All ER 961,

at para. 4.

48. White Paper of the Secretary of State of the Home Department, "Secure Borders, Safe Haven: Integration with Diversity in Modern Britain," HMSO (February 2002): 64-65.

49. *Id.* at p.66.

50. "Immigration white paper: Blunkett to shut 'outdated' and hated Campsfield," *The Independent*, 8 February 2002.

51. *HM Chief Inspector of Prisons Campsfield Report, supra* ntoe 46 at para. 1.01.

52. See for instance: <http://www.barbedwirebritain.org.uk/>; <http://www.closecampsfield.org.uk/>; <http://www.srcf.ucam.org/card/>; <http://www.corporatewatch.org.uk>; http://www.statewatch.org>; <http://<www.ncadc.org.uk>; <http://www.refugeecouncil.org.uk>; <http://www.closeoakington.org>.

53. *HM Chief Inspector of Prisons Campsfield Report, supra* note 46 at paras. 2.01-2.02.

54. S. Morris, "How fuse was lit for inmates with nothing less to lose," in *The Guardian*, 16 February 2002.

55. *HM Chief Inspector of Prisons Campsfield Report, supra* note 46 at paras. 2.03-2.04.

56. *Id.,* para. 7.09.

57. *Id.,* para. 2.04.

58. *Id.,* para. 7.12.

59. *Id.,* para. 2.04.

60. S. Morris, "How fuse was lit for inmates with nothing less to lose," *supra* note 54.

61. *HM Chief Inspector of Prisons Campsfield Report, supra* note 46 at paras. 2.05-2.06.

62. *Id.,* paras. 3.21-3.23.

63. Liz Peretz, "Social Exclusion - the case of refugees & asylum seekers," SCCD (Standing Conference for Community Development) Journal, Spring 2001 <http://www.closecampsfield.org.uk>.

64. *R. v. Secretary of State for the Home Dept., ex parte Quaquah*, QBD (Administrative Court), CO/1028/00, 1 September 2000.

65. *R. v. An Immigration Officer, ex parte Quaquah*, QBD (Crown's Office List), The Times, 21 January 2000.

66. *Id.*

67. *Quaquah v. Group 4 (Total Security) and the Home Office*, QBD (High Court of Justice), Case No. TLQ 340/01, 23 May 2001.

68. *R. v. Immigration Officer, ex parte Quaquah*, QBD (Crown's Office List), CO/4738/98, 4 February 1999.

69. *R. v. An Immigration Officer, ex parte Quaquah*, QBD, *supra* note 65.

70. *Id.*

71. BBC, Radio 4, 6 o'clock news, 15 February 2002; see also "Yarl's Wood Detention Centre - Burnt to the Ground" at <http://www.ncadc.org.uk>.

72. Steven Morris, "Violence continues at asylum centre," *The Guardian*, 18 February 2002.

73. Steven Morris, "*Inside Story:* Riot was ignited by rising desperation of failed asylum seekers aggrieved at immigration centre's prison-like conditions," *The Guardian*, 16 February 2002.

74. "Asylum centre staff 'to be doubled'," BBC News, 18 February 2002 <http://news.bbc.co.uk>.

75. "Australia's leader says he won't soften policy on asylum seekers," *AP World News*, 30 January 2002.

76. "Criticism grows over asylum seekers' detention," *Inter Press Service, supra* note 11.

77. Jim Hanna, "Australian immigration minister says UK 'copying our migration policies'," *AAP News*, 8 February 2002.

78. "Aylum seekers detained in Australia sew lips," *Xinhua,* 19 January 2002.

79. "Officer hurt in riot at detention centre," *Agence France Presse*, 22 January 2001.

80. "Australia: Government again under pressure over treatment of asylum seekers," *AP World News*, 23 January 2002.

81. Note, however, that section 158 of the Immigration and Asylum Act of 1999 makes it an offence for a detainee custody officer to disclose, otherwise than in the course of his duty or as authorised by the Secretary of State, any information which he acquired in the course of his employment and which relates to a particular detained person.

82. Corporate Watch, "Group 4: Cry Freedom," Magazine Issue No. 8, Spring 1999 <www.corporatewatch.org.uk/magazine/issue8/cw8g4.html>.

83. "Criticism grows over asylum seekers' detention," *Inter Press Service, supra* note 11.

84. G. Goodwin-Gill, "Article 31," *supra* note 4 at 2.

CHAPTER TWELVE

Worker Rights in Private Prisons

Joshua Miller

Introduction: The Evidence is Clear

Although private prison companies like Corrections Corporation of America (CCA) and Wackenhut Corrections claim they can operate prisons cheaper than governments can and still generate a profit, various studies have belied this assertion. In 1998 for example, CCA lobbied the Tennessee State legislature to allow it to operate up to 70 percent of the state's prisons. As part of its decision-making process, the legislature analyzed one of its existing contracts with CCA. The analysis revealed that the state did not save any money by contracting with CCA. The company however, reported a 2 percent profit by spending almost $2 million less on annual salaries and benefits for its employees than the state had spent.[1]

The Tennessee study illustrated what has been the *modus operandi* for private prisons operators: reduce labor costs to generate profits. At roughly 70 percent of all prison operating expenses, it makes sense that labor costs must be reduced to generate corporate profits.[2] In fact, the quest to dramatically slash labor costs drives everything from the selection of a private prison site to the design of the facility and its operating policies and procedures.

Much of what goes on behind the walls of a private prison is not only hidden from the public, but also from state corrections officials and legislators as well. The evidence in this chapter will demonstrate that private prison operators typically pay significantly lower wages and benefits than do public sector corrections systems, resulting in less qualified personnel and extremely lower employee retention rates. The companies also deliberately cut back on front line staffing, diminishing security and jeopardizing the safety of private prison guards, inmates and the surrounding community.

While private prison companies invest less in front line staffing, they generously reward wardens and company executives. According to a study by Abt Associates Inc., under contract with the National Institute of Corrections (NIC), "privatization changes the way taxpayer dollars are spent on prison inmates: less is spent on employees having direct contact with prisoners; more is spent on prison-level administration, monitoring activities by state officials, corporate overhead and corporate profits."[3]

Numerous national and regional studies have shown labor cost cutting to be endemic in the private prison industry. For instance, a national study by the National Council on Crime and Delinquency noted, "private prisons have a significantly lower staffing level, lower salaries and higher rate of assaults on staff and inmates than public facilities."[4] There are numerous audits and studies that corroborate the findings of the NCCD study. The following provides a description of three such reports:

- 30 April 2001; *Briefing Report–Florence Correctional Facility: Report of the Hawaii monitors for the CCA Florence Correctional Facility.*[5] After two inmate deaths, six inmate assaults and a riot that left one guard with six stitches – all of which happened in April–the state of Hawaii dispatched four auditors to inspect the privately owned Florence, Arizona prison, which opened in 2000 and housed some Hawaii inmates.[6] The Hawaii auditors attributed the hazardous environment to lack of experience of the prison guards (due to high employee turnover). The auditors also noted that employee morale was declining and that inmates and staff were frustrated with the staff's lack of commitment to provide a safe and secure environment. Moreover, the auditors discovered indications that the inmates were in control of the facility. For instance, there appeared to be widespread drug introduction into the facility by staff members, who were "working" for the gangs.

- February 2000; *A Review of the Jena Juvenile Justice Center, Jena, Louisiana.*[7] A US Department of Justice (DOJ) investigation found numerous violations at the Wackenhut-owned and operated juvenile prison in Jena, Louisiana. As a result of its investigation, the Justice Department sued Wackenhut alleging that the juveniles at the facility were subjected to excessive abuse and neglect. In the suit, DOJ asserted that juveniles at Jena were at a substantial risk of harm due to unreasonable levels of violence from juvenile-on-juvenile assaults and the use of excessive force and abuse from staff. The complaint also alleged that the juveniles at Jena were subjected to unreasonable isolation and restraints, inadequate medical and mental health care, inadequate general, vocational, and special education, and inadequate rehabilitative services. Federal investigators blamed many of Jena's problems on high staff turnover and poor guard training. The state eventually moved its inmates out of the Jena facility and decided to end its experiment with private juvenile prisons.

- 25 November 1998; *US Department of Justice Report on Northeast Ohio Correctional Center.*[8] This report became necessary after deficiencies, errors, and mismanagement at a CCA-run facility led to a series of disastrous occurrences, including disruptions, escapes, 20 inmate stabbings, and the deaths of two inmates all in a little over a year. Major findings included an absence of experience at the entry guard level (guards noted that turnover among their ranks was high), absence of experience at the mid-supervisory level and general insufficient training of personnel. Furthermore, a pattern of flawed security, attributable to both corporate and institutional management deficiencies, resulted in failures to meet the basic correctional mission of community, staff and inmate security.

In just these three reports, we can already see some common problems emerging in regard to prison employees. Chronic employee turnover and understaffing, poor training and a high rate of violence are just a few of the concerns that are raised over and over, and are the direct result of the cost cutting and profiteering that are the benchmarks of the private prison industry. The remainder of this chapter will explain how the mission to reduce labor costs creates poor working conditions in private prisons and puts employees, inmates and entire communities at peril.

Reverse Robin Hood

Employees in private prisons tend to earn considerably less than their public sector counterparts. Unfortunately, most of the information about employee salaries in private prisons is anecdotal because the companies are not held to any public disclosure requirements. *The Corrections Yearbook*, an authoritative source for corrections statistics, began to publish self-reported data from the private operators in 1998. The comparative data for public corrections officer (CO) versus private guard salaries is contained in the following table:[9]

Average Starting Salary

	1997	1998	1999
Public COs	$21,246	$21,855	$23,002
Private Guards	$17,344	$19,344	$17,719

Average Maximum Salary

	1997	1998	1999
Public COs	$34,004	$34,728	$36,328
Private Guards	$20,448	$21,790	$21,961

The disparity between public sector and private sector salaries is evident in the above table. The average starting salary for public sector correctional officers was approximately 28 percent higher than the starting salary for private prison guards in 1999, the most recent year that comparable data is available. Likewise, the average maximum salary for public sector COs was 64 percent higher than that of private prison guards in 1999. Maximum salaries don't mean much to private prison guards because most of them do not last long. However, it is also noteworthy that the average starting salary for public sector cos is greater than the average maximum salary for private prison guards in each year. Thus, it is easy to understand why private prison employees bolt when other employment opportunities become available. The data also indicates that the average starting salary for private prison guards decreased by approximately 8 percent from 1998 to 1999.

In labor markets where there are both publicly and privately operated prisons, the low pay offered by private companies makes it virtually impossible for them to compete with publicly run facilities for quality staff. For instance, in one of the above-mentioned studies, auditors in Florence, Arizona recently noted that the "Florence Correctional Center [operated by CCA] faces continuous staffing problems, due to competition with … state and federal facilities within the area."[10]

Competition for employees was also a problem at CCA's prison in Youngstown, Ohio, where the company was believed to have controlled its costs by hiring fewer guards, paying them less and prohibiting overtime. The starting wage at the Youngstown facility was $24,672 a year compared to $25,979 a year at an Ohio state prison. In addition, former CCA guards said employees were asked to pay a greater share of their health insurance premiums than state employees. There is also anecdotal evidence that CCA's employee retirement plan consisted entirely of company stock. According to Daniel Eshenbaugh, 42, who left CCA and now works at the state-owned supermaximum-security prison, "they [CCA] don't care about the corrections officers, and they don't care about the inmates. Everything there is about money."[11]

The low pay provided by private prison operators does not extend to management and company officers. According to one published report, for example, "the head of ... Wackenhut Corrections, made almost $500,000 in 1997 ... nearly four times the salary of the head of the Federal Bureau of Prisons."[12] In another example, taxpayers helped CCA pay Mike Quinlin, Executive Vice-President and Chief Operating Officer, a salary of $305,846 in 2000.[13] Mr. Quinlin earned an annual salary of $123,100 as director for the Federal Bureau of Prisons before moving to CCA.[14]

Even private prison consultants benefit from the skewed pay structure in the private prison industry. For instance, Charles W. Thomas pocketed a $3 million consulting fee for negotiating a merger involving CCA. The Florida Commission on Ethics later fined Thomas $20,000 for ethics violations stemming from his interest in the private corrections firms he was required to evaluate and regulate. At the time Thomas received the $3 million from CCA, he was earning $80,548 a year as a state employee at the University of Florida in Gainesville.[15] In privatized corrections, corporate executives, insiders and consultants receive exorbitant salaries while the front line prison staffs don't even earn market level wages.

A Green Workforce

There are many reasons why front line experience is an invaluable asset for corrections officers. The most important may be the interpersonal relationships that develop over time between corrections officers and inmates; they are essential for maintaining order in a prison, as well as for aiding inmate rehabilitation. High employee turnover impedes the development of such relationships. It also creates situations where employee naïveté can lead to severe security breaches in a prison.

A high turnover rate also creates a transient workforce. Private prison guards do not see corrections as a profession, but rather as a temporary place of employment until a higher paying job becomes available. These temporary workers have little incentive to deal effectively with the intrinsically dangerous and serious conditions of prison employment.

Constant employee turnover leads to what is known as a 'green' workforce. According to private prison researchers Scott Camp and Gerald Gaes, "the 'greener' the workforce, the more likely there will be lapses in fundamental security procedures. The 'greenness' of the workforce may pertain not only to line staff, but to mid-level supervisory staff as well."[16] Since private prison operators provide low pay and benefits, they tend to have green workforces. The significantly higher rate of employee turnover in a private prison leads to increased violence, riots and security compromises. As Alex Friedmann, a former inmate at a CCA-run facility, put it, "if you have a high turnover you have less stability. New employees come in; they don't know what's going on. That leads to conflicts with inmates."[17]

The Corrections Yearbook provides three years of national data on employee turnover rates for public sector COs and private guards from 1997 to 1999. The data indicates that the turnover rate for private prison guards is about 3 times as high as for public sector corrections officers.[18]

Average Turnover for State COs/Private Cuards

	1997	1998	1999
Public COs	15%	15%	16%
Private guards	41%	41%	53%

Furthermore, there is reason to suspect that turnover in the private prison industry is even higher than the self-reported data for the private companies in the above table. To illustrate:

• State audits and reports routinely show very high turnover rates at privately run prisons. For example, a report of employee turnover in private and public prisons for the calendar year 1999, prepared by the Tennessee Department of Correction Planning and Research, noted that the turnover rates at the CCA operated South Central Correctional Center and Harderman County Correctional Facility were 104.8 percent and 81.7 percent, respectively. Meanwhile, employee turnover for state corrections officers was 34 percent.

• Media reports have chronicled a track record of extremely high turnover in private prisons. For instance, Wackenhut Corrections accumulated a 300 percent turnover rate at its facility in Jena, Louisiana in a one-year period.[19] In a similar case, CCA experienced a 76 percent turnover rate at its Hernando County (Florida) Jail.[20]

• Reporting high turnover is bad for business. For example, in 1997 Genesis Merchant Group Securities lowered its Earnings Per Share[21] estimate for CCA because of its "high employee turnover at new facilities."[22]

Because of high employee turnover, the private prison industry often has to resort to hiring from the "bottom of the barrel." Due to a lack of available information, only anecdotal evidence exists about the industry's hiring practices. There have been enough reported instances, however, to infer a pattern of poor hiring procedures in the private industry. For example, media reports revealed that Cornell Corrections knowingly hired convicted felons to work as guards inside Santa Fe County, New Mexico's juvenile jail.[23] In another instance, a media report noted that CCA violated its contract with the Tulsa County Criminal Justice Authority by not performing background checks on about 40 percent of its employees. The same report also noted that the Tulsa County Commissioner was surprised by the number of jailers working for CCA who had arrest records.[24]

Private prison companies handsomely reward their wardens and executives, but there is growing evidence that high employee turnover also exists in the management ranks. For instance, at its recently closed juvenile facility in Jena, Louisiana, Wackenhut Corrections went through five wardens in one year.[25] In a similar situation, Ohio did not renew its $14.8 million contract with the CiviGenics Corporation of Marlboro, Massachusetts because "the prison had five different wardens in its first 18 months and did not meet minimum staffing levels."[26]

The private mode of operation is structurally flawed because low pay (driven by the profit imperative) leads to high turnover, which ultimately leads to danger in and outside the walls of a private prison. One remedy to this situation was suggested by researchers Camp and Gaes: "given the apparent relationship between staff separations, staff inexperience, and misconduct, private companies must ... increase pay and/or benefits to attract and retain experienced employees."[27]

Chronic Staffing Shortages

The staffing shortages that exist in privatized prisons are partially attributable to the high level of employee turnover. However, published reports suggest that deliberate understaffing is also at fault. For instance, some CCA employees told a news reporter privately that "the company leaves positions open to boost profits."[28] In another example, speaking before a legislative panel in Tennessee, Russell Boraas, the private prison administrator for Virginia, stated that some private prisons in Texas have made up for low reimbursement rates "by leaving positions vacant a little longer than they should."[29] According to *The Corrections Yearbook*, the average inmate-to-corrections officer ratio has historically been higher in privately run facilities and appears to be increasing. [30]

Inmates Per CO

	1997	1998	1999
Public	5.6	5.9	5.6
Private	6.2	6.7	8

Staffing shortages often lead to employees working extra hours, but the pioneers of the private prison industry did not think they would have to resort to employee overtime. Private prison firms do not like to pay overtime because it cuts into their profits. Former CEO of CCA Doc Crants explained the industry's philosophy when he told CNN News, "the real efficiency in operating a prison is to get everyone to come to work everyday, on time, work eight hours, and go home on time."[31] Evidently, Crants mistakenly thought a prison could be run like a corporate business office.

The reality of running a prison for profit turned out to be a different story. For instance, guards at Wackenhut's juvenile prison in Michigan told reporters that they were forced to work long hours—sometimes 70 to 80 hours per week—and that two or three guard posts routinely are left vacant. One day, Wackenhut locked the guards in, refusing to let them leave. Some guards have taken out their frustrations on prisoners, taunting them into fighting.[32]

Perhaps realizing that overtime is unavoidable, private prison firms may be utilizing other methods of reducing overtime costs. For instance, CCA employees at three privately run prisons in Mississippi recently sued the company for failing to pay overtime. The lawsuits "allege CCA required employees to attend meetings off the clock and prohibited workers from clocking out on days when they worked more than eight hours."[33] So much for Crants' original overtime philosophy.

In the final analysis, it seems some companies will do whatever they can to avoid paying overtime, sometimes even at the expense of public safety. For instance, private prison operators will often leave posts unattended rather than pay for overtime coverage. Such a scenario was recently played out at CCA's facilities in southeast Georgia. After ten months in operation, the two prisons failed to meet the state's minimum standards in inmate health care, staffing and security, according to a quarterly audit. The report noted that neither prison had enough guards and some "priority" security posts were not staffed as they should be. No overtime was paid and there was no indication that an effort was made to fill these positions or cover them in any way.[34]

In 1997, an analyst at Genesis Merchant Group Securities gave CCA some simple advice that other firms could also use to address chronic employee understaffing in private prisons: "it [CCA] can lower its operating margin by staffing its facilities with additional guards and support personnel."[35] Judging from the available data, CCA did not follow the advice of its analyst and it is unlikely that other private prison companies would either.

On-the-Job Training

The constant turnover in private prisons makes it difficult to adequately train staff because of the need to quickly fill vacant positions. Thus, employees are often put into dangerous situations without adequate preparation. For instance, according to New Mexico Corrections Secretary Rob Perry, a Wackenhut guard who was killed in a riot was not certified to work as a corrections officer. Five other Wackenhut guards working at the prison were not certified either.[36]

In a similar situation, high turnover caused CCA to hire uncertified prison guards at the Hernando County, Florida jail. According to one media report, approximately 44 percent of the guards were uncertified in 1999. The picture was similar at the Citrus County Jail, also operated by CCA.[37] In yet another example, inspectors for the Georgia Department of Corrections, inspecting a Cornell Companies facility in 1998, found, along with lax security and filthy conditions, non-certified corrections officers patrolling the prison's perimeter. They additionally cited the prison for poor record keeping and inadequate inmate tracking.[38]

The Corrections Yearbook contains data on the amount of pre-service training provided in private prisons; the data is self-reported by the private companies.[39] As the following table indicates, the average amount of pre-service training, which prepares inexperienced employees for work inside a prison, is less in private prisons than in public prisons. The data also shows that the amount of pre-service training in private prisons is decreasing. In contrast, the average amount of pre-service training in public prisons is increasing.

Pre-Service Training Hours

	1997	1998	1999
Public	232	240	250
Private	189	177	149

A staffing shortage can jeopardize an employer's ability to provide adequate pre-service training. Filling vacant positions with unqualified personnel is a dangerous and disturbing practice, but even more alarming is an abundance of evidence that private prison companies *purposely* avoid pre-service training to reduce personnel costs. For instance, former employees at CCA's prison in Youngstown, Ohio told reporters, "the company did not train its employees to use firearms because state certification can cost up to $3,000 a person."[40]

Such cost-cutting practices can have serious consequences. For example, after a 1995 riot at an Immigration and Naturalization Service (INS) detention center under contract with Correctional Services Corporation (formerly, Esmor Correctional Services), the INS found that "poorly trained and abusive guards preyed on immigrants." Their lack of training was evident when the riot began as guards adopted an "every person for himself mentality."[41]

Playing the Market

In an attempt to further reduce labor costs, some private prison companies have given employees company stock for retirement rather than a real pension. Former CEO of CCA, Doc Crants, once proudly told reporters, "the principal difference between CCA and government is that CCA makes every single employee a shareholder after a year through an employee stock ownership plan."[42]

Besides being an inexpensive form of compensation, the CCA stock plan was designed to instill a 'business' mentality into the rank and file. The drive for profit maximization thus moves down from corporate executives into the operating culture of its prisons. As one CCA staff member put it, "being a stockholder yourself ... you make sure you don't waste money on things like cleaning products. Because it's your money you're spending."[43] In reality, however, it is taxpayer dollars that are being spent.

The inherent uncertainty of such a risky 'retirement' plan can negatively affect the staff, as the value of one's retirement could evaporate overnight.[44] Frustration with CCA's stock performance became evident when shareholder litigation resulted from the company's convoluted reorganization into a real estate investment trust in 1999.[45] The following chart plots the tumbling closing share price of CCA stock from 1998 to 2000, when the company announced it would become a real estate investment trust and was later renamed Prison Realty Trust Inc.[46]

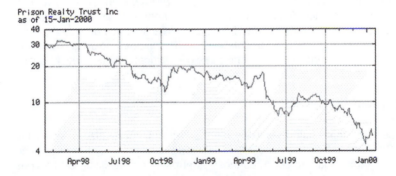

Prison Realty Trust Inc
as of 15-Jan-2000

CCA's stock bottomed at 18 cents per share in December 2000 (unfortunately, not shown in the preceding chart), after trading as high as $44 in 1998.[47] Somewhere along the way, management must have realized that CCA stock wasn't much of a benefit. According to the company's web page, it now offers its employees a retirement plan with more investment options than just CCA stock. Some of the other companies also appear to offer more diverse retirement investment plans as well.

Built-in Savings

The quest to keep staffing levels as low as possible actually begins as early as when the private facility is designed and built. Private companies claim the prisons they build and operate have modern designs, integrating technology more effectively than public prisons. It is no secret that these "advancements" are aimed at reducing labor costs. For example, in describing CCA's approach to constructing a facility in Bay County, Florida, a reporter noted that "it was designed, as are all jails CCA builds, to use as little labor as possible."[48] In another example, media reports describe Canada's first private prison as one that was "built to minimize staff costs." At Utah-based Management & Training Corporation operates the Canadian private prison at Ogden.[49]

Describing the construction of CCA's facility in Lawrenceville, Virginia, the private prison administrator noted that the prison has no guard towers, an "innovation" that saves the company $2.5 million in construction costs and eliminates twenty-five full-time positions.[50] These special designs help keep expenses down, but it is unclear if they help improve the delivery of service. There have been some noteworthy circumstances where private prison designs were flawed. Unfortunately, something terrible must usually occur before these scaled-down designs are thoroughly scrutinized.

CCA and Wackenhut Corrections have built the majority of prisons that are owned and operated by private firms. Both CCA and Wackenhut Corrections have been criticized for severe design flaws. For example, in the most publicized escape from a private prison, CCA's design did not prevent six maximum-security inmates from escaping from the Northeast Ohio Correctional Center in July 1998. Following the escape, CCA was forced to build three guard towers and additional fences around the facility to bring it up to acceptable security standards.[51]

After the death of four inmates and one Wackenhut guard in New Mexico's private prisons, the state reached out to a group of independent prison consultants for help. The consultants faulted Wackenhut for having inadequate and ill-prepared staff.[52] They also faulted Wackenhut's prisons for having ceilings that allowed inmates to hide themselves and weapons. Wackenhut was subsequently forced to make several costly augmentations to its prisons, including replacing ceilings, adding surveillance cameras and putting electrical outlets in every prison cell.[53]

No "Qualified Immunity"

In a decision that could eventually hamper efforts to privatize prisons, the Supreme Court ruled 5-to-4 in June 1997 that workers at privately run prisons do not enjoy the same legal protection as those at publicly run facilities. Corrections officers in the public sector are protected from inmate lawsuits that arise as the result of performing their lawful duties. Called "qualified immunity," this protection is critical for officers, and for all government workers.

Most industry analysts agree that the ruling will increase the cost of prison privatization. Private firms now carry liability insurance. The court's ruling will likely lead to increases in the cost and level of such insurance. Also, the knowledge that private prison employees are not entitled to immunity may spur more prisoners to file lawsuits–and lead to fewer of those suits being dismissed.[54]

Strike Out

State legislatures and courts have determined that a strike by corrections officers is not in the public interest. As a result, public corrections officers are prohibited from striking, as it would present a severe public safety danger. In contrast, private prison guards are covered by federal law–the National Labor Relations Act–which gives them the right to strike. There is little that can be done to prevent strikes by private prison guards because any state legislation to pro- hibit strikes would be federally preempted. In addition, private prison guards cannot be held subject to any existing legal prohibitions against strikes that apply to public employees.

This concern about private prison strikes is not hypothetical. In September 1999, for instance, in Tallulah, Louisiana, Correctional Services Corporation guards walked away from their posts to protest pay and working conditions, which even- tually caused the state to permanently take over the facility.[55] In April of 2001, Cornell prison guards narrowly avoided a strike by settling a contract dispute a day before the prison guards were scheduled to go out on strike in Rhode Is- land.[56]

Yes-In-My-Back-Yard

In economically distressed towns like Youngstown, Ohio, building a private prison has become a form of economic development. The biggest incentive for these towns is the lure of jobs that come with a new private prison. The city of Youngstown and the Mahoning Valley were struggling with the loss of more than 50,000 jobs during the 1970s and 1980s as the area's steel mills closed.[57] Youngstown was desperate for some economic improvement and it bent over backwards to get a CCA prison.

Youngstown, like other towns in America, let a private prison company import inmates into its community from another state. The wages at the privately run Youngstown facility were low and turnover was high, but poor jobs are superior to no jobs, so CCA got little resistance. Even after a rash of inmate stabbings and a major escape, the dangers of operating a prison solely for economic gain were always justifiied by the benefit of job creation.

Private prisons like the one in Youngstown are marketed as "recession proof," but that is not always the case. Excess bed supply and contract cancellations have caused some projects to fail. In Youngstown's case, for instance, more than 500 workers lost their jobs in the summer of 2001, when the facility lost its cus- tomer, the DC Department of Corrections.[58] In a similar scenario, CCA's Tallahatchie County, Mississippi Correctional Facility was forced to lay off approxi- mately 200 employees when it lost its contract in February of 2001.[59]

The above examples demonstrate that private prisons don't necessarily mean a steady source of employment. In many circles, there is growing debate about whether the economic drawbacks of a private prison overshadow the benefits. For instance, taxpayers often have to alter the existing infrastructure to accommo- date a private prison. Another possible consequence was revealed in a recent report by the Institute on Taxation and Economic Policy, a Washington-based research center, which documented the numerous taxpayer subsidies used for private prison projects. According to the authors of the study, "given the relatively low wages paid by the industry and its limited ripple effect on the larger economy ... private prisons may not provide much bang for the buck."[60]

Conclusion

Private corrections is structurally flawed. The profit motive drastically changes the mission of corrections from public safety and rehabilitation to making a quick buck. Chronic employee turnover and understaffing, a high rate of violence, and extreme cost-cutting make the private prison model a recipe for disaster. The conditions that exist within the walls of private prisons put entire communities at peril. The practices of the companies are predictable and their consequences are preventable, but the need to satisfy stockholders and Wall Street analysts preclude the industry from taking effective action.

Endnotes

1. Sheila Wissner, "Study Casts Doubt on CCA Savings," *The Tennessean* (1998).
2. Eric Bates, "Private Prisons," *The Nation* (1998).
3. D. C. McDonald, et al, *Private Prisons in the United States* (1998).
4. Ziva Branstetter and Barbara Hoberock, "When Trouble Strikes Prisons," *Tulsa World* (1999).
5. State of Hawaii, *Briefing Report – Florence Correctional Facility* (2001).
6. Hawaii, like some other states, exports prisoners to private prisons out of state because of prison overcrowding in its own state.
7. Nancy K. Ray, *A Review of the Jena Juvenile Justice Center, Jena, Louisiana* (2000).
8. John L. Clark, *US Department of Justice Report on Northeast Ohio Correctional Center* (1998): November 25.
9. Camille Camp and George Camp, *The Corrections Yearbook* (1998, 1999, 2000).
10. State of Hawaii, *supra* note 5.
11. Mark Tatge, "Employees Criticize Privately Run Prison Guards, Others Leaving, Calling Facility Unsafe," *The Plain Dealer Cleveland* (1998).
12. Peter Carlson, "Getting Behind Bars; In *Atlantic Monthly*, the Prison-Building Boom," *The Washington Post,* 1998.
13. Corrections Corporation of America, *Definitive Proxy Statement* SEC filing (2001), 30 April.
14. Joseph T. Hallinan, "Prison Business Makes Crime Pay," *The Plain Dealer Cleveland,* 1997.
15. "Ethics Fine $20,000 for UF Professor," Knight-Tribune News Service, 1999.
16. Scott D. Camp and Gerald G. Gaes, *Growth and Quality of U.S. Private Prisons* (2001).
17. Eric Bates, "Private Prisons," *supra* note 2.
18. Camille Camp and George Camp, *supra* note 9.
19. Scott Pelley, "Private Prison Comes Under Fire for Abusing Young Inmates," CBS News: 60 Minutes II, 2000.
20. Scott Calvert, "Past Officers Cite Warden For Turnover," *St. Petersburg Times,* 1999.
21. EPS is a measure of financial profitability. It is calculated by dividing net income by the number of shares outstanding.
22. "Genesis Lowers '98 EPS Estimate on Corrections Corporation of America," *PR Newswire,* 1997.
23. "Three Felons Hired as Juvenile Jail Guards," *Associated Press,* 1999.
24. Susan Hylton, "Some Jail Workers Have Prior Arrests CCA Warden Uses Discretion in Hiring Applicants Convicted of Misdemeanors," *Tulsa World* (2001).
25. Scott Pelley, "Private Prison Comes Under Fire" (2000)
26. Kera Ritter, "Utah-Based Firm May Run Low-Security Grafton Prison," *The Plain Dealer Cleveland* (2001).
27. Scott D. Camp and Gerald G. Gaes, *Growth and Quality of U.S. Private Prisons, supra* note 16.
28. Eric Bates, "Private Prisons," *supra* note 2.
29. *Id.*
30. Camille Camp and George Camp, *supra* note 9.
31. Donald van de Mark, "CEO of Corrections Corporation of America (CCA)" CNNfn: Entrepreneurs Only, 1999.
32. Ken Kolker, "Short Staffing, Long Hours Create Danger, Guards Say," *The Grand Rapids Press,* 2000.
33. "Overtime Pay Questioned in Lawsuit for Workers at Three CCA Facilities," *Associated Press*

Newswires, 2001.

34. Rhonda Cook, "Audit Blasts Private Prison Management 'Indifference': State Finds Faulty Conditions at Two Southeast Georgia Prisons" (1999).

35. "Genesis Lowers '98 EPS Estimate" (1997).

36. "Guard Not Certified to Work in Prison," *Associated Press,* 1999.

37. Scott Calvert, "Past Officers Cite Warden For Turnover" (1999).

38. Greg Burton, "Firm Not Guarded About Prison Profits," *The Salt Lake Tribune,* 1999.

39. Camille Camp and George Camp, *supra* note 9.

40. "Former Employees Say State's Only Private Prison Unsafe," *Associated Press,* 1998.

41. John M. Goshko, "INS Blames Riot On Mismanagement By Contractor At New Jersey," *The Washington Post,* 1995; Ashley Dunn, "U.S. Inquiry Finds Detention Center Poorly Run," *New York Times,* 1995.

42. Laurel Campbell, "Privatized Prisons: Keying In On Costs Has Lock On 8 Tennessee Facilities," *The Commercial Appeal Memphis, TN* (1997).

43. Eric Bates, "Private Prisons," *supra* note 2.

44. A similar situation was recently illustrated with the Enron Corporation

45. "Judge OKs Settlement of CCA Lawsuits," *Associated Press,* (2001).

46. <http://finance.yahoo.com>.

47. Peter Slevin, "Private Prisons Finding Out That Crime Doesn't Pay," *The Baton Rouge Sunday Advocate,* 2001.

48. Erik Larson, "Captive Company, Customer Service, Quality Control, Employee Morale" (1998).

49. John Lorinc, "Profits & Convicts: It's About Saving Money. No, It's About Doing a Better Job on Rehabilitation. That's Only One of the Contradictions as Ontario Makes its Pitch for Prisons-for-Profit," *The Globe and Mail,* 2001.

50. Eric Bates, "Private Prisons," *supra* note 2.

51. Amy Beth Graves, "Private Prison Shows Off New Security Measure," *Associated Press,* 1998.

52. James McNair, "Wackenhut Corrections A Prisoner of Its Own Problems," *The Miami Herald,* 2000.

53. Loie Fecteau, "Study Calls For Prison Pact Changes, Albuquerque Journal, 2000.

54. "Immunity from Suits Is Withheld for Guards in Privately Run Jails," *New York Times,* June 1977; "Private-Prison Guards Remain Prey to Lawsuits," *The (Memphis, Tenn.) Commercial Appeal,* June 1977.

55. David Jackson, "Broken Teens Left in Wake of Private Gain," *Chicago Tribune,* 1999.

56. "Correctional Officers at Central Falls Jail Threaten to Strike," *Associated Press Newswires,* 2001.

57. "Warden Anticipates Private Prison Will Be Used Again," *Associated Press,* 2001.

58. *Id.*

59. "Inmate Shift Means 208 Face Layoffs At CCA'S Prison in Tallahatchie," *The Commercial Appeal,* 2001.

60. Gina Holland, "Private Prisons Don't Pay, Report Says," *The Philadelphia Inquirer,* 2001.

CHAPTER THIRTEEN

"Get Tough" Efficiency: Human Rights, Correctional Restructuring and Prison Privatization in Ontario, Canada

Dawn Moore, Kellie Leclerc Burton and
Kelly Hannah-Moffat

Introduction

Since the mid-1990s, the Ontario government's penal rhetoric and policy reforms have shamelessly promoted a conservative agenda that advocates getting tough on crime within a broader framework of fiscal responsibility. 'Get tough' efficiency introduces super-jails, the demise of parole, the elimination of programming and the privatization of penal facilities. These shifts in how punishment is imagined and carried out in this province raise real and pressing concerns about justice and the basic human rights of those incarcerated. These concerns are especially distressing in Canada, a nation often praised for its attention to and respect for human rights, both within its borders and abroad, and internationally regarded as one of the more progressive countries with respect to the treatment of prisoners. While punishment in Canada, specifically at the federal level, has consistently de-emphasized punitiveness, centering instead on affirming the importance of rehabilitation and reintegration, the politics of punishment in the province of Ontario has moved in a different direction.

Recent changes in Ontario must be considered in their entirety in order to fully understand the potential threats to human rights we face. These changes, however, are very much in their infancy. It is an evolving task to write about actual infringements of the human rights of prisoners in Ontario, especially of those incarcerated in privately run institutions. Our purpose, then, is to consider the potential for human rights abuses as we move further along the trajectory of implementing these regressive policies.

We begin with a brief overview of punishment in Canada. Our goal here is to survey various new initiatives underway in other Canadian penal jurisdictions in an effort to provide context for the changes in question in Ontario. We then move on to explore the situation in Ontario, focusing on issues around privatization of penal institutions and emerging changes in the day-to-day conditions in provincial prisons and detention centers. We seek to understand these changes in the context of existing Canadian and international human rights mandates and guidelines pertaining to the treatment of prisoners.

Penal Practices in Canada

The international acclaim Canada enjoys in punishment arenas arises mainly out of its federal corrections system.[1] Unlike the 'get tough' trend evident in Ontario, the Correctional Service of Canada (CSC) rhetoric privileges rehabilitation and respect for diversity of incarcerated populations.[2] This orientation is congruent with a more general, liberal welfare mentality that is still used to characterize the Canadian state. The Corrections and Conditional Release Act (CCRA) (which governs federal correctional policy) clearly defines the purpose and principles of the CSC. This act explicitly and formally protects the human rights and dignities of those incarcerated in Canadian federal prisons. Sections 3 and 4 of the CCRA define the legal obligations of the CSC with respect to the confinement of prisoners:

> 3b) The purpose of the federal correctional system is to contribute to the maintenance of a just, peaceful and safe society by assisting the rehabilitation of offenders and their reintegration into the community as law-abiding citizens through the provision of programs in penitentiaries and in the community.

> 4c) That the Service use the least restrictive measures consistent with the protection of the public, staff members and offenders;

> 4d) That offenders retain the rights and privileges of all members of society, except those rights and privileges that are necessarily removed or restricted as a consequence of the sentence.[3]

Later sections of the CCRA define the roles and responsibilities of the Office of the Correctional Investigator, who is mandated to

> ... conduct investigations into problems of offenders related to decisions, recommendations, acts or omissions of the Commissioner [of Corrections] or any person under the control or management of, or performing services for or on behalf of, the Commissioner, that affect offenders either individually or as a group.[4]

Despite concerns about the practical implications of these ideals (see endnote 2), the program of punishment and incarceration at the federal level includes an official commitment to the rehabilitation and timely reintegration of the prisoner and maintenance of his/her rights in the least restrictive fashion. The CCRA also discusses the duty to 'act fairly' with respect to correctional decisions and correctional policies and practices. In accordance with the law, the CSC, under s. 4h of the CCRA, is expected to "... respect gender, ethnic, cultural and linguistic differences and be responsive to the special needs of women and aboriginal peoples, as well as to the needs of other groups of offenders with special requirements."[5] Any contravention of the CCRA can be directed to the office of the Correctional Investigator for resolution.[6]

Each provincial jurisdiction, conversely, is free to decide its own penal laws and policies.[7] Thus, each governing body has a great deal of leverage in determining the conditions under which an individual will experience punishment in a given jurisdiction. Governing bodies such as the Ontario Ministry of Correctional Services (OMCS) set policy on virtually every aspect of punishment including conditions of confinement, parole eligibility, rehabilitative programming and, of course, the contracting out of services.

Some provinces, most notably New Brunswick, evoke welfarist mentalities similar to those espoused by the CSC. New Brunswick has chosen to make changes to its penal policies that are in direct opposition to those taking place in Ontario. New Brunswick is now working in accord with the CSC and has adopted a firm policy of using incarceration only as a last option for punishment. The New Brunswick government claims that, as a direct result of this policy, the province has succeeded in significantly reducing its prisoner population. Where New Brunswick once had one of the highest rates of incarceration in the nation, it now ranks among the lowest.[8] Using much of the CSC's community programming, New Brunswick now has a heavy emphasis on community-based rehabilitation of those in conflict with the law. Interestingly, in early attempts to reorganize their correctional system, the government of New Brunswick proposed privatizing a youth correctional facility. The initiative met with such strong public opposition, however, that while Wackenhut was able to build the facility, the government decided to maintain public control over the new youth center.[9]

The government of Nova Scotia has also begun to revamp its system of incarceration. In 1995, they adopted a 'Co-operative Business Solutions' approach to their problems of overcrowding in a quickly decaying system. In 1996, the Nova Scotia government released a Call for Proposals to 'modernize' the system. This correctional overhaul included the construction of new prisons, the provision of programming for those incarcerated and the amelioration of working conditions of penal staff, all within strict budgetary confines.[10] As in New Brunswick, privatization was tabled but met with local resistance. The government has since abandoned plans to privatize.

British Columbia has just experienced a change in political leadership, from a labor-oriented NDP government[11] to a right-wing Liberal government. This new government's representatives suggest that the privatization of penal facilities in that province is not an impossibility, although, as yet, no plans have been made. Governments in other provinces have distinctly disavowed the possibility of privatizing prisons. Alberta, Manitoba and Saskatchewan have all reaffirmed their decisions to keep prisons under public control in their respective jurisdictions.

In 1995, the Progressive Conservative party came to power in Ontario under Mike Harris. Harris' campaign platform promised a 'common sense revolution' that would reorganize the ways in which virtually all aspects of governing were carried out in the province. In terms of punishment, the common sense revolution has combined neoliberalism with neoconservativism,[12] resulting in rhetoric of 'correctional renewal', promising fiscal responsibility at one end and the 'toughening' of the system on the other. The presence of this salient rhetoric within corrections in Ontario has facilitated the introduction of a bi-directional approach to corrections that simultaneously seeks to be both punitive and cost-effective. In practice, this has resulted in the introduction of several new initiatives in the penal system, including privatization. In their entirety, these changes raise real concerns about the rights of those incarcerated in Ontario.

Capitalizing on the Pains of Imprisonment: Ontario's Correctional 'Renewal'

Correctional renewal in Ontario marks a drastic departure from the ways in which punishment was previously imagined in the province.[13] Punishment now is organized around a mantra of 'get tough' efficiency that promises to cut the costs of punishment while offering more austere conditions for those incarcerated. While we can only hope that a schism will emerge between rhetoric and reality, much of this new ideology appears to be filtering down into the day-to-day practices of punishment in Ontario, creating real concerns about the welfare of prisoners.

What we are seeing now is an Americanization of the penal system, which draws on a now all-too-common set of themes including harsher sentences, the increased use of imprisonment, 'truth in sentencing', the decreased use of parole, austere and 'super-max' prisons, the revival of chain gangs, community notification laws and zero tolerance policies.[14] In effect, Ontario has abandoned the post-war notion of prison *as* punishment in favor of the more archaic and disavowed idea of prison *for* punishment.[15] This, despite the fact that this premise has been formally discredited in international human rights provisions such as the UN Minimum Standards for the Treatment of Prisoners, which explicitly states, "[t]he suffering that results from the loss of liberty and freedom by the fact of incarceration is punishment enough."

The correctional policies introduced by the Conservative government in 1996 were justified on the basis that they would create a 'modernized' correctional system. The slogan of creating 'safe, secure, efficient and effective' corrections with 'no frills'[16] is often evoked in public discourses to gather support for tougher and more austere penal conditions. One of the most significant initiatives currently underway is the Adult Infrastructure Renewal Project (AIRP).[17] This project, legitimated by corresponding claims about the need for improvements to the current 'decaying and inefficient system,' plans to close approximately 20 correctional facilities, detention centers and jails; to expand and 'modernize' the remaining facilities and to build two new prisons.

1) Punishment without Conviction: Detention Centers

Significant changes taking place in Ontario's detention centers are raising questions about the disregard for prisoners' human rights. In 1997, as part of the mandate to develop a 'no frills,' efficient system of punishment, the Conservative government cut virtually all programming in detention centers. Where prisoners used to have access to recreational, life skills, educational and social work-related programming, now all but those deemed to have 'special needs' have extremely limited access to programs. Those programs that are accessible to prisoners are almost exclusively offered by volunteers. Consequently, inmates remain locked in their cells from 16 to 23.5 hours a day and have no access to existing facilities within the detention centers. Recreation consists of a legislatively mandated 20 minutes of outdoor time that takes place without the benefit of basic equipment or recreation officers. Time out of cells is spent on units with minimal facilities and little to occupy prisoners. As a result of these changes, including the ban on smoking in 2000, the detention centers' overall safety and security has been compromised as boredom, extended exposure to less-than-favorable living conditions (including, in many instances, triple bunking and vermin infestations) and unassisted 'cold turkey' withdrawal from nicotine take their toll.[18]

Another result of the 'get tough' campaign is the retrofit of existing, now decommissioned gymnasiums into dormitories for additional prisoners serving intermittent sentences. Correctional officials have raised concerns about the possible negative impact of these retrofitted areas on inmate and staff safety, as visual obstructions are likely, making living in and patrolling these areas potentially dangerous.[19]

Correctional renewal in Ontario further dictates changes in the day-to-day operations of Ontario's prisons. Prisoners are expected to participate in work programs that offer no opportunity to gain marketable skills (like picking up trash by the side of the highway); they are stripped of personal effects upon admission; their hair is cut; they are made to wear bright orange prison issue jumpsuits in public (*i.e.,* to outside medical and dental appointments) and they are subject to random drug-testing. Inmates hoping for release face a much more restricted parole policy and increased community surveillance. These changes run contrary to the UN's Standard Minimum Rules (SMRs), which clearly detail the intended objective of punishment:

> The purpose and justification of a sentence of imprisonment or a similar measure deprivative of liberty is ultimately to protect society against crime. This end can only be achieved if the period of imprisonment is used to ensure, so far as possible, that upon his return to society the offender is not only willing but able to lead a law-abiding and self-supporting life.[20]

The United Nations mandates that punishment be forward-looking through offering developmental opportunities, especially to those incarcerated. Ontario has clearly disavowed these directives, devising instead a penal system that not only fails to offer real rehabilitative or developmental opportunities, but also subscribes to a method of punishment that serves only to amplify the dehumanizing and demoralizing effects of incarceration.

2) Generic 'Super-Jails': The 'New' Correctional Centers

Through the AIRP, Ontario has witnessed a surge in prison construction. The Maplehurst Correctional Centre near Milton was retrofitted and underwent massive expansions while two entirely new prisons have been constructed: the Central North Correctional Centre in Penetanguishene and a similar one in Lindsay. One of the main concerns about the new prisons is the move toward the 'super-jail'[21] design and pursuant operational strategies. Each of these two new maximum-security facilities (in Penetanguishene and Lindsay) are designed as clustered panoptic pods. Inside each pod, 192 prisoners are housed together. There are six identical pods in each prison, holding in total approximately 1,200 people. Each pod also holds its own admissions and discharge facilities, visiting room, programming rooms and 'recreation' area.[22]

These prisons allow for optimal visual surveillance with minimal staff. One or two guards are stationed in a central control tower from which all of the areas are either clearly visible or monitored by closed-circuit video surveillance. All doors are controlled from the tower, eliminating the need to have guards patrolling ranges or manage prisoner movement through keyed doors. This structure also minimizes 'front line' contact between prisoners and guards, which may compromise the therapeutic effect that prisoner-guard relations can have on prisoners, especially vulnerable populations like the self-injurious or suicidal, who can benefit from positive relationships with staff.[23] The elimination of prisoner/ guard interaction can serve to further dehumanize incarcerated men and women within these large institutions as they are denied the (albeit at times cold) comfort of contact with those connected to the 'outside'. This move away from individualizing prisoners and facilitating human interaction compromises both safety and the notion of 'humane' confinement.

In addition to the construction of the new prisons at Penetanguishene and Lindsay, 1,969 beds are being added to four different provincial correctional facilities, transforming one of them (Maplehurst) into a 1,500 bed 'mega-jail'. These beds are intended to compensate for the closure of approximately 20 smaller local jails and prisons in various locations across Ontario. The provincial government's move towards centralized and homogeneous mega-prisons replacing smaller institutions dispersed across the province dismisses earlier correctional trends towards gender and cultural sensitivity.

Women incarcerated in Ontario prisons will be housed in separate units within larger male facilities at Maplehurst and Thunder Bay correctional centers. This centralization and co-location of women's corrections within the larger men's institutions is in direct opposition to the federal government's approach to women's imprisonment, which supports the development of gender and culturally sensitive custodial models. This initiative fails on all counts to even remotely reflect the principles of the Women's Issues Task Force report[24] which emphasized the importance of smaller localized institutions and more personalized programming for incarcerated women. An essential part of the progression of women's federal imprisonment was the assertion that large, high-security, depersonalized institutions were not necessary or appropriate for women.

The new provincial units require women to be housed on ranges in cells with solid doors with small meal slots. There are minimal provisions for recreation beyond a small, enclosed concrete patio. This is contrasted with the current provincial women's institution in Brampton (slated to be transformed into a boot camp for young offenders) in which women are housed in cottage-style units with large facilities for recreation and programming. Because of the outcry by advocates for imprisoned women, the female unit at Maplehurst has a slightly different design and has been able to access more programming and social services than the male unit. However, these small victories have been compromised by a shortsighted backlash from men's corrections, which perceives female inmates as being treated preferentially and being given better services. With such a dearth of services and facilities beyond the absolute basics, advocates for male and female prisoners find themselves competing for basic human comforts, to the detriment of all prisoners.

The UN's guiding principles for prisoners under sentence, as outlined in the SMRs, clearly state that:

> Imprisonment and other measures which result in cutting off an offender from the outside world are afflictive by the very fact of taking from the person the right of self-determination by depriving him of his liberty. Therefore the prison system shall not, except as incidental to justifiable segregation or the maintenance of discipline, aggravate the suffering inherent in such a situation.[25]

Many of the changes being adopted by Ontario's Ministry of Correctional Services clearly compromise these guidelines. The new super-jails present grave concerns for both women and men in terms of geographic dislocation, as the jails are all located in small rural communities that are at least a half hour from any urban center, and the availability of public transportation to these sites is limited if it exists at all. The remoteness of the jails raises a number of concerns: access to legal counsel; access to court and the increased use of video testimony; access to families, particularly children; availability of and access to volunteers and limited opportunities for reintegration/release planning. For women, incarceration in these institutions heralds a return to the days of the Prison for Women (P4W)[26], when federally sentenced women might not see children and family for extended periods due to long distances and limited economic resources for travel. While this geographic dislocation was not the only reason for the demise of P4W, it was a significant contributor to the acute pains of imprisonment experienced by the women held at this institution.[27]

Access to volunteers is also an important service that inmates will lose by being housed in a remote location. Programs operated by Alcoholics Anonymous and other volunteer-run groups are increasingly the only services offered to prisoners and often the only community support these individuals have. Through contact with volunteers, prisoners are able to form relationships that can assist their reintegration into society. This is especially crucial given that volunteer groups offer important community-based services, (*i.e.* housing and relapse prevention) that can impact a prisoner's ability to form workable release plans and impact post-release success. These essential support-building activities are lost if volunteers cannot reach the inmates because they are too far away.

The super-jails are similarly insensitive to the needs of minority inmates. Countering the so-called 'club fed' approach,[28] the provincial super-jails do not allow space for the construction of sweat lodges or other services and sites of spiritual importance to a significant number of (particularly Aboriginal) inmates. The fundamental right to practice one's religion and participate in spiritual life is severely compromised by this lack of access and concern for the spiritual needs of provincial inmates. These omissions run contrary to the CCRA and the UN SMRs that state "[s]o far as practicable, every prisoner shall be allowed to satisfy the needs of his religious life by attending the services provided in the institution."[29] While the construction of a sweat lodge or other site of spiritual importance may be deemed 'unpracticable', in the past precedents have been set for attempting to accommodate various spiritual needs within the institution. The Ontario Correctional Institute (slated for closure under the AIRP) provides the Native Sons their own separate and private space in which to conduct spiritual practices. Current reforms allow for no such bid to accommodate differential needs.

3) Punishing for Profit

Perhaps one of the Harris government's most contentious initiatives with regard to the plan for correctional change is the privatization of one of the super-jails, the newly constructed Central North Correctional Centre in Penetanguishene, Ontario. The move to privatize the prison was not initially a central component of the government's efficiency agenda. In 1998, then Minister of Corrections Bob Runciman expressed strong reservations about the possible privatization of correctional facilities (largely based on experiences of privatization in other jurisdictions see below), assuring that the new correctional facilities (then in early stages of construction) would *not* be privately run. One year later, under the new corrections minister Rob Sampson, these original concerns were disregarded and plans for privatizing the Penetanguishene site were well under way.

In other international correctional jurisdictions, privatization has been related to deficiencies and inadequacies in correctional care.[30] In the United States, the incidents at Youngstown are well documented and serve as a cautionary tale for governments that seek fiscal efficiency through privatization of their correctional facilities.[31] In an open letter to Mike Harris,[32] Ohio State Senator Robert Hagan counseled:

> Ohio's experiences with private prisons has been to date eventful yet wholly regrettable. Given my district's history with private prisons and reports of similar events at other private prisons in the United States, I would respectfully urge you to reconsider your position on the construction of a private prison in the Province of Ontario.

Likely because of the ample and well-substantiated concerns that have been raised about the effects of privatization in the United States over the last few years, the Conservative government has exercised extreme caution, avoiding any concrete long-term or intractable commitment to further privatization of adult facilities. Instead, it initially proposed a five-year study of privatization, using Penetanguishene as the test site. The second super-jail, recently completed in Lindsay, is meant to act as a control in this experiment, mirroring Penetanguishene in every way with the one exception that Lindsay, for now, remains under public control. Upon completion of the study, a decision will be made to either return Penetanguishene to public control or, presumably, to privatize Lindsay and then other facilities. Despite this initial five-year plan and the fact that the study has yet to begin, Corrections Minister Sampson admits that he (and presumably the province) has prejudged the outcome and there are already preemptive plans to privatize another adult prison and several youth facilities.[33]

The Central North Correctional Center began taking prisoners on 10 November 2001. We completed writing this article two weeks later. In that extremely brief period of time, there have already been incidents that have raised concerns about the quality of care that Management and Training Corporation (MTC) (the private corporation currently holding the contract for operating the facility) has been providing to the 68 inmates who are the first to be held in the super-jail. Troubling incidents include a lack of coats for inmates to wear outside, lack of heat in the building, no extra blankets and staff who refuse to take messages for prisoners, even when calls have been described as "urgent and personal."[34] At some points since the jail opened, the phones have not been answered at all.[35]

Perhaps inevitably, prisoners held in Penetanguishene have reportedly gone on hunger strikes to protest these conditions, and 20 of the 68 incarcerated there rioted on 18 November 2001, causing damage to plumbing. A 'riot team,' presumably made up of external forces (perhaps the Ontario Provincial Police, although this remains under investigation) extracted the inmates involved and placed them in punitive segregation as a result of the alleged 'disturbances'. If these incidents are an indication of the future of Penetanguishene, fears about the consequences of privatization and its expansion are obviously well warranted.

Conclusion: In Pursuit of Human Rights

In her findings in the *Report of the Commission for Inquiry into Certain Events at the Prison for Women* (Arbour Report), Madame Justice Louise Arbour states,

One must resist the temptation to trivialize prisoners' rights as either an insignificant infringement of rights, or as an infringement of rights of people who do not deserve better. When law grants a right, it is no less important that such a right be respected because the person entitled to it is a prisoner.[36]

She continues on to highlight the ultimate vulnerability of prisoners, suggesting that it is precisely because of their disempowered status that their rights must be most vigorously protected. These statements underscore the importance of limiting the state's right to punish and ensuring that punishments conform to the rule of law.

In the aftermath of the Arbour Commission, prisoners' rights enjoyed a brief moment in the Canadian public spotlight. Predictably, public interest has since waned. This, coupled with an emerging and uncharacteristic quest for punitive 'justice' in Ontario, has created a system of blanket neglect of basic human rights and dignities with regard to prisoners. This indifference is made more acute given the context of profit-making and cost-cutting in which these changes occur. Although it seems trite to reach the conclusion that things will get worse before they get better, it is reasonable to forecast that, in Ontario, this is most likely the case. This prediction becomes an even greater inevitability when we consider that, in less than two weeks of operation, questionable human rights practices are already emerging from Penetanguishene. This, coupled with concerning broader changes in the punishment system that is becoming increasingly harsh, austere and vengeance-oriented, places Ontario on what seems to be a perilous trajectory.

Epilogue

In late September of 2002, reports of a riot at Penetang surfaced. While the riot was alleged to have included over 100 prisoners, it gained almost no media attention. When questioned about these events, ministry officials indicated that, because the institution is privately run, they had very little knowledge of what had occurred. This solidifies ongoing concerns about the lack of accountability within a privatized regime.

Endnotes

1. While Canadian law only allows for a singular, national Criminal Code, the task of carrying out punishment is divided amongst the provinces and the federal government. Thus, anyone given a sentence of two years or more is remanded to the federal penitentiary system. Anyone serving less than two years or probation enters into provincial custody.
2. This is not to suggest that CSC is without its blemishes or critics. Many argue that CSC has merely paid lip service to prisoner's rights, especially to the concerns of women and minorities. Further, its emphasis on rehabilitation raises yet another set of questions about human rights, particularly concerning intensive, state-enforced treatments and psychiatric interventions (See: Canada 1996; Culhane 1979; Hannah-Moffat 1991, 1995, 2001; Jackson 1988; Kendall 2000; Kolb 1983; Monture-Angus 1999).
3. Corrections and Conditional Release Act (1992: c. 20)
4. Correctional Investigator, *Annual Report of the Correctional Investigator, 1996-1997* Ottawa: Ministry of Public Works and Government Services, 1997): 5.
5. Corrections and Conditional Release Act, *supra* note 3.
6. Concerns have also been raised about the actual efficacy and resolutionary power of this position. See Kelly Hannah-Moffat, "Prisoners' Rights in the Canadian Correctional System" (2000).
7. This does not, however, mean that either provincial or federal jurisdictions are granted carte blanche with respect to devising penal policies. Canada's Constitution includes the Charter of Rights and Freedoms, which has ultimate legal authority in that all subsidiary laws must conform to its basic principles. The legal rights outlined in section 7 that among other things guarantee protection from cruel

and unusual punishments and unlawful detention, are particularly relevant to prisoners.

8. New Brunswick Department of Public Safety, *Achieving a Balance* (1999).

9. Robbie O'Neil, New Brunswick Department of Public Safety, personal communication with author(s).

10. Fred Hornsberger, "Nova Scotia Custody Configuration Project" (1998).

11. In general, there are three main provincial political parties in Canada. From right to left of the political spectrum they are: the Progressive Conservative Party, the Liberal Party and the New Democratic Party (NDP).

12. This trend is in keeping with broader penal trends that Pat O'Malley has termed the 'New Right Penality'. Pat O'Malley, "Volatile and Contradictory Punishments" (1999): 175-196.

13. From the 1970s until this change in government, punishment in Ontario followed an agenda of decarceration with a heavy emphasis on rehabilitation and community reintegration. Maeve McMahon, *The Persistent Prison? Rethinking Decarceration and Penal Reform* (1992); Dawn Moore & Kelly Hannah-Moffat, "Correctional Renewal Without the Frills" (*forthcoming*).

14. David Garland, *Punishment and Modern Society: A Study in Social Theory* (1990).

15. This distinction was clearly made by the Arbor Commission in 1996. Arbour argued that individuals are sentenced to a period of imprisonment as punishment. Engaging in amplified punitive practices (i.e. austere settings, corporal punishment, denial of rights, dignitiy etc.) with those already confined oversteps the boundaries of the sanction set out by the court.

16. This slogan abounds on the ministry's web site, as well as on all their publications and press releases.

17. Ontario Ministry of Correctional Services (OMCS), "Modernization of Jails Puts Public Safety First" (Elizabethtown Township, 2000), 5 May.

18. Barry Scanlon, Ontario Public Service Employees Union, personal communication with author(s).

19. *Id.*

20. United Nations, Standard Minimum Rules for the Treatment of Prisoners A/CONF/611, E/3048 (1957), E/5988 (1977).

21. This is a euphemistic term used to describe the overwhelming size and warehousing mentality of these prisons.

22. Ontario Ministry of Correctional Services. "Modernization of Jails Puts Public Safety First."

23. Correctional Service of Canada, "National Strategy for the Prevention of Suicide and the Reduction of Self-Injury" (1992); Hayes, L., *Prison Suicide: An Overview* (1995).

24. Women's Issues Task Force, *Women's Voices, Women's Choices: Report of the Women's Issues Task Force* (1995).

25. United Nations, Standard Minimum Rules, *supra* note 20 at Part II A, Section 57.

26. Until 1996, The Prison for Women in Kingston, Ontario, was the only federal institution for women in Canada. Women held at P4W were often thousands of kilometers from children, families and other support systems.

27. Canada, *Commission of Inquiry into Certain Events at the Prison for Women in Kingston* (1996).

28. The provincial Conservative government often juxtaposes itself with the federal so-called 'club fed' approach to punishment. Largely targeting the federal government's rehabilitative mandate, the Ontario government sees federal prisons as country clubs that coddle rather than punish.

29. United Nations, Standard Minimum Rules, *supra* note 20 at Part I, Section 42.

30. Stephen Nathan, *Private Adult Correctional Facilities: Fines, Failures and Dubious Practices*. (Toronto: Ontario Public Services Employees Union, 2000) <http://www.opseu.org/ops/ministry/report/section7.htm>.

31. The private prison in Youngstown, Ohio, is now regularly held up as a concrete example of the reasons why privatization should be approached with caution. Within its first year of operation, there were inmate stabbings and two prisoner murders. Inmates were teargassed by under-trained staff and six prisoners escaped and were eventually recaptured. Office of the Corrections Trustee for the District of Columbia, *Report to the Attorney General: Inspection and Review of the Northeast Ohio Correctional Center* (1998).

32. Dated February29, 2000.

33. John Lorine, "Profits and Convicts," *The Globe and Mail - Report on Business*, 28 September 2000.

34. Ontario Public Service Employees' Union (OPSEU), *Lock Talk: A Publication of the OPSEU Corrections Campaign* (2001), 23 November. According to the OPSEU report, the MTC staff apparently solved the coat problem by traveling to the local publicly run jail and taking some coats from that facility, as well as bulletproof vests and an OMCS van.

35. *Id.* Interestingly enough, OPSEU, the guard's union in Ontario, has been the most vigilant voice of dissent in the privatization scheme, seeking to illuminate the shortcomings of non-unionized labor practices and their impact on correctional practices. This illustrates a disturbing absence of traditional advocates in the debate. The John Howard Society is the only prisoners' advocacy group in Canada that has offered any resistance on the issue of prison privatization or correctional restructuring more generally. See John Howard Society (JHS)–Ontario. *Fact Sheet # 15 - The Changing Face of Ontario Corrections: An Assessment*. (Toronto, 2000).

36. Canada, *Commission of Inquiry, supra* note 27 at 183.

CHAPTER FOURTEEN

Prison Privatization
in the United Kingdom

Stephen Nathan

It is ten years since the first privately managed prison opened in the United Kingdom. This article provides a brief overview of how the UK has progressed from implementing one experimental prison management contract to having Europe's most privatized criminal justice system. Along the way it has contributed to the expansion of a multi-million dollar industry which is developing a long term stake in criminal justice systems throughout the world. The article also briefly profiles the role of one of the pioneering American prison companies, Corrections Corporation of America and its former British joint venture, UK Detention Services Ltd.

Introduction

Since the 1970s, there had been privately managed immigration detention centers in England, and an even longer modern history of private companies as well as not for profit agencies providing services within the criminal justice system. These experiences had proved largely non-controversial.

The implementation of prison privatization[1] in the UK, however, was an ideological step rather than anything to do with best criminal justice practice. The policy was revived and promoted in 1984 by the right-wing think tank, the Adam Smith Institute (ASI), which based its arguments on free market theory and the recent developments in the United States. The ASI suggested that the UK should privatize the building and running of prisons on the grounds that

> it would overcome both the spiralling costs of the prison system and the shortage of places by using innovative managerial and technological methods and by concentrating resources on capital investment rather than increased labour costs.[2]

Although shunned initially by the then Conservative government, the policy soon found favor. As one former cabinet minister in the Thatcher government confirms:

> [M]ost Thatcherites and many others in the Conservative party became as blindly dogmatic in their zeal to privatize everything in sight—even prisons—as had been the left wing socialists

of old to sweep all the major private industries into the state sector.[3]

There is no question that by 1986/87 the prison system in England and Wales was in need of an overhaul, not least since the prisoner population had reached record levels at nearly 51,000. Nevertheless, the former minister's analysis is not wholly correct: the reason for the state's nationalization of regional and local prisons over 100 years before was due to the abject failure of private provision.[4]

The Early Years

In 1986, the parliamentary Select Committee on Home Affairs examined the state and use of prisons in England and Wales. Its terms of reference included the ability to visit other countries as "we have been concerned with the possible applications to England and Wales of the penal reforms of other countries."[5] Although the committee had every country of the world at its disposal, the only trip they made was to the United States in October 1986. Their remit did not specifically include the examination of privatization yet the itinerary included "visits to two establishments run by the Corrections Corporation of America (CCA)." The committee did not report "how CCA came to have the necessary contacts to arrange this with the clerks who service the committee…"[6]

Members of the committee also visited two facilities run by the Radio Corporation of America, but it was CCA that impressed to the extent that, in its subsequent report, the committee relied heavily on what CCA had told them about privatization, taking at face value the assertion that this system of provision in the United States was now "a proven concept".[7] The committee stated that the principal advantages of contract provision of penal establishments were: 1) that it relieves the taxpayer of the immediate burden of having to pay for their initial capital cost; 2) it dramatically accelerates their building; and 3) it produces greatly enhanced architectural efficiency and excellence. The committee concluded that

> …the Home Office should, as an experiment, enable private sector companies to tender for the construction and management of custodial institutions. Such contracts should contain standards and requirements and failure to meet them would be grounds for the Government's terminating a contract. The standards should be made legally enforceable against contractors. We also recommend that tenders should be invited in particular for the construction and management of new remand centers, because it is there that the worst overcrowding in the prison system is concentrated.[8]

It is important to note that, although the policy was deemed an experiment, no recommendations were made as to how extensive that experiment might be, no time frame was set, and no evaluation process was prescribed. Nor were any of these conditions found in the eventual enabling legislation, the Criminal Justice Act, 1991, but Angela Rumbold, then prisons minister, said that "[i]f, and only if, the contracted-out remand centre proves to be a success might we move towards privatization of other parts of the prison service."[9] In January 1992, she told the *Financial Times* that she was "going to take it step by step so that we can test it properly."[10] Both of these statements turned out to be false.

Following a tendering process in which the public sector was barred from participating, a European security firm, Group 4, was awarded a contract to manage Wolds, a newly constructed 320-bed prison for unsentenced male prisoners. The prison had previously been earmarked for public management. Wolds opened on 6 April 1992, and even before it had taken its first prisoners, the government had made plans to contract out the management of two more facilities which would hold sentenced prisoners.[11]

On 3 February 1993, as if to signal the government's long term intentions, the application of the Criminal Justice Act, 1991, was extended from new prisons to existing facilities. The 'step by step' strategy was ignored even though there were indicators that all was not well at Wolds. In April 1993, a report by the Prison Reform Trust on Wolds' first year of operation concluded the following:

> We discovered many things which were positive but others which were not. We must therefore conclude that rather than the unqualified success that the government and the company are claiming, there is genuine cause for concern about aspects of the regime at Wolds.[12]

This was followed up by critical reports from the then chief inspector of prisons and the National Audit Office.[13] However, this did not get in the way of the government announcing in 1993 that all new prisons would be privately built and operated. By 1994, two further private prison contracts had been awarded and facilities opened: Blakenhurst, at Redditch in the West Midlands and Doncaster in the north of England.

It was not until 1996 that academic research which evaluated Wolds was published by the Home Office. This found that

> ...similar and, some might argue, better achievements are to be found in some new public sector prisons, showing that the private sector has no exclusive claim on innovation or imaginative management able to deliver high quality regimes to its prisoners.[14]

By then, any notion that prison privatization was simply an experiment, if that had ever been the case, had been long forgotten. The role of the emerging private prison industry in ensuring that state of affairs should not be underestimated.

As stated earlier, Corrections Corporation of America (CCA) influenced the Home Affairs Committee. In 1987, CCA formed a British company, UK Detention Services Ltd. (UKDS) as a joint venture with two long established British construction companies, Sir Robert McAlpine & Sons Ltd. and John Mowlem & Co. Both of these companies were regular contributors to the then ruling Conservative Party.

One of UKDS's stated aims was lobbying the government to implement prison privatization. In a memorandum signed on 19 January 1988, the parties agreed to "promote the private design, financing, construction and management by private contractors of prisons and remand facilities in the United Kingdom (including the acquisition of land and/or other property in connection therewith)."[15]

The company subsequently admitted that "it took us two or three years to finally convince government that this was indeed the right course of action ..." and that with regard to the enabling legislation "UKDS was very much involved in bringing forward the arguments in favour of the case."[16]

For example, Mowlem notepaper was used to lobby members of parliament to support enabling legislation for privatizing prisons. A letter to members of the House of Lords dated 7 March 1991, trying to drum up support, stated:

> We have actively promoted the introduction of private sector management of our prisons for four years ... the present UK public sector prison service is rightly under attack. UKDS wants the opportunity to show just how much better the best of the private sector can do the job ...I do hope for your support and I would welcome the opportunity to discuss the matter further if you so wished.[17]

The company had not been alone in its endeavors. As the *Guardian* pointed out:

> On September 15 [1988] the private prisons network came together at a dinner for more than 150 given by the Carlton Club political committee. All the various players were there: representatives of the ASI [Adam Smith Institute] and other right wing policy units, civil servants, John Wheeler and his colleagues, architects and people from the consortia ... a mood of satisfied ѕᴜᴩ₉ᴏᴛᴀᴛᴉᴏᴨ ᴡᴀѕ ʙᴇɢɪɴɴɪɴɢ ᴛᴏ ᴇᴍᴇʀɢᴇ."[18]

It is ironic, however, that given CCA's role in influencing the Home Affairs Committee in 1986/97 and the fact that it provided the technical expertise to UKDS, the company did not win a prison contract in the United Kingdom until 1992. This was to manage Blakenhurst prison at Redditch, in the West Midlands. The 649-bed medium-security prison opened in May 1993.

Ten Years On

Since the opening of the first privately managed prison, the UK has developed the most privatized criminal justice system in Europe. As at the end of October 2001, there were more than 6,000 adults and young offenders held in private prisons in England and Wales.[19] This represents around eight per cent of the total prisoner population. In Scotland, which has a separate prison service, one private prison holds 600 prisoners, around ten per cent of the total prisoner population.

No other European nation has commissioned privately financed, designed, built and operated prisons or contracted out the custodial functions in a prison.[20] In terms of the number of private prisons, the UK is second only to the United States. In addition to private prisons, the UK has privately operated secure training centers for young offenders, immigration detention centers, prisoner escort services, electronic monitoring programs, provision of a wide range of non-custodial services in publicly run prisons, as well as major programs for privately financed, designed, built and operated court complexes, police complexes and probation hostels.

In addition to Wolds, in this period three other prison management contracts have been awarded, but after tendering exercises at the end of the initial contract period, two have since been taken over by the prison service (see Table 1).

Central to the Conservative government's long term strategy of privatization was the implementation in 1992 of the Private Finance Initiative (PFI). The PFI is a

financial mechanism to obtain private finance which could satisfy the political need to increase investment in infrastructure
without affecting public borrowing, guarantee large contracts
for construction companies and new investment opportunities
for finance capital.[21]

The PFI was inherited by the incoming Labour government in 1997 and is
still the only option for procuring new prisons. Seven privately financed, designed,
built and operated prisons, each with 25-year contracts, have been commissioned and opened in England and Wales with two more due to open in 2003
and 2004 (see Table 2 notes). Meanwhile, the Scottish Executive is planning
three more private prisons to replace antiquated facilities. The combined capital
value of the contracts for the privately financed, designed, built and operated
prisons in England and Wales is £312 million.[22]   This figure excludes annual
revenue payments for the provision of the buildings and services.
       For an indicator of the growth in operations, one does not need to look any
further than the UK's largest private prison services operator, Premier Custodial
Group Ltd. Until May 2002, this was a joint venture between the American private
prison operator Wackenhut Corrections Corporation and a British facilities management firm, Serco plc. Formed as Premier Prison Services in 1992, the
company's revenue for the year ended 31 December 1994 was £7.52 million.[23]
For the period ended 31 December 2000, Premier's empire had extended to
some 16 companies with combined revenues of £160.9 million and pre-tax profits of £12.4 million.[24] The companies provide a range of services including prisons, a secure training center, an immigration reception center, prisoner escort
services and electronic monitoring.
       UKDS, however, did not win another prison contract until 1998. The 25-year
contract to finance, design, build and operate Forest Bank prison in Salford,
northwest England, was signed with the government on 6 July 1998. The prison,
which holds 1,100 prisoners opened in January 2000. But the company's early
lobbying and subsequent commitment to the UK market was rewarded at the
end of 2001 by its being chosen as preferred bidder for two new prison contracts
with a combined value of more than £478 million.

TABLE 1: UKDS - revenues and profits 1995 - 2000

	Revenues (£m)	Pre-tax profit (£m)
1995	10.9	0.54
1996	11.25	0.50
1997	10.9	0.48
1998	11.6	0.33
1999	11.9	0.75
2000	23.12	1.89
2001	17.96	0.25

NB: 2001 figures are for eight months ended 31 August 2001.

The United Kingdom has its own private prison industrial complex. The prison contracts are shared among the same companies that are marketing their services across the world: Group 4 Falck, Wackenhut Corrections Corporation/Serco, Sodexho and Securicor.

TABLE 2: Private prison contracts in the UK - July 2002

Prison/YOI	Opened	Contractor	Population
Contractually managed			
Wolds	1992	Group 4	390
Doncaster	1994	PPS	1,050
PFI (contracts to design, construct, finance and manage)			
Parc	1997	Securicor	800
Altcourse	1997	Group 4	800
Lowdham Grange	1998	PPS	500
Ashfield	1999	PPS	340
Kilmarnock	1999	PPS	506
Forest Bank	2000	UKDS	1,100
Rye Hill	2001	Group 4	600
Dovegate	2001	PPS	800
Ashford	2003*	UKDS	460
Peterborough	2004*	UKDS	840
Secure Training Centers (STCs, also DCMF)			
Medway	1998	Group 4	72
Hassockfield	1999	PPS	40
Rainsbrook	1999	Group 4	76

Notes:
• UKDS is UK Detention Services Ltd. In 1996, CCA bought out its original partners and immediately sold 50 percent of UKDS to Sodexho, a Paris-based multinational corporation. Sodexho was a logical partner since, in 1994, the two companies had signed an international joint venture agreement in countries outside of the US, UK, Australia, France and Belgium. In September 2000, Sodexho bought out CCA's share in UKDS, making it the 100 percent owner.
• UKDS is the preferred bidder for the contracts for a 450-place women's prison at Ashford, Middlesex and an 840-bed prison for men and women at Peterborough, Cambridgeshire.Peterborough will be the first private facility in England and Wales to hold men and women. There will be 480 places for men and 360 for women including a 12-place mother and baby unit. Financing for both prisons will be provided by Royal Bank Project Investments Ltd. and the construction partner is Interserve Project Services. The prisons were scheduled to open in 2003 and 2004 but contract signing has been delayed due to difficulties with obtaining insurance.
• From 1992, UK Detention Services Ltd held a contract to operate HMP Blakenhurst. The company lost its contract after a market testing exercise in 2000. From August 2001 the prison has been run by the Prison Service.

• PPS is Premier Prison Services Ltd, part of Premier Custodial Group Ltd.
• Premier Prison Services was a joint venture between Wackenhut Corrections Corporation of the US and Serco plc. Premier companies and their subsidiaries now form the Premier Custodial Group Ltd. In May 2002, The Wackenhut Corporation was acquired by Group 4 Falck. Group 4 is due to sell off the 57 percent interest that it acquired in Wackenhut Corrections Corporation. Premier is currently owned jointly by Group 4 and Serco. However, Serco believes it has the right to now own Premier and the dispute is in the hands of lawyers.
• The contract for Doncaster was retendered in 1999 and Premier Prison Services won a further ten year contract.
• Group 4's contract for Wolds was recently renewed for a further ten years.
• Group 4 opened HMP Buckley Hall in 1994. It lost the contract after retendering in 1999. The prison has been run by the Prison Service since June 2000.
• In 2000 the private sector also bid against the Prison Service for a contract to run HMP Manchester. In January 2001, it was announced that the Prison Service had retained its contract.
• Kilmarnock is in Scotland. The Scottish Executive is considering a further three private prisons.
• Rainsbrook STC originally had 40 beds. It has now been expanded to 76. Medway is being extended from 40 to 72 beds, with the new unit opening in November 2002.
• Five further STCs are planned for Essex, Nottinghamshire, Buckinghamshire, northwest England and Wales. In July 2002 Securicor was chosen as preferred bidder for a new 80 bed STC at Milton Keynes, Buckinghamshire. This is due to open in December 2003.
• By mid 2002 the prison population in England and Wales reached 71,000: Scotland has some 6,000 prisoners.
• As at 31 March 2001, there were 137 prison establishments in England and Wales.
• This list excludes contracts for immigration detention centers, court and police complexes and services such as electronic monitoring and prisoner escort services.

Labour's U-turn

Prison privatization may have been ideologically imposed by the Thatcher government and continued by successive conservative administrations. But the policy has not just survived the election of a Labour government; it has thrived.

In opposition, Labour Party leaders asserted that the policy was morally repugnant. For example, in 1994, John Prescott, now deputy prime minister, pledged that "Labour will take back private prisons into public ownership–it is the only safe way forward."[25] This position was endorsed in March 1995 by the then shadow home secretary, Jack Straw. He stated that "[i]t is not appropriate for people to profit out of incarceration. This is surely one area where a free market certainly does not exist..." and that "at the expiry of their contracts a Labour government will bring these prisons into proper public control and run them directly as public services."[26]

Labour's backtracking started soon after the general election on 1 May 1997. On 8 May, Jack Straw, by then the home secretary, said "...if there are contracts in the pipeline and the only way of getting the [new prison] accommodation in place very quickly is by signing those contracts, then I will sign those contracts." On 19 June, Mr. Straw announced that he had renewed UK Detention Services Ltd.'s management contract for Blakenhurst and agreed to two new privately financed, designed, built and run prisons. He also said that the recommendations of the Home Affairs Select Committee, which reported in March 1997,[27] were "still to be fully considered" and announced that he had ordered two reviews.

The full policy U-turn was announced in a speech to the Prison Officers' Association (POA) annual conference on 19 May 1998 when Mr. Straw revealed that he had reviewed the recommendations of the Home Affairs Committee and decided that all new prisons in England and Wales would both be privately built and privately run. The prison service review that he had commissioned found the option of using private finance to build new prisons while retaining the management function in the public sector was not affordable and did not offer value for money.[28]

Straw also endorsed another review, which concluded that "the immediate transfer of existing private prisons to the public sector is not affordable and cannot be justified on value for money grounds."[29] However, he said that "the prison service will be allowed to bid for the chance to take over the management of existing privately managed prisons on the next occasions that the contracts expire."

Despite the findings about costs and value for money, within two years, contracts for two privately managed prisons, Buckley Hall and Blakenhurst, had been won by the prison service by submitting bids which were lower on cost and higher on quality (see table).[30] Further, a market testing exercise for one public sector prison, Manchester, resulted in the prison service successfully beating off bids from the private sector and retaining the service level agreement (SLA), the public sector equivalent of a contract. Meanwhile, in 2001, an attempt to contract out the management of a so-called underperforming public sector prison, Brixton, failed when none of the companies submitted a bid.

In October 2001, the prisons minister, Beverley Hughes, answered a parliamentary question with the information that by 2005, she expected eight percent of the prison estate to be privately operated—11 of 138 facilities for adults and young offenders.[31] In the same month, there was a hint that a mixed management model might be considered for some new prisons when the director general of the prison service for England and Wales said that "it is now very possible that, at some point, we will have a prison designed, financed and built by the private sector but run by the public sector."[32] Although still a long way from their stated aspirations of operating at least 25 percent of the prison estate,[33] the prison companies' directors and shareholders will have afforded themselves a wry smile following a more recent revelation.

In January 2002, the prisons minister said that she was considering the closure of up to 28 English prisons built in the Victorian era. The land and buildings would be sold off and these facilities would be replaced by a program of regional super-jails.[34]

In February 2002, the prison service published the source of these ideas, a report commissioned some time earlier and completed as long ago as January 2001 to "consider how best to develop the contribution of the private sector, particularly PFI, to achieving the objectives of the prison service; and to make recommendations."[35] The author, Patrick Carter, also argued that 'new for old' schemes appeared affordable and that existing public sector prisons which cannot achieve appropriate standards should be contracted out.

As well as advocating continuing with privately financed, designed, built and operated prisons, Carter suggested that the prison service move beyond the traditional choice of public or private prisons and explore the mixed management approach adopted successfully in France.

France has 21 semi-private prisons to date, publicly financed and with the prison officers remaining state employees while the private sector builds the facilities and operates non-custodial services. The French government is also commissioning at least six more. If this model is implemented in England and Wales, there will be at least one difference: it is unlikely that the prisons will be publicly financed. The irony with adopting this model is that, like the American model imported into the UK before it, there is a dearth of independent research to prove that it is as successful as is being claimed.[36]

Costs, Fines, Failures and Secrecy

The original arguments for contracting out the management of prisons included cost savings. It has been shown, however, in at least three of the recent tendering exercises for prison management contracts that the public sector can be as cost effective and even more so than the private sector. In terms of privately financed, designed, built and operated prisons (PFI), there is no doubt that new facilities have been constructed more quickly than before. But the public sector has not been allowed the opportunity to prove whether it can now commission and construct more efficiently. As for the cost savings of the PFI prisons, due to the use of 'commercial confidentiality' by the government and the companies, and the lack of political will of the parliamentary Select Committee on Public Accounts, it has not been possible to fully scrutinize the claims.[37] However, there is a growing body of evidence from other PFI schemes in the criminal justice system that cost comparisons with hypothetical public sector projects are flawed and cost savings have been overstated.[38]

The National Audit Office (NAO) provided another example of how the claimed benefits of the PFI prisons have recently been promoted without independent substantiation. The NAO released a report stating that most public bodies involved in PFI projects believe that they are achieving satisfactory or better value for money from these projects.[39] The NAO also reported that there was generally positive feedback from service users. Included in the survey were the contractors that run Dovegate, Rye Hill, Forest Bank, Ashfield, and Lowdham Grange prisons in England and Parc prison in Wales. The NAO also canvassed the prison service's views.

The NAO used an external reference panel "comprising representatives from the Office of Government Commerce (treasury), departmental PFI units and the private sector ... to discuss and agree [on] the overall direction of the study; the proposed questionnaires ... the interpretation of the results of the surveys and the presentation of the information in this report."

The panel included the prison service's contracts and competition group and, from the private sector, WS Atkins (involved in Parc prison in Wales and private prison consultancy), Carillion (Group 4's prison construction partner), the CBI (Confederation of British Industry), the Business Service Association, the Major Contractors Group and the Construction Industry Council.

In short, the NAO provided a one-sided view. Notably absent from its survey and reference panel were the views of prisoners, prisoners' families, prisoners' advocates, criminologists, prison reform organizations, trade unions, NGOs working in the field, probation services and others who provide services to private prisons.

Another of the original claims for privatization was that it would help ease prison overcrowding. However, since the prison population has leaped from 51,000 in 1986/7 to some 71,000 in mid 2002, the number of new available places has not kept pace with the number of offenders committed to prison. Even the private prisons have been overcrowded. For example, the average number of prisoners held two to a cell designed for one in private prisons between April

1999 and February 2000 were as follows: Doncaster 589 (626 in 1998/99, 588 in 1997/98, 399 in 1996/97), Blakenhurst 371 (360 in 1998/99, 309 in 1997/98, 134 in 1996/97), and Altcourse 416 (203 in 1998/99, 309 in 1997/98). Lowdham Grange had 15 between April 1999 and February 2000.[40] As at January 2002, Altcourse and Doncaster were overcrowded by 212 and 303 prisoners respectively.

The companies are very quick to advertise their successes in the United Kingdom through press releases and other material used to promote their services around the world. Not surprisingly, their fines, failures and controversies do not find their way into the public domain through the same channels.

Yet there is much evidence that the private sector is no panacea.[41] First, the last ten years has seen Wackenhut (UK) Ltd. withdraw from a contract to operate the prison industries at a publicly run prison after failing to provide adequate services.[42] Second, between 1998 and 2000, companies incurred over £2.7 million in financial penalties for prison contract failures in England and Wales.[43] Third, Group 4 and its construction partner, Carillion, made a windfall profit of an extra £10.7 million after refinancing the loan for the construction of its Altcourse prison in Liverpool, northwest England.[44] Interestingly, the same prison had the distinction of being named "the jewel in the crown" of the English prison service by the chief inspector of prisons while, at the same time his report noted that

> a great number of ... cells have been fitted with an extra steel bunk bed reached by a vertical steel ladder and then used for two prisoners ... the additional bunk bed in the cells provided obvious convenient and substantial ligature points ... it could be held that the provision of such ligature points rendered the cells unfit for use at all.[45]

Fourth, despite topping the prison service's league tables for having the most incidents of prisoner self-harm between 1996 and 1999,[46] Premier Prison Services managed to retain its contract to manage Doncaster prison in 1999. Leaked tender evaluation documents relating to that contract led to allegations and, of course, a denial of a political fix.[47] Since then, the chief inspector of prisons has remarked that at Doncaster,

> Purposeful activity was mainly based on education programs with some skill training and employment. These activities were tightly controlled by contractual arrangements laid down by the prison service which demanded that each prisoner was given 20 hours purposeful activity each week. The total weekly hours (a multiplication of prisoners in the establishment x 20 hours) was, in fact, achieved. This came about by simply using an arithmetical figure to assess contractual compliance. The number of purposeful activity hours achieved by those prisoners who did participate equaled what was contractually required for all. In effect there were many prisoners receiving virtually no purposeful activity. There was a clear need for more training courses or work.

The chief inspector also noted "the many examples of good practice" and that at "this time it was still a good prison, not so well able to cater for the 1,100 prisoners for which it now has to cater, not least because of the continued lack of sufficient activity places."[48]

As for the idea that private prisons reduce recidivism rates, that was scotched in March 2000 when the then prisons minister admitted that comparative re-offending rates of former prisoners of public and private prisons did not exist: "...since prisoners may move between privately owned and publicly owned prisons on a number of occasions during their sentence, it is not possible to calculate the reoffending rates."[49]

Even the director general of the prison service for England and Wales, who has not been short of praise for the private sector, has remarked on the private sector's complacency. He said recently that companies have achieved a "massive step forward" in the flexible use of staff but

> they have become, in running prisons, a bit complacent. They have not been as imaginative as this [prison] service has had to become in terms of utilizing staff—and, of course, they have to take a profit out of this. It may be that one or two of them are looking backwards to the days of very much higher profit margins.[50]

Meanwhile, sweeping statements included in the Carter report of February 2002 such as "the results of recent market tests demonstrate beyond doubt the value of the competitive process..." and "... it is widely accepted, by management and unions alike, that the competition offered by new private prisons ... has made the prison system more efficient and effective ..." are supposed to add weight to the argument that competition from the private sector has driven down costs and stimulated performance in the public sector.

While it is a moot point whether the public sector could have improved without such competition, there is no independent academic research to prove 'beyond doubt' how far the private sector has influenced improvements or to assess the negative impact caused by competition.

In May 2002, the prison service took the unprecedented step of removing a company's prison director and installing public sector management at the Premier Prisons-run Ashfield, a prison for young offenders near Bristol, south west England. The action was taken because of concerns over the safety of staff and anxieties that Premier might lose effective control. On 23 May 2002, the director general of the prison service said: "I found that standards of care and control of prisoners were not as high as I would expect them to be. I considered that the prison was unsafe for both staff and the young people detained there and that urgent action was required ... my aim is that the prison should be made safe and constructive and that in due course we are able to hand management back to a director appointed by Premier."[51]

In Scotland, which has a separate prison administration, the first private prison has also proved controversial. In 2000, Kilmarnock prison was described by the chief inspector of prisons for Scotland as having made a promising start, but it was also "Scotland's most violent prison." He also set out a range of other concerns.[52] There was also an incident which epitomizes how 'commercial confidentiality', extensively used by government and the industry to keep fundamental information from scrutiny, overrides the public interest. After pressure from both the Scottish Executive and Premier Prison Services Ltd., the chief inspector was forced to have his first inspection report pulped at the printers because it included the company's staffing levels at the prison.

Kilmarnock has since received two further critical reports from the chief inspector. And following an investigation into a Scottish Executive review of the prison estate (which recommended that three new private prisons be commmissioned), a parliamentary committee found that "... major questions exist about HMP Kilmarnock ... which mean it cannot be used as a point of comparison. In particular, the committee has serious concerns about the low level of staffing at HMP Kilmarnock."[53]

HMP Blakenhurst: A 'Snapshot' of Fines and Failures

UK Detention Services Ltd. (UKDS) was the first private prison operator to be penalized by the prison service when it was fined £41,167 after losing control of Blakenhurst during a disturbance in February 1994. In May 1995, the then Chief Inspector of Prisons, Judge Stephen Tumim, published a report of his team's inspection of the prison eight months earlier. Acknowledging that 12 months is a "relatively short time for any establishment to develop a balanced culture," he said that "the most impressive feature was the quality, enthusiasm and potential of staff: the most disappointing feature was the comparative shortage of innovation." His 109-page report also included over 100 recommendations for improvement.

Also in May 1995, Jeffrey Titmarsh, a UKDS prisoner custody officer was jailed for 18 months for scheming to have two prisoners beaten up after he suspected they put drugs in his coffee.

But perhaps one of the most serious incidents to have taken place at the prison was when Alton Manning, a 33-year old black remand prisoner, was 'unlawfully killed' by prison staff in December 1995. On 21 March 1998, a Coroner's court jury returned its unanimous verdict of unlawful killing even though the company, supported by the government, had applied to the High Court to deny the jury this option. Seven UKDS staff were suspended on full pay although those allegedly involved in the incident have never been prosecuted. A Home Office pathologist who carried out a post-mortem examination reported that Mr. Manning's case fell "into the category of death resulting from respiratory impairment and restriction during restraint." A second independent examination concluded: "The appearance is definitely that of an asphyxial death. In my opinion death was due to the way he was handled."[54]

On 7 August 1996, when 25-year old prisoner John Cowley was found hanging in his cell, his was the fourth death at the prison within ten months.

According to the prison service, in 1997-98 Blakenhurst failed to meet its performance targets in respect of: assaults as a percentage of the prisoner population 14.2 (target 13.1), hours of purposeful activity per week 19.9 (target 22.2), percentage of prison population tested for drugs 9.6 (target 10.0), and percentage of positive drug tests 46.3 (40.9). The number of assaults was more than double either of the prison's comparators. In terms of education, Blakenhurst offered no accredited courses. In November 1998, the company received its second penalty when it was fined £25,000 for allowing a prisoner to escape from escort.

In January 2001, the government announced that UKDS had failed in its attempt to retain its contract bidding against the prison service, which won the contract. UKDS was reported to have been 12 percent more expensive and 13 per cent worse on quality than the prison service bid.[55]

Then, in a report published in May 2001, the chief inspector of prisons noted that "... of more immediate concern is the clear evidence that treatment of and conditions for prisoners at Blakenhurst had, at best, stood still since our previous inspection, and in some respects have become worse. It was disappointing to find so many previous recommendations still not actioned, and so many promising innovations stalled until it had become clear whether the contract had been won or lost."[56]

In August 2001, the prison service assumed control of the prison.

Conclusion

Although the overall claims for private prisons remain unproven, the government remains committed to private sector provision. According to Sir David Ramsbotham, the former chief inspector of prisons for England and Wales:

> ... private prisons have been delivering, by and large, a far higher standard of treatment for prisoners than the public sector. Each private prison has a compliance monitor who ensures that the terms of a contract are met and, if they are not, can levy hefty fines. In fact, these terms are often far more demanding than those that apply in the public sector. For example, all private prisons have to provide at least 30 hours of purposeful activity per prisoner each week as opposed to the public sector's target of 24 hours, which in reality is often less and has been progressively lowered over the past three years.
>
> As a result, several of our nine private prisons have been doing remarkably well. Over the past two years, neither Altcourse, Liverpool, nor Lowdham Grange, Nottingham, have cancelled a single lesson or evening activity. Altcourse so impressed Merseyside's chief constable, Norman Bettison, that he declared, 'this is the first time in my career I've left a prison feeling optimistic.[57]

Yet despite his above mentioned assertion, Sir David Ramsbotham also has reservations about the use of the private sector. In his words,

> [I] can accept the private sector looking after unsentenced prisoners because they are still innocent in the eyes of the law. But I do have questions about the sentenced. The state has awarded that punishment and the state should deliver it.[58]

On the other hand, Mike Newall, president of the prison governors' association (PGA),[59] wrote in his organization's magazine recently that

> Almost ten years on the private sector provides the most expensive prison places and its performance, in most areas, is well below what the best of the public sector can provide. Change has taken place in the public sector. Perhaps this is the legacy the experiment leaves behind but it has no more to offer in its current shape. The PFI projects are proving so expensive that, quite simply, we cannot afford any more privately run prisons. The long term debt already built up is crippling the [prison] service and it would be foolhardy and irresponsible to burden our successors with yet more debt.[60]

Early in 2001, the general public was brought into the equation for the first time and it seems that the majority sides with the prison governors. An ICM poll for the *Guardian* in March 2001 found, when asked if they thought prisons should be brought back into the public sector, that 60 percent of respondents said yes, 24 percent said no, and 16 percent were undecided.[61]

Clearly, the debate about what the private sector has achieved so far and what it can contribute to the United Kingdom's prison system is not yet over. But for the foreseeable future, the public is not going to get its way.

As ever, it appears that the industry sets the agenda. In evidence to the Home Affairs Committee's inquiry into the management of the prison service in England and Wales in 1996, representatives from Group 4, Premier Prison Services Ltd and UKDS had all said that they would like to see between 20 and 25 per cent of the entire prison estate shared among three to five companies.[62]

In its submission, UKDS stated that

> the prison service needs to have three to four healthy suppliers so that it has choice, competition and reliability. For these suppliers to be healthy, they need to have a minimum number of establishments to ensure there is scope for staff development and exchange in a demanding job and efficiencies of scale so that operational and overhead costs are minimized. A minimum of four establishments per supplier or an average of eight is necessary for this. Thus, assuming four suppliers, that leads to a total of 32 which is around a quarter of the estate.[63]

The company also proposed that:

> • the private sector should be invited to tender for the management of prisons on existing sites which are performing less well than average;
> • the public sector should not compete in market testing procedures until independent mechanisms are in place to measure contract performance and the same accountability can be applied ...
> • ... as part of the drive to improve value for money, the very old and inherently inefficient prisons should be closed and demolished and the private sector invited to tender for new design, build, finance and operate contracts on the same sites.

These recommendations were broadly incorporated into the Carter report's strategy for the future of the prison service in England and Wales. Carter also included the suggestion that the prison service should guarantee a continued and expanding role for a competitive private sector and that all new prisons should be privately designed and built.

Endnotes

1. This has taken the form of contracting out the management of prisons to the private sector as well as private finance, design, construction and management. In the first case, a company manages a prison commissioned and designed by the public sector; the original contracts lasted up to five years but, where contracts have been renewed, these are for ten years. In the latter, under the Private Finance Initiative, it is envisaged the facility will be handed back to the public sector at the end of a 25-year contract to provide the prison and all services. The prison industry does not regard this as privatization since accountability with the government is maintained.

2. Omega Report on Justice Policy, Adam Smith Institute (1984).

3. I. Gilmour, *Dancing With Dogma, Britain Under Thatcherism* (1993).

4. See M. Ryan & T. Ward, *Privatization and the penal system, The American experience and the debate in Britain* (1989).

5. House of Commons, Fourth Report from the Home Affairs Committee, Contract Provision of Prisons, 6 May 1987.

6. M. Ryan & T. Ward, *Privatization and the penal system, supra* note 4.
7. House of Commons, Contract Provision of Prisons, *supra* note 5.
8. *Id.*
9. Hansard, 25 February 1991.
10. "Tories plan to extend private prisons," *Financial Times*, 28 January 1992.
11. "Second prison to be privatized," *The Guardian*, 4 December 1991 and "Baker wants third sell-off before election," *The Guardian*, 13 January 1992.
12. Prison Reform Trust *Wolds remand Prison, Contracting Out: A First Year Report* (1993).
13. The chief inspector of prisons at the time was Judge Tumim.
14. Research Findings No.32, "Wolds remand Prison - An Evaluation," Bottomley, James, Clare and Liebling, April 1996. The research compared Wolds remand prison with public sector prisons, in particular, Her Majesty's Prison Woodhill.
15. Memorandum between the registrant [Corrections Corporation of America] and CCA International Inc, Sir Robert McAlpine & Sons Ltd and John Mowlem & company PLC, 19 January 1988.
16. RDN Hopkins, "The Formation of UK Detention Services" (1993).
17. Correspondence dated 7 March 1991, signed by Nicholas Hopkins, director of corporate communications. Mr. Hopkins is now a director of UKDS. In financial year 2000, UKDS paid Nicholas Hopkins Associates £80,000 (£77,000 in 1999) for public relations services. Source: UKDS Directors Report and Accounts for the Year Ended 31 December 2000.
18. D. Rose, "Big Money Turns The Key," *The Guardian*, 11 January 1989; John Wheeler was the chairman of the Home Affairs Committee in 1986/87. He was also chairman of the British Security Industry Association, whose members included Group 4 and Securicor, both of which subsequently won prison contracts. The Carlton Club is a Conservative political and social club.
19. Hansard, 6 December 2001.
20. France has a number of semi-private prisons which have been privately built. Belgium has one and the German state of Hesse is developing another. In these facilities, prison officers are state employees but maintenance and all other non-custodial services are privately provided. For a recent overview of the international development of prison privatization see S. Nathan, "Private prisons, an international overview," Prison Review International, Issue 2, January 2002, www.prisonreview.com.
21. D. Whitfield, *Public Services or Corporate Welfare* (2001).
22. Hansard, 18 December 2001.
23. S. Nathan, "Premier's loss," Privatization Factfile #11, Prison Report #32, Autumn 1995, Prison Reform Trust, London.
24. Premier Custodial Group Ltd, Directors Report and Accounts, 31 December 2000.
     For details of other British companies' revenues and profits see "Money Go Round," Prison Privatisation Report International # 44, November 2001 <www.psiru.org/justice>.
25. Speaking to the Prison Officers Association Annual Conference, 1994, reported in Gatelodge, June 1994.
26. "Labour gives pledge to end prison privatization," *The Times*, 8 March 1995.
27. While still under a Conservative government, the Home Affairs Committee held an inquiry and subsequently reported on the management of the prison service in England and Wales. See House of Commons, Home Affairs Committee, The Management of the Prison Service (Public and Private), 19 March 1997. Within the debate on the principle of contracting out (para. 47, conclusions and recommendations), the Committee concluded: "While we accept that contracting out is not universally welcome, we consider that the fears hitherto expressed over the principle of contracting out - that it would mean the abdication of state responsibility for public safety and the deprivation of freedom - have not proved justified and that the idea of privately managed prisons is undoubtedly now more generally accepted and should be allowed to develop further." Second Report, Volume 1 at para 162. In December 1997, seven months after the general election, the Labour government responded to the Committee's recommendations by stating that it wished to "give further and careful consideration to this issue." There were also comments on commercial confidentiality, the quality of provision in privately managed prisons, comparative costs, the effects of competition and the further development of the contracted out sector. The Government Reply to the Second Report from the Home Affairs Committee, Session 1996-97 HC57, The Management of the Prison Service (Public and Private), CM 3810, December 1997.
28. Prison Service, "Review of Private Financing of New Prison Procurement," unpublished document (1998).
29. Prison Service, "Public and Private Prison Management, Considerations on returning privately managed prisons to the public sector," unpublished document, April 1998.
30. Group 4 opened HMP Buckley Hall in 1994. It lost the contract after re-tendering in 1999. The prison has been run by the Prison Service since June 2000, see Prison Privatisation Report International #31, October 1999 <www.psiru.org/justice>. From 1992, UK Detention Services Ltd held a contract to operate HMP Blakenhurst. The company lost its contract after a market testing exercise in 2000. From August 2001, Blakenhurst has been run by the Prison Service, see Prison Privatisation Report International #38, January/February 2001 <www.psiru.org/justice>.

31. Hansard, 17 October 2001.

32. *Financial Times*, 2 October 2001.

33. In evidence to the Home Affairs Committee, 1996.

34. "Sale of Victorian jails to pay for 'super prisons'," *Daily Telegraph*, 19 January 2002.

35. P. Carter, "Review of PFI and Market Testing in the Prison Service" (2002). For a brief critique of the Carter report see S. Nathan, "Carter's wish list for industry?, The PFI Report, April 2002, <www.publicprivatefinance.com>.

36. In 1987, France introduced a program of 21 semi-private prisons. The government has recently re-tendered the contracts and is also commissioning at least six more of these facilities. Although a program of 30 new prisons has been announced, it has not yet been decided how all of these will be procured.

37. In 1998, the Select Committee on Public Accounts investigated, to a limited degree, the extent of claimed savings at Parc and Altcourse prisons. See "The PFI Contracts For Bridgend [Parc] and Fazakerley prisons [Altcourse], Select Committee on Public Accounts," Fifty Seventh Report <www.publications.parliament.uk/pa/cm1997/98/cmselect/cmpubacc/499/49903.htm>.
For a critique of that Committee's investigation see Centre for Public Services, Justice Forum, "Privatising Justice, the Impact of the Private Finance Initiative in the Criminal Justice System," London, 2002 <www.centre.public.org.uk>.

38. See, for example, Centre for Public Services, Justice Forum, "Privatising Justice, The Impact of the Private Finance Initiative in the Criminal Justice System," London, 2002 <www.centre.public.org.uk>.

39. Managing the Relationship to Secure A Successful Partnership in PFI Projects, Report by the Comptroller & Auditor General, HC 375, Session 2001-2002:29 November 2001.

40. Hansard, 22 and 27 March 2000.

41. There are too many examples to include in this article.

42. "UK: Audit slams Wackenhut contract," Prison Privatisation Report International #27, February 1999 <www.psiru.org/justice>; see also Prison Privatisation Report International #26, #25 and #23.

43. A table of financial penalties incurred by private prisons in England and Wales appeared in an answer to a parliamentary question, see Hansard 18 October 2001. However, the figures provided were incomplete and, in a couple of instances, miscalculated. For a short article discussing these figures, see S. Nathan, Privatisation Factfile 35, Prison Report 57, Spring 2002, Prison Reform Trust, London.

44. See "Cashing in on PFI prisons," Prison Privatisation Report International #36, July 2000 <www.psiru.org/justice>.

45. See "UK: ligature points in Group 4's 'jewel'," Prison Privatisation Report International #35, May/June 2000 <www.psiru.org/justice>.

46. S. Nathan, "Doncaster's self harm figures," Privatisation Factfile #30, Prison Report #51, Prison Reform Trust, June 2000.

47. See "UK: competition shrouded in secrecy," Prison Privatisation Report International #31, October 1999 and "Documents reveal tender facts," Prison Privatisation Report International #32, November 1999, both at <www.psiru.org/justice>.

48. "Report of an Announced Inspection of HMP& YOI Doncaster," 17-20 April 2001 by Chief Inspector of Prisons <www.homeoffice.gov.uk/hmipris/insrep.htm>.

49. Hansard, 20 March 2001.

50. *Financial Times*, 2 October 2001.

51. Public sector manages Premier's Ashfield, Prison Privatization Report International #47, May 2002 <www.psiru.org/justice>.

52. "Scotland's first is most violent," Prison Privatisation Report International #36, July 2000. For the chief inspector's follow up, see "Kilmarnock's second inspection," Prison Privatisation Report International #40, April/May 2001 <www.psiru.org/justice>.

53. The Scottish parliament, Committee News Release CJUSTI 08/2002, 2 July 2002.

54. For a full briefing on this case contact: INQUEST, email: inquest@compuserve.com.

55. "UK: firms lose two but market is safe," Prison Privatisation Report International #38, Jan/Feb 2001 <www.psiru.org/justice>.

56. "Report on a full announced inspection of HM Prison Blakenhurst," 22-26 January 2001 by HM Chief Inspector of Prisons.

57. *Readers Digest* <http://www.readersdigest.co.uk/magazine/CHAY-4TAQ9L.htm>.

58. "The government ignored my warnings about prisons," *Daily Telegraph*, 17 December 2001.

59. PGA is the trade union that represents public sector prison governors. Most, if not all, of the directors and senior managers working for the private prison companies have been drawn from the governor grades within the public sector and are no longer PGA members. If, however, a former governor returns to the public sector, he or she can rejoin the PGA.

60. *The Key*, Issue 56, Autumn 2000.

61. *The Guardian*, 21 March 2001.

62. "Fresh evidence," Prison Privatisation Report International, #5, November 1996 <www.psiru.org/justice>.

63. UK Detention Services Ltd, Memorandum to the Home Affairs Committee Inquiry into the Management of the Prison Service, 14 May 1996.

CHAPTER FIFTEEN

Prison Privatization: Developments in South Africa

Julie Berg

South Africa currently has two private prisons. The first private prison that was constructed, Manguang Maximum Security, opened in Bloemfontein and has been taking in prisoners since July 1, 2001. Kutama-Sinthumule Prison, located in Louis Trichardt, has been taking on prisoners since its opening on 19 February 2002. These two maximum-security private prisons were planned by South Africa's Department of Correctional Services in partnership with two international private corrections companies. The two successful international companies, which had been involved in negotiations with the South African government for a number of years prior to the construction of the prisons, are the Wackenhut Corrections Corporation (known as SA Custodial Services in South Africa) and Group 4 Securitas. The latter is responsible for the Bloemfontein private prison, while Wackenhut will look after the Kutama-Sinthumule Prison being constructed in Louis Trichardt, which is expected to be operational by early 2002.[1] Apart from a small detention facility for 'illegal immigrants', which happens to be a human rights disaster, South Africa's first-hand experience with prison privatization is virtually non-existent. Consequently, whether the government will continue its prison privatization endeavors will hopefully depend on the success of these two prisons.

What makes the development of prison privatization in South Africa noteworthy is the fact that South Africa is a developing country, new to the democratic ideal and the first African country to privatize prisons. South Africa's current prison system is in a critical condition and is in serious need of reformation. South Africa's prisons tend to be overcrowded, many prisoners have to tolerate squalid conditions and certain South African prisons are completely inadequate for prisoner development programs. Where some countries are able to modify their existing prisons, South Africa may have to do away with many of its old prisons as they are beyond modification. That is what makes South Africa's situation unique. It is a recently transformed country experiencing all the problems associated with a transformation, one of which is an increase in the crime rate, yet it is attempting to adopt a First World solution to its problems. The question is whether prison privatization in South Africa is a viable solution or a bad mistake. To fully understand the impact of a First World approach to imprisonment on South Africa, one has to gain an understanding of the current state of South Africa's prison system.

South Africa's Prison System

In a recent speech Ben Skosana, the Minister of Correctional Services, made the following observations:

> Over the years various factors have had a cumulative effect on the crime rate in South Africa and consequently the Department of Correctional Services finds itself faced with a prison population that far exceeds that which the current infrastructure is geared for. The overpopulation of prisons continues to be a problem and it is clear that the unacceptably high occupancy rate will continue to be a problem in the foreseeable future.[2]

Many countries have experienced an explosion in their prison population, but in South Africa the effects of the increase are much more serious due to the current state of the prison system, a prison system designed during the Apartheid era or what is called the Old Regime.

The Transformation Period

One can use the April 1994 elections in South Africa as the official end of the Apartheid Regime and the start of South Africa's democratic government. While it is useful to use the elections as the symbolic end of the Old Regime, it must be noted that the transformation process was a gradual one and was already taking place before the 1994 elections. As far as South Africa's penal system is concerned, the Old Regime prevented any monitoring or effective transparency of the correctional system. Consequently, many human rights abuses occurred without effective opposition or reformation. The running of the prisons by the military reinforced the institutional nature of the Apartheid dogma. The prison managers had wide discretionary powers and many incidents of racism and violence against prisoners (and among prisoners) took place even up to the 1994 elections. Fortunately the Prisons Department, as it was known until 1991 when it was renamed the Department of Correctional Services, had been slowly undertaking reforms since the mid-1980s. These ranged from changes in attitude towards previously harsh policies to the acceptance of prison unions.[3] Eventually, in 1993, the Interim Constitution of South Africa was introduced.[4] Both this Constitution and the 'final' Constitution, adopted in 1996, contain a Bill of Rights that pertains to the rights of society, including prisoners.[5] Issues dealt with by the Bill include greater access to courts, equality before the law, the right to life (thereby negating the death penalty), the right to proper treatment and the right not to be subject to forced labor. Other rights outlined include the right to privacy, freedom of association and therefore the right to petition, the right to vote and to gain access to information. Moreover, the rights included in Section 35 (1) are directly pertinent to detained persons. These rights are therefore related to the conditions within prisons, such as the provision of nutritious meals, medical attention, reading material and so forth.

In addition to the granting of rights, the Constitution also includes a provision that allows the limitation of rights, whereby constitutional justification is given for the restriction of certain constitutional rights by virtue of the conditions of incarceration. For example, freedom of movement and the right to privacy would necessarily be reasonably limited by the fact that prisoners are incarcerated and may be searched at any time. These restrictions must be consistent with dignity, equality and freedom to the degree possible in relation to conditions of confinement.[6] The promulgation of the Interim Constitution encouraged developments within the Department of Correctional Services, most of which occurred after the 1994 elections.[7] For example, on 1 April 1996, the demilitarization of the Department was enforced. By June 1996, it was announced in Parliament that the demilitarization process had been successfully implemented; however, despite the symbolic removal of the military from the penal system, the actual process of demilitarization took considerably longer. It was a gradual process as the institutional nature of the military structure had to be replaced by a civilian one.[8] The reasons for the removal of the military were based partly on Parliament's intention to comply with international law and because the Department's plans sought to avoid military-style prison management.

Altering such a distinctive style of prison management is not an easy task and some prisons even today are trapped in a style of prison management and prison design that is not in line with internationally accepted penal standards. Consequently, not only has the Department of Correctional Services been trying to cope with the huge numbers of prisoners awaiting trial, but it is also trying to alter a prison system designed merely to house prisoners. In fact, most of the prisons in South Africa are designed on a warehouse basis, holding a large number of prisoners in each cell. As it is now, prisoners' rights are not being fully upheld; in fact it would be almost impossible to do so without a greatly expanded budget. The government has consequently had to be innovative in coping with a difficult situation, as demonstrated in a speech given by the Minster of Correctional Services, who said that

> strategies will be put in place to find more cost-effective mechanisms to design and build prisons that would give us about 30,000 bed spaces in the next five years. Other strategies would involve the enhancement of rehabilitation programmes to reduce recidivism and marketing the community corrections system as an alternative to imprisonment.[9]

The privatization of prisons is the key strategy employed. To date, this strategy has engaged the Asset Procurement and Operating System (APOPS), which allows the private sector to design, build, finance, operate and maintain a prison while being paid by the government to provide the services for a fixed period of time.

Yet considering the heightened awareness of human rights in South Africa, it is strange that the untested practice of prison privatization would be so hastily employed. It is true that prisoners' rights are not currently being respected in a public system that is coping with the sheer difficulty of transforming the prison system and keeping up with prisoner numbers, but this does not license the government to implement a system that may, in South Africa, cause further violations of prisoners' rights. Before considering the future of private prisons in South Africa, it is necessary to look at the exact origin of this phenomenon.

The Origin of Prison Privatization in South Africa

Dr. Sipo Mzimela, South Africa's Minister of Correctional Services until July 1998, was very keen on the idea of privatization. Before becoming Minister he was a prison chaplain in the United States. His vision of prison privatization in South Africa was therefore most likely based on and influenced by developments in the United States.[10] He advocated full operational privatization, meaning that the finance, design, construction and management of South African prisons should be contracted out. He pointed out that the inclusion of the private sector in South Africa's prison system would not only save money but also improve future prison designs and security. He considered what he saw

> in the United States [to be] very good. The prisons that are run by the private companies are far more efficient in every sense because they are run by business people, unlike those in the Department of Correctional Services who are not necessarily trained to run businesses.[11]

In June 1996, Minister Mzimela announced to Parliament that the Department of Correctional Services was "looking for alternative ways of providing suitable accommodation to inmates".[12] He also stated that the private sector had been approached in this regard "which would lead them to finance, design, construct and maintain new facilities, and lease them to the Government over an agreed period."[13]

Although Dr. Mzimela outlined the advantages of private sector involvement in his address to Parliament, those witnessing it did not wholeheartedly accept the proposal for prison privatization. Carl Niehaus, who had been chairman of the Portfolio Committee on Correctional Services in 1995, pointed out the possible difficulties in seeking private sector assistance. Apparently the Correctional Services budget had not accounted for this new plan. Also, as pointed out by Carl Niehaus, the government would have to pay a higher interest rate after borrowing from the private sector. Another element that should have been taken into account by the government was highlighted in a document from the Department of Finance, which pointed out potential financial difficulties. These difficulties include the rise of inflation over the lease period and the subsequent costs for the government borrowing from the private sector. The document

> comes to the conclusion, on a particular suggestion presented by the Department of Correctional Services…that that particular proposal was too costly and hence unacceptable.[14]

It is interesting to note that the Correctional Services budget was increased from R2.5 billion to R3.3 billion for the 1997/1998 year.[15] Also in 1997, the relevant enabling legislation was enacted through the creation of the Correctional Services Amendment Act.[16] The Amendment Act empowers the Minister "to contract out prisons to private contractors".[17] On 27 November 1998, the Correctional Services Act was published.[18] It refers to the product of contracting-out as "joint venture prisons" and also states, in Chapter 14, that:

> The Minister may subject to any law governing the award of contracts by the State with the concurrence of the Minister of Finance and the Minister of Public Works enter into a contract with any party to design, construct, finance and operate any prison or part of a prison.[19]

From this process of initiation one can gather that prison privatization was introduced into South Africa based on a 'seeing is believing' notion. Organized visits to the USA may have bolstered the government's confidence in prison privatization, since it saw for itself what appeared to be the beneficial results of a privatized prison, but what the South African government failed to take into account, even at the legislative stage of development, was whether this same type of prison management would be suitable for a unique country such as South Africa. What may work in the US may not work in South Africa. In fact, important philosophical issues related to the functioning of a transitional society, especially one with a new Constitution advocating prisoners' rights, were never really discussed. It seems that the practical advantages of prison privatization, such as decreasing prison population and cost-savings, were the sole motivations for its introduction into South Africa. The Minister admitted that

> the main rationale behind the initiative is to improve cost-effectiveness of the remand system by making additional accommodation available more quickly and flexibly than would otherwise be possible, thus contributing to the reduction of overcrowding and improving conditions for prisoners.[20]

Controversy Surrounding the Decision to Privatize

A degree of criticism has surfaced concerning the way in which the government went about employing the option to privatize prisons. Some have criticized the speed at which the process has taken place. Only a couple of years after the process began, two maximum-security prisons are already in operation. This differs from other countries' experiences, beginning their developments in immigration detention and youth detention before embarking on medium to maximum-security imprisonment. By resorting first to pilot projects and proving their success over time in a number of other types of privatization services, the government could include the private sector in the operational and managerial aspects of prison administration. At that point, the private sector could then be invited to bid for the operation of an adult prison. In fact, the process was initiated before the legislation was analyzed and approved.

> Much to the chagrin of the Correctional Services Parliamentary Portfolio Committee, tenders for the first five private prisons were shortlisted months before the legislation empowering government to award such contracts was presented to Parliament.[21]

Criticism has also been leveled at the government for failing to include the views of interest groups, especially non-governmental organizations (NGOs), to among other things provide research on the topic of privatization so as to develop a better understanding of it. Chris Giffard, an independent researcher affiliated with the University of Cape Town, expressed the following opinion:

> I firmly believe that any good policy is arrived at by good hard debate, because somebody presents the idea, somebody opposes it, they sit down and they work against each other until

new ideas spring forth. And the Department and the Ministry have tried to avoid that as much as possible. Maybe they thought that the opposition would be absolute opposition that would try and stop the process rather than generate better ideas ... privatization can be a really positive force in prisons if there are certain safeguards which are installed and checks and balances. And the only way you are going to work out what those checks and balances are going to be is if people are involved in the debate.[22]

In general, political criticism leveled against the African National Congress (ANC) government from the opposition at that time, the National Party (NP) and Inkatha Freedom Party (IFP), was limited. The opposition seemed to support the privatization move. However, the NP (now known as the NNP–the New National Party) did question the involvement of the ANC Youth League in one of the consortiums that had tendered for one of the APOPS programs. At this early stage of prison privatization development, the transparency of the Department of Correctional Services was questioned as well as the potential financial benefits the Youth League, as a political party, could gain. In an address to Parliament, an NP representative made the following criticism:

The short-listing process surely does not speak of any transparency whatsoever. If the reports we have are true, it would seem that the ANC wishes to boost its Youth League's coffers with state money, something one should perhaps refer ... to the Public Protector.[23]

It must, however, be noted that the ANC Youth League did not put in a bid as such; they were merely involved in one of the consortiums that tendered. The international companies would ultimately be the core operators, not the local consortiums involved. At this time political opponents of the ANC were not completely aware of the extent to which the ANC Youth League would benefit from the contracts signed with the private companies. They therefore questioned and criticized the perceived threat of a political party becoming involved in a bid for a tender as this could lead to incarceration policies being amended to suit the needs of the party concerned. Despite the limited criticism regarding a potential abuse of power, the opposition has commended the government for its initiatives so far to implement prison privatization.

From this process of initiation of the privatization phenomenon one can predict problems arising out of the government's reasons for introducing privatization and its lack of interest in adequate debate on the matter. All the countries advocating prison privatization pointed to the practical benefits that privatization might offer without adequately assessing the underlying problems it may present. Now many problems are arising in these countries, problems that will most likely also arise in South Africa, since South Africa followed a similar route of introduction. Since South Africa is a developing country it may be even less able to manage these problems due to lack of resources and other problems associated with the prison system. However, now that the process of privatization has already begun, the government can only see the process through by adhering to basic strategies that may prevent future problems.

Strategies for Success

The government's shaky introduction of prison privatization into South Africa does not bode well for the future success of the private prisons. Nonetheless, by following certain basic guidelines suggested below, perhaps many of the pitfalls experienced overseas may be minimized in South Africa.

The Need for Experimentation and Debate

Unfortunately the government began by launching a full-scale privatization of two adult maximum-security prisons, each housing approximately 3,000 prisoners. Despite the enormity of the project, the government is calling it a pilot project. Initially the entire pilot project was to include a juvenile center and a remand prison. Ultimately, only the two maximum-security prisons were approved for development due to fiscal restraints. It would have been more beneficial for the government if the shallow-end facilities were built first since these facilities, especially the juvenile center, would have been on a much smaller scale. Mistakes are far more likely to occur in a 3,000 bed adult maximum-security prison than in a 1,600 bed juvenile center.

Even though the first private prison has already been opened, perhaps it is not too late to experiment, as well, with small-scale juvenile centers. Or if this is not possible, at least the government could open itself up to the suggestions of the academic world, which has largely been shut out from the entire process. Any feedback from learned professionals (not just those with business interests), especially those from countries already engaged in privatization, could help the government to avoid potential problems it may not have prepared itself for. As mentioned earlier, many non-governmental organizations could provide useful assistance to the government and incite public and political debate if allowed to participate in the project.

As it is now, the pilot project will hopefully remain just that, a pilot, instrumental in determining future decisions concerning the use and development of private prisons to guarantee that future private prisons are a success, even if the first two private prisons are a failure.

Upholding Prisoners' Rights

Currently the government cannot guarantee the rights of prisoners in its public prisons. One of its motivations for implementing prison privatization was the possibility that privatization would alleviate overcrowding, and consequently result in raising standards for those imprisoned. Even though it was not a primary motivation for employing private prisons in the first place, it was and is hoped by the government that a general improvement of the public prison system will eventually result, as well as an increase in the applicability of South Africa's Bill of Rights to detainees. Consequently the entire success of the private prison enterprise rests on the ability of the government to guarantee the rights of the prisoners within these private prisons. Therefore it is of vital importance that the government does not shirk its responsibility to ensure that rights are upheld at all times by the private companies running the prisons. Even though private prison personnel are, in theory, bound by legal and professional standards of performance, violations of these standards may take place. In the case of serious violations, the government must be able to terminate its contract with the private company.[24] Henk Bruyn, South Africa's former Commissioner of Correctional Services who is currently involved in the private security enterprise, emphasizes the importance of the government's duty:

> [The government] must oversee the [private contractors] on a day-to-day 24-hour basis. And they must make sure, from the government's point of view, that the service delivery coming out from that private contractor is up to scratch, that all government laws are being adhered to, that all specifications are being subscribed to and that it can be checked and measured...from a philosophical point of view, the government can never walkaway from its responsibility for incarcerating inmates.[25]

By simply carrying out its duty to incarcerate inmates in accordance with their Constitutional rights, the government may ensure the success of the private prison enterprise.

Ensuring Equality

Just as the rights of the prisoners are of utmost importance, so is the right that they be treated equally before the law. The newly created private prisons will naturally be of a higher quality than the public prisons in South Africa; after all it was the intention that they be of an international standard. Ironically, if the rights of prisoners are fully upheld in the private prisons, then the right to equality will not be maintained. A lot of South African public prisons are simply incapable of providing what the private prisons are and will be providing–education, inmate programs and other forms of rehabilitation. Public prisons are only able to provide these things until the prison becomes too overcrowded or resources dry up. In a society that promotes equality before the law and the use of prisons *as* punishment and not *for* punishment,[26] how does one account for this huge difference in prisoners' rights? The Commissioner of the South African Human Rights Commission, Jody Kollapen, elucidates this problem:

> ...in [private prisons], the standards and the quality and the hygiene etc is remarkably different. What does this mean in terms of a society that is trying to deal with questions of equality? Does it mean that there will be different forms of punishment for the rich and poor? Whereas in fact if people contravene the law, then the notion of equality requires that the law must punish them equally, and that means the conditions under which they find themselves must be the same for all prisoners, by and large.[27]

The only way that this problem can be solved is if the government keeps its promises and improves the state of all of South Africa's prisons. While this has always been the government's intention, however, the contracting of the two prisons has necessitated the use of a large amount of government funds, causing the public sector to do with even less. Simply put: the government has to improve the conditions of the prisoners incarcerated in its public prisons. There is no point in guaranteeing the rights of only a few prisoners in relation to South Africa's entire prison population. Also, the government should continue ardently with its endeavors to provide alternatives to imprisonment, since many petty criminals need not be imprisoned at all. Community service alone would be more beneficial than a stint in a prison or so-called 'university of crime'.

Avoiding the 'Revolving Door Syndrome'

Another pitfall the government should avoid is the 'revolving door syndrome'.[28] This term can be used in a general sense to refer to state officials who become involved with private, for-profit functions and in so doing, blur the distinction between these two functions.

South Africa's carefully constructed democracy could be undermined by profit-motivated companies indirectly or directly affecting policy decisions in the upper echelons of governmental power. Political leaders may become motivated by the needs of the private prison industry and inadvertently or purposefully affect sentencing policy. No country is completely immune from this problem. What is of concern is the degree to which undue private influence on policy decisions can be controlled and reduced. The government thus has to ensure that none of its members have a vested interest in the private prison enterprise.

Conclusion

So far, the two private prisons are operating without problems, but South Africa's government should, at the onset, have taken complete responsibility for its decision to privatize. From the start, the process of initiation was lacking in preparation and transparency. One can only hope that the start of the process does not reflect its possible future success. By following the simple guidelines suggested by many academics and those well versed in the advantages and disadvantages of private prisons, South Africa could perhaps avoid a potential disaster. In other words, if the government is able to learn from its own experiences and the experiences of other countries with private prisons, guarantee the rights and equality of all prisoners–in public and private facilities–and also ensure that public policy is never influenced by business interests, then private prisons may have a lot to offer South Africa as a developing country in serious need of correctional reformation.

Philosophically then, it is the author's opinion that private prisons are fundamentally wrong, but their possible practical advantages have led to the adoption of the belief that they could in the end promote the very constitutional rights of prisoners in South Africa that they are said to refute. Provided of course that the government retains control over the situation and does not lose sight of its ultimate goal: to improve South Africa's entire prison system. On a positive note then, private prisons have the potential to be more legitimate in South Africa than in other countries because of their inherent ability to demonstrate the type of prisons the South African government should be creating.

Endnotes

1. Department of Correctional Services Address by Minister of Correctional Services, Mr Ben Skosana MP, at the site visit of Kutama-Sinthumule Maximum Security Prison: Louis Trichardt on 23 August 2001 [*hereinafter* "address by Mr Ben Skosana MP"].

2. *Id.*

3. C. Giffard, *Out of Step? The Transformation Process in the South African Department of Correctional Services* (Master's Dissertation, Criminal Justice Studies,1997).

4. The Republic of South Africa Constitution, Act 200 of 1993.

5. Constitution of the Republic of South Africa, No. 108 of 1996 [hereinafter *Constitution*].

6. D. Kalinich and W. Clack, "Transformation: From Apartheid to a Democracy–South African Corrections," *Acta Criminologica*, Vol. 11(2), 1998, 64-71.

7. J. Kollapen, "Prisoners' Rights under the Interim Constitution" (1995): 74; Constitution, *supra* note 5.

8. A. Dissel, "The Passing-Out Parade: Demilitarisation of the Correctional Services" (1997): 17; Hansard, *Debates of the National Assembly of 1996, Republic of South Africa* (Cape Town: The Government Printer, 1996).

9. Address by Mr Ben Skosana MP, *supra* note 1.

10. C. Giffard, *Privatising Prisons in South Africa* (Unpublished Work, 1997); C. Giffard, *South African Corrections: Privatization Fact File* (Unpublished Work, 1997).

11. D. Nina, "Dr. Sipo Mzimela: A Minister with a Vision?" (1996): 20.

12. Hansard, *Debates of the National Assembly of 1996, Republic of South Africa* (Cape Town: The Government Printer, 1996): 3663.

13. *Id.*

14. *Id.*, 3677.

15. Hansard, *Debates of the National Assembly of 1997, Republic of South Africa* (Cape Town: The Government Printer, 1997).

16. Correctional Services Amendment Act, No. 102 of 1997 [hereinafter the Amendment Act].

17. Ministry of Correctional Services, *Parliamentary Media Briefing*, 1997.

18. Correctional Services Act, No. 111 of 1998.

19. Correctional Services Act, section 103(1).

20. Address by Mr Ben Skosana MP, *supra* note 1.

21. C. Giffard, "Privatising Prisons in South Africa" (1999): 339.

22. Interview with Chris Giffard, independent researcher, Institute of Criminology, University of Cape Town.

23. Hansard, *Debates of the National Assembly of 1998, Republic of South Africa* (Cape Town: The Government Printer, 1998): 1786.

24. H. Corder and D. Van Zyl Smit, "Privatised Prisons and the Constitution" (1998): 475.

25. Interview with Henk Bruyn, former Commissioner of Correctional Services and currently Chief Executive Officer of Command Security, based in Cape Town.

26. McDonald clarifies this phrase "as punishment and not for punishment" by pointing out that prisons are meant to administer a punishment as decided by a legal authority. However, due to the state of many prisons, the prisoners usually end up going to prison as punishment, as well as *for* punishment, due to the atrocious conditions in which they will have to live. For example, in South Africa, some prisons do not even have electricity and/or adequate nutrition, meaning that the prisoners have not only had their freedom taken away but their basic necessities of life as well. The loss of these necessities becomes an added punishment over and above the court's decision to imprison the offender. Ideally prisons should only be a means of administering a punishment not imposing an additional punishment due to prison conditions. See D. McDonald, "When Government Fails" (1990): 183.

27. Interview with Jody Kollapen, Commissioner of the South African Human Rights Commission.

28. D. Schichor, "The Corporate Context of Private Prisons" (1993): 113.

CHAPTER SIXTEEN

Private Prisons: Emerging and Transformative Economies

Stephen Nathan

This article briefly describes the development of the international 'market' for private prisons. It also focuses on Lesotho where Group 4 Falck, a European-based transnational corporation, has proposed privatization as a solution to the government's problems of prison overcrowding, inadequate facilities and lack of finance for new infrastructure.

Introduction

In an open letter dated 17 September 2001, the Director General of the Lesotho prison service, Mr C.L. Siimane, wrote to the international criminal justice community asking for help.

> We wish to inform you that we are under a terrible pressure to have the entire Lesotho Prison Service privatized by Group 4 from the UK. Our stance as the prisons management team regarding the above has been indicated in very categorical terms. We unitedly stand opposed to the prison model suggested by Group 4. Right now Group 4 is conducting a little research which will help them make a proposal to the ministry of justice quite soon. Presently there is no outright formal opposition to the proposed regime at the ministerial level and we strongly feel this proposal is very likely to be approved.

He requested recipients of the letter to

> do anything in your power and means to frustrate the wishes and efforts of Group 4 and its proponents. Our initiatives to improve this service are at an advanced stage .... we desperately look forward to international support ...[1]

Such a letter from a senior public official is unprecedented. It could be argued that this plea for help is based simply on a vested interest in maintaining the status quo. But it epitomises a modern dilemma when privatization of a core government function is mooted. In this case, the officials are caught in the crossfire of conflicting interests: they want to be part of a democratic, local solution to a problematic criminal justice system; prisoners want humane conditions; the government wants to implement a quick fix, meet the demands of the International Monetary Fund (IMF), aspire to human rights standards and maintain electoral kudos; and the western-based private prison industry wants to expand further into emerging and transformative economies.

1. Developing Global Aspirations

Soon after the modern private prison industry emerged in the United States in the 1980s, the pioneering companies, Corrections Corporation of America (CCA) and Wackenhut Corrections Corporation (WCC) looked to the international market for growth. They were subsequently joined by European-based security firms Group 4 and Securicor as well as facilities management company Sodexho which also set up subsidiaries to exploit the burgeoning correctional services market.

Through the parent companies' established international operations or, in the case of CCA and Wackenhut, through joint ventures, these corrections companies made it clear that their market was the world's criminal justice systems. For example, in 1994 CCA and Sodexho of France formed an international strategic alliance. The deal gave Sodexho a stake in CCA and the companies agreed that the joint venture would bid for and, if successful, manage projects outside of the United States, United Kingdom, Belgium and Australia, splitting profits 51/49 per cent in favour of CCA in English-speaking countries and favoring Sodexho in the rest of the world.[2] CCA's then president and chief executive, Dr. R. Crants, is reported to have said the following:

> Our partnership links two premier service providers with the expertise to make a significant impact on the global corrections market at a time when every criminal justice system is seeking fiscally sound, technically innovative ways to solve their corrections problems.[3]

Also in 1994, Wackenhut Corrections Corporation stated in its annual report that "in preparing for the third millennium and the globalization of privatized corrections, WCC has taken a number of important steps."

After winning contracts in the United Kingdom and Australia, CCA eventually withdrew from the international market in 2000 to concentrate on its domestic operations. Sodexho, having previously bought out CCA's interests in joint venture companies in the United Kingdom and Australia, sold its eight per cent stake in CCA in May 2001.

But since its launch in 1988, Wackenhut Corrections Corporation has become the second largest private prison operator in the United States and it also claims 57 per cent of the international market. The company promotes what it describes as "its highly acclaimed, comprehensive correctional solutions and diversified services world-wide." In addition to its operations in the US, UK, Australia, Canada, New Zealand, South Africa and the Netherlands Antilles, it is "aggressively seeking further opportunities in economically and politically stable countries."[4] It has been helped in this project by the fact that its parent company, The Wackenhut Corporation, has operations in 56 countries.

Of the European security firms, Denmark-based Group 4 Falck has operations in 50 countries, including what it describes as "many emerging markets".[5] To date, its prison contracts are in the United Kingdom, Australia and South Africa.

However, in May 2002, Group 4 Falck acquired the Wackenhut Corporation. It remains to be seen what form Wackenhut and Group 4's prison operations will take and what impact any restructuring will have.

Securicor is in 40 countries but, so far, it only has one prison contract in the UK, a detention center contract in the Netherlands, and it manages two juvenile facilities in the United States. Sodexho, which is a more diversified facilities management company, is in over 70 countries, but operates five semi-private prisons in France, one private prison in the United Kingdom and another in Australia. It also provides food services to prisons in Spain, Italy and the Netherlands. The company has recently won further prison contracts in the United Kingdom and Chile.

In addition to prisons, the industry's current contracts range from electronic monitoring, prisoner transportation, health care, and the operation of immigration detention centers to financing, designing, building and operating court complexes and police custody centers.

Increasing International Interest

Although the 1996 prediction by stock analysts Prudential Securities that "the private management of prisons, jails, detention centers and, ultimately, the full spectrum of corrections services could be a worldwide movement..." has yet to come to fruition, an increasing number of countries have become sold on the idea that privatizing prisons is more cost effective, innovative and produces lower recidivism rates than public sector provision. This is despite the weight of evidence which indicates that, overall, the claims made by the industry have not been substantiated.[6]

The United States has the most private prisons and is still the largest potential single market. Australia and the United Kingdom were the first countries outside of the United States to establish first privately managed and then privately financed, designed, built and operated prisons. South Africa now also has two private prisons based on the UK model while New Zealand has one privately managed prison and Ontario recently became the first province in Canada to open a privately managed prison for adults.

In 1987, France launched its program of 21 semi-private prisons. These were built privately with all non-custodial services contracted out but the prison officers remain state employees. These contracts have recently been re-tendered and there are plans for at least six more semi-private facilities.

This French model is gaining wider acceptance, particularly in jurisdictions that do not want to, or cannot for legal reasons, devolve responsibility to privately employed prison officers. Belgium has one semi-private prison and the German state of Hesse is developing its first. Brazil is now experimenting with two mixed management medium-security prisons, and Chile has embarked on a program of ten privately financed, designed, built and maintained facilities in which all the prison officers will remain state employees.

In 2000, the Netherlands Antilles government awarded a one-year contract for the design, construction and management consultancy for a new public facility.

Meanwhile, South Korea's ministry of corrections has launched its first prison tendering process, inviting religious organizations as well as private companies to bid for a 300-bed facility management contract. Governments of countries as diverse as Cost Rica, Venezuela, Lebanon, Thailand and Mexico are at various stages of feasibility studies or contract tendering processes. The Netherlands has not ruled out a public-private partnership for at least one prison and in Israel, long regarded by industry analysts as a potential market, the current minister of justice says that he supports full privatization of the prison service and the immediate establishment of private prisons.

Other governments such as Poland, Malaysia, Hong Kong and Japan are closely watching developments, particularly in the United Kingdom.

Where Next?

Commercial confidentiality and fierce competition make prison companies notoriously secretive about contract negotiations, and exactly where they are promoting their services or lobbying for legislation that would enable prison privatization. By his own admission in a recent interview, a Group 4 Falck spokesperson would only offer "something fairly anodyne" about his company's international prospects and refused to be drawn out on the company's activities in Lesotho. He said the following:

> There appears to be continued interest in various jurisdictions around the world in exploring the applications of PPPs [public-private partnerships] using the UK model of an agreed contract and measurable standards and management fee structure as opposed to payment per head. There is also great interest in the private financing of projects.[7]

Fiona Walters, Securicor's director of development, was also circumspect.

> Our approach is slightly different [from the other companies]. We are not going for new business in areas where there is a high degree of interest, such as South America, which appears to be more interested in the French semi-private model. We are looking at markets closer to home.

Nevertheless, she added: "We don't want to contribute to environments where there is a negative culture of prison management. Eastern Europe is not a priority."[8]

Utah-based Management & Training Corporation now manages two prisons outside of the US, one in Queensland, Australia, and the other in Ontario, Canada. The company's president told the Australian media in January 2001 that " MTC hopes to run other private jails in Australia, Britain, Canada and, eventually, South America."[9] MTC is currently negotiating a contract in Costa Rica.

Correctional Services Corporation (CSC) of Florida has so far tried but failed to break into the UK and Australian markets. In the light of the company's recent restructuring in the US, it is not clear what CSC's international aspirations are.

Sodexho does not state its global corrections aspirations although its latest annual report for 2001 notes that one of its senior executives has the title of 'worldwide correctional services market champion'. The company's annual report for the year 2000 noted that "the number of inmates in creditworthy democratic countries is estimated at 2.5 million, of which two million are in the United States." Only recently, Sodexho developed and published a corporate policy which includes providing services to prisons "only in those countries which are established democracies, where the death penalty is illegal and which have rehabilitative policies for inmates." It will also not provide services requiring its employees to carry firearms.[10]

Fortunately, despite company secrecy, there are other important clues to where the industry is headed: in the direction of emerging economies. In April 2000, Mexico called on the Organization of American States, whose membership excludes Cuba but includes the US, Canada and 33 Caribbean, Central and South American countries, to look into the possible advantages of prison privatization.

Then, in September 2000, the government of Puerto Rico with sponsorship from the private sector held the first Corrections Summit of the Americas at which ministers and officials from the Caribbean, Central and South America heard presentations from Wackenhut and CCA. Notably, at that San Juan summit, Wackenhut promoted itself as operating in accordance with the criteria of both the UN and the European Committee for the Prevention of Torture and Inhuman and Degrading Treatment or Punishment (CPT).[11]

Group 4 was invited to make a presentation to a conference attended by the heads of correctional services from southern, central and eastern Africa at Windhoek, Namibia, in September 2001. In October 2001, the industry was able to make another sales pitch to ministers and officials from 20 countries in the Asia/Pacific region when they attended the Asian and Pacific Conference of Correctional Administrators (APCCA) in Chiang Mai, Thailand.

In October 2001, the private sector was given another international platform at the 2001 conference of the International Corrections and Prisons Association for the Advancement of Professional Corrections (ICPA) which attracted delegates from 32 countries. Presenters of workshops included representatives from Wackenhut Corrections Corporation, Group 4 and UK Detention Services Ltd.[12]

Private Finance: Debt by Another Name

Countries with emerging and transformative economies have some of the worst human rights records and prison conditions. They are, in many cases, in need of new infrastructure and assistance with criminal justice reform. These are also the countries that already have serious debt problems. They also face demands from the IMF and World Bank to cut public spending and privatize assets and services in return for financial aid. It is no coincidence, therefore, that the private prison industry is offering governments privately financed solutions based on the 'success' of privatization in the United States, United Kingdom and Australia. Companies, banks, think tanks and other agencies are all promoting private finance rather than public borrowing for new infrastructure.[13]

As an indication of the African market's importance, in December 2000, Cape Town hosted a Public Private Partnerships (PPP)/Private Finance Initiative (PFI) global summit. At the event, South Africa's minister of finance, Trevor Manuel, said: "... if we are to reduce our dependence on debt as a source of finance for public sector capital formation, we have to engage formally and contractually with private sector partners or investors."[14]

For many governments, and emerging economies in particular, the PFI or PPP proposition appears, on the surface, to be both fiscally and electorally attractive. Some penal reformers, too, might argue that private finance is the only option if it provides new infrastructure quickly. Private finance schemes mean that a government contracts with a consortium for the finance, design and construction of a new facility and the provision of related services. Under this arrangement the consortium is due to receive monthly fees over, usually, 25 years. Governments have no up-front capital costs as the consortium provides the necessary finance, albeit at a higher interest rate than if the government borrowed the money itself.

However, there is a terrible irony here. As experience in the United Kingdom and, in particular, Victoria, Australia, has already shown, such schemes have dire social, economic and political implications, including the loss of public account-ability, poorer wages and conditions for employees, fewer jobs than before, and inadequate service provision. Moreover, money that could be allocated to services gets creamed off in profits and fees for consultants and advisors to schemes, the private sector becomes even more entrenched in criminal justice policy making, and the fuse is lit on a financial time bomb. After all, a 25-year contract is nothing more than a long-term debt.[15]

Significantly, governments of emerging economies seeking advice on privatization from the United Nations will be disappointed. The development of private prisons has gone largely unscrutinized by the international human rights organizations charged with creating, monitoring and enforcing legal standards, safeguards and conditions in prisons. The United Nations Commission on Human Rights provides a case in point.

As far back as 1989, Cuba initiated a proposal that the United Nations Sub-Commission on Prevention of discrimination and Protection of Minorities should appoint a Special Rapporteur and set up an inquiry into prison privatization. A feasibility study was carried out and in 1993, the Sub-Commission requested authorization from its parent body, the Commission on Human Rights, to appoint one of its members to undertake a special study.

In 1994, the Commission asked the Sub-Commission to reconsider its request. Then in 1997, the Sub-Commission asked its parent body again for authorization to appoint a Special Rapporteur and undertake "an in depth study on all issues relating to the privatization of prisons, including the obligation to respect and implement the legislation in force in the country concerned and the possible civil responsibility of enterprises managing private prisons and their employees."[16] In 1998, the Commission on Human Rights repeated its request that the Sub-Commission reconsider its recommendation.

In August 1999, the Sub-Commission was due to debate the issue again but there was no discussion. Its original proposal had been consistently blocked—most notably in 1998 by the delegate from the United States supported by the delegate from the Netherlands.[17] The issue has not been raised again for discussion.

2. Lesotho's Prison Service–A Suitable Case For Privatization?

The decisions by the ANC government of South Africa to not only adopt free market reforms but also become the first on the continent and the first major transformative economy to commission private prisons has been a coup for the private prison industry. When the government tendered for its original program of four new private prisons, which was later reduced to two due to financial constraints, it short-listed five consortia which included Group 4 from Europe, Wackenhut Corrections Corporation, Management & Training Corporation and Youth Services International from the United States, and the Banapuri Group from Malaysia.

Group 4 was one of the two companies to win a contract. The 3,024 bed maximum security Mangaung prison in Bloemfontein has been financed, designed and built, and is being run by a Group 4-led consortium.

For the successful bidders, South Africa has provided a crucial launch pad from which to try to 'open up' the rest of the continent as well as the platform on which to argue that prison privatization is acceptable across the ideological divide. Both of South Africa's private prisons are currently larger than any other project in the world. That record could be shattered, however, if a proposal from Group 4 to the government of Lesotho is implemented.

Lesotho has some 3,000 prisoners and, according to the director general of the prison service, its prisons are 20 percent overcrowded. There is a policy of using parole to try to keep prison numbers down, but overall this has had little impact.

The economic backdrop to the government of Lesotho considering prison privatization includes its dependence on loans from the International Monetary Fund (IMF) and the OECD, as well as assistance from the World Bank. For example, in announcing a review of Lesotho's economic performance and the release of a further tranche of US $4 million under a poverty reduction program, the IMF stated that Lesotho's

> policies are geared to the ultimate goals of sustaining rapid economic growth, boosting employment opportunities and reducing poverty, relying primarily on the private sector. The authorities aim progressively to improve the environment for private sector economic activity through limiting the role of the public sector and making it more efficient, continuing to improve governance and the judicial system, and maintaining financial stability.[18]

Group 4's Proposal

A confidential 12-page report dated March 2001 by a consortium comprising Group 4 Correction Services SA (Pty) Ltd. and the South African construction firm, Murray and Roberts, offers an insight into the private sector's marketing efforts in an emerging economy such as Lesotho's.[19] It reveals how Group 4's operations are presented in their best light. For example, it makes no mention of any of the problems that have occurred at Group 4-operated prisons in the UK and Australia or any of the fines, contract failures, lawsuits and other scandals involving private prison companies generally in the United States, United Kingdom or Australia.[20]

The report also indicates the weight given to both private prisons and private financing for the provision of new infrastructure: traditional public procurement methods are dealt with in two paragraphs while the Private Finance Initiative warrants two pages.

Yet the consortium fails to mention any of the conceptual or practical flaws in the Private Finance Initiative, which are increasingly being exposed in the United Kingdom. Nor does it mention the case of a privately financed, designed, built and operated prison run by Corrections Corporation of Australia in Victoria, Australia, which had to be taken into public ownership in 2000 after the operator failed to rectify persistent problems.[21]

The report also shows how fast negotiations between a company and a government can take place, thus setting the political agenda and the terms of any debate. This, in turn, makes it difficult for the consideration of a locally based alternative criminal justice strategy, a crucial matter in emerging economies, to be considered. This is especially the case in Lesotho where there has been no public debate about prison privatization in general or the company's proposal in particular.

According to Group 4, on 25 August 2000, officials from the Department of Justice, Human Rights and Rehabilitation in Lesotho visited the Group 4 prison then being built for the South African government in Bloemfontein. The report does not mention which party prompted the visit. Following this visit, the company received a formal request to put forward draft proposals for a 1,000-place facility in the capital, Maseru, to house both sentenced prisoners and those awaiting trial.

On 5 October 2000, the company met with the minister for justice, the director for prisons and other state officials and made a presentation on the proposed new facility. The minister asked the company to continue a dialogue with officials to develop the proposals to the point at which they might be presented for Cabinet consideration. On 12 December 2000, the company was asked to prepare a further report addressing the general background and progress to date, design philosophy and operating procedures, funding and procurement options, and next steps.

Following discussions about centralizing all of Lesotho's prison population within one prison complex, the capacity of the proposed prison was increased to 3,500. The plan was for existing facilities to be closed, offered for alternative use, or, if commercially viable, sold off to private interests.

The consortium went on to provide further guidance for the government of Lesotho. It advised that when

> looking to the government's central spending budget, minis-
> ters must take account of many competing demands as they
> address the needs of the people. Not everything can be af-
> forded at the same time, no matter how desirable this might be.
> On the other hand, things which are important both to sustain-
> ing public confidence on the one hand and to meeting the pres-
> sures of international opinion on the other, cannot be put off
> continually.
>
> In this respect governments around the world are turning
> increasingly to the private sector in their efforts to meet as many
> of their service delivery and infrastructural needs as possible.
> These procurement strategies are called by many different terms
> although essentially they all come down to the same thing: that
> of using private sector money to procure state assets, the pay-
> ment for which is then linked to long term service contracts.
>
> In the United Kingdom for example, this process–known
> as the Private Finance Initiative–has been used to procure bil-
> lions of pounds worth of infrastructure, buildings and services...
> perhaps the most successful example of this has been new
> prisons... other related services are also contracted to the pri-
> vate sector including the transportation of prisoners to and
> from courts, the management of prisoners at court throughout
> their trials and the electronic monitoring of offenders in the com-
> munity.
>
> ... to summarise, the purchasing of assets and services in
> areas traditionally restricted solely to government is increas-
> ingly being replaced by recourse to private sector skills, finance
> and resources and is rapidly becoming the procurement method
> of choice.[22]

The document then set out the possible procurement options and suggested that the consortium could start the project "very soon" and complete it within 18-20 months.

The Alternative Strategy

While Group 4 was negotiating with the government, another initiative to solve Lesotho's problems of overcrowded and inadequate facilities was taking place. The initiative led to a report by independent consultants working with the United Kingdom's Department for International Development (DFID), which found that there was a viable alternative to privatization.

> In the five institutions visited around Maseru, there appeared to be space for initiatives, relations appeared to be relatively good with prisoners (the degree to which power is abused could not be gauged) and there was a clear sense of people knowing what needed to be done to improve the situation.[23]

A round table meeting of over 30 stakeholders including senior staff from prisons headquarters, officers in charge, rehabilitation officers, NGO representatives and police

> came up with ready 'no-cost' suggestions for reducing over-crowding in prison. These constitute positive indicators of a willingness and ability to change. They should be taken seriously and the Lesotho Prison Service should be supported with resources to manage and implement the change programme.[24]

Group 4's proposal was also commented on by the consultants, who said that if accepted, the proposal

> will inevitably arrest the flow of ideas and process of change currently experienced by the Lesotho prison service (LPS). It will present, at a stroke, a private solution to a public problem. The privatisation of the LPS is a matter for serious consideration as the implications are far-reaching and do not appear to have been fully aired.[25]

Their report went on to raise a number of questions which the government, in its haste, had not considered, as well as a range of issues that Group 4 had not addressed in its report. For example, they pointed out that Group 4 had based their proposal on solutions for wealthy countries and had not provided evidence showing that developing countries had implemented private prisons. Nor had they provided details of the promised 'latest programs in prisoner development' or substantiated the claim that such programs actually reduced reoffending rates. The consultants also asked the fundamental question, whether there are any known disadvantages of the model being proposed. They concluded that

> In the event that the government of Lesotho rejects the Group 4 proposal, the change agents are to be found in the LPS. The reform programme outlined above is both practicable and sustainable.
> There is a growing momentum across the continent for penal reform that can be traced from the Kampala Declaration

on Prison Conditions in Africa (the importance of which was recognised by the Economic and Social Council–ECOSOC–of the United Nations and adopted as a formal UN document in 1997), the establishment by the African Commission on Human and Peoples' Rights of a Special Rapporteur on Prisons and Conditions of Detention in Africa, the Kadoma Declaration on Community Service Orders in Africa 1997 (also adopted in the following year by ECOSOC) and the Arusha Declaration on Good Prison Management 1999.

Best practice models are growing in number around the world and groundbreaking initiatives are being developed across Africa. DFID has recognised that justice sector reform is relatively recent and that it is a 'long-term project'. There are no quick fixes, even if there are steps that can be taken immediately to ameliorate existing conditions.[26]

In the consultants' view, there was clearly a great deal of merit in allowing the local solutions to be developed. They feared, however, that Group 4's proposal would simply ride roughshod over that strategy.

The Director General's Plea for Help

As a result of the negotiations between the government and the company and the findings and recommendations of the consultants, the Director General of the prison service took the step of writing his letter to the international criminal justice community.

A position paper accompanying the letter set out the management's "total opposition" to privatization.[27] It pointed out that Lesotho is a member of the United Nations, the Commonwealth, Organization of African Unity and the Southern African Development Community. These bodies fully promote and protect democratic principles and a human rights culture in correctional services. Lesotho is also a party to the International Covenant on Civil and Political Rights, as well as the Convention on the Rights of the Child, and most importantly, it has acceded to the guarantee of prisoners' rights on the basis of United Nations Standard Minimum Rules for non-custodial measures. According to the position paper, "none of these instruments have accommodation for the privatization of prisons." The paper also referred to the regional conventions and declarations mentioned by the consultants and added that these "are all proponents of diversionary measures and all forms of non-custodial options as well as post sentencing dispositions for prison regime."

The position paper reminded the international community that

> Lesotho has acceded to all aforementioned instruments. Our constitution, parent legislation, policies and practice are all in line with these instruments; and for all the past five years, a headway is noticeable due to recognition and full utilization of these instruments.

It went on to consider other arguments against privatization. Some were general, such as the idea that "privatization is too extreme a reform measure". Others were more specific to Lesotho's circumstances, such as the argument that the public would have to travel over long distances at terrible expense to visit their next-of-kin in such a prison; remandees and convicts in Qacha's Nek and Mokhotlong would have to travel over a great distance at an unbearable public cost in a country whose economy is already shaky. So, more expenses will be incurred by the taxpayer/public or the government to run this model.

Then, as if the possibility of such a proposal was so farfetched, they stated that "privatization of the entire prison service would be tantamount to commercializing the police service or the entire ministry of justice and human rights, given the complexity and the size of the Lesotho prison service."

The prison service noted that the LDF (the Lesotho Defence Forces), NSS (the National Security Service), and LMPS (the Lesotho Mounted Police) have, on a number of occasions, been subjected to vigorous review and reform championed by the government in consultation with internationally recognized specialists and organizations. As a result, their administration, level of service provision and professionalism had "improved very positively". So it urged the government to consider whether "a vigorous penal reform with special and particular attention to prison reform would be enough to effect visible change in so far as the efficiency of our prisons is concerned." The prison service also urged the government to finalize a draft prison bill which should be "urgently effected as it incorporates UN standards. This draft already received commendation from the United Nations Center for Human Rights in 1998."

Recent Events

In a letter to the author dated 8 October 2001, the Director General said:

> Group 4 has been allowed to conduct research on our prison regime by the ministry. We asked them whether they would permit any public debate on their proposal. They replied that it might not be necessary as the Cabinet can approve their system on behalf of the entire nation. It should be noted that the Lesotho prison service management team has not, at any stage, been consulted; and it does not look like this will happen in the future. The entire model is being imposed on us...

Since then, a general election has taken place and whatever negotiations there have been between the government and Group 4 have continued without the prison service's input.

However, in September 2002, a government spokesperson said that a director of Group 4 was due to make a presentation on its proposal to the government "very soon".[28]

Conclusion

For almost 20 years, the private prison industry has developed on the back of an increasing trend towards privatization of public services. Having established itself in the west, this industry will expand further into the emerging and transformative economies as long as governments are tied to the diktats of the IMF,

World Bank and other agencies that demand privatization as a condition of assistance.

In countries like Lesotho, efforts to develop local solutions for improving the criminal justice system could be hijacked for generations to come if services are tied to privately financed and operated infrastructure and corporate interests rather than those of society as a whole.

Endnotes

1. Prison Privatisation Report International #43, Sept/Oct 2001 <www.psiru.org/justice>.

2. S. Nathan, "US companies expand corrections market overseas", (Summer 1995), *National Prison Project Journal,* American Civil Liberties Foundation.

3. CCA/Sodexho Alliance, Privatisation Factfile No.7, in Prison Report No.28 (Autumn 1994), Prison Reform Trust.

4. Annual Report 2000, Wackenhut Corrections Corporation.

5. Annual Report 2000, Group 4 Falck.

6. See for example: Paul Moyle, *Profiting from Punishment* (Australia, Pluto Press, 2000); A. James, A. Keith Bottomley, A. Liebling E. Clare, *Privatizing Prisons: Rhetoric and Reality,* (London, Sage, 1997); Abt Associates Inc., *Private Prisons in the United States: An Assessment of Current Practice,* (Cambridge, Mass. 1998); *The Evidence Is Clear: Crime Shouldn't Pay,* (Washington, American Federation of State, County and Municipal Employees, AFL-CIO, 2000); *Private Adult Correctional Facilities: Fines, Failures and Dubious Practices,* (Canada, Ontario Public Service Employees Union, 2000); and Prison Privatization Report International, issues 1-43 (1996-2001) Prison Reform Trust and issues 44 (2001) onwards, Public Services International Research Unit, University of Greenwich, London, all at <www.psiru.org/justice>.

7. S. Nathan, "Private prisons, global aspirations" (June 2001); The PFI Report, Centaur Finance Intelligence <www.publicprivatefinance.com>.

8. *Id.*

9. Courier Mail, 9 January 2001, reported in Prison Privatisation Report International #38, Jan/Feb 2001 <www.psiru.org/justice>.

10. Reported in Prison Privatisation Report International #41, June 2001 <www.psiru.org/justice>.

11. S. Nathan, "International prison privatisation" (November 2001), Socio-Legal Newsletter No. 35, Socio-Legal Studies Association, Cardiff.

12. For a summary of the discussion, details of the industry's overall strategy and Wackenhut's suggestions for emerging economies in particular, see Prison Privatisation Report International #48, April/May 2002, <www.psiru.org/justice>.

13. See, for example, "Global Push for PFI" in Prison Privatisation Report International # 42, July/August 2001 <www.psiru.org/justice>.

14. S. Harrington, "The internationalisation of PPP: the Cape Town summit," (Dec 2000/Jan 2001), The PFI Report, Centaur Finance Intelligence, *supra* note 7.

15. See "What Future For Public Services: the PFI and Public Private Partnerships" (2001) <www.centre.public.org.uk/briefings>; see also S. Nathan and D. Whitfield, "PFI and Europe's most privatised criminal justice system" (February 2000), The PFI Report, Centaur Finance Intelligence, *supra* note 7.

16. Annotation to the provisional agenda of the 51st Session, United Nations Sub-Commission on Prevention of Discrimination and Protection of Minorities, August 1999, E/CN.4/Sub.2/1999/1/Add.1

17. Author's interview with clerk to the Sub-Commission reported in Prison Privatisation Report International # 32, November 1999, <www.psiru.org/justice>.

18. "IMF Completes Lesotho's Review Under Poverty Reduction and Growth Facility," IMF News Brief No. 91/65 20 July 2001, Washington.

19. Report On The Proposed New Central Prison Complex for the Government of Lesotho by Group 4 Correction Services SA (Pty) Ltd, Murray & Roberts and Paul Silver, March 2001.

20. Annual Report 2000, Group 4 Falck, *supra* note 5.

21. S. Nathan, "Victoria' flagship, PFI prison sinks" (February 2001), The PFI Report, Centaur Finance Intelligence, *supra* note 7.

22. Report on the Proposed New Central Prison Complex for the Government of Lesotho, *supra* note 18. See also Prison Privatisation Report International #41, June 2001 <www.psiru.org/justice>.

23. Department for International Development "Lesotho: Safety, Security and Access to Justice, Penal reform Policy Choices," DFID, April 2001.

24. *Id.*

25. *Id.*

26. *Id.*

27. "Private Prison as an Alternative to Lesotho Prison Regime," Lesotho Prison Service, September 2001.

28. Prison Privatisation Report International #49, August/September 2002, <www.psiru.org/justice.org>.

CHAPTER SEVENTEEN

Women Prisoners as Customers: Counting the Costs of the Privately Managed Metropolitan Women's Correctional Centre: Australia[1]

Amanda George

In October 2000, the Victorian government used emergency powers under the Corrections Act to step in and take over management of the Metropolitan Women's Correctional Centre (the MWCC was known as Deer Park Prison) from Corrections Corporation of Australia (CCA). The government intervention came after a scathing report on the prison's management by the Victorian Corrections Commissioner.[2]

This 'step in' put a stop to the former liberal government's most controversial prison privatization–signing over 80 percent of Victorian women prisoners to the Australian subsidiary of the world's largest private prison corporation, Corrections Corporation of America. Prison privatization, the government said, would reduce the 'risk' to government. This risk proved a disaster for women from the moment the prison opened.

In her September 2000 Report, the Commissioner cited as concerns the levels of self-harm, assaults on officers and the continuing failure of the prison to have adequate suicide prevention procedures. She cited the tear gassing of women twice in three months in 1999 as a concern and was also critical of extraordinarily high levels of women–as high as 29 percent–being kept on protection.[3]

Yet if we look back at Commissioner's Reports from 1996 when the prison opened, these problems were already evident. Key issues in four years of Commissioner Reports have been self-injury, assaults between women, 'at risk' assessments,[4] children's issues, prescribed medication levels, and the misreporting of incidents by the prison. These Commissioner Reports clearly document four years of escalating crises which could and should have been stopped much earlier.

After the government's September intervention, CCA protested that the use of this power, agreed to by all parties in the contract, was unfair and politically motivated.[5] What CCA failed to acknowledge was that for four years, a politically motivated decision was made to keep paying them, notwithstanding their continuous breaches of the contract.

What I will discuss in this paper is the costs of privatizing women prisoners' lives, who paid the price and how this 'radical social experiment' was allowed to go on for so long.

In August 1996, amid much community protest, the Victorian liberal government opened the first private women's prison outside of the US. At the time, Victorians were spending $2.00 each a year on women prisoners;[6] by privatizing prisons, the government said it would save each of us 20 cents a year. Along with this massive saving, women prisoners were promised better conditions and society was promised greater prison accountability through parliamentary scrutiny. It is a sad indictment of the secretiveness of most governments that public scrutiny of what goes on in prisons is used as a carrot for privatization, when it should be a staple of good government.

Any government that wishes to set up a prison system that on every count—cost, conditions and accountability—was a failure, need look no further than Victoria. More disturbingly, if the intention of a society is to abrogate responsibility for how women prisoners live by throwing them to the compassion of the wolves of profit, then emulate Victoria.

The first step and cost of prison privatization was to hobble democracy. In a promise booktlip, the former Kennett government legislated to actually prevent parliamentary scrutiny of prisons.[7] In four years of prison privatization, except for the report justifying the removal of CCA from the MWCC, there has been no reporting to Parliament on the experiment, even though each year the government pays $180 million a year to private prison corporations.[8]

After hobbling the democratic principle of parliamentary scrutiny, the next step in privatization was to claim that what government requires of prison operators and what goes on in prison, is a commercial secret. The commercial secret exemption to disclosure under Freedom of Information legislation was subsequently was waived by government and three prison corporations in a court case that went on for three years. Using the Freedom of Information Act, a community legal center sought disclosure of the standards required of prison operators, the prison operating manuals, prison contracts and the Commissioner's monitoring reports. The legal center ultimately won its case in the Victorian Supreme Court the day before the election which toppled the Kennett government. The decision affirmed the imperative of public disclosure surrounding prisons.[9] Unfortunately the most revealing forum for discovering what went on at Deer Park Prison was at the coronial inquests into the deaths of two women who died in the prison.[10]

The legal costs accrued by the government and the corporations in fighting, over the span of three years, to prevent the disclosure of information and the government's consequent denial of public accountability, came in at over a quarter of a million dollars. The community legal center ran its case on minor philanthropic funding, and on an overwhelming majority of volunteer work. Such costs, financial and social, do not feature in the government's cost-saving analysis of twenty cents.

In addition to legislated secrecy and commercial secrecy, those who pushed for privatization wanted to gag public debate, and relied on corporate heavyweights to do so. Threats of defamation from these corporations served to silence their critics in a similar manner that domestic violence silences its victim. First came the bullying, followed by the threats of further bullying, designed to control behavior by instilling fear. This has dangerous consequences for open and vigorous discussion about what practices we permit in prison in the name of punishment and control.

Corrections Corporation of Australia, the managers of Deer Park Prison, sent their last defamation threat in 1997, the day after an Australian Institute of Criminology conference on private prisons was held, sponsored by the AIC and Group 4, another prison corporation.[11] In this instance, CCA's complaint concerned an article that had been published in a newspaper two weeks before the conference. It reported on the tear gassing of women at Deer Park and the escalating crisis in management at the prison.[12] It seemed CCA didn't want the community to know what was going on or going wrong in the prison. And things were going very wrong, which was partly evidenced by the tear gassing, signaling the first time tear gas had been used on women in Victorian prisons. The women subjected to tear gas were the same women whom the state system previously managed without resort to chemical weapons.

The first use of tear gas targeted three women in an enclosed prison van who were handcuffed and who had refused to move. They had stepped through each other's handcuffs, forming a single mass, and could not easily move. Gas was used to force them to move. Tear gassing women who present no threat, carry no weapons and who are in handcuffs, merely to force movement, would never happen in the outside community. Nor should it happen in prison.

Since then the use of tear gas has escalated–the first gassing in May 1997 was of three women, the second in August 1999 of 5 women, and the third in October 1999 of 18 women. On each occasion the government held hands with CCA, because it is the government that has authorized and administered the gassing for CCA. The incidents that preceded all of the gassings, came about after festering complaints by women about management and conditions at the prison.

As well as having to resort to the use of chemical weapons to control women, Deer Park staff had problems protecting women. Deer Park has had the highest number of women 'on protection' in Australia. At any given time, 25 percent of women were on protection, whereas in other eastern states the figure is as low as 3 percent.[13] These high numbers of women living in fear of other women is another sign of the abject failure of the company.

The fact that the CCA was allowed to continue at length to cause women to live in a state of fear may be explained in part by the government's decision to contract itself out of direct control over its prisons. Low numbers of staff, high turnover, and resource starvation, which were the root of the prison's problems, could no longer be affected by the government. Moreover, CCA was not particularly encouraged to prevent violence between inmates because the contract merely called for a negligible performance penalty which prevented the corporation from being penalized for under- or misreporting incidents.[14]

Even when certain contractual breaches enable the government to act, this is an enormously long, complex, legalistic and expensive process against powerful global prison corporations. The current Corrections Minister described the contracts as

> a dog's breakfast. It's not the way to run a prison system. I mean it's bizarre when you have very urgent situations in the prison and you have to each time talk to lawyers to ascertain what you actually have to do about it.[15]

Through privatization, the government hampered its ability to make policy on prison as any policy change requires agreement between all prison providers. In 1996, community legal centers wrote to the Commissioner asking for rules related to the retention of prison camera videotapes. Deer Park relies on at least 55 cameras in its prison management. First the government refused on the basis that it did not want overly prescriptive contracts and that the issue should be left to the providers to resolve. In 1999, the auditor general recommended uniform electronic surveillance rules.[16] The policy is still under review because the government is obliged to negotiate with each of the four corrections operators to come to a mutually accepted uniform procedure. Meanwhile the videotape of a woman in a camera monitored cell, having her clothes cut off, forcibly injected, put into a canvas nightie and having her knee broken in the process, is lost. Videotapes of assaults and tear gassings are missing, but videotapes of women picking up drops over the fence never seem to disappear.

Their fettered ability to change policy is exacerbated by the fact that the government is required to compensate operators for any change in policy.[17] If government regained full control over prisons, it could create policy or re-allocate resources whenever the need arose, but with private operators it cannot do this. As a consequence of privatization, it took five months of haggling between government and the operators of the Port Phillip private men's prison to decide who would pay for the removal of hanging points. Meanwhile, another four men died by hanging themselves.

When Deer Park had problems with levels of self-harm in its first year, the government did nothing to force the operator to change its practices. To make matters worse, it gave the corporation $70,000 to help it along. How concerned was the Commissioner the next year when Paula Richardson, who had a documented history of suicide attempts and self-harm, was found hanging by a shower curtain in a management cell?[18] Not only does the Commissioner's quarterly report for that period ignore Paula's death, but it gives the prison a "☺", a Mr. Smiley face, for their improved levels of self-harm that year.[19]

The promise of improved prison conditions and accountability that apparently only privatization could deliver was to come about from the setting of standards and service delivery outcomes. These outcomes are quantifiable measures, such as the number of assaults, self-harms and positive urine tests. One flaw with these measures, however, is that they are based on prison operators' self-reporting. Government monitoring processes rely largely on these prison-generated reports. Because performance is assessed for example on how many self-harms are reported, there is a clear incentive for the prison to underreport, and minimize the problem. The result at Deer Park was that there were ongoing disputes about what constituted self-harm and whose responsibility it was to write up self-harm reports, even though there were very clear rules and definitions in the prison's operating manual. This was revealed in the Paula Richardson inquest, in which prison officers' notes were found to have recorded Paula's statement that she wanted to do worse than self harm. The prison's reports to the Commissioner's office did not list the injuries to her forearm as self-harms, as required by the operating manual. More disturbingly, with the operator and the government focusing on what constituted self harm and how it was to be reported, everyone except women prisoners could pretend that the incidents were fewer than they really were. The problem of self-harm has become masked, with government unable, and the prison unwilling, to act. This is one of the costs of prison privatization for women.

In each year the MWCC operated, it exceeded the levels of assaults permitted under the contract. They were often twice as high.[20] Moreover, we know that the recorded levels of assault are a drop in the ocean, because it is up to the eyes and honesty of the prison staff to report these assaults. So, the stand-overs, bashings and burnings went on. Likewise, the levels of self injury were often twice as high as the contract permitted.[21] Those who have any experience in women's prisons know that the levels of self-harm are the barometer of the health of the prison. But with privatization, government intervention is hampered, while women suffer the costs.

In the past there have always been surges of self-harm in women's prisons. In the late 1980s, the Fairlea prison was in crisis, which many outside organizations forced government to acknowledge. Research was commissioned, resources were provided or reallocated, changes made, programs implemented and rates of self-harm dropped. In the private system though, the government seems powerless to act to effect change, except by removing the operator entirely. So as a consequence, the inability of the government to force the operator to act and the failure of the operator to act, has resulted in privatization fostering violence, self harm and suicide attempts. For four years, the government and CCA met and talked between themselves while the slashings, hanging attempts and bashings went on, and the CCA pocketed $40 million.

The claim of increased accountability about incidents at Deer Park has not been verifiable, particularly because there is no contractual penalty for under or misreporting, so the Commissioner's Reports, which merely regurgitated the prison's own reports, could not be believed. Moreover, staff left at such high rates that allegations of poor reporting and record keeping could be blamed on individuals who were no longer there rather than the prison's overall management systems. The MWCC had the revolving door syndrome not just in relation to prisoners but to staff too. In its four-year existence, the CCA says it had four general managers. In fact, that represents only half the story since five other casuals managed while new general managers were found. This staff turnover occurred from top to bottom.[22] For women prisoners, this constant staff turnover meant there was even greater uncertainty in the rubbery rules that characterize any prison. In terms of standardized record keeping, rarely did staff remain employed long enough to know how to do it.

The prison's medical center had three different subcontractors over four years.[23] Each of these contractors relied on nursing agency staff because the working conditions were too difficult to keep permanents. This meant that there was no continuity of health care for women, and that formal complaints about health care were ignored and ultimately fell away.

At times, the levels of prescribed medication at Deer Park have been astoundingly high. What did the government do about this? It monitored it, expressed its concern and monitored it again. The Commissioner, in her September 2000 Report which justified the removal of CCA, documented the enormous number of overdoses at the prison, but she failed to report that over 95 percent of MWCC women are on prescribed medication.[24] The illegal drugs that come into the prison in dribs and drabs are not the prime cause of overdoses, but rather the fact that women are having tastes of illegal drugs in bodies that are already saturated with anti-psychotics, antidepressants, major tranquillizers and methadone.

In terms of accountability, the health service was particularly bad. Brimbank Community Legal Centre made complaints regarding allegations that the medical center was crushing women's medication to stop women storing it in their mouths. Such a practice is dangerous, crude and unnecessary. Crushing pills and putting them in water not only produces a foul-tasting liquid, it removes the protective coating around many medications which exists to protect the stomach's lining and this can seriously affect the absorption process. In health facilities where swallowing via the mouth is a problem, a pharmacist can be asked to produce the medication in suspension form, as is the general practice with methadone dispensing. However, pharmacists cost money and MWCC would not employ one.

Community legal centers complained about the medication crushing from the time the prison opened, but each time the prison denied it was happening, assured us that it would not happen again, or proclaimed that the particular health provider had left. Brimbank Community Legal Centre then obtained medical center logbooks where nurses described doing it and documented women's complaints about it. Nothing happened. Why is it that we could find the evidence of medication crushing, yet the government prison health monitors apparently could not? There are two reasons. First, the government never intended to spend the money on proper prison monitoring because that would eat into their 20 cents saving.[25] Second, proper monitoring could reveal problems in the experiment.[26] If you don't really want to see and don't make resources available to look, you never will find.

In terms of accountability, the structure of the Commissioner's office has its own conflicts. It is the role of the Commissioner to monitor and advise the minister on contract compliance. As stated previously, tear gas has now been used three times at MWCC. On every occasion the government's elite prison squad, the Special Emergency Security Group (SESG) were brought in wearing dark overalls, helmets and shields. Although the contract for the women's prison specifically prohibits the use of tear gas on pregnant women,[27] in October 1999 the Commissioner herself authorized the use of tear gas on 18 women in the protection unit at Deer Park, one of whom was eight and a half months pregnant. A complaint to the Commissioner—that she had authorized a serious breach of the contract she was supposed to monitor—rested with her and was dismissed. The Commissioner's willingness to authorize such a breach and her appraisal that her own actions were justified, demonstrate how she pandered to the perspective of the corporation, failing in her role as a purportedly independent public servant meant to monitor and enforce a contract in the public interest. When the woman had her baby soon after the gassing, she was faced with an unenviable 'choice' of whether to bring her baby back to a prison of fear and violence or go through the pain of separation, and send the baby out. These are costs women and their children pay.

It is with respect to the rights of women and their children that the government and the company have shown the most contempt. Victoria was the first state in Australia to allow children up to school age to live in prison with their mothers. This occurred in the early 1980's. Victoria was also the best state at providing extended visits for children. The all-day visits used to take place in the relative privacy of women's cells or units, and allowed woman and children to have less artificial time together, cooking, cuddling, and running around, unlike visits that take place inside a room with other people under the watch of cameras. When the government drafted the Deer Park contract, it did nothing to ensure the continuance of the private extended visits which had been practice for years. Instead, it left extended children's visits entirely up to the prison operator. When the women were moved to Deer Park, the prison decided it would not provide them. The women protested immediately by organizing a sit-in, and for a time these visits were reinstated, but later they were stopped. The government did not intervene.

There have been other costs for women and their children. At Fairlea, with a population of eighty women, there would sometimes be four children living there;

many were three- and four-year olds. At Deer Park with twice as many women, there are only three children and they are all babies. The reason women do not want their children there is because the environment is unsafe and resources non-existent. Many women do not want their children witnessing women bashing each other, they do not want them living in an environment of fear and they do not want them to face tear gas. In terms of resources, children create extra problems for prison managers, problems that require money and frankly, the prison operators prioritize corporate profits over the need of women and their children.

Visitors to the prison have also experienced the costs. Thirty thousand people have visited women at Deer Park over four years,[28] yet there is no public transport to the prison. It is a three kilometer walk from the bus on a road used by quarry trucks with no footpath. The land was formerly a defence industry rocket fuel testing site which the government purchased for a song. The government chose the site even though it had no public transport access, and the CCA kept it that way. Having fewer visitors at the prison made it possible to operate with less staff. Moreover, fewer visitors meant that fewer people knew what was going on.

If you want to create a prison system that is completely unresponsive to what is going on in a prison, privatize it because privatization 'Victorian-style' burdens government with a spectacular contractual inability to act when a prison is in crisis, except to take the extraordinary step of terminating the contract and paying out the operator. There was little in the way of financial stick in the contract to force operators to address problems. The payment structure of the contract meant that as long as the operator housed prisoners and performed required correctional functions, such as preventing escapes, they were paid. A component of the contract was a 5 percent payment stream for 'performance', called the performance linked fee, which was based on an extremely complicated calculation. Despite the ongoing and increasing failure of the operator to meet the contractual performance indicators, CCA lost only $70,000 from the $40 million contract as penalty.[29]

Moreover the threat of legal action by companies over the interpretation of the contract and contractual breaches means that government and companies engage in lengthy squabbles, while women live in a decaying prison filled with fear, despondency and violence.

So what did we get for the eighty cents we may have saved over four years? Cheryl Black is dead. Cheryl was a 43 year-old intellectually disabled epileptic woman. She started institutional life in the Darling Babies Home followed by 39 years in state institutions where she was abused. Her first prison was Deer Park, where she died within two months of natural causes.[30] Her incarceration shows the preference for prisons as the place for people already pushed to the margins. Paula Richardson, a 23 year-old woman of aboriginal heritage is dead by hanging. In the last year, fifteen women died within days and weeks of leaving prison, most as a result of combined drug toxicity overdoses.

The cost to the community was years of struggle to force the disclosure of promised information and to expose what was going on at Deer Park. There was enormous cost to the individuals and organizations picking up the pieces of women's lives and those of their children. The cost for women prisoners included being forced to live in a environment of violence and despair: women living in fear of bashings, repeatedly committing harm to themselves, weeping at the loss of meaningful contact with children, and happily accepting medication from the prison to dull the pain.

For eighty cents, the government bought itself shackles, and the largest private prison corporation in the world laughed all the way home from the New York Stock Exchange, having cashed in its shares which then suffered a spectacular demise from a high of $68 to $1.00.[31] But it was women prisoners who were burned, by the contempt of government and the god of profit. But then, they are the criminals.

Endnotes

1. This paper has been written drawing on the work of the Corrections Working Group of the Victorian Federation of Community Legal Centres. This small group of unfailingly dedicated people are an inspiration to work with. We also rely on and thank the women and men in prison who work with us. As always, thank you to Malcolm Feiner, the OCSC librarian.

2. "Correctional Services Commissioner's Report on Metropolitan Women's Correctional Centre's Compliance with its Contractual Obligations and Prison Services Agreement" (2000).

3. 'Protection' is where a prisoner who is in fear of other prisoners is kept separate from them. At MWCC there was a separate fenced protection unit, which at times housed forty women.

4. 'At risk' assessments are the tools the prison uses to decide whether a woman is at risk of harming herself.

5. Mark Forbes, "Prison operator 'aided opposition'," *The Age*, 24 October 2000: 6. This report on leaked media briefing documents between CCA's media representatives and the (liberal) opposition on the prison default notices detailed a strategy to 'curry favor' with key journalists.

6. "Commonwealth Grants Commission Report on General Relativities" (1999): vol. III, p.83.

7. In a press release on 16 December 1993, the former government promised to appoint the contract monitors under Section 9D of the Corrections Act. Section 9D(3) incorporates monitors' reports into annual reports to Parliament. Instead, the monitoring occurs as a function of the Commissioner under Section 8A which carries no legislated reporting responsibilities. The only information tabled in Parliament is contained in Justice Ministry Annual Reports, which comprise a couple of pages on prisons and extensive statistical tables.

8. Disappointingly the new Bracks Labor government in Victoria, which was elected on the promise of transparency and accountability, has made no move to legislate parliamentary reporting by the Corrections Commissioner, despite recommendations of the former auditor general. See Victorian Auditor-General, "Victoria's prison system: Community protection and prisoner welfare" (1999): 55; Bracks government's own Russell Review: Prof. B. Russell, "Contracting, Privatisation Probity and Disclosure in Victoria 1992-1999" (2000): 39.

9. *Coburg Brunswick Community Legal and Financial Counselling Centre* v. *Department of Justice Australasian Correctional Investment Ltd., Corrections Corporation of Australia Pty Ltd., Group 4 Correction Services* (1999) VAR 208. On 17 September 1999, the Supreme Court of Appeal affirmed the VCAT decision requiring disclosure.

10. Inquest into the death on 30 March 1997 of Cheryl Fay Black, Victorian Coroners Court, findings 5 August 1998; Inquest into the death on 11 September 1998 of Paula Richardson Victorian Coroners Court (part heard).

11. Australian Institute of Criminology Conference, *Privatisation and Public Policy: A Correctional Case* Study, Melbourne, June 1997.

12. Amanda George, "Women Gassed in Prison," *The Republican,* 30 May 1997: 1.

13. Information from NSW and Qld Corrective Services, 23 October 2000.

14. B. Russell, "Contracting, Privatisation Probity and Disclosure in Victoria 1992-1999," *supra* note 8 at 21.

15. Stateline ABC TV Victoria, 21 July 2000.

16. Victorian Auditor-General, "Victoria's prison system: Community protection and prisoner welfare" (1999).

17. B. Russell, "Contracting, Privatisation Probity and Disclosure in Victoria 1992-1999," *supra* note 8 at 16.

18. A management cell is used for prisoners who are being punished for an internal prison offence. Paula was in the cell because she had thrown a dustpan and broom around, tipped over a chair, and refused to pick them up.

19. MWCC Commissioner's Compliance Quarterly Report, September to November 1998.

20. *Victorian Commissioner for Corrective Services Quarterly Reports 1996-1999.* All Commissioner's reports are not provided until twelve months after a performance year because of the desire "not to prejudice the perception of performance by releasing quantitative information part way through a performance year," see P. Kirby, *Independent Investigation into the Management and Operation of Victoria's Private Prisons,* (2000): 46. This deliberate time lag makes it impossible for outside bodies to know what the prisons are telling government about their performance and compare it to the story told by prisoners.

21. *Victorian Commissioner for Corrective Services Quarterly Reports 1996-1999, supra* note 20.

22. B. Russell, "Contracting, Privatisation Probity and Disclosure in Victoria 1992-1999," *supra* note 8 at 33.

23. It has never been revealed, but it is believed the subcontractor turnover is because of the

impossibility of providing adequate health services at CCA's price.

24. Department of Human Services, MWCC Medication Audit 1997-1999. The percentages varied from 87-98 percent of women on some form of medication.

25. The debates in Parliament assured everyone that monitoring would be thorough, yet the government did not allocate nearly enough resources. It appears that no written guidelines for health monitoring were drawn up, and the monitoring program was not actually developed until they were into the running of the contracts.

26. See Victorian Auditor General Report, *supra* note 16 at 84-86. The first Correctional Services Commissioner, John Van Groningen, unsuccessfully requested more money for contract monitoring.

27. Metropolitan Women's Correctional Centre Policy Manual 9-100.6.

28. Three CCA Monthly Service Reports to the Commissioner for 1998 have been released. The author has used those figures to approximate the visitor numbers.

29. B. Russell, "Contracting, Privatisation Probity and Disclosure in Victoria 1992-1999," *supra* note 8, Attachment 1.

30. David Elias, "A Death Undeserved. Cheryl Black is dead. Does anyone care?" *The Age*, 12 April 1997: A19.

31. CCAustralia formerly owned by CCAmerica, has now been bought out by Sodhexo a French private prison company. CCAustralia was already taking orders from Paris, as referred to in Correctional Services Commissioners Report, *supra* note 2 at18. In November 2000, the Victorian government announced a complete buy back of the Deer Park Prison from Corrections Corporation of Australia for $A20.2 million.

Conclusion

Andrew Coyle

The topic of prison[1] privatization cannot be separated from a wider consideration of the nature of imprisonment and its use. On that basis, it is no surprise that this volume concentrates on the situation in the United States. The love which the US has for incarceration is something which its friends in other countries find very difficult to understand. In the US there are two million men, women and children in federal and state prisons and local jails. In 2001 the US overtook Russia as the country with the greatest proportion of its citizens in detention. The US has just under 5 percent of the world's total population[2] but has 23 percent of its prisoners.[3] In the States of Louisiana and Texas and the District of Columbia, over 1 percent of the entire population is in prison or jail custody.[4] These are figures which set the United States apart from the rest of the democratic world and which are a constant source of perplexity for academics, corrections professionals and public commentators in other countries.

In most countries prisons reflect the values of the societies in which they exist. In a number of countries, such as Canada[5] and the Netherlands[6], a genuine attempt is made to use them as places of last resort. In these countries there is a reluctance to deprive citizens of their liberty since this is not regarded as an effective form of punishment nor as an efficient way to increase public safety. In some countries where there has been an increasing use of imprisonment in recent years, politicians and senior public officials are now openly questioning the wisdom of what is happening. For example, in a recent major speech the Director General of the Prison Service in England and Wales said:

> As I have told the Home Secretary, no one, including me, thinks that locking more and more people up is a sensible way of spending public money. Many of the people we are locking up will not benefit in any way from their sentence. Many of them will lose jobs, accommodation and family support and will become more criminal. Meanwhile, the very significant numbers in prison who we can change, whose lives can be given a new direction, get too little of our attention as we struggle to cope with the insanity of a prison population that may hit 70,000 this summer.[7]

Similar views are being expressed in the countries which made up the former Soviet Union, which until recently had even higher rates of imprisonment than the US. Speaking at a conference of European Ministers of Justice, the Russian Minister Yuri Chayka, a man with a reputation as a hardliner, called on his European colleagues to take common action to stop the increase in lengthy prison sentences, by which he meant sentences over five years:

> The expansion and tightening of modern punitive practice leads
> to a higher load on the penitentiary system, overcrowding of
> prisons, personnel shortage and an increase in the spending
> of society as a whole.[8]

These are not sentiments likely to be voiced by senior officials or politicians in the US. So, the first question to be asked in this context is about the value system of a society which is content to lock up so many of its citizens.

Further questions arise when one looks at the composition of the prison population. In any country, if one wishes to discover who are the marginalized groups in society, one need only look at the composition of the prison population. In many countries there will be disproportionate numbers from racial and ethnic minority groups: Roma in Central Europe, Aboriginals in Australia and, as graphically described in a number of the chapters of this book, African Americans and other minorities in the US. In many prisons and jails one will also find large numbers of men and women who are mentally disordered and who have alcohol or drug addictions. Significant proportions of people who are in prison will have been previously unemployed and homeless. For these groups, as several authors in this book argue, prison is a place of social control, replacing the poor houses and asylums of previous centuries.

The need to consider prisons within the wider context of society does not apply only to prisoners. It applies also to the way in which prisons are organized and managed. In modern democratic societies, the task of government is to ensure that all citizens have equal access to a decent, humane and secure lifestyle. It often achieves this, not by providing essential services itself, but by ensuring that they are provided by others in as equitable a manner as possible. This can be done in a wide variety of ways, encompassing a wide spectrum of options. In respect of some essential services, such as health care, education and utilities, including electricity and water, there is likely to be a mixed economy in which some services are provided by private companies and others by public agencies. Those who are able and who so choose may purchase these services for themselves and their families. The task of government is to make fiscal arrangements which ensure that everyone has appropriate access to these services; citizens should not be excluded from them simply because they cannot afford them. There are a small number of contexts in which the state is not prepared to permit a mixed economy. National defence is an obvious example. All armed services remain under the direct control of the government. Private or mercenary armies are not permitted in democratic countries. The judiciary is another example where private enterprise is not permitted. Protection of the public has become a slightly greyer area in recent years. Private security firms now abound and in some areas outnumber the police but the core responsibility for public order and for investigation of crime still lies with state officials.

All of these, national defence, the judiciary and the police are what might be termed monopoly providers. The equal provision of these services is regarded as being so essential for the good of democratic society that this overrules other considerations, such as profit or loss. President Bush has made this abundantly clear in respect of the security of the US since September 11, 2001. That is not to say that in providing these services there is no need to take account of efficiency or value for money. On the contrary, since these services are all provided from the public purse close attention should be paid to these matters. The point is that finance is not the bottom line. Instead, the good of civil society is the final consideration.

In the modern era, until fairly recently, the task of depriving citizens of their liberty was another function which was regarded as a state monopoly for similar reasons. Individual freedom was so sacred that only the state could take it away after due process and only the state could administer the punishment passed by its own courts.

The chapters in this book have described how the state monopoly on the administration of punishment has been eroded in recent years in a number of countries, especially in the US. What is usually described as "privatization" of prisons covers a wide spectrum.[9] This starts with generally non-contentious areas such as issuing commercial contracts for the prisoners' canteen or commissary. Even here, there is room for concern. In the US a single payphone inside a prison can earn $12,000 a year for its owner. In 1997, $21.2 million commission was made from phone calls made by prisoners in New York, $17.6 million from prisoners in California and $13.8 million from prisoners in Florida.[10]

The next stage in privatization is that in which specific services, such as drug treatment or other programs for prisoners, are delivered by commercial companies or not-for-profit organizations. Moving along the spectrum, in some cases contracts are issued for the central services within the prison; these can include catering, health care, education and work for prisoners. The most advanced example of this is in France where a number of prisons are run under a system of dual management, with prison service personnel carrying out what are described as the public service duties (supervision, rehabilitation, registration and management) and commercial companies being responsible for all other functions (maintenance, transportation, accommodation, food service, health services, work and vocational training)[11].

A further phase of privatization is that in which the entire operation of a prison is contracted to a commercial company or a not-for-profit organization. In this case the state builds and continues to own the prison buildings and enters into a contract with the company about the way in which the prison is to be managed. A number of the earliest examples of prison privatization outside the United States followed this model. They included the Wolds prison in England[12] and Borallon in Queensland.[13] Thereafter the state takes no part in the daily management. The ultimate stage of privatization, so far, is that in which a commercial company takes a prison from drawing board to final operation. This includes its design, its construction, its financing and its management. The latest example of this is the prison at Bloemfontein in South Africa.[14]

Technically, none of these models should be described as privatization. The legal responsibility for the prisoners who are held in them remains with the state, which contracts out their daily management to the differing degrees described above. Full privatization would exist only if the state handed over complete responsibility for the citizens sentenced to prison to a commercial company. However, as far as the prisoner in the prison which is managed by a commercial company is concerned, this is a semantic distinction. For all practical purposes, such a prisoner is in the hands of a commercial company. The best of these companies may well set out to treat the prisoners under their control in a decent and humane manner. A few of them succeed better than their counterparts in the public sector. Despite this there is no escaping the fact that the final responsibility of these companies is to their shareholders; they must deliver a profit or they will cease to trade. This is the ultimate difference between a private prison and a public one.

In considering these issues, this volume is an important addition to the growing literature on the private prison industry. Some of the authors consider the issue within a human rights context. Others place it within a wider political and economic environment. The failures and abuses which are documented are shocking. It is clear that many of the inequalities and wrongs which exist in public sector prisons can be magnified in badly managed private prisons. Yet this book also demonstrates that in a broad sense the concept of private prisons has not been widely successful. Compared with other privatization initiatives in selling public transport systems and public utilities such as electricity and water, prison privatization has been marginal as a process. One example of the consequences of getting one of these privatizations wrong is the furore which has surrounded the provision of electricity in California.[15] This book takes a comprehensive look at the prison privatization experience. Yet in reading it one is continually reminded how narrow this experience is. Authors refer to the same examples. There are a limited number of companies involved and a small number of key players. One is not left with a vision of an indestructible monolith. Rather there is a sense that the whole edifice depends on a small number of individuals operating the private prisons and an equally small number of figures in public service who are pursuing the concept of private prisons for a variety of pragmatic or ideological reasons, such as the need to do something to cope with massive increases in prison populations or a determination to curb the power of public sector employees

The events of September 11, 2001 may well provide a temporary boost to private prisons in the United States as the federal government looks for additional spaces to hold the expected increase in illegal immigrants and others held in detention. In the long run, however, there may be grounds for concluding that the trend towards privatization which began in the early 1980s with commercial companies in the US providing detention facilities for illegal immigrants has already peaked in other developed countries and is likely to wane in the near future.

The use of private prisons has remained an anglophone phenomenon. No country in continental Europe has shown any real interest in developing a private prison sector. In most of these countries the concept is completely unacceptable. The closest any such country has come to it is in France but significantly even there the state has firmly retained control of the actual deprivation of liberty. After almost twenty years, one is left with the conclusion that its progress in the countries which have espoused it has been less than spectacular. In the US, only 5.8 percent of state prisoners are in private prisons,[16] predominantly in the southern states. The exception to this has been the fairly recent conversion of the Federal Bureau of Prisons to privatization as a means of solving the problem of having to provide new prisons and staff as quickly as possible. Canada, the northern neighbour of the US, as in other prison issues, has steadfastly refused to embrace any notion of privatization, with the exception of one provincial government, as described in the chapter by Dawn Moore and her colleagues.

At one point in the late 1990s Australia had the highest proportion of its prisoners in private hands: this peaked in 1999 with 15 percent of the country's 20,000 prisoners.[17] For a period it looked as though England and Wales might follow suit.[18] The picture has changed in more recent years. Amanda George describes in her chapter how the State of Victoria in Australia took one private prison back into public control in October 2000. Concern has also been raised at the management of some other privately controlled prisons in Australia. In England and Wales when contracts for existing private prisons have come up for renewal the public sector has been allowed to compete against the private sector and in two recent instances private prisons have been returned to public hands.[19]

The Director General of the Prison Service in England and Wales recently foresaw a future in which private companies would design and construct new prisons but they would be managed by the public sector.[20] In New Zealand a change of government has meant that a move towards privatization has been halted.[21]

An important consideration, at least outside the US, has been the manner in which governments have monitored delivery by the private prison companies of their contractual obligations. In England and Wales, for example, contracts have required high levels of delivery of prisoner programs and general quality of service, in many cases, as the private contractors have pointed out, higher than those expected in the public sector. These contracts have been vigorously enforced, with strict financial penalties when failures occur.[22] In addition statutory functions such as the disciplining of prisoners have often been left in the hands of government-appointed monitors.

What then is to be said about the future of prison privatization? There is little evidence to suggest that it will spread to other countries of the developed world. In those countries where it already exists, the potential for further expansion is likely to be limited. However, there has been one recent development which gives cause for considerable concern. Faced with the reality that profit margins in the developed world are likely to be restricted in future and the fact that returns on investment have to be balanced against greater levels of public scrutiny and potential for embarrassment, the small number of companies involved in the business of prison privatization are beginning to turn their attention to developing and newly democratic countries. Many of these are countries which are faced with rising prison populations and with terrible prison conditions. Governments are under increasing pressure from international agencies like the United Nations and regional organizations such as the Inter-American Commission on Human Rights and the Council of Europe to improve the conditions of their prisons, while knowing that they have no resources to do so. These are fertile grounds for private prison companies, who can come into a country, promising to relieve the government of unbearable commitments to capital funding in exchange for a revenue commitment which is attractive in the short term but which will have crippling implications in the longer term. This often suits the wishes of politicians who have short term agendas rather than long term ones.

A further attraction for private prison companies is that in such countries it will often be possible to prepare a contract which meets the needs of the private contractor much better than those of the contracting state in both financial and operational terms. In many developing countries, there is a real problem with corruption in the public and private services. This can be found at an institutional level and at an individual level. The potential for corruption of government officials and of prison employees in impoverished countries is always a matter for concern. When prisons are operated on a for-profit basis, the danger of this happening is likely to be considerably increased. In addition, the strict monitoring arrangements which exist in some developed countries will be absent, leaving the contracting company free to interpret the conditions of the contract to its own advantage.

No commercial company will lay claim to being altruistic in its operation. That is not to say that it cannot work for the common good. The present author leads an academic institution[23] which has extensive connections with prison systems in the countries of Eastern Europe and Central Asia, where there are some of the worst physical conditions for prisoners. A few years ago he was contacted by a company which is a leading player in the private prisons field. The pitch was a simple one: "Your institution works tirelessly to improve conditions for prisoners and prison staff in these countries. Why not combine your human rights approach with our pragmatic desire to provide prison conditions which are decent and humane. We will give your center financial assistance to develop your human rights work if you will endorse the potential of our company to provide new prison facilities in the region. The outcome will be better conditions for prisoners." The approach was not taken up, tempting though it was. A similar dilemma faced the Department of Correctional Services in South Africa a few years ago. In the newly democratic society of South Africa, crime rates were spiralling out of control, the prison population was increasing significantly, yet appalling prison conditions were attracting widespread criticism. The Department was short of funds, yet it desperately wished to build new prisons to alleviate the conditions of the prisoners. Two consortia of commercial companies, led respectively by Group 4 Correctional Services and Wackenhut Corrections Corporation have been contracted to design, finance, build and manage new prisons.[24] The first one in Bloemfontein has over 3,000 beds, making it by far the biggest prison in the republic. The potential for things to go wrong is significant at many levels. Yet one can understand why the government sees this as a short term solution to what appears to be an intractable problem.

The problems faced by a country such as South Africa are compounded if one looks at the situation of its impoverished neighbour, Lesotho. The prison population of Lesotho is less than 3,000.[25] The government acknowledges that the conditions in its prisons are appalling and have to be improved, yet it lacks the resources to realize its ambition. Enter Group 4 Corrections Services SA (Pty) Ltd with a solution which is completely alien to the traditions of the country. It offers to build a prison with 3,500 places which will be of a high physical standard. The price to be paid is that all the prisoners in the country will be located in this single mega prison, very far from their homes and in an environment which will be completely alien to the culture of the country. Group 4 apparently developed its proposal at the request of the Lesotho Department of Justice, Human Rights and Rehabilitation. The head of the Lesotho prison system is not in favor of this plan and in September 2001 issued an extraordinary open letter asking for help to defeat the plan:

> ... we wish to inform you that we are under a terrible pressure to have the entire Lesotho Prison Service privatised by Group 4 from the UK. Our stance as a prisons management team regarding the above has been indicated in very categorical terms. We unitedly stand opposed to the prison model suggested by Group 4.[26]

At the time of writing (February 2002) it is known that the Minister who invited Group 4 to develop its proposal has been replaced but it is not known whether the government intends to pursue this matter.

Venezuela has some of the most dangerous prisons in the world, with management having largely abdicated control in favour of powerful prisoners. In an attempt to regain control the government is considering the option of privatization.[27] The government of Costa Rica has recently announced its intention to construct a private prison.[28] Having looked at models in the United Kingdom and France the government of Chile has now decided to construct ten new prisons following the French example.[29]

From the evidence available it is clear that prison privatisation schemes in the developed world, including the US, have not been generally accepted across the spectrum and on present performance it begins to look as though their use is likely to be reduced rather than increased in the future. In this respect the critics of prison privatization can claim considerable success in putting the case against this form of prison management, consistently pointing out the deficiencies of the providers, the costs and the dangers to the point where governments have become wary of going down that path.[30] For some of the consortia involved in prison management, prison is a relatively small part of their business. As the returns on investment become increasingly small and the danger of poor publicity greater, they can make the commercial decision simply to drop this part of their portfolio and to concentrate on more lucrative areas of business. For other companies, prisons are their sole business or at least a significant part of it. They cannot afford to leave this work without putting their very existence at risk. In future, these companies are likely to turn their attention increasingly to countries where the possibility of short term financial gains, coupled with maximum operating freedom and little independent monitoring of their performance, are greater. The danger in these developments is that the treatment of prisoners is likely to deteriorate even below present levels. In the long term the governments involved will be left with ever increasing fiscal burdens, causing a substantial drain on other public expenditure.

Having mentioned South Africa in this respect, it is appropriate to end with a quotation from the world's most famous former prisoner, who became president of that country. In his autobiography, Nelson Mandela wrote:

> It is said that no one truly knows a nation until one has been inside its jails. A nation should be judged not by how it treats its highest citizens, but its lowest one.[31]

It is not too farfetched to interpret this comment as an argument against the privatization of prisons. It is the responsibility of the "nation" to treat its prisoners; that responsibility should not be delegated to commercial companies.

Endnotes

1. The word "prison" is used throughout in its generic sense to describe prisons, jails and lock-ups. The word "prisoner" is used in the same way.
2. US Census Bureau <http://www.census.gov>.
3. Walmsley R, 2001. An Overview of World Imprisonment: global prison populations, trends and solutions, A paper presented at the UN Programme Network Institutes Technical Assistance Workshop, Vienna, May 2001 <http://www.prisonstudies.org>.
4. World Prison Brief Online <http://www.prisonstudies.org>.
5. See speech of the Solicitor General, October 1998 <www.sgc.ca>.
6. P. Tak, "The Dutch Criminal Justice System" (1999).
7. Martin Narey speaking at the Prison Service annual conference, February 4, 2002 <www.hmprisonservice.gov.uk>.
8. Yuri Chayka speaking at a meeting of European Ministers of Justice, Moscow, October 4, 2002: ITAR-TASS news agency, Moscow, 4 October 2001.
9. Goyer, K.C., 2001, Prison Privatisation in South Africa, Institute of Strategic Studies <http://www.iss.co.za/Pubs/Monographs/No64/Contents.html>.
10. J. Hallinan, "Going Up The River" (2001).
11. <http://www.justice.gouv.fr/minister/sceri/indexgb.htm>.
12. A. James, Bottomley , Liebling and Clare, "Privatizing Prisons" (1997)
13. P. Moyle, "Profiting from Punishment" (2000).
14. Goyer, K.C., *supra* note 9.
15. See Reason Public Policy Institute website <http://www.rppi.org/electricity/>.
16. A. and H.D. Beck, Karberg, "Prison and Jail Inmates at Midyear 2000" (March 2001): 4.

17. D. Biles and Dalton, "Deaths in Private Prisons 1990-99": 1-3.

18. V. Stern, "A Sin Against the Future" (1998): 294-296.

19. Prison Privatisation Report International, No 41, Public Services International Research Unit, University of Greenwich, London <www.psiru.org/justice>.

20. Martin Narey, *supra* note 7.

21. Prison Privatisation Report International, *supra* note 19, No. 34.

22. In 1999 the Prison Service of England and Wales submitted the following evidence to Parliament: "To date the Prison Service has deducted the following sums from contractors in respect of under-performance against terms of the contract: £363,136 from Securicor at Parc, £83,347 from payments to Premier Prison Services (PPS) at Lowdham Grange an £28,089 from payments to Group 4 at Altcourse. A further deduction of £440,338 in respect of 1998-99 will be made from payments due to Securicor during 1999-00. Further deductions may be made from payments to Group 4 at Altcourse in respect of 1998-99." Memorandum of evidence from HM Prison Service (PAC98-99/180) to House of Commons Select Committee on Public Accounts <http://www.parliament.the-stationery-office.co.uk/cgi-bin/htm>.

23. The International Centre for Prison Studies, King's College, University of London, UK.

24. Goyer, K.C., *supra* note 9.

25. Lesotho prison administration <http://www.prisonstudies.org>.

26. Prison Privatisation Report International, *supra* note 19, Nos. 41 and 43.

27. *Id.*, No. 40.

28. *La Nación* newspaper, Costa Rica, 10 and 11 January 2002.

29. Prison Privatisation Report International, *supra* note 19, No. 38.

30. Kahn, Si, Grassroots leadership community assets campaign 2000: stopping for profit private prisons, Prison Moratorium Project at <www.nomoreprisons.org> and the newsletter, Prison Privatization Report International, have been indispensable tools for anti-privatization activists.

31. N. Mandela, *Long Walk to Freedom* (1994).

Notes on Contributors

Elizabeth Alexander
Ms. Alexander is the Director of the National Prison Project of the American Civil Liberties Union Foundation. A graduate of the Yale Law School, she has litigated many cases challenging health care in prisons and has argued three cases before the United States Supreme Court.

Julie Berg
Ms. Berg is a researcher, affiliated with the Institute of Criminology, University of Cape Town, who has been studying the origin and monitoring the development of prison privatization in South Africa.

Allison Campbell
Ms. Campbell is a Master of Arts candidate in the Department of Sociology at Simon Fraser University, in the area of women's corrections and state ruling practices. Her work examines the changing shape of corrections for federally sentenced women during the 1990s in Canada, looking at how institutional processes maintained and reinforced the relations of ruling, despite discourse to the contrary.

Andrew Coyle
Dr. Coyle is the Director of the International Centre for Prison Studies in the University of London, UK. He has had 25 years' experience at a senior level in the prison services of the United Kingdom. He has a PhD in criminology from the University of Edinburgh. He is the author of a number of books and articles on issues concerning criminal justice and prisoners rights and has extensive international experience on prison matters, having visited prison systems in many countries as an expert consultant for bodies such as the United Nations and the Council of Europe.

Alex Friedmann
Mr. Friedmann is a former contributing writer for *Prison Legal News*, former resources editor for *Prison Life* magazine, two-time PEN prison writing award winner and member of the Public Safety & Justice Campaign–a coalition dedicated to the abolition of the private prison industry. He served 10 years behind bars, including six years at a private facility operated by Corrections Corporation of America.

Amanda George
Ms. George is a Victorian community lawyer who for 20 years has been a prison activist. She has received various awards for her work on women in prison including the Australian Avon Spirit of Achievement Award. She has written numerous articles on women in prison and in particular has been active against the privatization of prisons.

Judith Greene
Judith Greene, a criminal-justice-policy analyst, has researched prison privatization under fellowships from the Open Society Institute of the Soros Foundation and the Institute on Criminal Justice of the University of Minnesota Law School.

Donna Habsha
Ms. Habsha is a second year student at the University of Windsor, Faculty of Law. She maintains a commitment to the protection and promotion of children's rights through research, writing and the facilitation of youth empowerment workshops.

Mark Erik Hecht
Mr. Hecht is a lawyer and Executive Director of HRI, an international human rights NGO located in Ottawa, Canada. Mr. Hecht is also Senior Legal Counsel for Beyond Borders: Ensuring Global Justice for Children and a Board member of ECPAT International, a campaign to end child prostitution, child pornography and the trafficking of children for sexual purposes. Mr. Hecht's area of specialization is international child law. He teaches the subject at the University of Windsor and has published related chapters in *Human Rights and the Internet* (MacMillan Press, 2000) and *Child Abuse on the Internet* (Berghahn Books, 2001).

Kelly Hannah-Moffat
Dr. Hannah-Moffat is Assistant Professor in the Department of Sociology, University of Toronto Mississauga. She worked as a researcher and policy advisor for the Commission of Inquiry into Certain Events at the Prison for Women in Kingston and is a past president of the Toronto Elizabeth Fry Society. Her book *Punishment in Disguise: The Governance of Canadian Women's Federal Imprisonment* has just been published by the University of Toronto Press.

Kellie Leclerc Burton
Ms. Leclerc Burton is completing her second year as a Doctoral Candidate at the Centre of Criminology, University of Toronto. Her interests include critical race theory, with a specific focus on Canadian women in conflict with the law, the racialized subject in the criminal justice system and prisoners' rights.

Joshua Miller
Mr. Miller is a corrections specialist with the American Federation of State, County and Municipal Employees' (AFSCME) Department of Research & Collective Bargaining Services. The union represents approximately 80,000 corrections employees in the United States.

Bente Molenaar
Ms. Molenaar is a graduate of Development Studies from the Universities of Carleton (B.A.) and Cambridge (M.Phil). She has worked on human rights issues in association with a number of NGOs.

Dawn Moore
Ms. Moore is completing her PhD at the Centre of Criminology, University of Toronto. She is currently studying the experiences of probationers and parolees in state mandated substance 'abuse' treatment programs. She has been active in attempts to resist the privatization of prisons in Ontario and has written critically (with Kelly Hannah-Moffat) on the overhaul of Ontario's correctional system. Other

publications cover issues including date rape drugs, drug testing and alcohol intervention programs.

Monique Morris
Ms. Morris is a senior research associate with the National Council on Crime and Delinquency, where she has led several projects since 1998 designed to address racial and gender disparities in the juvenile justice system. Morris has written and spoken extensively on the plight of African American and urban youth, and is the author of the critically-acclaimed novel, *Too Beautiful For Words* (Amistad Press: 2001). Morris received her Bachelor of Arts and Master of Science degrees from Columbia University in the City of New York.

Stephen Nathan
Mr. Nathan is a journalist, researcher and editor of Prison Privatisation Report International (www.psiru.org/justice). The writing of both articles has been made possible through financial support from the Open Society Institute.

Rodney Neufeld
Mr. Neufeld is a research associate at the Lauterpacht Research Centre for International Law at the University of Cambridge where he works on diverse issues of public international law. He is a graduate of the University of Manitoba (B.A.) and the University of Ottawa (LL.B.),

Christian Parenti
Dr. Parenti is the author of *Lockdown America: Police and Prisons in the Age of Crisis*; he is a Soros Justice Senior Fellow of the Open Institute and has a PhD in Sociology from the London School of Economics. His writing appears regularly in *The Nation, the San Diego Union Tribune, New York News Day*, the *Washington Post,* and *Salon.*

Sir Nigel Rodley
Sir Nigel Rodley is Professor of Law at the University of Essex. He has recently stepped down from his position as United Nations Special Rapporteur for Torture. He is a member of the Advisory Board of the International Centre for Prison Studies. In 1999 he was awarded a knighthood in recognition of services to human rights and international law.

Jeff Sinden
Mr. Sinden is a Research Associate at Human Rights Internet and is Managing Editor of HRI's *Human Rights Tribune*. He is currently a Master's student in International Development at the Norman Paterson School of International Affairs.

Frank Smith
Mr. Smith has been a legislative advocate and community organizer in criminal justice reform and decriminalization of substance abuse for over three decades. In semi-retirement he remains an Alaskan court-appointed Guardian *ad litem*, representing the best interests of children. He is heavily involved in disability advocacy and labor, peace and social justice activism. In the past ten years he has helped a succession of communities in Alaska and other states to defeat private prison proposals. He has visited prisoners and public and private penal institutions throughout the United States and Sweden.

Katherine van Wormer

Dr. van Wormer did a participant-observation study at the women's prison in Alabama and is a Professor of Social Work at the University of Northern Iowa, Cedar Falls. She is the author of six books including *Women and the Criminal Justice System* (with C. Bartollas) (2000) and *Counseling Female Offenders and Victims: A Strengths-Restorative Approach* (2001), as well as *Addiction Treatment: A Strengths Perspective*, in press.

Phillip Wood

Dr. Wood was educated in Canada and the UK, and teaches Comparative and American Politics at Queen's University. His other research work includes projects on the transformation of American politics since the 1970s; the politics of political science research methods; structure, agency and disfranchisement in the Florida fiasco of November 2000; globalization, uneven development and the restructuring of southern textiles; and on the social structure of agriculture and racial politics in the American South before the Voting Rights Act.

H.R.I.

(Human Rights Internet)

8 York St., Suite 302, Ottawa, Ont., K1N 5S6, Canada
Tel. 613.789.7407 • Fax. 613.747.7414
Email. hri@hri.ca

Founded in 1976, HRI is a leader in the exchange of information within the worldwide human rights community. Launched in the United States, HRI has its headquarters in Ottawa, Canada. From Ottawa, HRI communicates by phone, fax, mail and the Internet with more than 5,000 organizations and individuals around the world working for the advancement of human rights.

Mission Statement

HRI is dedicated to the empowerment of human rights activists and organizations, and to the education of governmental and intergovernmental agencies and officials and other actors in the public and private sphere, on human rights issues and the role of civil society.

HRI seeks to accomplish the above by:

- Facilitating the application of new technologies toward the furtherance of human rights through transferring knowledge and expertise particularly to Southern non-governmental organizations (NGOs) and other civil society organizations;
- Producing and providing access to human rights databases and a unique and comprehensive documentation centre;
- Carrying out human rights research and disseminating the results to concerned institutions and activists;
- Producing human rights resources including the Human Rights Tribune, annual publications and directories in digital, hard copy and microfiche formats and making them available to NGOs and international institutions;
- Fostering networking and cooperation among NGOs, as well as other civil society organizations, to integrate human rights with social and sustainable development issues; Strengthening civil society and NGO access to and participation in international fora; and
- Supporting the role of NGOs in the promotion of civil society and assisting governmental and intergovernmental organizations in the application of good governance practices and the protection of human rights through technical assistance, training and educational programs.

Capitalist Punishment Team:

Allison Campbell: Associate Editor
Andrea Chow, Project Assistant
Andrew Coyle: Senior Editor
Donna Habsha, Project Assistant

Mark Erik Hecht: Project Supervision
Rodney Neufeld: Associate Editor
Jeff Sinden: Managing Editor
Danielle Young: Project Assistant and Researcher

Bibliography

Abramson, B. *Juvenile Justice: The 'Unwanted Child' of State Responsibilities.* International Network on Juvenile Justice, 2001.

Acoca, L., and J. Austin. *The Crisis: Women in Prison.* San Francisco, CA: National Council on Crime and Delinquency, 1996.

Adam Smith Institute. *Omega Report on Justice Policy.* London: Adam Smith Institute, 1984.

Alt, James E. "The Impact of the Voting Rights Act on Black and White Voter Registration in the South," In *Quiet Revolution in the South,* edited by Chandler Davidson and Bernard Grofman. Princeton, NJ: Princeton University Press, 1994.

American Federation of State, County and Municipal Employees. *The Evidence Is Clear: Crime Shouldn't Pay.* Washington: AFL-CIO, 2000.

Amnesty International. *Not Part of My Sentence: Violations of the Human Rights of Women in Custody.* New York: Amnesty International, 1999.

Angel, W.D. *The International Law of Youth Rights: Source Documents and Commentary.* Dordrecht: Martinus Nijhoff Publishers, 1995.

Applebome, Peter. *Dixie Rising: How the South is Shaping American Values, Politics and Culture.* New York: Harcourt, Brace, 1996.

Austin, J., and G. Coventry. *Emerging Issues on Privatized Prisons.*Washington, D.C.: US Department of Justice, Bureau of Justice Assistance, 2001.

Austin, James, et al., *The Consultants' Report on Prison Operations in New Mexico Correctional Institutions.* Santa Fe, NM: Special Advisory Group. 2000.

Bates, Eric. "Private Prisons." *The Nation.* January 5, 1998.

Beck, Allen, and Lauren Glaze. *Correctional Populations in the United States, 1980-2000.* Washington, D.C.: US Department of Justice, Bureau of Justice Statistics, 2001.

Beck, Allen and Karberg, J. *Prison and Jail Inmates at Midyear 2000 March.* Washington, D.C.: US Department of Justice, Bureau of Justice Statistics Bulletin, 2001.

Beckett, Katherine, and Theodore Sasson. *The Politics of Injustice: Crime and Punishment in America.* Thousand Oaks: Pine Forge Press, 2000.

Bellon, Bertrand, and Jorge Niosi. *The Decline of the American Economy.* Montreal: Black Rose Books, 1988.

Beardsley, Philip. *Whose Country America?.* Encino, CA: Dickenson, 1973.

Biles, David and V. Dalton. "Deaths in Private Prisons 1990-99: A Comparative Study." *Trends & Issues in Crime and Criminal Justice* no. 120, June 1999.

Bloom, B., and D. Steinhart. *Why Punish the Children? A Reappraisal of the Children of Incarcerated Mothers in America.* San Francisco, CA: National Council on Crime and Delinquency, 1993.

Booker, C. "The Profits of African American Male Criminalization." *African American Male Research* 1, no. 2 (1996).

Bowles, Samuel, David M. Gordon, and Thomas E. Weisskopf. *Beyond the Waste Land: A Democratic Alternative to Economic Decline.* Garden City, NY: Anchor Press, 1984.

Bonczar, Thomas P., and Allen J. Beck, *Lifetime Likelihood of Going to State or Federal Prison.* Washington, D.C.: US Department of Justice, Bureau of Justice Statistics, 1997.

Brenner, Robert. "Uneven Development and the Long Downturn: The Advanced Capitalist Economies from Boom to Stagnation, 1950-1998," *New Left Review* 229, (1998): 1-264.

Bridges, G., and S. Stevens. "Racial Disparities in Official Assessments of Juvenile Offenders: Attributional Stereotypes as Mediating Mechanism." *American Sociological Review* 63 (1998).

Burton-Rose, D., D. Pens and P. Wright. *The Celling of America: An Inside Look at the US Prison Industry.* Common Courage Press, 1998.

Cahill, D. "The Global Economy Behind Ohio Prison Walls." *Prison Legal News* 6, no. 3 (1996).

Camp, Camille, and George Camp. *The Corrections Yearbook.* South Salem, NY: Criminal Justice Institute, 1998, 1999, 2000.

Camp, Scott D., and Gerald G. Gaes. *Growth and Quality of U.S. Private Prisons: Evidence from a National Survey* (Washington, DC: Federal Bureau of Prisons, 2001).

Cappelaere, G. "Juvenile Justice 10 years after the CRC." *Juvenile Justice Worldwide* Spring 2000.

Carcach, Carlos, and Anna Grant, "Imprisonment in Australia: Trends in Prison Populations and Imprisonment Rates, 1982-1998." *Trends and Issues in Crime and Criminal Justice* no. 130 (1999).

Carter, Dan T., "Legacy of Rage: George Wallace and the Transformation of American Politics." *Journal of Southern History* LXII, no. 1 (1996): 3-26.

Carter, Patrick. *Review of PFI and Market Testing in the Prison Service.* Prison Service, 2002.

Casarez, N.B. "Furthering the Accountability Principle in Privatized Federal Corrections: The Need for Access to Private Prison Records." *University of Michigan Journal of Law Reform* 28, no. 249 (1995): 264-272.

Chesney-Lind, M. "Girls, Delinquency, and Juvenile Justice: Toward a Feminist Theory of Young Women's Crime." In *The Criminal Justice System and Women: Offenders, Victims, and Workers,* edited by B.R. Price and N.J. Sokoloff. New York: McGraw-Hill, 1995.

Chesney-Lind, M., and J. Pollock. "Women's Prisons: Equality with a Vengeance." In *Women, Law, and Social Control,* edited by A. Merlo and J. Pollock. Boston: Allyn & Bacon, 1994.

Churchill, Ward and J. J. Vander Wall. *Cages of Steel: The Politics of Imprisonment in the United States.* Washington: Maisonneuve Press, 1992.

Clark, John. *Report to the Attorney General: Inspection and Review of the Northeast Ohio Correctional Center.* Washington D.C.: Office of the Corrections Trustee for the District of Columbia, 1998.

Commonwealth Grants Commission. *Report on General Relativities.* vol. III, Canberra, 1999.

Commonwealth Ombudsman. *Report of an Own Motion Investigation into the Department of Immigration and Multicultural Affairs' Immigration Detention Centres.* March 2001.

Corder, Hugh, and Dirk Van Zyl Smit. "Privatised Prisons and the Constitution." *South African Journal of Criminal Justice.* 11 (1998): 475-490.

Correctional Investigator. *Annual Report of the Correctional Investigator, 1996-1997.* Ottawa: Minister of Public Works and Government Services, 1997.

Correctional Services Commission. Report on Metropolitan Women's Correctional Centre's Compliance with its Contractual Obligations and Prison Services Agreement. Victorian Government Printer, 2000.

Correctional Service of Canada. "National Strategy for the Prevention of Suicide and the Reduction of Self-Injury." Forum on Corrections: Prison Violence and Inmate Suicide and Self-Injury. 4, no. 3 (1992).

Covell, K. and R.B.Howe. *The Challenge of Children's Rights for Canada.* Waterloo: Wilfred Laurier University Press, 2001.

Culhane, Clair. *Barred From Prison: A Personal Account.* Vancouver: Pulp Press, 1979.

Cummings, Stephen D. *The Dixification of America: The American Odyssey into the Conservative Economic Trap.* Westport, CT: Praeger, 1998.

Cunningham, William, and Todd Taylor. *Crime and Protection in America: A Study of Private Security and Law Enforcement Resources and Relationships.* Washington, D.C.: U.S. Department of Justice, National Institute of Justice, 1985.

Danner, M. J. E. "Three strikes and it's women who are out: The hidden consequences for women of criminal justice policy reforms." In Miller, S. L. (Ed.), *Crime control and women: Feminist implications of criminal justice policy.* Thousand Oaks, CA: Sage Publications, 1998.

Davis, Angela. "Race and Criminalization: Black Americans and the Punishment Industry." In *The Angela Davis Reader,* edited by Joy James. Malden, MA: Blackwell Publishers, 1998.

Davis, Angela. "Globalism and the Prison Industrial Complex." *Race and Class.* 40, no. 2-3 (1998-99).

Davis, Angela. "Masked Racism: Reflections on the Prison Industrial Complex." *ColorLines* 1, no.2 (1998).

Davis, Mike. "Hell Factories in the Field: A Prison industrial complex." *The Nation* 260, no. 7 (1995).

Department of Justice, Canada. "Toward Safer Communities." In *Canadian Delinquency,* edited by J. Creechan and R. Silverman. Scarborough: Prentice Hall, 1995.

Dilulio, J. "The duty to govern: A critical perspective on the private management of prisons and jails" in *Private Prisons and the Public Interest,* edited by D. McDonald. New Brunswick: Rutgers University Press, 1990.

Dissel, Amanda. "The Passing-Out Parade: Demilitarisation of the Correctional Services." *Acta Criminologica.* 10, no. 1 (1997):17-27.

DiMartino, K. "Juvenile Justice...ten years on..." *Juvenile Justice Worldwide* Spring 2000.

Ditton, P.M. *Mental Health and Treatment of Inmates and Probationers.* U.S. Department of Justice Bureau of Justice Statistics, Special Report 2, 1999.

Dooley, S.W., et al. "Multidrug-Resistant Tuberculosis." *Annuals of Internal Medicine* 117, no. 257 (1992).

Downes, David. "The Macho Penal Economy: Mass Incarceration in the United States: A European Perspective." In *The Global Third Way Debate,* edited by Anthony Giddens. Cambridge, UK: Polity Press, 2001.

Dunn, Tim and Jose Palafox. "Border Militarization and Beyond: The Widening of the War on Drugs." *Borderlines.* 8, no. 4 (2000).

Edsall, Thomas B., and Mary D. Edsall, *Chain Reaction: The Impact of Race, Rights and Taxes on American Politics.* New York: Norton, 1991.

Egerton, John. *The Americanization of Dixie.* New York: Harper's Magazine Press, 1974.

Evans, Linda and Eva Goldberg. *The Prison Industrial Complex and the Global Economy.* Berkeley: Agit Press, 1998.

Fellner, Jamie, and Marc Mauer. *Losing the Vote: The Impact of Felony Disfranchisement Laws in the United States.* Washington, D.C.: Human Rights Watch and the Sentencing Project, 1998.

Fletcher, Beverly R., Lynda Dixon Shaver, and Dreama G. Moon (eds.). *Women Prisoners : A Forgotten Population.* Westport, Connecticut: Praeger, 1993.

Flood, Philip. *Report of Inquiry into Immigration Detention Procedures.* An independent inquiry commissioned by Hon. Philip Ruddock MP, 23 February 2001. Gainsborough, Jenni, and Marc Mauer. *Diminishing Returns: Crime and Incarceration in the 1990s.* Washington, D.C.: The Sentencing Project, 2000.

Gandy, J. and L. Hurl. "Private sector involvement in prison industries: Options and issues." *Canadian Journal of Criminology* 29 (1987): 185-204.

Garland, David. *Punishment and Modern Society: A Study in Social Theory.* Chicago: University of Chicago Press, 1990.

Gentry, J. "The Panopticon Revisited: The Problem of Monitoring Private Prisons." *Yale Law Journal* 96, no. 353 (1986): 356-357.

Gerhardstein, A. "Private Prison Litigation: The Youngstown Case and Theories of Liability." *Correctional Law Reporter* 62 (2000).

Giffard, C. *Out of Step? The Transformation Process in the South African Department of Correctional Services,* Masters Dissertation, Criminal Justice Studies (1997).

Giffard, C. *Privatising Prisons in South Africa.* unpublished work (1997).

Giffard, C. "Privatising Prisons in South Africa." In *Between Unity and Diversity: Essays on Nation-Building in Post-Apartheid South Africa,* edited by Gitanjali Maharaj. Idasa: David Philip Publishers, 1999.

Giffard, C. *South African Corrections: Privatization Fact File* (Unpublished Work, 1997).

Gilmour, Ian. *Dancing With Dogma, Britain Under Thatcherism.* London: Simon & Schuster, 1993.

Goodwin-Gill, Guy. "Article 31 of the 1951 Convention relating to the Status of Refugees: Non-penalization, Detention and Protection." A paper prepared at the request of the Department of International Protection for the UNHCR Global Consultations, October 2001, at p.34.

Gordon, David M. *Fat and Mean: The Corporate Squeeze of Working Americans and the Myth of Corporate Downsizing.* New York: Free Press, 1996.

Government of Canada. *Commission of Inquiry into Certain Events at the Prison for Women In Kingston.* (Arbour Report). Ottawa: Public Works and Government Services of Canada, 1996.

Government of New Brunswick. *Achieving a Balance: The Successful Transition from Incarceration as a First Option to Incarceration as the Last Option.* St. John: Department of Public Safety, 1999.

Greene, Judith A. "Comparing Private and Public Prison Services and Programs in Minnesota: Findings from Prisoner Interviews," *Current Issues in Criminal Justice* II, no. 2. (1999).

Hallinan, Joseph T. *Going Up The River: Travels in a Prison Nation.* New York: Random House, 2001.

Hammett, T.M., P. Harmon and L.M. Maruschak. *1996-1997 Update: HIV/AIDS, STDs, and TB in Correctional Facilities.* Washington, D.C.: National Institute of Justice, 1999.

Hannah-Moffat, Kelly. "Creating Choices or Repeating History: Canadian Female Offenders and Correctional Reform." *Social Justice.* 8, no. 3 (1991): 184-203.

Hannah-Moffat, Kelly. "Feminine Fortresses: Women-Centred Prisons?" *The Prison Journal.* 75, no. 2 (1995): 135 – 64.

Hannah-Moffat, Kelly. "Prisoners' Rights in the Canadian Correctional System" In *Corrections in Canada: Social Reaction to Crime*, edited by J. Winterdyk. Toronto: Prentice Hall, 2000.

Hannah-Moffat, Kelly. *Punishment in Disguise: Penal Governance and Federal Imprisonment of Women in Canada.* Toronto: University of Toronto Press, 2001.

Hawaii Department of Public Safety. *Briefing Report – Florence Correctional Facility.* State of Hawaii, Department of Public Safety, 2001.

Hayes, L. *Prison Suicide: An Overview.* Washington, D.C.: United States Department of Justice, National Institute of Corrections, 1995.

Haymes, S. Nathan. *Race, Culture, and the City: A Pedagogy of Black Urban Struggle* Albany, NY: State University of New York Press, 1995.

Herrnstein, Richard J., and Charles Murray. *The Bell Curve: Intelligence and Class Structure in American Life.* New York: Free Press, 1994.

HM Chief Inspector. *Campsfield House Detention Centre.* A report by Her Majesty's Chief Inspector of Prisons following an unannounced short inspection, 1998.

Hopkins, RDN."The formation of UK Detention Services." a paper submitted to Private Gevangissen In Nederland conference, Utrecht, 1 December 1993.

Hornsberger, Fred. "Nova Scotia Custody Configuration Project." in *Privatizing Correctional Services*, edited by Stephen Easton. Vancouver: The Fraser Institute, 1998.

House of Commons, *Fourth Report from the Home Affairs Committee*, Session 1986-87, Contract Provision of Prisons, HC 291, 6 May 1987.

House of Commons, Home Affairs Committee, Session 1996/97, *The Management of the Prison Service (Public and Private)*, 1 / 2, no. 19 (1997).

Hudson, R.B., "Aging and Criminal Justice: Images and Institutions." *The Public Policy and Aging Report* 10, no. 2 (2000).

Human Rights Watch. *All too familiar: Sexual Abuse of Women in U.S. State Prisons.* New York: Human Rights Watch, 1996.

Human Rights Watch. *Nowhere to hide: Retaliation against women in Michigan state prisons.* New York: Human Rights Watch, 2000.

Human Rights Watch. *World Report, 2001: United States.* New York: Human Rights Watch, 2001.

Jackson, M. *Justice Behind Walls: A Report to the Canadian Bar Association Committee on Imprisonment and Release.* Vancouver: University of British Columbia Law Review, 1988.

Irwin, John and James Austin. *It's About Time: America's Imprisonment Binge.* Belmont: Wadsworth Publishing, 1997.

James, A.L. et al. *Privatizing Prisons: Rhetoric and Reality.* London: Sage, 1997.

John Howard Society of Ontario. *Fact Sheet # 15 - The Changing Face of Ontario Corrections: An Assessment* Toronto: John Howard Society, 2000.

Kalinich, Dave, and Willie Clack. "Transformation: From Apartheid to a Democracy–South

African Corrections." *Acta Criminologica*. 11, no. 2 (1998):64-71.

Karaagac, J. *Between promise and policy: Ronald Reagan and conservative reformism*. Lanham, Md.: Lexington Books, 2000.

Kassebaum, P.A. *Substance Abuse Treatment for Women Offenders: Guide to Promising Practices* Rockville, MD: US Department of Health and Human Services, 1999.

Kassindja, F. *Do They Hear You When You Cry?*. New York: Delacorte Press, 1998.

Kawai, Patrick. Memo to HCF Warden Nolan Espinosa. "Summary of identified Security Threat Group (STG) at Florence Correctional Facility (FCC)." Hawaii Department of Public Safety, April 16-20, 2001.

Keating, J. "Public over Private: Monitoring the Performance of Privately Operated Prisons and Jails" in *Private Prisons and the Public Interest*, edited by D. McDonald. New Brunswick: Rutgers University Press, 1990.

Kendall, Kathy. "Psy-ence Fiction: Governing Female Prisons through the Psychological Sciences." in *An Ideal Prison? Critical Essays on Women's Imprisonment in Canada*, edited by K. Hannah-Moffat and M. Shaw. Halifax: Fernwood, 2000.

Key, V. O. *Southern Politics in State and Nation*. New York: Vintage, 1949.

Kirby, Peter. *Independent Investigation into the Management and Operation of Victoria's Private Prisons*. Victorian Government Printer, 2000.

Kolb, C.E.M. "The Riot and Deaths of Archambault Penitentiary, Saint-Annes-des-Plaines, Canada on July 25, 1982-A Report to the International Human Rights Law Group." *New England Journal on Criminal Law and Confinement*. 9, no. 1 (1983): 125 - 43.

Kollapen, Jody. "Prisoners' Rights under the Interim Constitution." *Acta Criminologica*. 8, no. 2 (1995): 74-78.

Ladipo, David. "The Rise of America's Prison industrial complex." *New Left Review* 7 (2001): 109-123.

Lee Gifford, Sidra. *Criminal Justice Expenditures and Employment*. Washington, D.C.: US Department of Justice, Bureau of Justice Statistics, 2000.

Lesotho Prison Service. "Private Prison as an Alternative to Lesotho Prison Regime." September 2001.

Lichtenstein, Alex. "Through the Rugged Gates of the Penitentiary: Convict Labor and Southern Coal, 1870-1900," In *Race and Class in the American South since 1890,* edited by Melvyn Stokes and Rick Halpern. Oxford: Berg, 1994.

Lowi, Theodore J. *The End of Liberalism: The Second Republic of the United States*, fifth ed. New York: Norton, 1979.

Lyson, Thomas A. *Two Sides to the Sunbelt*. New York: Praeger, 1989.

Mandela Nelson, *Long Walk to Freedom*. London: Little Brown & Co, 1994.

Mann, C. Richey. *Unequal Justice: A Question of Color* Bloomington: Indiana University Press, 1993.

Mara, C. Massie, and C. McKenna, "Aging in Place in Prison: Health and Long-Term Care Needs of Older Inmates," *The Public Policy and Aging Report* 10, no. 1 (2000).

Marable, M. "The Political Cultures of Incarceration." *Souls: A Critical Journal of Black Politics, Culture, and Society* 2, Winter (2000).

Marash, M., T. Bynum, and B. Koons. *Women Offenders: Programming Needs and Promising Approaches*. Washington, D.C.: U.S. Department of Justice, National Institute of Justice, 1998

Marglin, Stephen A., and Juliet B. Schor. *The Golden Age of Capitalism: Reinterpreting the Postwar Experience*. New York: Oxford University Press, 1990.

Martinez, John. *After Action Report — Florence Correctional Center, June 4, 2001–June 6, 2001*. Honolulu: Hawaii Department of Public Safety, 2001.

Maruschak, L. *HIV in Prisons and Jails, 1999*. Washington, D.C.: U.S. Department of Justice, Bureau of Justice Statistics, 2001.

McConnell, Grant. *Private Power and American Democracy*. New York: Knopf, 1966.

McDonald, Douglas. *Private Prisons and the Public Interest*. New Brunswick: Rutgers University Press, 1990.

McDonald, Douglas, et al., *Private Prisons in the United States: An Assessment of Current Practice*. Cambridge, MA: Abt Associates, 1998.

McMahon, Maeve. *The Persistent Prison? Rethinking Decarceration and Penal Reform*.

Toronto: University of Toronto Press, 1992.

Messina, N.P., and L. Prendergast. "Therapeutic Community Treatment for Women in Prison: Some Success, but the Jury is Still Out." *Offender Substance Abuse Report* (2001).

Moore, Dawn and Kelly Hannah-Moffat. "Correctional Renewal Without the Frills: The Politics of 'Get Tough' Punishment in Ontario." In *Disorderly People: Law and the Politics of Exclusion in Ontario,* edited by Joe Hermer and Janet Mosher. Fernwood: Halifax, forthcoming.

Monture-Angus, Patricia. "Women and Risk: Aboriginal Women, Colonialism and Correctional Practice." *Canadian Women Studies.* 19, no. 1/2 (1999).

Morrow, Phyllis. "Yup'ik Eskimo Agents and American Legal Agencies: Perspectives on Compliance and Resistance." *Journal of the Royal Anthropological Institute.* 2 (1996): 405-423.

Moyle, Paul. *Profiting from Punishment: Private Prisons in Australia–Reform or Regression?* Sydney: Pluto Press, 2000.

Muscroft, S. *Children's Rights: Reality or Rhetoric?* London: The International Save the Children Alliance, 1999.

Nathan, Stephen. *Private Adult Correctional Facilities: Fines, Failures and Dubious Practices.* Toronto: Ontario Public Services Employees Union, 2000.

Nathan, Stephen. "Private prisons, an international overview." *Prison Review International.* Issue 2, Broadcast Publishing Ltd, 2002.

Nathan, Stephen. "US companies expand corrections market overseas." *National Prison Project Journal.* American Civil Liberties Foundation, Summer 1995.

Nathan, Stephen. "International prison privatisation." *Socio-Legal Newsletter.* No. 35, Socio-Legal Studies Association, November 2001.

National Crime Prevention Council Canada, *Economic Analysis Committee Report* March 1996.

New World Border. Produced by Casey Peek. 28 min. Casey Peek Productions, 2001. Videocassette.

Nina, Daniel. "Dr. Sipo Mzimela: A Minister with a Vision?" *Imbizo.* no 2 (1996): 20-25.

Nixon, Ron. "The Dixification of America," *Southern Exposure* XXIV, no. 3 (1996): 19-22.

O'Malley, Pat. "Volatile and Contradictory Punishments." *Theoretical Criminology.* 3, no. 2 (1999): 175 - 96.

Ontario Public Service Employees' Union *Private Adult Correctional Facilities: Fines, Failures and Dubious Practices.* 2000.

Ontario Public Service Employees' Union. *Lock Talk: A Publication of the OPSEU Corrections Campaign.* November 23, 2001.

Parenti, Christian. *Lockdown America: Police and Prisons in the Age of Crisis.* New York: Verso, 1999.

Perelman, Michael. *The Pathology of the U.S. Economy.* New York: St. Martin's Press, 1996.

Poe-Yamagata, E., and M. Jones. *And Justice For Some: Differential Treatment of Minority Youth in the Justice System* Washington, D.C.: Youth Law Center, 2000.

Pratt, Travis C. "Are private prisons more cost effective than public prisons? A meta-analysis of evaluation research studies," *Crime and Delinquency* 45, no. 3 (1999).

Press, Aric. "The Good, the Bad and the Ugly: Private Prisons in the 1980's." In *Private Prisons and the Public Interest,* edited by D. McDonald. New Brunswick: Rutgers University Press, 1990.

Prison Service. "Public and Private Prison Management, Considerations on returning privately managed prisons to the public sector." unpublished document, April 1998.

Prison Service. "Review of Private Financing of New Prison Procurement," unpublished document, 1998.

Prison Reform Trust. *Wolds Remand Prison, Contracting Out: A First Year Report.,* London, April 1993.

Pugh, Ralph. *Imprisonment in Medieval England.* Cambridge, UK: Cambridge University Press, 1968.

Radzinowicz, Sir Leon. "Penal Regressions." *Cambridge Law Journal* 50, no.3 (1991).

Reiman, J. *The Rich Get Richer and the Poor Get Prison: Ideology, Class, and Criminal Justice* Boston: Allyn & Bacon, 2001.

Rolison, G. "Toward an Integrated Theory of Female Criminality and Incarceration." In *Women Prisoners : A Forgotten Population*, edited by Beverly R. Fletcher, Lynda Dixon Shaver, and Dreama G. Moon. Westport, Connecticut: Praeger, 1993.

Ross, Luana. *Inventing the Savage: The Social Construction of Native American Criminality*. Austin: University of Texas Press, 1998.

Rural Ethnic Institute. *Western Dakota's Pilot Project of the Evolving Roles of Tribal People in Nation States*. Rural Ethnic Institute, 1997.

Russell, B. *Contracting, Privatisation Probity and Disclosure in Victoria 1992-1999*. May 2000.

Ryan, Mick and Tony Ward. *Privatization and the penal system, The American experience and the debate in Britain*. Milton Keynes: Open University Press, 1989.

Savas, E.S. *Privatization and Public-Private Partnerships*. New York, N.Y.: Chatham House Publishers, 2000.

Shaw, M. "Women in Prison: A Literature Review." *Forum in Corrections Research* 6, no.1, (1994): 1-7.

Shichor, D. "The Corporate Context of Private Prisons." *Crime, Law And Social Change*, 20 (1993): 113-138.

Shichor, D. *Punishment for Profit: Private Prisons/ Public Concerns* Thousand Oaks, CA: Sage Publications, 1995.

Shafer, N.E. *A Comparison by Race of Juvenile referrals in Alaska: Phase II Report*. Anchorage: Anchorage Justice Center, 1998.

Silverstein, Ken. "America's Private Gulag." *Prison Legal News* 8, no. 6 (1997).

Sinden, Jeff. "Capitalist Punishment: Prison Privatization in the United States" Human Rights Tribune 7, no. 2&3 (2000): 15-16.

Smith, Hedrick. *The Power Game: How Washington Works*. New York: Ballantine Books, 1988.

Snell, T., ed. *Survey of Inmates of State Correctional Facilities* Washington, D.C.: Bureau of Justice Statistics, 1996.

Stern, Vivien. *A Sin Against the Future: Imprisonment in the World*. Harmondsworth: Penguin Press, 1998.

Sturm, S.P. "The Legacy and Future of Corrections Litigation." *University of Pennsylvania Law Review* 142, no. 639 (1993): 662-681.

Sudbury, Julia. "Globalisation, Incarcerated Black Women/ Women of Colour and the Challenge to Feminist Scholarship." In *Millennial Visions: Issues for Feminism*, edited by Women's Studies Network. Cardiff University Press. (1998).

Sudbury, Julia. "Transatlantic Visions: Resisting the Globalization of Mass Incarceration." *Social Justice*. Fall 2000, 27, no. 3 (2000).

Tak, Peter J.P. *The Dutch Criminal Justice System*. The Hague: Ministry of Justice, 1999.

Thomas, C. *Corrections in America: problems of the past and the present*. Newbury Park: Sage Publications, 1987.

Thomas, Jennifer. "Adult Correctional Services in Canada, 1998–99." *Juristat*. 20, no. 3 (2000).

U.K. Secretary of State for the Home Department, *Prison Statistics, England and Wales 2000*. London: HMSO, 2001.

UNICEF, *The State of the World's Children 2002*. New York: UNICEF, 2002.

U.S. Department of Health and Human Services. *Mental Health: Culture, Race, and Ethnicity* (Rockville, MD, 2001).

U.S. Department of Justice, Bureau of Justice Statistics. *Women Offenders* (Washington DC: U.S. Department of Justice, 1999).

U.S. Department of Justice, Bureau of Justice Statistics. *Correctional Populations of the United States 1997*. (Washington, D.C.: GPO, 2000).

U.S. Department of Justice, Bureau of Justice Statistics. *American Indians and Crime*. (Washington, D.C.: GPO, 1999).

U.S. Department of Justice, Office of Juvenile Justice and Delinquency Prevention. *Census of Juveniles in Residential Placement Databook*. (Washington, D.C.: GPO, 1997).

U.S. General Accounting Office. *Private and public prisons–studies comparing operational costs and / or quality of service*. (Washington, D.C.: GPO, 1996).

Van Bueren, G. *The International Law on the Rights of the Child.* Hague: Kluwer Law International, 1998.

Victorian Auditor-General Report. *Victoria's prison system: Community protection and prisoner welfare.* Special Report No. 60, May 1999.

Victorian Commissioner for Corrective Services Quarterly Reports 1996-1999.

Walmsley, R. *World Prison Population List.* London: UK Home Office Research, 2000.

White, A. "Rule of Law and the Limits of Sovereignty: The Private Prison in Jurisprudential Perspective," *American Criminal Law Review* 38, no. 3 (2001).

White Paper of the Secretary of State of the Home Department. "Secure Borders, Safe Haven: Integration with Diversity in Modern Britain." HMSO, February 2002.

Whitfield, Dexter. *Public Services or Corporate Welfare.* London: Pluto Press, 2001.

Wilcock, K., et al. *Tuberculosis in Correctional Facilities 1994-95* Washington, D.C.: National Institute of Justice, 1996.

Williams, M., and I. Sapp-Grant. "From Punishment to Rehabilitation: Empowering African American Youths." *Souls: A Critical Journal of Black Politics, Culture, and Society* 2, Winter, (2000).

Women's Issues Task Force. *Women's Voices, Women's Choices: Report of the Women's Issues Task Force.* Toronto: Ministry of the Solicitor General and Correctional Services of Canada, 1995.

Wood, Phillip J. *Southern Capitalism: The Political Economy of North Carolina, 1880-1980.* Durham, NC: Duke University Press, 1986.

van Wormer, K. *Counseling Female Offenders and Victims: A Strengths-Restorative Approach* New York: Springer, 2001.

van Wormer, K., and C. Bartollas. *Women and the Criminal Justice System* Boston: Allyn & Bacon, 2000.

van Wormer, K., and D. Davis. *Addiction Treatment: A Strengths Perspective* Belmont, CA: Wadsworth, 2002.

Wright, P. "Slaves of the State." *Prison Legal News* 5, no. 5 (1994).

Yeoman, Barry. "Steel Town Lockdown: Corrections Corporation of America is trying to turn Youngstown, Ohio into the private-prison capital of the world," *Mother Jones* May/June 2000.

Zembik, Cheryl. "Briefing Report – Florence Correctional Facility, 4/16 – 4/20 Monitoring Trip." Department of Public Safety inter-office memo to Ted Sakai, April 30, 2001.

Index